USER NEEDS IN INFORMATION TECHNOLOGY STANDARDS

General Editors:

C.D. Evans

B.L. Meek

R.S. Walker

with the assistance as technical editors of

A. Hopkinson (Section 2)

Dr B. Jerman-Blažič (Section 5)

Dr I.A. Newman (Section 8)

I.H.A. Johnston (Section 9)

BUTTERWORTH
HEINEMANN

Butterworth-Heinemann Ltd
Linacre House, Jordan Hill, Oxford OX2 8DP

ℛ A member of the Reed Elsevier group

OXFORD LONDON BOSTON
MUNICH NEW DELHI SINGAPORE SYDNEY
TOKYO TORONTO WELLINGTON

First published 1993

British Library Cataloguing in Publication Data

A catalogue record for this book is
available from the British Library

ISBN 0 7506 1559 1

Printed and bound in Great Britain

User Needs in Informati...
T...

Contents

Attribution

This book owes its existence to USFIT, the User Standards Forum for Information Technology. USFIT was established in the early 1980s as the outcome of discussions in the Working Group on Standards of NCUF, the National Computer Users Forum in the UK. NCUF is a federation of computer users' associations and other interested bodies. USFIT was established primarily as a forum for individuals on standards committees representing user as distinct from supplier interests, but is open to any persons with a user interest in IT standardization. USFIT became a (largely autonomous) wing of ITUSA, the IT Users Standards Association, a UK organization representing corporate users and organizations.

In the late 1980s, IT standardization within BSI, the British Standards Institution, was reorganized into DISC ("Delivering Information Solutions to Customers"). USFIT decided that it was time to gather together in a single volume a selection of the considerable quantity of material on user needs in IT standardization which was known to be widely scattered in committee documents, published articles, private reports and so on. The task began of collecting material and recruiting contributors, and this book is the result. It is hoped that this compendium of views will be of continuing use to those who represent user interests within BSI/DISC, international IT standards committees, or elsewhere.

Once DISC was established, ITUSA decided to wind itself up as a separate organization and to merge its activities into DISC. USFIT, however, continued in existence in its own right, and is now back under the aegis of NCUF and the NCUF Working Group on Standards of which the general editors of this book are members.

After initial payments to authors and editors, all royalties from the sale of this book will go to the Working Group on Standards and be used to support further activities to promote the user interest in IT standardization, both in the UK and elsewhere.

Preface

The motivation for producing this book is explained in the preceding *Attribution*. As general editors, we undertook to collect together material related to user needs, and assemble it into book form.

This has been no easy task. The material was known to exist, but finding it was not always straightforward. Even when found, we were not always able to use it, for one reason or another: the authors felt it was too out of date, and did not have time to update it; it was written for a specific purpose or readership and would be difficult to adapt for a more general audience; or it was simply "against the rules" to let others use such material. In some cases we could have used material but decided against, usually because it was too technically detailed for the purposes of the book.

Inevitably, the collection we have ended up with is uneven in level and approach, simply because of the number of authors and the variety of purposes for which the original material was produced. Inevitably, given the vastness and complexity of the subject, and the fact that we were limited to using what was available, there are some gaps in coverage. If your favourite topic seems not to have been given the attention it deserves, this is probably because no-one (including you?) provided us with suitable material. We urge you not to dismiss the book as therefore "not for you", but instead to read it and use lateral thinking on the topics that are covered, to see how the discussion might apply to yours. Very often in standards-making the experiences in one area provide lessons for other areas, but far too commonly those lessons are not learned.

As well as gaps there are also overlaps – recurrent topics which different authors have all treated in one way and another, and reappear in various places throughout the book. The Open Systems Interconnection area is one such, because of its high profile in the technology, and its wide scope. We have tried, by editing, cross-referencing, and using extracts rather than complete texts, to reduce the amount of repetition, but often it was not possible to eliminate all repetition without doing violence to an author's line of argument.

We have also tended to use extracts rather than complete texts in the case of older material, the earliest dating back to 1980: selecting what still seemed to remain relevant in the 1990s, and only retaining material which was otherwise technically out of date if it was needed to make the context clear. (The fact that there is any material at all of that vintage which is still relevant in 1992 of course demonstrates how much of an uphill struggle it is for users to get their needs addressed.)

Other contributions, however, were written or extensively revised especially for this book. We have also done our best to avoid the limitations of simply a collection of distinct contributions (a "connectionless service"?) by providing introductory and linking passages, also especially written for the purpose, as commentary and explanation.

The technical editors drafted the linking material for their sections as well as assembling and organizing the contributions. We are grateful to them for their assistance, and of course to all those who supplied contributions. Brian Meek as coordinating editor took on the technical editor role for the other sections apart from Section 4, where Cliff Evans undertook the task. Ray Walker and Cliff Evans did much of the work of seeking out potential material and reading and commenting on large numbers of documents. As coordinating editor Brian Meek dealt with the mechanics of putting together the complete text as material arrived, and acting as the link with technical editors and contributors. We take collective responsibility for the end product.

We have already expressed our thanks to the technical editors and contributors, and more formal acknowledgements appear elsewhere. However, we should also like to thank our colleagues, too numerous to list individually, whom we consulted during the course of this project and who gave much helpful advice. Finally, a special word of gratitude to the other members of the NCUF Working Group on Standards, not just for their help, but for their unfailing support and encouragement.

Cliff Evans

Brian Meek

Ray Walker

Acknowledgements

Use of copyright material

We are grateful to the following copyright holders for permission to use material appearing in this book:

The **Association for Computing Machinery** for permission to include its Code of Conduct in Section 9.

The **British Standards Institution** for permission to include the diagram from BS 2481-1:1982 as Figure 3.1 in section 3, and the extracts from BS 7002:1989 in Section 8 and from BS DD210:1992 in Section 10. (Copies of BSI pubiications may be obtained from the BSI Sales Department, Linford Wood, Milton Keynes, MK14 6LE. UK.)

The **Computing Services Association** for permission to include its Code of Conduct and its Code of Practice: Consultancy in Section 9.

Datamation for permission to include the extracts from the article by Jeff Moad in Section 1.

Ellis Horwood Limited for permission to include the extracts from the book *Programming Language Standardisation* [Hill and Meek 1990] in Section 1.

Elsevier North-Holland for permission to include, in Sections 1, 6 and 10, material from papers by Brian Meek published in *Computer Standards and Interfaces* and in the INSITS conference proceedings [Berg and Schumny 1990], and, in Section 5, the paper by Fred Cole and Heather Brown published in *Computer Networks and ISDN Systems*.

The Chairman and Secretariat of **ISO/IEC JTC1** for permission to include the extracts from the TSG-1 working paper N94 used in Section 1.

The **Joint Network Team** for universities and research councils (as sponsors), together with the **Science and Engineering Research Council** (as the funding body for the work) for permission to include extracts from David Cannon's Posix reports in Section 6.

Trademarks

Lego is a registered trademark of Lego System A/S.

OSF, OSF/1, OSF/Motif and DCE are registered trademarks of the Open Systems Foundation.

Posix is a registered trademark of the Institution of Electrical and Electronic Engineers.

TeX is a registered trademark of the American Mathematical Society.

Unix is a registered trademark of Unix Systems Laboratories.

Word is a registered trademark of the Microsoft Corporation.

WordPerfect is a registered trademark of the WordPerfect Corporation.

WordStar is a registered trademark of WordStar International Ltd.

X/Open is a registered trademark of X/Open Company Ltd.

All other products and brandnames are trademarks of their respective companies or organizations.

Contributors

Nigel Bevan is head of the Human-Computer Interaction section of the National Physical Laboratory, Teddington, UK, and chairman of the WG9U User Interface subgroup of ISO/IEC JTC1/SC18/WG9.

David Blyth is an independent consultant. Formerly with the National Computing Centre, he has served on BSI committees concerned with programming languages, magnetic media, text interchange and OSI. A founder member of the BCS Specialist Group in Formal Aspects of Computing, he is also vice-chairman of the BCS working party on formal methods in standards. He is author of a book on cryptanalysis and compiler of a dictionary of mathematical terms in computing.

Heather Brown is Professor of Electronic Publishing in the Computing Laboratory of the University of Kent at Canterbury, UK, and an "expert monitor" for the European PODA-SAX project.

David Cannon is a systems and networking programmer in the Computer Unit at Exeter University, UK, and is convenor of the BSI Posix panel and principal UK delegate to the JTC1 SC22 WG15 Posix working group.

Fred Cole is a research fellow working on document structures at the Computing Laboratory of the University of Kent at Canterbury, UK, currently (1992) working on a project funded by British Telecom.

Cliff Evans is the Technical Computer Manager in the Research Division, Kodak Ltd, Harrow, UK. He has been active in promoting the "user view" in IT for over ten years. He represents Kodak on a number of IT standards committees and is currently (1992) chairman of the Working Group on Standards of the National Computer Users' Forum.

Dr Jordi Farrés is a European Space Agency researcher at ESRIN, the European Space Research Institute at Frascati in Italy. His main research interests are formal development of software, verification methods and software engineering.

Ron Fiddes is a chartered European Engineer (Eur Ing) and has been a member since 1974 of the BSI committee which developed BS 7002. In that role he represented the Central Computer and Telecommunications Agency for ten years before taking the British Computer Society's seat on the committee. He is an active participant in the work of IEC TC74 and its Working Group 8.

Ken Holdaway is from the User Interface Technology department in IBM's Entry Systems division at Austin in Texas, USA, and chairman of ISO/IEC JTC1/SC18/WG9.

Alan Hopkinson is Systems Development Officer at the Tate Gallery in London and is also a chartered librarian. He has worked in library automation since 1972, specializing particularly in the exchange of records between bibliographic systems, which demands rigorous implementation of standards. He has undertaken numerous consultancies for UNESCO and other UN agencies.

Dr Borka Jerman-Blažič is from the Computer Science department at the Institut Jožef Stefan of the University Edvard Kardelj in Ljubljana, Slovenia, and a member of JTC1 SC2 having chaired the Yugoslav national standards committee on character sets and information coding.

Ken Johnson is a principal consultant with Neville-Clarke Ltd, a management consultancy company in the UK.

Iain Johnston is a consultant at the Centre for Software Engineering Ltd, UK, involved in the assessment and management of a wide variety of software systems in safety critical or safety related applications. His main research interest is in safety integrity and safety critical systems.

Peter Judge is managing editor of OSN, the Open Systems Newsletter, published by Technology Appraisals, Twickenham, Middlesex, UK. He has written on open systems for many trade journals and national papers, and has produced two books, *Introduction to open systems* and *Guide to IT standards makers and their standards*.

Timothy Lam is a datacommunications engineer in the Department of Technology of the London Metropolitan Police Service, working on local area networking and with responsibility for computer network security.

Brian Meek is an assistant director of the Computing Centre at King's College London. He has been actively involved in IT standardization work since the mid 1970s including a period as chairman of the BSI programming language standards committee. He currently represents the British Computer Society on that committee and on IST/-/10, BSI/DISC's technical advisory panel on IT standards.

Dr Ian Newman is a Reader in the Computer Studies department at Loughborough University of Technology, UK, and was chief editor of JTC1 TSG-1 (Interfaces for Applications Portability).

Dr Harald Nottebohm was head of the Communication department of Hoechst AG, the German-based multinational chemical company. He represented the German Association of Chemical Industry in DIN and took a leading role in the formation of OSITOP, the European user association for the promotion of IT standards.

Bruce Paterson is an independent consultant. He is active in the development of standards for IT product internationalization, character coding, keyboard layouts, and exchangeable data media. He worked for ICL as a systems and standards designer for over 25 years.

A.L. Phillips is a chartered European Engineer (Eur Ing) and is Group IT Security Manager for Yorkshire Bank plc, and is the founder and chairman of the British Computer Society Computer Security Specialist Group. He was an active contributor to ITUSA and to the Department of Trade and Industry's IT Security Advisory Group.

Dr George Sudbury is director of technology projects, with responsibility for communications and computing projects, at the London Metropolitan Police Service.

Dr Peter Swann is Reader in Economics at Brunel University, Uxbridge, UK. He is currently coordinator of the ESRC/DTI research initiative on "New Technologies and the Firm", and Managing Editor of the journal *Economics of Innovation and New Technology*. His research interests are in the economics of innovation generally, and the economics of standards in particular.

Professor Harold Thimbleby is Professor of Information Technology at Stirling University, Scotland. He has over 100 publications in user interface design, his main concern being the principles of sound design that are applicable in the early design phases.

Ray Walker is managing director of Data Accord Ltd in the UK, a consultancy specializing in the practical application of IT standards, particularly for ISDN, EDI and X.400. Formerly Secretary-General of ITUSA and chairman of BSI's EDI committee, he is secretary of the DISC UK ISDN User Forum, UK MHS Forum and document interchange action group.

Anthony Wood works with Iain Johnston at the Centre for Software Engineering Ltd, UK on the assessment and management of software systems in safety critical or safety related applications. His main research interest is in software metrics.

General bibliography

[Berg and Schumny 1990] BERG, J.L. and SCHUMNY, H. (eds.), *An analysis of the information technology standardization process*, North-Holland, Amsterdam

[Cargill 1989] CARGILL, C.F., *Information technology standardization: theory, process, and organizations*, Digital Press, Bedford, Massachusetts

[Dahlstrand 1984] DAHLSTRAND, I., *Software portability and standards*, Ellis Horwood, Chichester

[Hill and Meek 1980] HILL, I.D. and MEEK, B.L. (eds), *Programming language standardisation*, Ellis Horwood, Chichester

[Judge 1991] JUDGE, P., *Guide to IT standards makers and their standards*, Technology Appraisals, Twickenham, Middlesex

[OECD 1991] *Information technology standards: the economic dimension*, ICCP (Information Computer Communications Policy), No 25, Organization for Economic Cooperation and Development, Paris

[Smith 1990] SMITH, J.M., *An introduction to CALS: the strategy and the standards*, Technology Appraisals, Twickenham, Middlesex

[Spencer 1987] SPENCER, J., *Computing standards: a practical guide for data processing management*, Blackwell Scientific Publications, Oxford

[Wichmann 1990] WICHMANN, B.A. (ed.), *Software in safety-related systems*, British Computer Society, Swindon, and John Wiley, Chichester

A note on references in the text

For each Section, all references for all contributions are collected together at the end of the Section. Listings are divided into two parts, with standards and other documents from standards bodies coming first, followed by all other references such as books and technical papers. Consistent referencing has been done throughout the text so that the same item has the same designation wherever it is referenced.

To avoid excessive repetition, the full attributions "International Organization for Standardization, Geneva" and "International Electrotechnical Commission, Geneva" have been omitted in the case of ISO, IEC and joint ISO/IEC documents. Similarly, "British Standards Institution, Milton Keynes" and "American National Standards Institute, New York" have been omitted in the case of BSI and ANSI documents respectively.

1

Users, standards and the standardization process

This opening section collects together material relating to user needs with respect to the properties of standards in general, rather than specific technical content; to the importance of users getting involved in the standards-making process; and to the properties which that process itself needs to have in order that user participation can be effective.

First, however, two questions need to be addressed – what is actually meant by the words "standard", and "user"? The first is easy enough: for the purposes of this book, "standard" means an official, published, public standard produced by a recognized standards institution: the International Organization for Standardization (ISO) or other international bodies in many cases, since IT is inherently an international activity; national standards bodies like the American National Standards Institute (ANSI), the British Standards Institution (BSI), the Deutsches Institut für Normung (DIN), the Association Française de Normalisation (AFNOR), and so on; or accredited professional bodies like the Institution of Electrical and Electronic Engineers. What is not meant by "standard" is a "company standard", adopted internally in an enterprise, or a so-called "industry standard", i.e. a proprietary product which has gained wide acceptance in the marketplace.

What is meant by "user" in rather more difficult. From reading the literature – of IT generally, not just standards – it is clear that the word is used very differently by different people and in different contexts. Even the term "end user" is used rather imprecisely or in different ways, though here we shall use it in its most common form, that of an individual human user of an IT product. This is not intended to imply that this said user is not an IT professional. In many cases this will be so, but (for example) an end user of a CAD/CAM system could be an electronics engineer, working for an IT hardware manufacturer and designing a new circuit element for the next systems range.

What an "end user" is not, with this usage, is a "customer" where the customer is a company rather than a private individual; one does come across such usages for the term "end user", especially in sales literature and press releases, but that is not intended here. The OECD report *Information technology standards: the economic dimension* [OECD 1991], being especially concerned with governments, companies and other organizations, distinguishes between *users* and *buyers*.

Nevertheless, corporate users do have requirements too, whether they be academic or other public institutions, clubs and societies, non-IT commercial firms like chemical companies or banks, or IT companies using the products of others (such as software houses as users of hardware). Where the intent is to refer to the needs of corporate users instead of or as well as individual users, this will either be pointed out explicitly or will be apparent from the context.

In fact, most of the contributions to this book discuss the needs of individual end users, the people who have to use the products built to the standards that are produced – or not to standards, either because no standards exist or those that do are ignored by the producers. Again, we shall tend to use the term "producers", where possible, to cover the makers of products. In Europe the term "suppliers" is often used, and in the USA "vendors", and this is reflected in many of the contributions reproduced here; we have not thought it appropriate to edit out and replace all such references. However, "vendors" certainly, and usually in practice "suppliers" also, tends to imply IT manufacturing (hardware, software or service) companies. The term "producers", used by Peter Swann in his contribution later in this section, is rather more general, including the individual designers and implementors of products. It does have the consequence of excluding dealers in IT products, who are customers of the producers who supply them with their goods, but are themselves suppliers to the eventual users rather than necessarily users themselves.

The book will include discussion of user needs for standards that do not exist, or the need for producers not to ignore those that do – including, of course, why standards are sometimes ignored by producers. Is this because the standards were defective, or the standards-making process was ineffective, or was it the users' own fault? These too are issues that will be discussed.

However, we provide as the first contribution some further discussion of what the term "user" means; even at the individual level, there are still differences, as the following paper shows. It is based on an early US contribution [TSG-1 1989] to the work of JTC1's Technical Study Group (TSG-1) on Interfaces for Application Portability. JTC1, Joint Technical Committee 1 of the International Organization for Standardization (ISO), and the International Electrotechnical Commission (IEC), is the primary world body dealing with IT standards, and will frequently be mentioned in these pages, as will CCITT, the Comité Consultatif de Télégraphie et Télécommunications, which collaborates closely with ISO and JTC1 on the computer communications side.

Promoting portability is, of course, an important aim of standardization, though not the only one as we shall see, and while portability of applications is only one aspect even of that, this analysis of the different kinds of user seems generally applicable and appropriate for this section. Indeed, the "short description" on the cover page of the original document reads (slightly edited): "We" [i.e. TSG-1] "need a categorization scheme for user requirements – user requirements to identify the things that have to be portable, and the degree of portability that is required". This book needs that also.

Since TSG-1 was concerned primarily with interfaces for application portability, most of the work of that group relevant to user needs is covered in Section 7 on human-machine interfaces. This contribution is substantially edited from the original TSG-1 document, which was directed primarily at members of the group and not for general publication, but apart from that, and some further presentational changes to improve continuity, the original source has been followed as closely as possible and is gratefully acknowledged.

User views of application portability

The study and formulation of standards for Application Portability (AP) are both extremely complex and pervasive. There is little in the field of information technology that is unaffected by AP. This is particularly true of the scope of AP that is within the province of JTC1. The following categories of JTC1 work are expected to be related to AP work:

> character recognition;
> media;
> programming languages;
> documentation;
> data representation;
> data communication;
> systems technology.

There are issues concerning users throughout the functional spectrum of JTC1 standards. These user issues must be effectively addressed by the work on AP. The term "user" in this document refers not just to the so-called end users/terminal operators (i.e. the people who actually use an application in the execution of their daily work). There are four other classes of user whose requirements of AP need to be provided. Those are the system administrators, the providers of support and services, developers, and non-humans.

Views of multiple, diverse users can be a tool for the identification and analysis of user requirements. While the five groups (or types) of users share some common requirements, each has additional unique requirements. As a consequence of these unique requirements, it is useful to analyse those requirements according to five user "views".

In order to understand fully the requirements revealed by any user view, one must first understand what users of that type require in order to perform their day to day work. Additionally, to achieve a comprehensive and consistent treatment of each user view, the preferred practice is to describe the AP requirements as though the users are experiencing a complete change of environment, that is, as though their hardware and system software are changing.

End users/terminal operators use the computer system to simplify or speed up their work. End users are the ones who use the solutions of developers to do their job. System activities are transparent to the end user view. Typically they see the system through the set of tools with which they interface. As a result their requirements tend to concern consistency of interface. They want the user interface to the applications to look and feel the same after the change as before. The predominant feature of AP required by this view is accessibility. The AP standards areas which this type of user is likely to stress first include graphics, user interface, and security.

System administrators are those people who maintain the integrity of the environment. System administrators may be considered to be a special subtype of end user since their predominant requirement is accessibility. Consistent security and data representation are high priority requirements of AP standards.

The support and services view is held by those users who establish and maintain the environment. They make the environment available for use. This includes personnel both on and off-site. This includes not only field engineers diagnosing and repairing the hardware elements of the system, but also the technical software analysts handling the operating system elements. An important feature of users with this view is that they handle problems on all aspects of the environment from all types of users. The requirements from system support and services include not only those necessary for day-to-day, steady state operations but also requirements derived by the transition from one system environment to another. Support and services users will emphasize AP standards in the areas of interconnection, media, and data communication.

In essence a developer is anyone who develops a solution to a problem. The developer view, therefore, spans not only the applications and system software developers but value-added resellers and systems integrators as well. This conclusion results from the observation that the developers of application and system software use similar tools (i.e. compilers, text editors, debuggers, etc) although their work products differ. Developers require that the functionality of their tools be portable and that the interface with those tools is consistent across environments. (It is recognized that many individuals operate sometimes in the developer mode and at other times in the end user mode.) Standards for the following are most important to developers:

> programming languages;
> programming language bindings;
> supporting functions bound to programming languages;
> data representation.

Non-human users present a unique view of the requirements of AP. A non-human user's information processing system is entirely closed and operates without human intervention. Embedded systems and process control systems are representative examples of non-human user systems. The non-human users will stress the AP standards efforts in the areas of interoperability, communication, and interconnection.

There are several requirements of AP shared by all user views. That is, there are some categories of user requirements that span multiple user views.

Examples of categories of user requirements spanning multiple user views include:

> operating system resources;
> distribution services (i.e. networking);
> data management;
> graphics.

In summary, masking the entire scope of AP through the user views will simplify the study and promote completeness and quality. In addition, this breakdown will likely reveal heretofore hidden requirements.

Though this survey of the different kinds of user does not adopt the same definition of "end user" that will be adopted generally, being more specifically applications-oriented, it does highlight the fact that, even among individuals, there are different requirements that they have for standards, depending on the work they do. In that all of us process information all the time, in myriad different ways, it would be surprising, perhaps even disturbing, were this not the case. This particularly arises in the case of human-machine interfaces, so we shall return to this topic in Section 7, in particular in the contribution there by Harold Thimbleby.

If the term "user" causes some difficulty, one might expect that, if words are to have any meaning at all, there should be some consensus on what a "standard" should deliver. However, even there the situation is not completely straight-forward.

Even in terms of portability, the portability of applications is only one aspect: people also want to transfer data from application to application, physical media from machine to machine, equipment from one machine to another, themselves (or their staff) from one system to another. They want to do that, and would like to be able to do it trouble-free. If the IT standards of the early 1990s ensured that they could indeed do it trouble-free, then the need for this book would be greatly reduced – but of course it is far from trouble-free. Whether it be due to the lack of standards, the lack of adherence to standards, or the inadequacy of standards, it is not trouble-free.

Nevertheless, portability is not the whole story, as far as what standards should deliver is concerned. A simulated discussion on standardization issues in [Hill and Meek 1980], extracts from which follow, addressed this question, and even though taking place in the context of the programming language standards existing or being developed at the beginning of the 1980s, still makes some generally applicable points.

What are standards *for*?

[The participants in the extracts quoted from this "discussion" were **Tony Addyman,** of Salford University, UK; **Ingemar Dahlstrand,** of Lund University, Sweden; **David Fisher**, then of Leicester University, UK; **David Hill**, then of the Clinical Research Centre, Harrow, UK; **Brian Meek**, then of Queen Elizabeth College London, now of King's College London, UK; and **Mike Sykes**, then of ICI, Wilmslow, UK. Ellipses {.....} indicate omissions from the full discussion, including in some cases remarks by other participants. The full discussion can be found in the sequence *The Purpose of Standardisation* in [Hill and Meek 1980], pages 182-192.

Fisher: I think it can be summed up in one word: communication. Communication at all levels – between organization and organization, programmer and programmer, program and program – and between levels – programmer and organization, programmer and program, and so on. Communication in the full sense of the word, with the aim of helping to achieve portability, to help in education, and to reduce or control unnecessary duplication.

Dahlstrand: The key purpose must be portability. Suppose we got to the point where you could expect your program to run anywhere as a matter of course – that would have a tremendous impact on data processing.

Hill: Portability is not the only thing. Even if there were only one model of computer in the world, so that portability was trivial, question of responsibility would still make standardization necessary. If a program fails to work correctly, it can be checked against the appropriate standard. If it is incorrect by the standard, that is the programmer's fault and it must be rewritten. If it is correct, however, a fault by the compiler writer is indicated. In either case the action to be taken is clear because the responsibility is clear.

Addyman: Strictly speaking, all that is needed in that case is a language definition. Although a standard for a programming language is often little more than a language definition, there is a growing demand for it to contain more. A standard could, for example, specify the performance criteria, error diagnostics etc.....

Sykes: I believe it is worthwhile distinguishing between two kinds of purpose for a standard. In the first kind we are looking for sameness for its own sake. In many such cases, quality is hardly a consideration – as for example the side of the road on which we drive, the arrangement of instruments in an aircraft, the frequency of the electrical supply. In other cases the uniformity issue dominates – screw threads, plugs and sockets, etc. Notice that the question is usually one of fit. The second kind of purpose is to guarantee a property which the user would have difficulty in assessing for himself. Although sometimes this will guarantee uniformity, usually it is a minimum which is specified. One gets uniformity (within limits) in sizes of eggs, fruit etc. but more often one gets a minimum of some property which is not conveniently measured. Electrical or mechanical safety is the best example, but there are others – the corrosion-inhibiting power of ethylene glycol for motor car cooling systems, the percentage of duds in ammunition, for example. So the motivation for standards are: fit, to make communication possible; safety, to reduce the risk of injury to human (or other) beings; protection, from poor quality; and cost saving and the reduction of inconvenience. Most of the benefits of programming language standardization fall into the last category. But..... the cost reduction is hard to estimate and long term, so the motivation is therefore weak.....

Dahlstrand: When I started to work on portability, I was asked to make an estimate of the costs attributable to lack of portability of computer programs. It was quite easy to show that the costs simply of rewriting programs and retraining programmers were amounting to several millions of dollars a year in Sweden alone. But there is more to portability than just the costs. Portability is vital to creating an information network, just as a standard gauge was vital to creating a railway network or a standard voltage to creating an electrical network. Railway networks transformed industry and commerce in a way that single railways could never have done. How much reloading between railway wagons of different gauges was actually done in – say 1850? – we don't know, and I suggest we don't really care, because the immediate cost saving, though an important effect of standardization, was not the most important effect. When we have portability, we shall see a whole new dimension of machine sharing, people sharing and program sharing. We probably want to design better programs than now, because a program's usefulness will no longer be bounded in space and time to a single installation.....

Dahlstrand (later): .....to get back to the purposes of standardization, I agree..... that portability of programs is only one of them. For instance, in industrial real-time control portability of programs is only a secondary consideration; the important thing is what we might call portability of people, a common language and a shared set of concepts to start working from. A third important purpose is the setting of quality standards (where we have not yet got very far), minimum levels of things like generality, consistency, naturalness in languages. We would not be very happy with a standard which did allow programs to be transported, but made them unreasonably hard to write.....

Meek: .....Even while we have been discussing portability, the point has come up that mere transferability is not enough – an element of predictability about what happens when you transfer a program is also needed. Or, to put it another way, what is wanted is not just compatibility, but some measure of safety as well..... If I buy a piece of electrical equipment which says that it is to some British Standard specification, I expect that standard to guarantee to me not merely that the equipment will perform the desired function when plugged in and switched on, but will not blow up or otherwise do damage, and also perform its function at a reasonable minimum level of efficiency. At present I cannot write a standard-conforming program or, more important, buy a standard-conforming compiler with anything like that sort of assurance. Surely the purpose of standardization should include such aims? But there doesn't seem to have been any attempt even to think about such aspects. Am I being unfair?.....

Sykes: Where I think Brian Meek was being unfair was in asking for a measure of efficiency, because efficiency, as we all well know, is almost impossible to measure. Besides this, there are often trade-offs between translation time and execution time – sorting programs are notorious for this – which cannot fairly be dictated. In any case the user can surely do some tests before he buys. Safety standards – for example that no implementation should ignore overflow – are much more important.....

So, standards need to address quite a wide range of matters – but where does one start? There is a school of thought which says that it is the marketplace that determines the need, and that standards should therefore be based on regularizing existing practice as it has become established through usage. The question begged is whether the means of determining the need should also be the means of determining how that need is best satisfied. In the following contribution, **Brian Meek**, of King's College London, UK, argues that a process based on existing practice cannot be relied upon to meet user requirements. It is a revised amalgam of two papers: *Is standardisation just regularisation?* [Meek 1988b] and *Product-based v. product-oriented standardisation* [Meek 1990a].

Existing practice – template or prototype?

Introduction

In the programming language standards field, a question which comes up from time to time is whether a standard can be permitted to contribute to language development, by innovation (for example, introduction of new language facilities), or must be confined to regularizing what already exists in current implementations. No doubt arguments that standards should be based on existing practice come in other fields too – not just in other aspects of computing, but generally; it is, after all, a fairly fundamental issue for the standardization process. It comes up particularly in language standardization because languages are essentially abstract entities capable of limitless variation. Constraints are imposed primarily by people either running out of ideas or exercising self-discipline. Hence, comments like "the committee is doing language design, not language standardization" are not infrequent.

The purpose of this note is to argue that the view that standards must not innovate, must not do development, but may only regularize, is mistakenly narrow – certainly in our own rapidly-developing field.

Standardization as a design activity

We can begin by noting that all standardizing involves in some sense an element of design, even if only at the minimal level of making a design choice between possibilities. To give an analogy, an interior designer may well not actually design the carpet to be laid in a room, or the individual pieces of furniture which will be put into it; the process is very likely to be one of selection. Nevertheless the activity is still a design activity. Selecting which to adopt of available existing practices for inclusion in a standard is also still a design activity – though not a development activity.

Another point to note is that virtually the whole of the Open System Interconnection (OSI) standardization activity has been design and development. Certainly for the upper levels of the OSI reference model [ISO 7498:1984], no products existed in the first half of the 1980s for much of what was going on; and the reference model itself is very much a design document. In such circumstances the question did not arise of standardizing on the basis of regularizing what already existed, because nothing existed. Indeed, some manufacturers were actually waiting for the standard to become stable, before proceeding with products; the emerging OSI standards were what are now termed anticipatory standards.

Here another suitable analogy exists, in urban planning. Anticipatory standardization, where the standards developments come before the products, can be compared with planning a new town on a previously undeveloped, uninhabited site. Access roads, estate roads, layouts and facilities can all be planned in advance without encountering problems like objections from affected existing residents, or finding that there are legal restrictions (from trust deeds and the like) on how the site can be used. When the plans are implemented, there is no previously established infrastructure to have to contend with, such as existing roads, foundations, sewers, gas pipes, power cables and the like.

A few years ago, much OSI standardization was akin to developing a hitherto uninhabited site. More recently it has had to cope with a different kind of standardization, where developed, marketed products already exist; the standards are no longer anticipatory. This, of course, is a much more usual form of standardization. That is certainly mostly the case with standardization of programming languages, and it is the normal situation, not just in the IT field but elsewhere.

The great advantage of anticipatory standardization is that it avoids divergence of existing practice that tends to occur elsewhere, and hence it also avoids the pressures towards compromises, options and deliberate ambiguities that can frequently take place at standardization time. There is, however, a price to be paid. The price is the absence of experience of actually implementing the projected standard and building actual products. It may later be found that, with hindsight, some parts of the standard should have been written differently – there is some evidence of this occurring with OSI. Yet at least this limits the diversity of existing practice when the products start coming, and it provides a sensible, limited agenda for revision of the standard. However, most standardizers will inevitably not have the equivalent of a previously undeveloped site to build on; there will be existing products and practices to take into account, and there will be the corresponding vested interests to contend with and to try to reconcile.

This is a difficult problem, and one with no easy answer, as the history of standardization in all fields shows. Every such situation, eventually, has to be treated on its merits. However, there can be guiding principles – and the main point that is made in this note is that one of these should not be "standardize only on the basis of existing practice".

The major problem is not, in fact, the conflict of divergent existing practices, even though this sometimes leads to compromises being arrived at, in order to achieve consensus, which undermine the objectives of standardization. It is not adequate as a guiding principle even when there is only one existing practice.

The reason why it is not adequate is that it implies that only the suppliers of products, not their purchasers, can take development initiatives or introduce innovations. The suppliers will therefore determine the philosophy, direction and pace of development, and in effect specify the limits of the standardization agenda, even before the standards committee has been formed. Taken completely literally, it means that the standard can reflect only the "state of the art" as it was a few years ago, because it takes that time for an innovation to become established in products and hence to qualify as "existing practice". It means that users, or purchasers, who wish to benefit from new developments will have no alternative but to use unstandardized products. Of course, users or potential purchasers with new ideas or requirements are always free to suggest them; but if standards have to be based only on existing practice, these ideas, however good, will never reach the standard unless or until enough suppliers have agreed to implement them.

The most undesirable consequence of adopting "existing practice" as a guiding principle would be that it would prevent users and purchasers from identifying, during standardization, deficiencies in the existing practices and products and introducing needed improvements in conforming products. Though it might not prevent, it would certainly inhibit even a "levelling-up" process to ensure that the standard reflected the best quality in existing practice.

Product-based standardization

Let us examine this approach further, even in the case mentioned earlier when there is only one "existing practice" so no conflicts exist.

Actual products have built in a whole lot of construction decisions – ad hoc, or in response to external commercial or technical factors which are extraneous to the purpose of the standard. It is hard to separate out factors like that. Once one starts thinking in terms of an actual product, it provides the conceptual model, it determines the approach taken, and its limitations get built into the standard. The properties that a standard-conforming product should have, and how they should be provided in an actual product, get confused. If a question is under dispute, this approach inevitably generates pressures to compromise in favour of the existing product. If there are competing actual products, rather than just one, then pressure is generated to build options or "implementation dependence" into the standard, instead of proper levels of abstraction.

Product-oriented standardization

In contrast, the product-oriented approach to standardization is to think of the properties (at this level of abstraction) that relevant products should be re-quired to have – with especial reference to conformance requirements, and properties whose presence or absence can be determined objectively through testing of conformance. (Note that a third possibility, of standardization which does not address properties of conforming products verifiable by testing, is omitted altogether from this discussion.)

In this approach, products are used as the basis for abstractions, not as models. Existing products merely provide evidence of the existence of marketable entities with a collection of properties which together represent a means of satisfying a need, the solution to a user problem. Levels of abstraction are separated out, so that any can be changed without affecting others, or at most only the adjacent ones. (Note that "levels" do not refer to the layers in the OSI reference model; the approach is far more general than that.) If there are options, they are in the details of the properties to be provided for the user, between which the user can choose. The options are not options for the producer, of the means of provision of the properties, in any sense which would permit these to be included merely to permit existing products to be able to claim conformance.

Where optional properties to be chosen by the user entail portability and interface issues, under this approach these are separated out and examined at the appropriate level of abstraction; any needed interfaces and conversions between options are defined alongside the options themselves. Note that no options should appear in a standard without such interfaces, and conversions between them, being defined: these are essential to ensure interchange and interoperability. This, however, is a state which is hard to arrive at with the product-based approach, where very often options, if not explicit, exist in the form of omissions – things being left undefined in the standard, effectively giving open choice to implementors to fill in the gaps. This is acceptable if the choice is invisible to the user, but all too often the user is affected, either through limitations which inhibit interchange, or by the introduction of outright incom-patibilities.

Why the product-based approach is inadequate

The product-oriented approach of top-down functional specification of properties will be dismissed by some as being too "theoretical" or "impractical" – or worst of all "academic"! However, this is hard to sustain if the requirements are firmly based on practical user need, and there will always be sufficient interested people from the producer side to look at the lower level implications of such requirements, in terms of technical feasibility, cost and performance.

Product-based standardization is producer-oriented and product-driven; it is hard to avoid extraneous factors entering into decisions concerning the content of the standard. In particular it is hard to separate out the functionality supplied and the way in which the particular product supplies it, the result often being that the standard tends to address too many different levels of abstraction. Product-based standardization also makes it harder to plan ahead for new developments; almost inevitably, it is backward-looking.

Product-oriented standardization, in contrast, is user-oriented and function-driven. It makes it possible to build on the best available experience of all relevant products. Limitations in existing products can be identified and avoided. However, the user-orientation of this kind of standardization process does not inhibit producer involvement to anything like the extent that product-based standardization inevitably inhibits user involvement. There is still ample scope for practicalities of implementing the requirements to be explored and taken into account.

The difference is that the process does not start from existing products, with users having to make out a case for new or changed facilities, it starts from user requirements, with producers having to make out a case that including them is not practicable. Discussion of the producer-user "divide" in standards-making often seems to assume that the relationship is symmetrical and equal, but of course it is not. Making the process one that is led by user requirements actually helps to correct an inbuilt imbalance in the relationship, without depriving producers of a significant and proper role.

In short, the product-oriented approach to standardization forms a sensible basis for the planned development of standards and dealing with the problems of obsolescence, while giving due weight to the interests of all parties concerned. In contrast, the product-based approach is essentially ad hoc, makes planning ahead almost impossible, and biases the standards-making process in favour of established vested interests.

Compromise: producer-user, not producer-producer

A standard always has to be a compromise, but it should not be just a compromise between the interests of the different suppliers. It should be a compromise between the requirements of the users and purchasers of products, and the ability of suppliers to meet them. Users can be unreasonable in their expectations; in programming languages there is the special problem, already mentioned, that the entities being standardized are not physical but abstract, and are capable of variation limited only by the inventiveness of people in devising new language constructs. However, even here most users are willing to withdraw proposals if it can be demonstrated that the cost implications for products, in terms of price or performance, would be disproportionate.

(However, such statements have to be properly backed up with evidence. There is a story in standards circles that a supplier representative on a standards committee once claimed that certain facilities would be too expensive to implement, only to have it pointed out by an informed user representative that some of them were already provided in his firm's product range.)

The argument remains to be dealt with, that such problems can be left to market forces to decide, that what people buy will show what they want, so the laws of demand and supply provide the answer. One part of the response has already been given; but even without the delays in innovations qualifying as existing practice, it is still not a tenable proposition. Purchasers as well as suppliers have to face economic pressures. They have to buy the best available they can afford, not necessarily quite what they need. Even the best available that they can afford may not fit in with other requirements. Their selection of products necessarily has to take into account many factors not related to what they would like, in the realm of a particular standard, to become the "existing practice".

Suppliers, naturally and understandably, like to see their customers committed to their product range, and there is consequently an inbuilt pressure to resist complete standardization. But even without such factors, market forces, as a mechanism to ensure that existing practice will reflect the needs of purchasers and users, are too cumbersome, too uncertain, and too slow-moving in areas as precise and specific as those covered by standards, however effective they may be on a large scale.

The arguments presented here may appear to be heavily weighted towards the user and purchaser interest in standards, so it is worth pointing out that there are advantages to suppliers as well. Many vendor companies spend a great deal of time, energy and money to discover what the needs are of actual or potential users of and customers for their products. A standardization project, involving both user and supplier interests, provides the opportunity to find out needs from technically aware representatives of the users and purchasers of related products (and the users participate at their own expense!). Indeed, there is evidence that many of the technical representatives from the suppliers do indeed welcome that opportunity; possibly little more is needed than to translate such feelings into accepted company policy.

Analysis of existing practice is an important part of standards activity. As a starting point, existing practice, rather than some imagined but untested ideal, has much to be said in its favour. However, correcting shortcomings and defects in existing practice is also a part of standards work – it is one of the most effective ways for purchasers and users to have their voices heard, and to contribute to development. But regularization of existing practice alone, without such opportunity for improvement, is not an adequate basis for the standardization process.

That is one user's challenge to the widespread view, or assumption, at least on the producer side, that standards can be anticipatory if there is general (producer) agreement to that and there are as yet no products, but otherwise should be based on existing practice. Whatever one's views on this issue, there is wider agreement that user involvement in standards-making is desirable and ought to be more effective than it is. The charters of standards bodies like ANSI and BSI do refer to the need to maintain a balance between producer and consumer interest on standards committees. For example, the rules for ANSI accredited standards committee X3 (Information Processing Systems) say that "voting members of X3 are classified as Producers, Consumers or General Interest, and no one classification shall be dominant". For subgroups, members are not so classified but "both the user and the producer points of view are desired", and the key Standards Planning and Requirements Committee (SPARC) is limited to 20 voting members "and a majority must be from nonproducer category organizations".

In practice, either at national or international levels there is little evidence of systematic effort to achieve and maintain a balance of user and producer views in the technical committees where the real work of standards-making is done, at least in the IT field; and see also the extracts below from an article in *Datamation*.

The most obvious solution to the lack of a coherent user view is the establishment of user associations. To be sure, the traditional, manufacturer based user associations have in the past seemed to have been concerned as much with demanding extra facilities as extensions to standards, or additional unstandardized products, than with demanding adherence to standards, but the 1980s saw a considerable shift as the importance of Open Systems Interconnection (OSI) and other interworking standards became more widely appreciated. In the next contribution, **Dr Harald Nottebohm**, of Hoechst AG, Germany, stresses the importance of user associations, with particular reference to OSI. Note that, in this contribution, "users" mostly means "corporate users".

What is the use of a users' association?

Introduction

Most users or user companies approached to participate in a users' association of any kind react in a quite natural way. They ask, what are the benefits of my involvement, either in form of financial contribution or manpower? The more the benefits of being a member relates to easing the daily work, the more readiness for participation we find. On the other hand, the more the association aims at long-term strategic goals the more reluctance we find, at least at the level of the users running the daily business. It is here that there is the challenge to the top managers.

Before trying to give an answer to the question in the title, we must recall the needs and requirements of IT users.

Needs and requirements of users

Most users feel more or less uneasy, if not to say helpless, when it comes to judging IT alternatives and deciding on the choice of software/hardware systems. Fast changing hardware technology now results in a revolutionary change of complete systems architecture, in the direction of distributed systems. Thus any decision in the present should not be made without checking if the decision possibly blocks the evolutionary way to an anticipated future system or structure.

Therefore users need reliable information enabling them to judge alternatives and their potential for evolution. Based on good judgement, users will be able to develop and follow a strategy of migration which does not lead into a blind alley.

One of the shortcomings is good and reliable information. The flood of information reaching the users is often incomprehensible and contradictory. Therefore many users tend to follow the market leader almost blindly. In a technical sense this may be a safe way. But is it really in the interest of users, considering economic aspects? Surely not. Here we have a problem, because the awareness of many users is not developed: the technical staff of user companies tend to go the way they think is safe, and the top executives do not understand the issues and therefore do not realize that these are management issues.

It is commonly agreed that the standards-making process is too slow and that it needs acceleration. It is also common understanding that the reason for this is seen to be the lack of available experts. What is not seen is that there are at least two factors which might accelerate the process considerably:

Firstly, very often standards are compromises reached by only vendors sitting at a round table, each of them trying to minimize his own costs of adaptation. Naturally this is a long and time consuming process which would be dramatically shortened by having some user representatives sitting at the table. This is especially true with standards which are near the users' application side, e.g. upper layer functions in the OSI model.

Secondly, the standards-making experts are certainly not aware what the most urgent needs of the users are, especially with respect to migration aspects. Input from users could therefore set priorities for their work, an effect which would bring the most needed standards sooner than by the present method of working.

There are numerous fields where the absence of approved standards and related products heavily impede the needed progress of implementing more communication links between incompatible systems. These are needed, for example, for the transmission of data files, documents (including graphics and different character sets) and EDI data, or for access to databases or for program-to-program communication. Likewise the evolving standardization in the Unix scene and in the field of user interfaces is of greatest concern. This list is certainly incomplete (e.g. no word about ISDN), but it presumably shows the gravitational centre.

As can be seen from the foregoing, the individual user or user company is in a way helpless. He plays the role of a spectator, watching with interest what is happening in the IT field. He does not have the feeling that he might be in the position to influence the play. On the other hand, it is he who orders IT equipment and its software, and pays for it. Thus he contributes to the creation of a "market demand". Why does he not use it in a way that helps him to meet his requirements? The answer is obvious. He can only expect success if he allies with other users. Only the joint use of market demand will be able to accelerate the process of standardization and counterweight the individual interests of vendors to be a little more equal than others.

As soon as a user decides to follow a migration strategy towards open systems and begins to implement products for linking systems of different architectures and from different vendors he embarks on an adventure: he has to manage a multivendor network without possessing a full set of tools for network management. These are not yet available. His decision may be based on his perception that an early start into the open world will gain him a competitive edge. Nevertheless, the decision may become easier if he could get some external help or support. Vendors will not be likely to be able to give this support.

What do users expect from a users' association?

This can clearly be deduced from the above requirements.

The association should be a source of reliable information, which must be given in a way that managers at the level of decision really understand the issues and are able to judge them.

The association should function as a relay between users and standardizers: it should be a focal point for user needs and priorities and should be in the position to influence the standardizers' work.

The association should support users to develop migration strategies and to give advice in implementing related products or prototypes and in managing heterogeneous networks. Aside from other activities, this can be done by appropriate projects preferably funded by public authorities, in Europe by the CEC.

The association should raise wide public awareness to become distinctly visible as a pressure group. This would certainly convince further users to join the association. Both – public awareness and growing membership – would broaden the market demand for open systems and consequently motivate software houses to develop and market interface products to ease migration.

What are the most important success factors?

The association should only admit direct membership of companies and not of other associations. It should also admit vendors – especially the leading ones – as members. However, its constitution must guarantee that it stays a user driven association, e.g. by stipulating an appropriate quorum of users and vendors in its steering committee.

The number of user members must be large enough to represent a real user community within a region of say Europe to be heard and followed. Promotional activities to acquire more members must be made on a professional basis. Professionalism of marketing would involve analysing the target group, address management effectively by using their notions and to care for a perpetual atmosphere of awareness of user companies and above all the public. I believe that a sufficient number of larger companies could be motivated to invest in such an association if the economic issues of IT standardization could be made clear to them and if the phenotype of the association could be made to appear trustworthy for an effective acceleration of the standardization process.

One of the factors to gain trustworthiness is the potential of actual influence the association has on standardization bodies, e.g. on JTC1 (S-Liaison) or EWOS and ETSI in Europe. Influence is not so much sought on technical details but more on priority of work plans and narrowing of options.

A great problem is to make users actively contribute to the association's technical work and to participate in working groups in a way that results may represent real users' attitudes. Questionnaires are often poorly answered. On the other hand, all the necessary expertise is more or less hidden somewhere within the association. Therefore suitable techniques of coordination, interviewing etc. must be used to motivate experts to contribute their knowledge without having to write something, speak an unfamiliar language or spend time on meetings if they don't like it or are not allowed to.

It is important to find out the interests of the members including the new ones from time to time and to adjust the scope of work accordingly. If the scope of work is to be widened beyond the initial intentions, care must be taken not to exceed the potential of the association.

Another part of good marketing is to polish up all documents issued by the association by giving them a unique layout, and to make them or part of them readable for managers (management summaries). This implies the use of professional editors for editing and publishing documents.

The above success factors can only be met if a professional management crew runs the organization. It reports to the steering committee. National secretariats in the main countries for national activities will help to promote the ideas and results of the association's work effectively. Their work would have to be coordinated by the main management. National secretariats are not identical with national chapters which are not recommended. An association with national chapters tends to divert and thus loses impact.

Conclusion

In Europe we already have a user association which has the potential to develop further in the sense outlined above. It is OSITOP, founded in February 1987 and now with approximately 120 members. Its original field of work – support of OSI only in the field of clerical and technical office environment –

has meanwhile widened beyond this scope and includes for example ISDN, and especially all topics related to migration of the members' present systems with proprietary protocols to open systems. OSITOP also runs its own OSI based network which is used not only for information transfer but also for the development and demonstration of business scenarios.

Starting from the "nucleus" OSITOP by a professional awareness campaign it should be possible to attract more "participating" members rendering the financial means to recruit a professional management to run the association more effectively and improve its public relation.

OSITOP has already signalled its willingness to eventually merge with other associations if its main principles are not violated, the most important ones being "direct membership" and "user-driven".

With all the above in mind I think that the question in the headline is duly answered: users aware of and in need of open systems will have to organize themselves in order to pursue their interests unless they don't mind financing a whole industry of interface and gateway systems.

In Nottebohm's paper, it is envisaged that producers, in particular supplier companies, would be involved in user associations, and that of course is the pattern for many of the associations for users of the products of the major manufacturers. One attempt to form a "pure" users association was the Information Technology User Standards Association (ITUSA) in the UK, an association of corporate users (and mainly large companies at that). ITUSA set up various "action groups" of technical IT experts from user companies to study and identify needs. However, after a few years, in the early 1990s these activities were subsumed in DISC (Delivering Information Solutions to Customers), an autonomous wing of BSI which undoubtedly has heavy involvement from the supplier side. We shall hear more about DISC in later sections of this book.

Most associations are in fact producer-user or producer-only consortia. The 1980s saw an explosion in the number and activities of such consortia, including actual standards development. This has been interpreted variously as an expression of dissatisfaction with the conventional standards-making machinery (by users, producers or both), and as a threat to the authority of the official, formal standards bodies. As well as in the preceding paper, the activities of these groups are referred to in [Cargill 1989], and in [Rankine 1990] and several other contributions to the 1989 INSITS proceedings [Berg and Schumny 1990], but it is contrary to the aims of this book to discuss the details of the activities of specific groups of that kind and their relationships with official standards bodies, especially as these are changing all the time. What matters here is the more general question of the effectiveness of consortia of this kind in meeting user needs.

A controversial article in *Datamation* [Moad 1990] discussed the phenomenon of the growth of such consortia, under the somewhat dramatic headline *The standards process breaks down.* While for the bulk of the article, consortia are referred to in terms such as "users and vendors", without differentiating between their differing needs and motivations, towards the end "users" start getting separated from "consortia" in the discussion, and the following extract is of interest. It has been lightly edited here to match the altered context from the original complete article. The discussion is in the context of the US standards process, and in particular it is that of ANSI Accredited Standards Committee X3 which is claimed to be "breaking down".

An uncomfortable fit for users

Many users who have tried to participate directly in X3 committees have found it difficult to fit into the process. At Chicago oil giant Amoco Corp., for example, information systems (IS) planning officials convinced their management to let them join the X3 SQL (Structured Query Language) committee four years ago in an effort to leverage the influence the company could have on the design of products from a number of vendors. For three years, Amoco sent some of its top data management technicians to about six committee meetings a year, at a cost of about $1,200 per meeting. Amoco submitted proposals for 10 features it wanted to see in the new SQL standard. Six of them were accepted.

Last year (1989), however, just as the X3 SQL committee set out to decide on the new SQL-2 and SQL-3 features that should be implemented, Amoco IS management decided to pull out of the committee.

"We were unable to convince management that the process still had enough relevance to us to continue," says Alan Hirsch, Amoco's representative on the committee.

Some longtime X3 participants say that that kind of user experience is unavoidable. "The truth is that, although we are now involved more in anticipatory standards, the process really hasn't changed greatly. But what we have now is pretty much the only way it will work given the constraints of our organizational structure in the US," says SQL committee chairman Don Deutsch. "All vendors are there representing their best understanding of user requirements, anyway."

Some users, however, say that's not good enough. Users like Michael A. Kaminski, General Motors Corp.'s manager for computer-integrated manufacturing (CIM) and networking technology, say X3 committees need to get requirement definitions directly from users. And users need to have an ongoing place on the technical committees.

"The process is much too slow, and part of the reason is that the committees are composed for the most part of vendors who have a base of products to protect, be it SNA [IBM's Systems Network Architecture] or something else," says Kaminski.

At least one consortium and a user group are currently defining a new standards role for users that Kaminski and others think could serve as a model for X3. The Corporation for Open Systems (COS), a consortium focused on the certification and testing of standard profiles, recently joined forces with the Information Technology Requirements Council (ITRC), an OSI-focused user group best known for defining the MAP/TOP profile (Manufacturing Automation Protocol and Technical Office Protocol, perhaps the outstanding example of effective standards originally conceived outside the formal standards process, though now absorbed into ISO). ITRC members... have become COS members and formed what the group calls a "requirements interest group". The first requirements interest group will help COS' technical committees understand the detailed technical requirements of MAP/TOP manufacturing users.

COS officials say they intend to add requirements interest groups from other industrial areas such as financial services, utilities and airlines. Already at least one other user group, a recently formed collection of aerospace, oil and other companies known as the "Houston 30," is considering joining COS as one or more requirements interest groups.

"Users are looking to leverage their common interests and influence standards development," says Bud Huber, manager of advanced networks integration at Hughes Aircraft Co. and a member of the Houston 30. "The changes being discussed by X3 are just a part of this trend."

So far, however, X3 hasn't come up with a plan for bringing users into the base standards-making process. But some in the organization are working on it. As a result of its review of the standards development life cycle, X3's two-year-old Strategic Planning Committee is expected to issue a report soon that suggests ways to carve out roles in the X3 process specifically for users and the consortia....

Many users would disagree with Deutsch about the vendors' "best understanding" of user requirements, and agree with Kaminski that it is not an adequate mechanism. So it would seem that the growth of user-producer consortia is a response to concern about the apparent dominance of producers in the standards process, and many users, particularly large corporate users, see this as the way to redress the imbalance referred to earlier in Meek's contribution. Nevertheless there a residual worry: what if the user-producer consortia gradually become producer-dominated – perhaps if the user participants relax once the immediate problems that motivated them to join have been addressed? And what of the activities of explicitly producer-only consortia, which certainly exist?

One aspect that makes users nervous is the recent adoption in the ISO JTC1 area of the so-called "fast track" procedure, for rapid adoption as international standards of existing documents deemed suitable for that purpose. This procedure was originally conceived to shorten the protracted, multi-stage formal review period that international standards normally go through, in cases where all the development work on the document had already occurred and did not need repeating. The institution of fast-tracking was primarily motivated by the wish to be able to give rapid endorsement by ISO to certain national standards, and standards produced by other international bodies like CCITT. However, the procedure is open more widely than that, including industry consortia, and including producer-only industry consortia.

A case in point is a standards produced by a producer-only consortium, for use by their members, which they were considering putting forward for fast-tracking in 1991. A presentation was made to representatives of a number of interested official standards committees. Afterwards, a user representative from one of these asked the consortium presenter, "what means did you use to ascertain the acceptability to users of what you are proposing?" There was a pause (slightly embarrassed) before the presenter answered "er – well, we didn't". It is things like this that make users involved with standards sceptical of the effectiveness of producer-only or producer-dominated consortia in meeting user requirements.

There remains to be considered the role of governments – who are, at least in all developed countries, themselves major corporate users. Many look to governments to give a lead to all users, and point to the effectiveness of the US government's Federal Information Processing Standards (FIPS), of initiatives such as that of the US Department of Defense in promoting the development of the programming language Ada, and later initiatives by the European Commission in the run-up to the Single European Market of 1992. On the other hand, equally there has been concern that national governments can sometimes subordinate their "IT user" role to a wish, in the major manufacturing nations, to promote their country's indigenous IT industry (see for example [Reynolds 1990], and also [OECD 1991]).

We shall not pursue this further here, but will return the role of governments in the last section of the book, which looks at "the way forward". For the moment, we shall conclude this opening section with a comprehensive survey, by **Peter Swann** of Brunel University UK, of how user needs might be reflected in the standards process.

How can we ensure that users' votes are counted?

Introduction and summary

One of the themes of this book is that the standardization process pays inadequate attention to user requirements. This paper examines from an economic point of view why this should be, and what (if anything) might be done to make standardization processes more sensitive to users' votes. In discussing this issue we concentrate on why users in particular are under-represented, and why it is so difficult to change the rules of the game so that users can be more heavily involved.

The paper starts by recognizing that participation in standards institutions is subject to economic rules of demand and supply. The establishment of good standards requires widespread participation, but widespread participation slows the process of negotiation; if participation is seen to be a very time consuming activity, many will drop out. In particular, it will be the users who choose not to participate, as they do not have the same resources as large producers to participate in what is often a long drawn out process. Partly in consequence of this, many of the standards that do emerge do not seem to be widely used in the market; instead, the best selling products are frequently based on proprietary standards rather than public domain standards.

For this reason, it is suggested that there is trade-off between the speed of standards setting and the quality of the resultant standard – in terms of its overall acceptability. Three natural ways of increasing participation are: (a) to subsidize participation of marginal participants – though it may be far from easy to distinguish the marginal participant from the stalwarts; (b) to improve committee structures to speed up the process of reaching consensus amongst a group – again this is not a trivial matter; (c) to design a more segmented institutional structure where small scale participation is valuable and worthwhile, if without the pay-off of longer term participation.

With growing demands on standards institution and growing costs associated with their work, some commentators ask why market processes can't be left to do some of the work. We explain why the oft quoted ability of competitive markets to attend to diverse user needs does not really apply in the establishment of standards; briefly, this is because users cast their votes in sequence, and the votes of the pioneers determine the choices available to later voters – but not vice versa. Indeed, we show that user involvement in setting market-defined standards may be very limited.

Moreover, we show that the existence of a (potential or actual) market process can undermine the work of a standards institution. First, it is very likely to push the institution to a more rapid consensus, and to achieve such a consensus rapidly, the number of participants must be kept down – and hence the quality of the standard will fall. Second, the coexistence of the market process and the standards institution can lead to the worst of both worlds. The existence of the first process (market) can undermine the momentum of the second (institutional negotiation), and in the face of a loss of confidence in the first, participants will flock to the market solution. It is arguable that the market process will work less well if it commences after the break up of a negotiating process, than if all parties were committed to the market process from the start.

To achieve widespread participation in standards negotiation calls for time, and if market pressures restrict the time available, then an increase in user involvement may require that market pressures be neutralized. One way is by devising schemes to discourage participants from breaking rank. The second is by the use of "pre-standards" as a means to strengthen resolve of those involved in the negotiation process, and as a means of giving the final standard more credibility.

The remainder of the paper is organized as follows. We make a vital distinction between horizontal and vertical standards issues, and examine the trade-offs between time and representation in standards setting. Then we ask whether user involvement in standards setting might be increased, or whether it may be nigh impossible. Next we look in contrast at market processes to generate standards, and examine the pressures that a rival market process will place on institutional standards negotiation. Indeed, we conjecture that the two processes may undermine rather than reinforce each other, and we explore two ways in which the negotiation process might be strengthened.

The paper does not attempt to address the distinct, though very important, issue of why it is so difficult to find a voting scheme that handles diverse votes in a satisfactory way. This last question has its roots in several well-known paradoxes and problems of social choice theory. In short these imply that it is impossible to find a voting method that satisfies certain apparently innocuous properties, and is applicable to a wide range of choice situations. This is a very real problem in counting votes, but need not particularly mean that users' votes are ignored in voting processes. The paper concentrates on why users may not even get into the voting booths, so to speak.

Horizontal and vertical standards issues

It is often argued that the non-responsiveness of the standardization process to user needs is a result of insufficient resources being spent on standardization institutions. This need not necessarily be so. To see why, it is helpful to make a distinction between two types of standards activities. One is concerned with horizontal definition of the standard, the other with vertical definition.

An example of the horizontal aspect of standards is the competition between two competing specifications from two opposed manufacturers, neither specification being obviously superior to the other on technical grounds, but which are inherently incompatible with each other. The vertical aspect of standards is concerned with enhancements to the scope, quality, comprehensiveness and flexibility of a standard. In making this distinction, it is assumed that there would be general agreement amongst users and producers as to what constituted an improvement in the vertical definition of a standard, while there would never be agreement on what was the best horizontal definition.

In the case of a contest over horizontal standards alone, the standards negotiation may fail to reflect user needs, but not because there is insufficient expenditure on standards; indeed, from one point of view it is arguable that there is too much spending on the standards negotiation. However much is spent on the negotiations, there will be (in a two sided contest), one winner and one loser, or else a compromise is struck. Economists often use the term *zero sum game* to describe contests of this sort. From the users' point of view it is the fact of the standard rather than its form that matters. From the companies' point of view, however, it is strategically vital to spend resources on trying to ensure that their specification is the winner – without such expenditure they are bound to lose. But this spending has little value to the user, and in that sense the expenditure is too high from a social point of view. (For a fuller discussion of this point, see [Swann 1991].)

Moreover, in this case of a horizontal contest the standardization process need not necessarily achieve the users' needs for standards. Two firms may fail to reach a compromise even when the joint benefits from agreeing a common standard exceed modification costs, because whichever compromise position standard is chosen, it is still better for one (or both) firms to break rank and revert to their own proprietary design, in which they have accumulated experience. The full details of this argument are somewhat technical, but the essence is this. A compromise will only survive if each party's share of the mutual benefits exceeds its modification costs; but in practice there may be no compromise solution in which this condition is satisfied for all parties.

One further reason why producers may fail to negotiate a common standard as required by users, is simply that from the producers' point of view such standardization increases the risk of price competition. The user demand can effectively be for an increase in competition, and not surprisingly producers would not be willing to supply that.

The vertical aspect of standardization is the making of (unambiguously) better standards. Here (to a first approximation) expenditure by any party leads to an improvement in the overall standard achieved, and hence there are positive spillovers to others whenever any parties spend on participation in standards setting. (This may seem an unrealistically pure form of participation, but the concept is useful in what follows.)

In this sense, time invested in improving the vertical quality of a standard is a public good. The standard economic analysis of public goods suggest that there would tend to be underinvestment in this aspect of standardization. This arises because the investor does not recoup the full dividend from his investment, with some of the dividend accruing to others (sometimes called free riders) who do not reimburse the investor. Thus from the point of view of the IT community as a whole, investment in this aspect of standardization tends to be too low – that is, there are inadequate resources being spent.

To recap, then, it appears that in horizontal standards contests, producers may not achieve the compromise standard required by users (though not from lack of expenditure on negotiations); while in the case of vertical aspects of standards, user requirements for standards may not be met because insufficient resources are devoted to the standards negotiation.

Participation, time and quality

Cargill, in his book *Information technology standardization: theory, process and organizations* [Cargill 1989], notes that diversity of participants is both an advantage and a problem for standards institutions. Reaching consensus in a diverse group takes time – the more diverse, the longer it takes. At the same time, it is the consensus from a diversity of opinions that gives the negotiated standard its strength and quality [Cargill 1989, pp 233-4].

It can be argued that participation in standards setting institutions is subject to the normal economic conditions of demand and supply. The process may not seem to adhere perfectly to this simple model, but the model still yields some useful insights.

Participation is costly (in terms of time) for the participants. As cost (the time a negotiation is expected to take) increases, then a number of previously willing participants find the time commitment too great and drop out, so that demand falls. This demand curve is the downward sloping line DD' in Figure 1.1. It may also be that as the number of participants increases, the expected quality of the standard increases, and hence each agent sees an additional reason for participation. Effects of this sort can easily be incorporated into the model, and they tend to make the demand curve less steep.

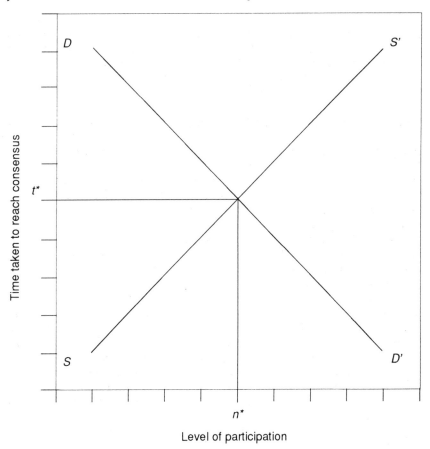

Figure 1.1 *Demand and supply in standards setting*

On the other hand, the cost (time taken to reach consensus) can be expected to rise as the number of participants (i.e. supply) increases – the line SS' in Figure 1.1. This supply curve – indicating time taken to reach consensus as a function of the number of participants – suggests a trade-off between speed and quality.

The implication of this is that there will be a "market clearing" price – that is a time for negotiation – and an associated level of participation. The equilibrium or outcome is summarized by n^* and t^* in Figure 1.1. Expecting the process to take time t^*, n^* people participate, and reaching consensus amongst n^* takes t^*; consensus amongst that number can just be reached within the time expected. If one extra person were to join, then t^* would have to increase to achieve consensus in this larger group, but then someone will want to drop out.

Those who do not come forward are unable to make the necessary time commitment. The likelihood is that most users will be unable to meet a large time cost. The reason for this lies in the inherent economies of scale in committee participation, and the costs of coordinating large and diverse groups to provide a delegate.

Large manufacturers have very large incentives to participate: the value to them of a small influence on the final form of the standard can be multiplied by the large number of units sold, while the single user would need to make a substantial influence on the choice of standard given that the value of this is to be multiplied only by one system.

In principle, a group of users with common interests might collectively sponsor one representative, so that the costs of participation are defrayed across a large group of users, while the benefits are enjoyed undiluted by each of that group. The practical problem with this always seems to lie with coordination costs, and the possibility of free riding described above. Individual users can benefit from such an action without contributing to the costs of representation; thus the amount contributed to such a representation is likely to fall well below the financial benefit of it. Large firms need not suffer such a problem, as they do not face such coordination costs. Consortia of medium and small sized firms lie somewhere in the middle; they do not face such serious coordination costs, nor is free riding so serious as for users, but such consortia are still at a disadvantage compared to large firms.

In short, the non-participation of users is a matter of time, or the speed with which standards can be set. But why does speed matter? Does it really matter? At first these questions may seem absurd; if institutions are too slow, users will just resort to the market solution – see under *Standards institutions in the face of market pressures* below. And speed matters for competitiveness, because once one party moves, there is competitive pressure to follow rapidly. Yet at a deeper level the questions are not so absurd. It is well recognized that markets can exaggerate the need to adopt technologies rapidly. If all users could confidently expect others to wait for the superior negotiated solution, then none will need to break rank and adopt prematurely. And the outcome for all will be better for having waited.

How to increase involvement

The implication of this last discussion is that unless time were unlimited, or negotiations a formality – both very far from that – there will always be some who would benefit from participation but chose not to participate because the time commitment is too large. Lack of user representation may simply be a consequence of this. To achieve broader user involvement would involve reducing the cost of access, or meeting some of those costs.

One method, then, is to subsidize users to participate. The rationale for this is that user participation generates valuable spillovers that go beyond the users themselves, and hence the beneficiaries of these spillovers should be willing to contribute to the costs of user participation. We set aside the institutional question of exactly how the subsidies would be financed, and concentrate on two more basic difficulties.

The first problem is the issue of additionality: how much of the subsidy finds its way to users who are thus enabled to participate, and who without the subsidy would be unable to participate? More generally, for any practical scheme of participation subsidies, what proportion goes to increasing participation, and what proportion simply goes as an arguably wasted subsidy to those who would have participated anyway? Economic analysis of some subsidy schemes suggests that additionality can in many cases be quite low.

The second problem is the implication of a subsidy for the time taken to achieve consensus. Using the model of the previous subsection, extra participation must mean that it takes longer to reach consensus. Whether this matters or not will depend on whether negotiation is proceeding without undue market pressure. If so, then there may be no reason why people will not wait. But if markets exert pressure for a quick solution, then the problem is more serious. This issue is addressed under *Standards institutions in the face of market pressures*.

A second method of increasing participation is by reforming committee structures. This bland statement immediately poses the question of whether pure improvements in committee structure can be achieved, and how, or whether, any such reforms will inevitably involve a compromise between the interests of different parties. One suggestion for reform is the use of informal working groups or subcommittees with a low time commitment that feed into the central standards committees. In this way participants can select the level of participation they wish: either a full time commitment with the expectation of substantial influence, or a more modest time commitment with more modest expectations about what that will achieve. Such schemes would in economist's language be called discriminatory, but while that term generally has a pejorative sense, it can be shown that – properly designed – such schemes lead to improvements over what can be achieved by a one-tier structure.

Our discussion of user involvement would not be complete, however, without a mention of the risks of filibustering in committee. This is one of the reasons why those of a very free market philosophy are sometimes suspicious of standards committees dominated by producers, and in which users play a modest role.

There can be incentives for producers to filibuster. In the absence of market pressure, the negotiation process can be prolonged (by filibustering) to a point that some participants (with views and preferences so different from those who filibuster) drop out and so have no influence on the outcome. In economist's language, this is called a strategy of raising rivals costs. And even in the presence of market pressure there can be an incentive, albeit more destructive, for filibustering: to neutralize the effect of the negotiated process so that participants have to resort to market process – an outcome which would suit those who filibuster.

Market processes to generate standards

Market processes can generate standards, though many would dispute that these are standards in the generally accepted meaning. Market defined standards are usually proprietary (rather than open), they are not written down as a publicly accessible specification, and it is common to find that the originators of these designs will eventually start to assert their proprietary rights.

But even setting aside these difficulties, the oft quoted ability of competitive markets to serve user needs does not really apply in cases such as this, where users cast their votes in sequence, and the votes of the pioneers determine the choices available to later voters – but not vice versa.

In the standard free market argument, competitive entry to the market ensures that any user need that can be served profitably will be provided, and competition will drive prices down to the minimum cost of production. In this case, all users are treated equally by the market, and serving the needs of one user need not deny serving the needs of others.

The difference when markets are called on to set standards is that different users are not treated equally. The choices of early users determine the choices available to later users. A sophisticated standard may be required by most later users, but if early pioneers have settled for a "crude" standard, then it may quite quickly become unprofitable (if not plain impossible) to sell a sophisticated standard – and hence producers abandon their attempts to market any new standards. In short, there can easily be an excessive and pervasive bandwagon effect that reinforces an early product's position as de facto industry standard.

Indeed, it may well be that the market-defined standard is effectively set by the actions and choices of a small proportion of users and producers, in ignorance of the requirements of those who follow later – see [Swann and Lamaison 1990]. Those who come later will effectively have little or no say in the matter. For a detailed economic analysis of the market process generating standards, the reader is referred to [Farrell and Saloner 1987, Farrell 1989, David and Greenstein 1990].

Standards institutions in the face of market pressures

Figure 1.2 illustrates how market pressure may constrain the action of the standards institution. It superimposes on Figure 1.1 a curve (*TT'*) showing the maximum time a standards institution can take to derive a standard before users lose patience, and defect en masse to the de facto standard offered by a market process. The derivation of this curve is a little complex – see [Swann 1991] – but the basic idea is simple enough: as more participants are involved in negotiations over the standard, the expected quality of that standard increases, and accordingly users and producers are prepared to wait longer before resorting to the market process. But the returns to increasing participation are diminishing, and the acceptable time delay starts to grow only very slowly.

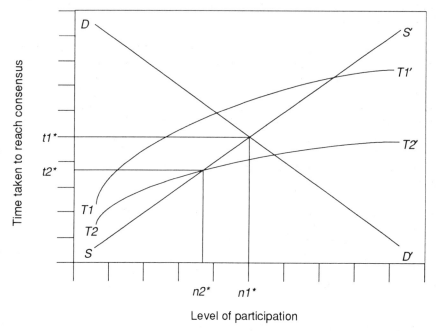

Figure 1.2 *Time constraints in standards setting*

In case 1 (*T1T1'*), the equilibrium outcome in the standards institution is a timescale *t** for a negotiated standard that is fast enough to prevent defection to the market process. In that case, market pressure does not constrain the standards committee. In case 2 (*T2T2'*), however, the timescale *t** is too slow to prevent defection to the market process. In this case, the market pressure does act as a constraint on the standards institution.

In this latter case, some would argue that the market pressures will sharpen up standards committees, and that must be a good thing. Market pressure certainly raises the cost of prevarication, and can exhort participants to make rapid decisions. It can also reduce the perceived time cost of involvement: if the committee is going to achieve anything, it will have to do so quickly. [Farrell and Saloner 1988] find that not only are negotiated standards superior to market defined standards, but that the mixed process is superior to the negotiated process alone. This arises because the existence of the market option puts more pressure on parties to reach agreement.

On closer inspection, however, the argument is not so clear cut. Market pressure may indeed force the institution to achieve a consensus more rapidly. But the value of that will depend on how it is achieved. Some optimists would suggest that the existence of this market pressure brings a pure improvement in institutional efficiency, so that faster standards setting is possible with no compromise on quality. Others would be more pessimistic. More rapid consensus may demand that expectations of the compromise standard reached must be lowered. And in this case the outcome is not an unambiguous improvement. Those who value timeliness more highly will consider it an improvement; those who value quality more highly will not.

Returning to Figure 1.2, we can explore these two possibilities. The optimists are arguing in effect that the SS' curve swivels downwards to cross DD' below the line $T2T2'$. The pessimists would argue that the SS' curve does not move; participation must be reduced to $n2^*$, where it will take only $t2^*$ to reach consensus, and accordingly the quality of the resultant standard must decline. It is worth noting incidentally that if the time to reach consensus is expected to be only $t2^*$, then more will wish to participate than can be accommodated given the time constraint. In such cases, membership of the standards committee will have to be rationed – perhaps by charging an entry fee which again brings demand in line with supply.

In conclusion, it is worth restating that from this perspective that, when they bite, market pressures must in general divert a committee away from further work towards a negotiated standard and towards something closer to the market solution. And it is worth remembering that the starting point in the whole process – part of the underlying rationale for standards institutions in the first place – is that the market solution is in several regards unsatisfactory.

Two processes that may conflict rather than reinforce

The two approaches to reaching standards – institution and market – are themselves rather like two competing standards, with pre-announcements on the part of the institution. The market process is available at an early stage, and users and producers alike can always adopt a market solution if they tire of waiting for the negotiated standard. The negotiated standard is pre-announced, and expected to be better, but may arrive too late. Thus, if a bandwagon starts around the market process, then people will desert the negotiation process in increasing numbers, even though the latter promises a better standard.

Participation in the negotiation process involves some sort of commitment not to go to market until a consensus is formed; but if the consensus is slow, some participants – those perhaps who attach less value to the ultimate quality of the standard – break rank away from the negotiated process and go to market. By doing so they put pressure on the (as yet incomplete) negotiated standard, and can easily destabilize what would otherwise be a satisfactory process of negotiation leading to a good standard. This is not to deny the fact that one of the reasons for institutional standards setting is that markets sometimes fail to generate any sort of standard. But the point is that if it works the market process is fairly quick to act, and a de facto standard will emerge quickly, necessitating rapid pursuit.

One example of this is the case of gateway products to connect different LANs. It is generally recognized that a system of LANs interconnected by gateways is technically a much inferior solution to a more global ISDN solution. In particular, critics of "gateways" point out that they never offer 100% compatibility. But this may not be enough to deter many users, who do not require perfect standardization. And in adopting the gateway solution, these users (unwittingly perhaps) undermine the momentum of ISDN as a marketable system [David and Steinmueller 1990].

It is arguable that the outcome of an interrupted negotiation process is worse than would have been the case had all parties committed themselves to the market process from the start. If all players commit themselves to the market from the start, then within the rules of the market process (themselves by no means ideal) the "best" standard will win. But if all players are committed at the start to negotiations, it is quite likely that the first to break rank will be one who produces a "bad" standard (in terms of its vertical quality). For a "bad" standard would never win if the process of negotiation can be prolonged as required, so the producer of the "bad" standard has greatest incentive to break rank. And given that the market process for setting standards puts great emphasis on bringing a product to market early, this "bad" standard may be well placed to win the market contest.

Discouraging participants to break rank

We have seen that achieving greater user representation in standards setting may involve allowing the process to take longer. But we have also seen that market pressure may deny institutions that time, as there will be growing incentives for some participants to break rank – effectively undermining the negotiation process.

A common argument in economic analysis is that there are adverse reputation effects that will provide adequate disincentive to break rank. Thus if all producers agree to adhere to a common quality standard, and one of their number cheats, then he will eventually be found out and users will ever after be wary of his produce. But reputation may count for much less in a fast moving industry. It is, for example, rare to see software and computer companies boast about their distant date of foundation. A long history of reputable trading may be a treasured boast in more stable industries, but is often irrelevant in rapidly changing industries.

To further discourage participants from breaking rank requires a mixture of "stick" and "carrot". The "stick" is to discredit those who do break rank, but that alone will not work in the absence of widespread user knowledge and compliance. If some users (it need not be all that many), are content to buy the "rogue standards" from the market, rather than wait for the agreed standard, then labelling alone will not be sufficient to prevent the negotiated standard from being undermined. It requires that users be educated that their "precipitate" choices may have adverse implications for their longer term IT investment and for the IT community as a whole.

Such education is not without difficulties. Most users simply cannot be aware of the extent to which their purchases are substandard, and of the implications of their purchases for the quality of choices available to later users. And, moreover, scepticism quickly sets in. Some users may grow weary of strictures not to buy precipitately before a standard has emerged, and start to suspect that these strictures are simply crude attempts to discourage purchase.

The "carrot" is a judicious use of pre-standards – preliminary outline specifications of what can be expected from the negotiated standard. If these are sufficiently widely publicized, they may carry sufficient credibility to both discourage producers from breaking rank and discourage users from resorting to the market solution. Pre-standards would work rather like pre-announcements of products. They can deter users from investing in today's inferior market solution, but instead to plan their investment around the specifications in the pre-standard. They can also deter producers from attempting to introduce their own non-standard systems, but rather to ensure that these conform to the outline specification.

Conclusions

This paper has set out to explore from an economic point of view why the standards setting process may pay insufficient attention to user needs for standards. We saw that this could arise for several reasons. First, in a contest over the horizontal definition of a standard (i.e. between the equally good but incompatible standards of two producers), producers might not be able to agree on a common standard even if the mutual benefits of doing so exceeded the modification costs. Second, there was reason to expect that the IT community would make insufficient investment in the vertical aspects of standards (i.e. the unambiguous improvements in the standard).

Third, we observed that users might be excluded from the standards process because the time commitment was too great. While they might be encouraged to participate if such participation were somehow subsidized, this would of itself further prolong the time required to reach consensus in the standards committee. Fourth, we noted that market pressures might constrain the institution to reach consensus more rapidly, but this of itself would require the committee to limit membership of the committee. Moreover, we argued that the combination of negotiated standards setting and market pressures might sometimes lead to the worst of both worlds. Finally, we noted that the market process for setting standards does not achieve universal suffrage either: the de facto standard that emerges may reflect the preferences of only a relatively small number of early users and producers.

The paper suggested that user participation might be enhanced by the use of informal working groups or subcommittees, reporting to the central standards committees; in addition, the early and widespread promulgation of pre-standards might deter users and producers alike from resorting prematurely to the market process.

Many of the issues raised in this section will be revisited at the end, when we consider "The way forward". Meanwhile, we proceed to the details of IT standards themselves, and user views of them, beginning with the most basic aspect of all: the information itself, that is the reason for the technology.

References

Standards and standard body documents

ISO 7498:1984 Open Systems Interconnection – basic reference model

[TSG-1 1989] User views of application portability, US contribution to JTC1/TSG-1, document ISO/IEC JTC1/TSG-1 N94

Other references

[Berg and Schumny 1990] *see general bibliography*

[Cargill 1989] *see general bibliography*

[David and Greenstein 1990] DAVID, P.A. and GREENSTEIN, S., The economics of compatibility standards: an introduction to recent research, *Economics of Innovation and New Technology*, Vol 1, Nos 1/2, pp 3-41

[David and Steinmueller 1990] DAVID, P.A. and STEINMUELLER, W.E., The ISDN bandwagon is coming, but who will be there to climb aboard?: quandaries in the economics of data communication networks, *Economics of Innovation and New Technology*, Vol 1, Nos 1/2, pp 43-62

[Farrell 1989] FARRELL J., The economics of standardization: a guide for non-economists, in [Berg and Schumny 1990], pp 189-198

[Farrell and Saloner 1987] FARRELL J. and SALONER, G., Competition, compatibility and standards: the economics of horses, penguins and lemmings, in GABEL, H.L. (ed.), Product standardization and competitive strategy, North-Holland, Amsterdam

[Farrell and Saloner 1988] FARRELL J. and SALONER, G., Coordination through committees and markets, *RAND Journal of Economics*, Vol 19, No 2, pp 235-252

[Hill and Meek 1980] *see general bibliography*

[Meek 1988b] MEEK, B.L., Is standardisation just regularisation?, *Computer Standards and Interfaces*, Vol 7, No 3, pp 257-259

[Meek 1990a] MEEK, B.L., Product-based v. product-oriented standardisation, in [Berg and Schumny 1990], pp 95-97

[Moad 1990] MOAD, J., The standards process breaks down, *Datamation*, 15 September 1990

[Rankine 1990] RANKINE, J.I., Information technology standards – can the challenges be met?, in [Berg and Schumny 1990], pp 41-48

[Reynolds 1990] REYNOLDS, P.E.M., Workshop W1 – Buyers, sellers and standards, in [Berg and Schumny 1990], pp 429-441

[Swann 1991] SWANN, P., Horizontal and vertical standards, user requirements, standards institutions, and market pressures, unpublished paper, Brunel University

[Swann and Lamaison 1990] SWANN, P. and LAMAISON, H., Vertical product differentiation, network externalities and market defined standards: simulation of the PC spreadsheet software market, CRICT Discussion Paper, Brunel University

2 User needs in information standards

This section consists of a single contribution by **Alan Hopkinson** of the Tate Gallery, London, UK. Ultimately, what matters most of all in an IT system for the user is the information the system holds; the way in which is is held and accessed, and what can be done with it, are also important but the means are of no value if the information itself is not what is needed. Alan Hopkinson discusses the problems of standardizing so various and elusive an entity, and how these problems have been approached in various applications. The author and editors are grateful to Ray O'Connor for access to an unpublished paper which was a valuable source of ideas.

Standards for information and the control of information

Information

Information is notoriously difficult to standardize and even more difficult is the standardization essential to improve the efficiency of the retrieval of information stored in computer databases; information is, of course, no use unless it can be appropriately selected or retrieved. Many standards in the field are quite well established and some pre-date automation.

Another feature of information is its international nature. Information generally knows no bounds, though its expression through the medium of a language limits its use to those conversant with that language. Indeed, it is the universality of information that makes it necessary to conduct IT standardization at the international level.

What does the I of IT really mean on its own? The Concise Oxford English Dictionary defines *information* as "items of knowledge"; *knowledge* as "familiarity gained by experience, person's range of information"; *data* means "facts of any kind". Data in fact can exist without being known by anyone. Most people would agree that a computer could contain some calculated figures which no human knew about. These would be data; could be information if read by some person; and would become knowledge if they were stored in the person's own "knowledge base", the information system contained, it is believed, in the brain. Information, then, seems to be data with a potential for being knowledge. Information must be structured to become knowledge. Data might be badly structured and never become even information. Knowledge seems to imply a usage of the information (unless qualified by a term like "useless knowledge" which means knowledge of the answer to questions like those in Trivial Pursuit games which are of no real benefit to the person with the knowledge beyond any kind of benefit gained in a competition).

Information standards

Information technology standards for Information are standards necessary for ordering information in such a way that it will be potentially useful. In the UK, the DISC Mission Statement for Information and Documentation Standards (the BSI Committee that deals with information standards) has as its objectives to "facilitate clear, unambiguous recording and transfer of information in all areas of documentation". *Documentation* means here the control of information in any way whether it be publishing, libraries, archives, records management and similar organizations.

Storage and retrieval of data are the two areas where general standards are needed and have been developed. Analysis of information is still an activity which requires human rather than computer attention, though in many scientific areas computers can pre-digest the information. Nevertheless, these are areas specific to a particular subject and general standards have not been developed to cover these areas.

Data storage implies a structure. A user needs a methodology for storing the letters of the alphabet on any computer medium ranging from computer memory to paper tape. The standard character sets of which ASCII is the best known and most widely used example have been developed for this purpose and are covered more fully by Borka Jerman-Blažič in *Character handling and computer communication* in Section 5.

Certain elements of information (information itself as opposed to its representation) lend themselves to standardization. Time and place come to mind but are notoriously difficult to represent in a standardized way as we shall see later. A user also needs a methodology for storing printed texts on a computer. He needs a methodology for storing indexes in machine-readable form and for displaying them in print. This leads to the subject of library catalogues which are a different kind of index. Here there exist cataloguing codes, rather like legal codes, which tell the librarian what element of the description of a document to include on a catalogue card (or nowadays in a library database) and the form in which to record them, for example, surname before forenames, separated by a comma.

The publishing world also needs standards; not just for phototypesetting or for displaying characters but for the layout of keyboards and for every aspect of book production. The International Organization for Standardization (ISO) has a Technical Committee on Information and Documentation (TC 46). The term *documentation* is used to mean all aspects of published or related unpublished material, including its storage and retrieval. In layman's terms, it is any standard that concerns a library, archive, museum, publisher, or bookseller and does not belong already to any other area. These are terms used in their widest sense so publisher means anyone who produces any kind of document, such as a small company producing documents on a word processor, not only the large commercial publishers.

Computers brought with them the possibility of information technology. In the publishing and library worlds, legal requirements and practical necessity had led standardization even prior to the introduction of computers. The invention of printing brought about a standardization of spelling and of type-faces. Later, most books acquired printed title pages which included certain details including the name and address of the publisher or printer. This was partly for legal reasons so that someone propagating blasphemy, revolution, or other scurrilous material could be chased. Paper sizes have been standardized for a long time (though admittedly metricized standards are not so old), an example of commercial necessity; and also for commercial reasons the concept of copyright evolved. Already in the 18th century, printers in Dublin were reprinting illegally texts produced in England and selling them in English bookshops at a lower price. Libraries also needed standards and cataloguing codes originated with the Bodleian Library in Oxford in the 17th century and the best known rules before this century were those developed for the British Museum Library by Panizzi in the 19th century. So even before formal standardization activities began with the establishment of national and international standards bodies, there were a number of conventions and standards highly valued by the information world.

In the area covered by ISO TC 46, there are a number of standards which are not really within the ambit of information technology and therefore do not belong to this volume. Conversely, the storage of information in machine-readable form (as opposed to in books) is becoming more closely related with its production which is often by means of computers, so computing standards themselves are becoming more relevant to documentation. In the past, one went through a book fairly sequentially or in the case of a reference work used a printed index. Now with computerized databanks replacing printed documents in some areas, one can go straight to any word in the text.

Standards for information elements

In the scientific world, many attempts have been made at standardization. The chemical elements all have standard abbreviations which have been accepted for a century. Objects in Natural History have been classified and assigned Latin names in order to standardize international discussion of them. Colours are given standard descriptions, but here we enter a very specialized area and only scientists working in the field of colour are interested in the standards. Weights and measures have also been subject to standardization, and here there is little disagreement. Areas of particular interest are place, time and currency. It is possible to be fairly precise when and where most events occur, but it is not so easy to record this in a standard way on a computer. Computers can usually store or print out the date and time, so it is possible to find the earliest version of a file. However, there is no standard way of doing it, so when data are transferred from one system to another there is room for confusion. There are no widely-accepted standards, though there is an international standard ISO 8601 for the representation of dates and times. Taking into account only date, there are pictured below methods of displaying this data element (12 March 1992).

12-3-92	3-12-92	92-3-12	12-3-1992	3-12-1992	1992-3-12
12-03-92	03-12-92	92-03-12	12-03-1992	03-12-1992	1992-03-12
12/3/92	3/12/92	92/3/12	12/3/1992	3/12/1992	1992/3/12
12/03/92	03/12/92	92/03/12	12/03/1992	03/12/1992	1992/03/12
12.3.92	3.12.92	92.3.12	12.3.1992	3.12.1992	1992.3.12
12.03.92	03.12.92	92.03.12	12.03.1992	03.12.1992	1992.03.12
120392	031292	920312	12031992	03121992	19920312

Additionally, the month could be replaced by either the word in any language or an abbreviation of it.

Bearing in mind that any of the above could be confused with 3 December 1992, communication of dates is extremely precarious.

When it comes to standardization of spatial concepts, attempts are made more difficult by the fact that our use of space varies. There are standard abbreviations of American states. Each place can also be identified by a zipcode or postal code. Geographical coordinates can also be used for identification, whether they be a national system, or based on latitude and longitude. Though they are the most objectively applied, coordinates may not always be what is required, since some systems are analysing only the built environment. Postal codes, in countries where they exist and are specific enough, are perhaps more appropriate there.

Time and time again, information is transferred not directly from one computer to another but by being printed out and then by being rekeyed. Take invoices, for example; they could easily be sent by telecommunications, yet about 95% of invoices are sent by post and treated as above, with manual rekeying of data. Perhaps it is as well, since the human eye can do a huge amount of analysis, avoiding problems that would occur otherwise. There are standard methods of denoting currency, but these are little used. They are in fact unfamiliar and "unfriendly" but they are precise. They are formed from the international standard country code followed by a "currency letter" so we have USD for US dollar and GBP for pound sterling. Anything else can be confusing. £ may be used for Italian lira, $ for any number of countries' dollars. But additionally these are often represented differently by the printer from how they are displayed on the screen. Invoices are often received with # instead of £, and sometimes $ is used instead of £, reducing the value of the invoice by almost a half! The reason for this is that currency symbols are given different representations in the different national character sets, so if you are transferring a file from one computer to another when each has been set up with different national character sets, you will have a problem.

Standards for electronic publishing

Information cannot exist in the abstract; it has to be broadcast or published. The book publishing world established its own conventions long ago, but had always done most of its work using hard-metal printing or, more recently, photographic techniques. These standards do not concern us here. The advent of information technology has meant that many more individuals have become involved in the publishing process, and the need for standards to enable them all to intercommunicate has had to be satisfied.

Electronic publishing relies on standards for character sets. Other standards are also involved. International standard ISO 8879, *Standard Generalized Markup Language* (SGML), includes notes on analysing a document before writing a formal document type definition as well as giving examples from office applications, mathematics, mixed text and graphic applications and languages using non-Latin character sets. There are conventions for inserting codes into text to indicate that certain elements are to be indexed. This is an area where user needs require a lead from the standardization infrastructure. The development of such a convention is required before computer programs can be written interpreting it and producing ultimately eye-readable printed copy products. However, this kind of standard is nowhere in the same class as hardware standards where small changes to a standard can produce expensive manufacturing costs. When contrasted with programming languages, it is clear that the development has started with the involvement of standards committees, so we do not have a situation in which there are rival versions. None of the many relatively small organizations (small by comparison with the giants in the hardware field) involved in the publishing field could ever have individually developed their own standard. Given the situation where resources for standardization in IT are being stretched, it is difficult not to sermonize and say that SGML is an area where it is cost effective to devote public money. The many small organizations which will use the standard will benefit financially overall, though none could ever have committed enough funding to do the job individually, and even collectively it would have been difficult because it is always difficult to point out the benefits of standardization except in the face of the chaos that almost inevitably appears in its absence.

Standards for libraries and bibliographic information systems

The above principle is applicable to many standardization activities in the field of information and documentation. Outside the publishing world, the users of these standards are predominantly public sector, particularly in education. Consequently, public sector ethos has tended to colour the tone of the standardization activities. Cooperation rather than competition is the order of the day. This stretches beyond the national into the international arena.

Formats for exchanging data

One of the best known standards in the field of documentation is concerned with data sharing. This is represented by ISO 2709, defining the format for bibliographic information interchange on magnetic tape. This standard is used mostly by libraries and organizations (often called secondary services or abstracting and indexing services) which make bibliographies of journal articles and books in a specific subject field. The standard was also recommended in the United Kingdom by BEDIS (the UK Book Trade Electronic Interchange Standards Committee) as the vehicle for bibliographic as opposed to commercial and financial data.

The ISO 2709 standard, formally agreed in 1973, has many failings, but it is a good example of the existence of a mediocre standard being better by far than having no standard at all. Its origin lay in a joint United States Library of Congress / British National Bibliography project dating from 1967 to exchange data in order to build up their own catalogues and union lists. The British National Bibliography was a limited company set up in 1950 and funded by a consortium of libraries to produce and publish a listing of printed materials submitted under the Copyright Act to what was then the British Museum Library. In 1973 it was absorbed into the newly established British Library. The data were to be exchanged on half-inch magnetic tape and a format was established known as MARC for Machine Readable Cataloguing [British Library 1989]. This consisted of a record structure and codes to define different data elements; some of these codes were field identifiers (known as tags) which were held in a record directory and pointed to the text so that tapes could be more efficiently processed; other codes, like the subfield identifiers, were embedded in the text. All this was aimed purely at bibliographic references, not the full text, and indeed one of the main aims of the format was to produce catalogue cards in appropriate numbers to include the added headings needed for extra authors, titles and the like. The record structure became a US ANSI standard, but the tags and other identifiers were not accepted by all the members of the ANSI working group. They were included as an appendix though they were an integral part of the application used by the Library of Congress when preparing tapes for other US libraries and for transmission to the British collaborators. In the US other producers of machine-readable bibliographic records like the Chemical Abstracts Service had their own requirements for field definitions, hence the lack of agreement on the field identifiers. As an aside, it is worth noting that the British National Bibliography immediately diverged in its precise use of field and subfield identifiers and so the field identifiers have never been established as US, British or International standards. Naturally users needed a standard, but it was left to the distributors of tapes to establish these. As mentioned, information is notoriously difficult to standardize, so the leading institutions imposed standards. Although some of their customers would argue that this should have been done more democratically or even with greater technical competence, this reflects rather on the perfectionism inherent in cataloguing and the differences between parties have been relatively trivial. In the US, a committee structure has been established and the former Library of Congress standard (LC MARC) is now called US MARC. This has never happened in Britain where UK MARC [British Library 1989] is used by UK libraries because the British Library uses it and most records come from them; it is the British Library standard rather than the UK standard though they do consult with organizations like the Library Association and various user groups when they plan to make deep-rooted changes.

Within the MARC standard, there are a number of points at which disagreements can take place. One is in the definition of the data elements. Though MARC does not pretend to incorporate a data element dictionary, it has to assume one, since the data elements have to be defined to make transfer meaningful. In the UK, all libraries involved in data exchange use the Anglo-American Cataloguing Code, so this is the source for the "data element dictionary", albeit implicitly. However, the level of detail which should be incorporated in the records is contestable. Other areas of contention are mechanisms for updating records and methods of linking records. The latter is not of too much concern to libraries as books tend to be the entities at the level of the exchange of data. Anything below that level such as the individual copy is treated purely internally within a system and is of no concern to exchange activities. Relationships between a paperback and a bound copy have been embedded in the unit record. Relationships between one edition and an earlier edition are merely indicated as a note in the text.

This does not suit the secondary services so well. This brings us to consider their needs. In the early 1970s they saw the advantages of the MARC format and there were moves to copy the idea basing it on the standard record structure. Few secondary services could agree to the adoption of the MARC format as it was designed for books and periodicals. Some services began to use MARC and others called for a format of their own and looked to an initiative by the International Council of Scientific Unions which was receiving support from Unesco. Though an unofficial standard was established under the auspices of Unesco known as the Reference Manual for Machine-Readable Bibliographic Descriptions [Martin 1974], it was never adopted as an international or national standard, as far as is known, and eventually, reflecting commercial interests that became paramount in this area in the late 1970s and 1980s, many of the original participants withdrew their interest. The activities in database creation became more commercialized and cooperation was replaced by competition. There was much more success with UNIMARC [IFLA 1988] which was established by the International Federation of Library Associations and Institutions (IFLA) as an international interchange format to counter the problem that every country was developing its own national format taking as a precedent the fact that UK MARC had initially diverged from its parent LC MARC. Even so, UNIMARC achieved in its early days more usage as a model for a national format than as a carrier for the exchange of data internationally, though IFLA remained an enthusiastic supporter of the format to serve its original purpose. More recently, Unesco has discontinued further development work on the Reference Manual in favour of a new Common Communication Format (CCF) [Unesco 1988] which has been devised to take into account the requirements of the secondary services but in a way that is compatible with the MARC format. This has seen quite extensive use, particularly in developing countries where the level of precision of MARC and Anglo-American Cataloguing Rules are unaffordable luxuries. Microcomputers have extended the scope of computerized systems to much smaller institutions and the needs of users have become more diverse. Unesco's involvement in the CCF has filled a need created by advances in technology. Indeed, Unesco has developed a software package, known as CDS/ISIS, that encourages the use of standards in the creation of bibliographic databases. It implements the ISO 2709 standard and databases can be created based on the record coding found in MARC formats and the Common Communication Format.

In this field, then, the leading players, rather than national and international standards bodies, have led the way, organizations such as the Library of Congress, the British Library and Unesco. There has been little opposition to their work. This is partly because organizations not interested in standardization have ignored it and those that are interested are willing to go along with the work of the leading organizations because it is not a predominantly competitive field.

One final point to note is that ISO 2709 has never been formally adapted to the exchange of data on other media; now that it is becoming increasingly used for exchange between microcomputer systems, this is causing some problems. Implementors have to make some assumptions since the standard is based on half inch magnetic tape and the international standard character sets. Microcomputer users naturally use magnetic diskettes and variants of the IBM PC character set, but these are not taken into account by the standard.

Character sets

This brings us on to the next class of standards. There is actually more to exchanging records than the tape standards and the record formats. There are the character sets. The best known is the ASCII character set which is essentially a 7-bit character set allowing 128 combinations of bits and 128 different characters some of which are reserved for special purposes so that about 96 may be used for graphic purposes. This can be extended into a 256 byte character set and there are standard mechanisms available for the inclusion of characters from other character sets. Since the information field is international, there is a need for diacritics (also known as accents) on letters of the alphabet. Moreover, the library and information sector was one of the first fields where printouts in upper case characters only were regarded as unacceptable, since they have a history of sophistication in the display of characters. ISO has developed a number of standard character sets for bibliographic use. There is ISO 5426, *Extension of the Latin alphabet coded character set for bibliographic information interchange*; ISO 5428, *Greek alphabet coded character set for bibliographic information interchange*; BS 6438, *African coded character set for bibliographic information interchange*; and ISO 5427, *Extension of the Cyrillic coded character set for bibliographic information interchange*.

An example of the problems of standardization in this field may be of interest: although the British Standards Institution accepts the extended character set provided for Cyrillic, the United Kingdom has never agreed to the basic set. This is because whereas in the Latin character sets upper case has lower values than lower case ("A" is 65, "a" is 97), in the Cyrillic (as originally developed by GOST, the Soviet Union Standards Organization and later adopted as the ISO standard), it is the other way round. The extended Cyrillic set does not raise any such issue. Other countries have accepted the basic set. Additionally, ISO has a character set for bibliographic control characters (ISO 6630:1986). A coded character set for mathematics and one for Hebrew are, in 1992, nearing completion.

Industry standards did not catch up with the requirements of users in the information field until the microcomputer entered into widespread use. The extensive use of microcomputers in word processing meant that accented character sets had to be provided, both for the computers themselves and for printers. The different national versions of the character set developed for the IBM PC is probably the most extensively used, but they are non-standard, because they use character values 128 to 160 for characters when these are reserved for control characters and space in the international standards.

For many years, the library and publishing field were ahead of other areas in their requirements for characters. Even today, many commercial French systems ignore accented characters, though they are essential for easy reading of French text. Nevertheless, systems are now regarded very much as second class if they cannot manipulate lower case characters and a number of accented characters and other signs. The library world has developed its own solution to these problems, by developing standards specially for a particular need and, in programs developed to use these, calling in character sets by means of escape sequences; but there is now the promise of a new standard which is dealt with elsewhere in this volume (see Borka Jerman-Blažič, *Character handling and computer communication*, in Section 5). Any new methods may prove slow to be accepted in the library and publishing fields which have already made large investments in the existing standards which they have developed themselves.

Data elements

In the information field, as elsewhere, the transfer of data between systems is becoming increasingly common. Standardization is more difficult in this field than elsewhere but certain data elements have been created for the computer environment. Those that are used totally within the library and publishing trade come under the Information and Documentation Committee. Most notable of these are ISBN and ISSN.

ISBN

The ISBN (International Standard Book Number) originated as the Standard Book Number developed by the UK publishing house Whitakers as an 8-digit number with the addition of a check digit. The number consisted of a publisher prefix, and a running number, so that publishers could apply their own ISBN having been issued with a prefix. Most publishers have applied it well, though there has always been some uncertainty as to whether a new impression should get a new number; librarians would prefer a new number to be applied only to new editions since for them a new impression is not a different work. The number was expanded to 9 digits when it was adopted as international standard ISO 2108 with an international maintenance agency based in Germany. The first digit was allocated as a country or in some cases language code, with 0 being for publishers in English-speaking countries (Australia, Britain, Canada, Ireland, New Zealand, United States), 2 for French-speaking countries including Quebec, 3 for Germany. Numbers beginning with 9 have been allocated to multi-digit country codes for countries with lesser publishing output, and codes for international organizations. There were few attempts to include the ISBN on publications as a bar code because by the time that technology had been developed other products such as baked beans were requiring the same kind of number for automated warehousing and point-of-sale systems. The ISBN has been incorporated into the standard product numbering scheme, by removing the final check digit and applying the scheme's own system of check digit.

ISSN

Following the success of the ISBN, the International Centre of the International Serials Data System (ISDS) developed the International Standard Serial Number (ISSN). The ISDS was established by Unesco in 1974 (serials is a technical word used by librarians to include not only journals, newspapers, periodicals but also monographic series). It could be asked why there is a need to establish formally standards in this area when there are internationally respected maintenance agencies. The answer probably lies in the fact that Eastern European countries usually had difficulties in adopting practices which were not governed by formally agreed international standards. On the other hand, some national standards bodies have taken a completely different view: the British Standards Institution never adopted the ISSN standard or the ISBN; it dropped the SBN when it became international on the grounds that there was no need to revalidate a standard established by a competent body.

Under discussion at the moment are ISO standards for an International Standard Technical Report Number and an International Standard Music Number.

Other codes

Codes have also been developed for countries and languages. It is useful in library systems to have a code rather than a country name, not only because it saves space to have a two-digit code but also because official country names might change. There is an international standard ISO 3166, *Codes for the representation of names of countries*. Some libraries use codes developed by the Library of Congress or their own national library; and others use the motor car country identification codes; few use the international codes, though it is an easy matter to convert to these from another set for international exchange purposes. None of these codes is really intended to be historic, but represent the political situation as at the present time: when the German Democratic Republic was absorbed into the German Federal Republic in 1991, the code for the former immediately became obsolete. Work is taking place on codes for historical purposes, so that codes will continue to be available for such countries as Prussia and the German Democratic Republic.

Although language codes have been developed by ISO (ISO 639, *Codes for the representation of names of languages*), these are not much used, since they have only recently been upgraded from a very sparse list including only the major world languages with bias towards the European languages. Libraries, particularly at the national level, tend to include a very wide selection of languages, and they have been using in their computer databases a set of codes developed by the US Library of Congress. These are also used by Unesco and in many bibliographic systems of the UN. Language codes need a good maintenance agency as, surprisingly, every year a number of languages go into print for the first time and a new code is needed.

Filing order

Information technology has brought with it the need to standardize filing order. In days gone by, the telephone directory, the catalogue card or the bibliography were produced by traditional typesetting, and the human eye and mind were responsible for ordering entries in a catalogue or bibliography. This changed with the introduction of computers. When the ASCII character set was devised, it was developed in such a way as to make filing by the ASCII numerical value a reasonable method for most purposes so long as correction was applied to align lower case with upper case and so ignore case in filing. Libraries, and the documents they produce listing bibliographic works, tend to have more complex requirements than these. ISO Technical Report 8393 is entitled *ISO bibliographic filing rules: exemplification of bibliographic filing principles in a model set of rules*, which is based on ISO 7154, *Bibliographic filing principles*. In the past, numbers in a title in a catalogue were often spelled out, either in the language of the catalogue or the language of the document; now there is a tendency to file them at the beginning of the catalogue before the alphabetical sequence.

Open Systems Interconnection

Open Systems Interconnection (OSI) has had, as might be expected, a profound influence on the standards being developed in Information and Documentation. One facet which has defied standardization, attempted even before OSI came on to the scene, is the specification of a common command language. This refers to codes used to initiate searching on computerized databases, usually though not exclusively in the bibliographic field. The European Community took an interest in this many years ago and a consultant produced a draft "language" but nothing was ever accepted. The problem is that codes need to be specified not only for activities such as search and print but also for each data element. These tend to differ between systems as there is no common data element directory. One system may separate author and editor, another may distinguish between persons as authors and institutions as authors. Even the activities and functions may be system-dependent. The many librarians and workers in the information field who have to keep switching between search languages will be pleased to know that a Search and Retrieval Specification is, at the time of writing (mid 1992), being developed within the context of OSI. This is going to be absolutely essential if it is to be possible for computer systems to switch search enquiries from one computer system to another. Commands for interactive text searching are also being developed. The acceptance of a standard data element directory, noted in its absence from the ISO 2709 data structure standard, is in part being resolved. Agreement has been easiest to reach in Interloan applications (ISO 8459-1). The next section of the data element directory is to cover acquisitions applications. The two parts achieved first are those relating not so much to information retrieval as to the transfer of known items (books, journal issues) between libraries and book suppliers. At the same time, ISO is developing an "Interlibrary Loan service definition" and an "Interlibrary loan protocol specification", and the same for search and retrieval, to be the basis for OSI work in the area.

These OSI standards are being formulated through official standardization channels, but – and it is particularly true of interlibrary loan – they could equally well have been developed by one or more of the major organizations in the international field acting alone or in partnership but outside the ISO infrastructure, and they would most likely have been as acceptable to the community at large. The OSI standards and the organizations involved in developing them are discussed in greater detail in later sections.

Standards for defining the intellectual content of information

Lastly, there are standards for defining the intellectual content of information. These were all developed before computerization and are known as controlled vocabularies, thesauri and classification schemes. Over the last decade (i.e. since the the early 1980s), work has been going on to investigate their suitability or otherwise in computerized systems and make suggestions for changes in the light of computerization. Unfortunately, all too often, it is difficult to make changes because the systems were developed in a particular way in order to assist linear searching. Since the computer can make different kinds of searches, much of the basic presumptions of these systems are no longer valid. BSI maintains the English edition of the Universal Decimal Classification, BS 1000, a scheme for classifying knowledge, which has been developed continuously since the 19th century, mostly used to shelve books in libraries. This scheme orders facets of a subject in such a way as to bring the code for the most important one to the fore so that it can be retrieved in an ordered list. It is not very easy to write a computer program to enable it to retrieve the other facets that are embedded in the strings which represent the subject in a coded form. A scheme which was developed today would take into account retrieval by the computer. Thesauri include relationships like broad terms and narrow terms as well as having terms which should be used in preference to others. As regards preferred terms, one thesaurus includes "Female manpower: use Women workers" and all thesauri include similar recommendations. A narrow term search would automatically retrieve documents which had been indexed as being about "Town Halls" and "Art Galleries" when the user made a search for "Public Buildings". These relationships can be included automatically in a searching program, but this may result in too much retrieval. These standards do not seem to have yet been influenced by information technology, and do not properly belong in this discussion.

Conclusion

User needs for information technology standards in the information field have been served only partially by the formal standardization channels. Since there are clearly defined leaders in the library field, that has not been a problem, but in the publishing field absence of official standards may have contributed to delays in making use of information technology and may yet reveal incompatibilities in the future.

Having dealt with the "information" in IT we now turn to the "technology". The question of character coding, from the IT point of view, will be returned to in Section 5, but first we deal with the basic technology – hardware in the next section, and communications in Section 4.

References

Standards and standards body documents

BS 1000 Universal Decimal Classification (n.b. various dates for different versions and parts)

BS 6438:1983 African coded character set for bibliographic information interchange

ISO 639:1988 Codes for the representation of names of languages

ISO 2108:1978 International Standard Book Numbering (ISBN), 2nd edn.

ISO 2709:1981 Format for bibliographic information interchange on magnetic tape, 2nd edn.

ISO 3166:1988 Codes for the representation of names of countries, 3rd edn.

ISO 3297:1986 International Standard Serial Numbering (ISSN), 2nd edn.

ISO 5426:1983 Extension of the Latin alphabet coded character set for bibliographic information interchange

ISO 5427:1984 Extension of the Cyrillic coded character set for bibliographic information interchange

ISO 5428:1984 Greek alphabet coded character set for bibliographic information interchange, 2nd edn.

ISO 6630:1986 Bibliographic control characters

ISO 7154:1983 Bibliographic filing principles

ISO 8459-1:1988 Data element directory – Part 1: interloan applications

ISO 8601:1988 Representation of dates and times

ISO 8879:1986 Standard Generalized Markup Language (SGML)

Other references

[British Library 1989] UK MARC manual, 3rd edn., British Library, 1989- (loose-leaf and issued in parts), London

[IFLA 1988] UNIMARC manual, office of Universal Bibliographic Control and International MARC (UBCIM), International Federation of Library Associations and Institutions (IFLA), London

[Martin 1974] MARTIN, M.D. (ed), Reference manual for machine-readable bibliographic descriptions, Unesco, Paris

[Unesco 1988] CCF: the Common Communication Format. 2nd edn., Unesco, Paris

3

User needs in hardware and physical media standards

When considering user needs for hardware standards, then apart from safety standards, dealt with as a whole in Section 9, it might be thought that they are unnecessary. The way things are in the industry, and have been for many years, the obvious factors which users regard as important – speed, capacity, cost of acquisition, cost of operation, ease of use – are all things which suppliers, whether on the design side or on the marketing side, seem to have fallen over themselves to provide, with no standards requiring them to do so. Certainly, advances in speed and memory capacity, and in capital cost per unit of each, have been staggering in their magnitude, almost embarrassingly so, while operating costs and ease of use have shown improvements, more modest but noticeable enough. Concerns about ease of use have been about software rather than hardware.

As far as it goes, this analysis is undoubtedly valid. The interests of suppliers in competing for market share and of the engineers in designing bigger, better and faster machines have served the users well, to date. Nevertheless there are some areas worthy of further scrutiny, and it is these that are the subject of this section.

User satisfaction with the basic processing and memory hardware does not extend quite so far with peripherals, and still less to physical media, especially machine-readable media, a major factor in portability short of the direct interconnection which is the subject of the section which follows. Both of these aspects will be discussed here.

However, even with basic central processing there are pockets of concern, and towards the end of the section we shall be looking at the question of "performance" standards – not because "performance" has not improved dramatically year after year, but because of the difficulties users still have in determining just what "performance" they are going to get out of a system they buy.

But we begin with something so fundamental that it is often taken for granted: indeed, it is precisely that it is taken for granted which is part of the trouble. It is, machine arithmetic. The first short contribution to this section is by **Brian Meek**, a member of the ISO working group responsible for language-independent arithmetic standards in the programming languages area.

Standards for machine arithmetic

From the very first experimental machines, arithmetical operations have been the essence of computing; indeed the very word suggests it. Even in the 1990s when computing has long since extended its scope into all forms of processing of information, it is still a commonly held view, among laypeople, that computers mainly "do arithmetic". That computers can do arithmetic accurately and with incredible speed is so basic to them that it goes without question. But though the speed can be granted, the accuracy cannot, at least automatically – something that comes as a great shock when first encountered. We are not talking about the familiar jokes about bills being sent for negative amounts, and so on, which are the result of poor software design and human error. We are talking about the basic hardware operations.

In the early days of computers, unwary programmers often came to grief and found out the hard way that it was not always possible to take the accuracy even of integer arithmetic wholly for granted. They would be startled when answers came out wildly wrong, because the machine said that the sum of two positive numbers was sometimes negative! Had they thought about it at all, which of course they hadn't, they would probably have taken it for granted that the machine would not allow a result larger than the capacity available to hold it. However, there were no standards to say that overflow had to be detected and reported. When standards for high-level languages began to appear, even they did not necessarily insist on the implementation supplying the user with this protection, by software tests if the hardware did not provide it (see discussion in [Hill and Meek 1980], p 184 ff).

This of course reflected the prevailing culture in the industry of speed at all costs, and though people are perhaps now more aware of the problem, things are hardly a great deal better in the 1990s. Certainly as far as "real" (i.e. approximate) arithmetic is concerned, users still cannot rely on hardware design engineers taking fully into account all of the factors that numerical analysts would wish, especially with respect to minimizing accumulated errors. Error analysis is a very specialist and difficult area, even in mathematics; one cannot expect people trained as electronic engineers necessarily to be aware of all its intricacies. All the more reason for hardware suppliers to take specialist advice!

In fact it is not, generally, that hardware is incapable of meeting quite strict requirements with regard to accuracy and predictability. The problem for users is usually a combination of hardware design and the way that implementors of languages and packages exploit it. But it is not unreasonable for users to wish that the hardware will not even *permit* the software writers to use it in an arithmetically unsafe way – or at the very least make it much easier for them to use it safely than unsafely. Yet still there are no standards to require this.

There is, to be fair, one honourable attempt which has gone a long way towards this goal – the floating-point standard ANSI/IEEE 754:1985. This does provide the required properties, including means for detecting spurious results. Since its inception it has been widely adopted for the powerful workstations increasingly used in the late 1980s and 1990s by professional scientists and engineers. There are, indeed, some who advocate its universal adoption, as a permanent solution to the unsafe arithmetic problem.

The critics of such a policy base their arguments on two main points. One is that the IEEE standard is not just an arithmetic standard but a hardware architecture standard, albeit an abstract one; it may have become popular for workstations (though its penetration into other areas has been limited), but there is no need to specify hardware architecture precisely in order to achieve safe arithmetic. That is a classic example of the all too common practice in IT of confusing levels of abstraction and purposes of standards. The other point is that while the IEEE standard does indeed make it likely that arithmetic will be safe, it does not actually guarantee it, because of that perpetual bugbear of IT standards, the presence of options. Sensible use of the options will preserve arithmetic safety, but you cannot be sure, and it is above all certainty that users need.

At the beginning of the 1990s a different approach is being taken, of developing a standard to define an abstract set of required properties for arithmetic operations and functions which will ensure arithmetic safety. Indeed, its abstract nature is such that it might not be regarded as a hardware standard at all, and it is in fact being developed in an ISO software committee, that for programming languages. Much software that is critically dependent on heavy "number-crunching", particularly in the scientific and engineering fields, is still written and maintained in traditional programming languages like Fortran and Ada; it is in those fields that the need is felt acutely and hence where the work is being done. The title of the project is "Language Independent Arithmetic" and it does not directly address hardware at all, which is outside the scope of the committee concerned. It does assume a floating point format for approximating to real numbers, but this does not mean that underlying hardware supporting a language implementation has to provide it, even though that might be expected. For the purely language point of view, how the requirements are implemented is irrelevant, even if they may be of interest to the programmer for a particular application. Language definitions found in standards are just that; assumptions may creep in or underlie a provision in a language standard, but basically it is immaterial to the definition whether implementation is by hardware, software, or any combination. For arithmetic, however, it clearly is of interest how readily current or proposed hardware can handle the requirements.

The Language Independent Arithmetic (LIA) standard is in three parts, and in early 1992 the first part, on the basic arithmetic operations, has been published in draft form as ISO/IEC JTC1 CD 10967, while the other two parts on mathematical procedures and complex arithmetic are still being prepared. An early draft of part one, under its original title of "Language Compatible Arithmetic", is available in the general literature [Payne, Schaffert and Wichmann, 1990]; while many details have changed during the formal development to CD 10967 stage, the basic principles can be obtained from that.

Because of its implications for hardware and its potential impact on numerical software, LIA part 1 has engendered a good deal of interest and comment, some of it quite trenchant (see for example [Kahan 1992]). Doubts were raised about motivation, in that one of the large suppliers was providing a good deal of support for the project. It is not unusual for substantial involvement in a standards project by one major supplier to be looked at with suspicion by other suppliers and by users! In all branches of politics "guilt by association" is sometimes resorted to as a line of argument so such concerns can perhaps be dismissed, unless of course backed up by technical arguments. There are enough instances in IT of standards being little more than a standards body wrapping round a thinly-disguised product manual, but even the earliest versions of LIA are a far cry from that.

Some critics argued that LIA would undermine IEEE 754, or weaken it in some way; supporters of LIA argued in return that it actually *strengthened* IEEE 754, and the combination of the two standards was the best that could reasonably be hoped for given the state of the art in the 1990s; yet it also offered hope and support to those who for one reason or another did not have the benefits of IEEE 754 to support them.

Fortunately all this controversy generated constructive as well as destructive comments, light as well as heat, and many suggestions for improvements have already been acted on and genuine technical concerns addressed by the project editors and the responsible working group. It will be some time before we know how effective LIA will be; what is sure is that there is nothing yet on the horizon to fill the gap should it not succeed.

We now turn to peripherals, or more precisely to the one aspect, apart from safety-related issues concerned with eyestrain from visual displays, which seems to cause users greatest trouble: keyboards. The contribution that follows comes from **Bruce Paterson**, formerly of International Computers Limited and now an independent consultant.

Standards for keyboard layouts – the origins and scope of ISO/IEC 9995

Historical background

The information technology products and systems that are available today, when compared with those of 30 years ago, provide a dramatic illustration of the speed at which change has occurred during the intervening time. The remarkable increases in performance, versatility, convenience, and variety have been matched by equally remarkable decreases in the size and cost of comparable products.

Keyboards have been, and still are, the principal means by which user personnel can enter text and data for processing, storage, or communication by IT systems. They have always formed an integral part of IT system installations. But while the general appearance and styling of keyboards, and the internal technology that they utilize, have changed substantially over 30 years the layouts of the keys on successive keyboard products have evolved relatively slowly. In fact the layout conventions used today by the keyboards of IT products have a long history, dating from well before the era of electronic computers.

Before giving a little of that history it is useful first to state what the term "keyboard layout" covers since it appears frequently throughout this chapter. A keyboard layout means the physical configuration and relative positions of the keys on a keyboard and the allocation of letters of the alphabet, numbers and other symbols, and associated control functions (such as shift or tabulation) to those keys.

The layout of the alphabetic section of almost all keyboards in use in English-speaking countries today incorporates the QWERTY convention, so-called because this sequence appears along the upper row of letters when reading them from left to right. This convention first came into use over 100 years ago on one brand of typewriters in the USA, and by the 1890s was already overtaking the alternative layouts that were provided on some other brands. The manner in which each row of alphabetic keys is slightly offset from the row next to it also originated at that time, due to the mechanical constraints of typewriter construction. There is no technical reason to perpetuate it now, and it is retained simply because users are familiar with it. Even the layout of the small rectangular group of numeric keys found on many keyboards today, and arranged as on a pocket calculator, is derived from a key-punch for punched cards that came on the market in about 1900, although at that time the layout was inverted with the zero key in the back row (furthest from the user), keys for 1, 2, and 3 in the next row, and so on.

Evidently the suppliers of typewriters and other keyboard products have recognized over the years that users prefer keyboard layout conventions to remain stable when new models of keyboard become available. Substantial changes of layout have sometimes been introduced when a new model of keyboard was designed to support new types or mixes of task. But in many respects the layouts of the keyboards that are on the market today are the result of a long succession of relatively small changes.

Along with these changes of keyboard layout conventions, since the early 1950s a succession of related national and international standard specifications for keyboard layouts has been published by BSI and ISO respectively. National standards have also been published in other European countries, in the USA, and elsewhere. Usually these standards have attempted only to recognize and give a precise description of the principal conventions adopted by current and forthcoming products in the marketplace, but they have enabled a wider harmonization of layouts between the products of different suppliers to be steadily achieved. The serial numbers of the published standards have also provided a convenient short form of reference to particular layout conventions, as an alternative to the proprietary product references which are so often used for this purpose.

User roles

By the 1960s several different types of keyboard were in use in offices, information processing installations, and elsewhere to support the sharply differentiated tasks that users were required to do. Keyboard operators were usually specialists in the use of one particular type of keyboard, and were trained so that they could achieve high productivity in their assigned task. The principal types of keyboard in use included typewriters (mechanical and electric), data-entry devices (for punched cards and other media), accounting and calculating machines (some for one-hand, others for two-hand operation), and telex and teletype machines for telecommunication of messages. Teletype machines were also in use on computer control consoles, and were increasingly provided for users of multiaccess computer systems who were typically scientific and technical specialists or programmers; however, in these roles their users generally did not need such a high productivity of keyboard operation.

Naturally the published standards for keyboard layouts made allowances for these distinctions of user role. In consequence, during the 1970s several different standards were published by ISO covering the main types of keyboard layouts that the ISO keyboards committee considered would continue in widespread use during the coming years. The principal distinction made by the standards was between two-hand keyboards and one-hand keyboards. Within two-hand keyboard layouts a further distinction was made between layouts for typewriters and layouts for data-entry using the ISO 7-bit (95-character) code for information interchange. Layouts for one-hand keyboards were intended for adding and calculating machines. The weak point of most of these standards, especially those for two-hand keyboards, was the lack of specification of control key functions suitable for use in information processing tasks, and of corresponding positions for them in the keyboard layout.

These standards each cover a carefully restricted scope, specifying some significant features of the layout but not the layout as a whole. For example, Part 1 of BS 2481 for typewriters (last reissued in 1982) specifies a layout of between 44 and 48 character keys, in which the positions of the letters of the alphabet, the digits 0 to 9, and 18 specified symbols and punctuation signs are fixed, but up to 16 further symbols may be more or less freely chosen for the remaining places on the keys (see Figure 3.1). The positions of shift keys and carriage return are specified in Part 3, but other controls such as backspace or tabulation are not mentioned. Part 2 specifies keytop symbols for 20 different functions, any of which might be present on a particular keyboard, but gives no indication of where the keys for these function should be placed relative to the layout of the character keys. Keyboards conforming to this standard will therefore not all have identical layouts, although the most frequently used characters and controls will always appear in the same relative positions on all conforming keyboards. The user must discover the placing of any additional characters and controls on a keyboard by observation whenever necessary. This arrangement was intended to provide a compromise between the need of users to achieve a high productivity of keyboard operation, and to maintain that productivity when they move from one model of keyboard to another, and the need for some variety in the repertoire of characters and controls included on different models of keyboard intended for different categories of document content.

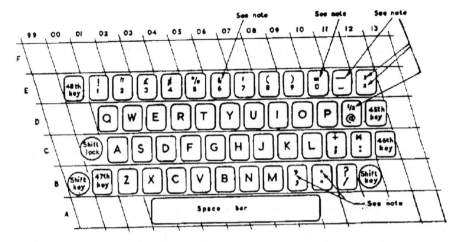

Figure 3.1 *Character Layout for Typewriters from BS 2481*
Note: The indicated characters may be replaced by others when required.

No standard was published for the widely used data-entry keyboard layout, based on the IBM Model 029 card-punch convention. This layout provided one-hand and two-hand operation on the same keys and a limited character repertoire with capital letters only. Because it was intended for tasks in which a high productivity was demanded, suppliers generally avoided providing variant layouts which might impair productivity, and a standard was considered to be unnecessary.

Also during the 1970s, and subsequently, national standards were published in many countries to specify a precise layout for all 95 characters of their national version of the ISO 7-bit code. These layouts typically included positions for the commonly-used accented letters in the national language, and sometimes also for separate accents intended to be combined with letters when required. In countries where the national language uses a different alphabet or script, such as Arabic, Cyrillic, or Greek, national or regional standards for corresponding keyboard layouts were also published.

Visual-display/keyboard devices

The availability of these ISO and national standards helped to bring about a considerable measure of harmonization of keyboard layouts on the new VDU/keyboard computer terminal products that were then coming on the market from many different suppliers. By this time such keyboards often included a two-hand alphanumeric block of keys and a separate one-hand numeric block to the right of it, mounted on a single base. For each of these blocks of keys suitable standards were available for adoption with little or no deviation. But initially there was little experience of the many and varied ways in which VDU terminals, interacting with computer application programs, might be used. Therefore the control functions provided, and their positions within the overall keyboard layout, were correspondingly diverse among the products that appeared on the market. The choice depended on the judgement of the individual supplier as to the user roles and tasks that the terminal should support and the layout conventions which those users might already be familiar with.

As the potential of VDU terminal devices became more broadly recognized and exploited, a bewildering variety of keyboard layouts could be seen among the numerous new products that emerged. Some products were designed as dedicated word-processors; their layouts were derived from the typewriter standards and conventions. Other products were intended as general purpose computer-access terminals; their layouts were derived from the adding-machine and the ISO 7-bit code layout standards. But many models of keyboard incorporated large numbers of additional control keys, arranged in blocks at either side of the alphabetic or numeric blocks, or in a long row across the top. These keys were allocated to a great variety of special functions, some associated with direct editing of data on the VDU screen, and others for interacting with the supporting applications in local or remote information processing systems. In these circumstances the user, once familiar with a particular keyboard model, might have to spend a significant amount of "learning time" before attaining a similar level of proficiency on a keyboard from a different supplier, on which the layout of control keys might be different.

The great variety of keyboard layouts tended to limit the choice of product for use in high-productivity tasks, and some purchasers chose to buy all their keyboards from suppliers who could offer layouts identical to those of the keyboards already installed, to ensure uniformity throughout a department or organizational unit. However, increasing numbers of users by now were using VDU terminals for applications where speed of keying was not such a critical factor. These users could allow themselves a little time to look at the positions of keys during normal use of the keyboard, but would still benefit from the fact that different models of keyboard adopted similar layouts for the character keys, and also for the block of numeric keys when provided. Thus the lack of standards for the control key positions was for some users a relatively minor inconvenience.

The number of keyboard users, and the variety of applications that they made use of, grew rapidly during the 1980s following the arrival of the "personal computer" and its widespread takeup in offices of all kinds. By this time it had become clear that the majority of control functions needed by keyboard users are quite specific to the individual applications that they are using at the time. When in addition a keyboard can be used for many different applications in turn, perhaps from different suppliers of application software, the allocation of such functions to particular keys clearly cannot all be known in advance nor marked on the keyboard during its manufacture. Instead the handbook for the application became the place where the allocation of control functions to key positions was described. A keyboard overlay to label the allocations might also be provided. Many suppliers of keyboard products concluded that in this situation convergence towards a common convention for the overall arrange-ment of keys on keyboards would be beneficial for all concerned, even though not all keyboards would be able to carry application-specific markings. The opportunity now existed for agreement on a new ISO standard to cover the layout of the modern office-system keyboard as a whole, and at the same time to bring up to date the existing ISO standards which were no longer properly applicable.

Outline of ISO/IEC 9995

In April 1986 the ISO keyboards committee, which had been relatively inactive for several years, was instructed to review the existing ISO standards for keyboards to determine if they were still valid, to assess if harmonization was achievable among them, including removal of the distinctions between text applications and data applications, and to advise on the requirements for new work items in this area. The work was soon under way and the outcome was a new and comprehensive standard for keyboard layouts (ISO/IEC 9995, *Keyboard layouts for text and office systems*) which was approved in June 1992 and is due for publication later in the year.

With the publication of ISO/IEC 9995 a standard directly applicable to the keyboard layouts of today's information technology products will at last be available. It aims to cover the field as widely as possible, including personal computers, workstations, computer terminals and so on. It aims to provide a single harmonized standard for the keyboards of IT products and of typew-riters, replacing the previous standards for typewriters and adding machines. It also provides harmonization with the numeric keypads of other products in everyday use such as calculators, telephones, and automatic bank teller ma-chines.

The new standard will allow some flexibility in the overall configuration of a keyboard layout, and while fixing some details of layout quite strictly will allow a certain degree of freedom in other details. As with the previous ISO standards which are to be replaced, this standard aims to provide a com-promise between the varied needs of different users. It provides commonality of layout for frequently-used keys, so that users' skills will still apply when they transfer between different keyboards, but at the same time it allows freedom for different models of keyboard to be produced to suit different classes of application; for example, multifunction workstations or compact dedicated word processors.

The standard identifies four main sections within a keyboard layout, any or all of which may be present. The arrangement is firmly based on the keyboard layout of the popular personal computers now on the market or already installed (see Figure 3.2). The sections defined are a typewriter-like alpha-numeric section, a calculator-like numeric section placed to the right of it, a small rectangular editing section placed between them, and a function section comprising one or more rows of keys across the back or at the left-hand side (or both) of the rest of the layout. Each of the sections is regarded as consisting of a central core of keys, known as zone zero, which is surrounded by other zones which may include keys for supporting or related functions. In general the layout in zone zero of a section is specified more tightly than in the surrounding zones.

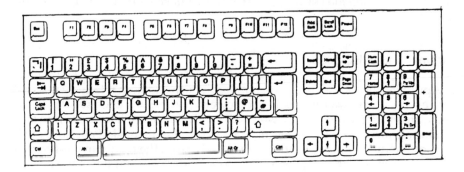

Figure 3.2: *Typical keyboard layout conforming to ISO/IEC 9995*

Each of the four main sections of a keyboard layout is specified in a separate part of the standard. There are additional parts to specify the overall configuration and general principles, the symbols that may appear on keytops, and the layout of a character set to supplement the Latin alphabet for multilingual use. The parts are numbered as follows.

1. General principles governing keyboard layouts.

2. Alphanumeric section.

3. Common secondary layout of the alphanumeric zone of the alphanumeric section.

4. Numeric section.

5. Editing section. Function section.

6. Symbols used on keyboards to represent functions.

A conforming keyboard must meet the requirements of Part 1, and of all other parts which are relevant to that particular model of keyboard. Claims of conformance must identify which parts of the standard are met.

The allocation of the principal set of characters to the keys in the alphanumeric section is not specified in Part 2 of the standard, but is assumed to be specified by a national standard or convention. Any claim of conformance that lacks a reference to such a standard will leave one of the main features of the layout undefined. Within the editing section the only functions that are identified and allocated to keys are the four cursor controls, although some additional recommendations are made. Within the function section only the Escape function is allocated. The allocation of all other keys in both of these sections is assumed to be defined by the application that is in use at the time, and is not specified by the standard. The functions of these keys may be identified by means of corresponding legends or symbols on the keytops. Alternatively, non-specific legends may be shown, such as the legends F1 to F12 commonly seen on personal computer keyboards. The specific functions for each application must then be identified in some other way.

It will be clear from the preceding outline that ISO/IEC 9995, in conjunction with related national standards, goes a long way towards promoting a desirable degree of harmonization between different models of keyboard. Users will increasingly benefit from its provisions as non-conforming models of keyboard already installed become obsolescent and are taken out of use. However, the standard on its own will generally not meet the needs of the staff in a purchasing department when they wish to issue a purchase specification for keyboards that are identical, or very similar, to those already in use in the organization. Reference to the relevant parts of the standard will not provide a sufficiently precise specification for that purpose.

The parts of ISO/IEC 9995

The following paragraphs give a brief summary of the scope of each individual part of ISO/IEC 9995, together with an indication of the impact on keyboard users.

Part 1 (General Principles) defines the four main sections of a keyboard layout, as already described above. It defines the various ways of indicating to the user the allocation of characters and functions to the keys, and defines how the characters and other visible symbols should be placed when they are marked on the keys. It requires that when an allocated character or function is not marked on the key the corresponding information should be made available to the user in some other way, such as in an accompanying product description document. It also defines a numbering system for key positions which is used for reference purposes throughout all parts of the standard, although this system is not usually of direct interest to the keyboard user.

A significant innovation in Part 1 is the concept of group shift, to supplement the traditional concept of up and down shifts on typewriters. It enables additional characters or control functions to be allocated to any key position. The group shift can be thought of as a "horizontal" shift. For example, when the keys are marked with characters both from group 1 (the primary character layout) and from group 2 the group 2 characters will be shown to the right of the group 1 characters on the key. Within a group there are three levels of shift, instead of the traditional two. Thus for each group that is provided in a particular keyboard layout up to three characters may be allocated to each key. Group shift as well as level shift keys must be provided to enable this feature to be used. The feature will be particularly useful for keyboards that support multi-alphabet operation.

All ergonomic and dimensional aspects of the keys and the layout of keyboards are now outside the scope of the standard. They are covered instead by ISO/IEC 9241-4, *Requirements for office work with video display terminals, Part 4: Keyboard requirements*. This standard specifies the dimensions of the keytop and the keytop shape, the distances between keys, the distance of key depression and the key force required, and the overall slope of the keyboard surface.

Part 2 (Alphanumeric Section) defines the permitted configurations of keys in the alphanumeric section of a keyboard layout. Most keyboards today provide 47 or 48 character keys to accommodate all 95 characters in one of the national versions of the ISO 7-bit code. However, Part 2 allows a minimum of 45 such keys, and also allows for possible expansion beyond 48 keys. As already mentioned, the allocation of characters is assumed to be specified by an appropriate national standard, but typical allocations for the letters A to Z and the digits 0 to 9 are given for guidance when a national standard needs to be newly developed.

Two British standards for character key allocations are available at present, BS 2481:1982 for typewriters, mentioned previously, and BS 4822:1980 for the UK version of the ISO 7-bit code (i.e. the version that includes the pound sterling sign). Of these standards BS 4822, equivalent to ISO 2530:1975, was widely adopted in the past for VDU terminals. However, since the mid-1980s the keyboards of many models of personal computer sold in Britain have adopted a layout in which many of the less frequently used symbols have been moved to other keys, mostly quite close to their previous positions. This layout is derived from the US standard ANSI X4.23:1982. That standard was published after an extensive survey of the opinions of users in many different market sectors. It has the advantage of a harmonized layout based on the long-standing typewriter conventions but also includes all of the characters of the ISO code. The adoption in Britain of the ANSI-based layout virtually eliminates the previous small but irritating differences between the character layouts of American and British versions of the same model of keyboard. It may thus be beneficial in the longer term, although, until well into the 1990s, coexistence with the BS 4822 and other layouts will be equally irritating to many users. Suitable amendments to BS 4822 are now planned.

Part 2 also defines the positions of the principal control functions such as the shifts, return (i.e. new-line, enter data, etc.), tabulation, and backward erase. Guidance is given for other common functions. The traditional offset between one row of keys and the next in the alphanumeric section is recognized, but the layout does not have to adopt it, nor is the dimensional pitch of the offsets defined. A keyboard in which the character keys were arranged according to a strictly rectangular grid, like the arrangement of the numeric block, would still conform to the standard. Although it would look and feel distinctly odd to most users initially, it might have some ergonomic benefit.

Part 3 (Common Secondary Layout) is derived from ISO 8884:1989, *Keyboards for multiple Latin alphabet languages: layout and operation*. This part defines a layout of supplementary characters for allocation to group 2 shift (described above) on the keys of the alphanumeric section. In conjunction with any suitable national standard character layout for group 1 it enables the user to key in any character from the 333-character repertoire of ISO 6937, *Coded graphic character set for text communication using the Latin alphabet.* This repertoire supports 40 different languages that use the Latin alphabet. 155 characters in the repertoire are letters of the alphabet with accents or other diacritical marks, and may be entered by keying the accent followed by the letter. While this layout fills a specialist need it is unlikely to prove very popular. Some keyboards on the market have adopted an alternative layout which provides a similar capability but, by reducing the amount of level shifting needed in group 2, on average requires fewer keystrokes.

Part 4 (Numeric Section) defines the small rectangular block of keys that includes the digits 0 to 9. It defines various alternatives for the symbols and functions that may be allocated to the surrounding keys, to suit different applications such as numeric data entry, general purpose calculator, or telephone number entry. Unfortunately there are two widely-used but conflicting conventions for the arrangement of the digits. In the "7-8-9" layout, adopted by pocket calculators and derived from the ISO adding-machine standard, the keys for 7, 8, and 9 are in the top row (i.e. furthest from the user), but in the "1-2-3" layout specified for the digit keys on telephones (in CCITT E.161) the keys for 1, 2, and 3 are in the top row. Although attempts were made to reconcile this difference, they were not successful. Accordingly Part 4 permits either layout to be adopted on a keyboard, depending on the predominant type of use intended. A keyboard which allows the user to select which layout he wants by means of an associated shift-lock key would also be in conformity. Although Part 4 expresses a preference for the telephone keys convention it is unlikely to cause the calculator convention to fall out of use. Users who rely on one of these conventions in high productivity tasks would need time to adjust if required to change over to the other convention.

Part 5 (Editing Section) defines a small rectangular area, between the alphanumeric and numeric sections, for the keys used for manipulating text and data on the VDU screen. Two alternative configurations are specified for the four cursor control keys, and recommendations are given on the placement of functions Delete, Insert, Next Page, and Previous Page. There is thus great freedom in the choice of functions provided within the editing section of a keyboard, and in their allocation to specific key positions.

Part 6 (Function Section) defines a long narrow area above (i.e. beyond) the top row of the of the other three main sections of the keyboard. It may alternatively, or additionally, extend along the left-hand edge of the alphanumeric section. Keys in the function section are intended for interactions with the application(s) in use, and accordingly Part 6 does not specify particular functions for them. Individual keys may be marked either with application-specific legends or symbols, or with legends that merely act as references to information provided elsewhere, as already mentioned above. The only exception is the Escape function which, if present, must be allocated to the key at the top left corner of the keyboard.

Part 7 (Symbols used to represent functions) defines a collection of over 50 symbols for individual functions which may be allocated to the keys on a keyboard. The corresponding symbol may be marked on the keytop as an alternative to marking with a legend to identify the function. Marking of keytops with symbols has the advantage that the functions can be recognized by users who are not familiar with the language of the user population for which that particular national version of keyboard product was intended. Since in most installations this is not an important consideration, legends for the less frequently used function keys are probably more convenient than symbols, particularly for the occasional user.

Conclusion

Publication of ISO/IEC 9995 does not imply that the task of standardization in its field has been completed. Extensions can be envisaged both to specify the relatively undefined features in greater detail and to recognize alternative features or configurations of layout that might offer benefits to users.

The present standard ensures that conforming keyboards have many features in common. They are suited to a wide range of applications, user roles, and differing levels of operating skill. When users transfer between different models of keyboard, they will find much that is already familiar. Coexistence of different models in the same installation will not seem quite so daunting. On a worldwide perspective the standard enables conforming keyboards to adopt character repertoires and languages suited to users in other countries. But the keyboard is only one component in the overall man-machine interface to information technology equipment. At present many other features of that interface are not covered by standards at all. Standardization of further details of keyboard layouts would probably not bring comparable benefits, and could stifle useful innovation.

Many features of keyboard layouts have evolved slowly over a long period of time. Users can adapt quite quickly to small changes, but large changes require an investment in retraining or familiarization which must be commensurate with the expected benefits. The new keyboard standard records the main features of today's keyboards; it does not point the way ahead. Ergonomics experts have in the past devised new physical configurations of keyboard intended to reduce the physical strain of keyboard operation, particularly on intensive users. They have also devised rational character layouts to replace the deliberately clumsy QWERTY, with the aim of improving the productivity of trained users or of easing the learning and memorizing process for the untrained or occasional user. Because of the difficulty of introducing these new features in an evolutionary way they have not been widely accepted in the market. Today's keyboard technology provides a better opportunity for them. For example, the multi-alphabet capability of a keyboard with group 2 shift could be harnessed to provide an optional substitute for the QWERTY layout that the user could switch on or off at will; not exactly evolution, but cautious coexistence. If users welcome such innovations the standards will soon follow.

Standards such as ISO/IEC 9995 represent a consensus of good practice in the IT industry. They are not backed up by any legal sanction. Suppliers will offer conforming keyboards as long as the demand exists in the marketplace. Users who regard the standard as beneficial must remember, or remind their purchasing agents, to ask about conformance to standards when considering new purchases.

A recurrent theme of this book, and indeed of all standardization work, is how to cope with diversity, and allowing justifiable diversity while restraining unnecessary diversity. In the case of keyboards it is primarily a matter of reducing the burden of coping with unnecessary diversity for the human user. Humans being capable of learning and adapting to change, the question of being able to cope at all hardly arises. It is a different matter when it comes to physical diversity of equipment. If a plug does not fit a socket or a nut does not fit a bolt, it takes more than human adaptability to cope with it.

Since keyboards are rarely moved from machine to machine that aspect is not a major factor there. Output peripherals are more commonly moved; users wanted to retain still serviceable devices while updating their processing power, or to share expensive or infrequently used devices between more than one system. This situation began to appear on a significant scale in the 1960s, and can be seen now as the first tentative step towards the now major concern of general interworking and Open Systems Interconnection. Even then there was the "physical layer" aspect – the plug on the printer had to fit the socket on the computer – and even then the pernicious effects of options in the standards, when the standards came to appear, were soon recognized, even if less readily acted upon. (A useful survey of the problems current in the early 1980s, which particularly if not exclusively discusses the problems of standards for microcomputers and their peripherals, can be found in [Nicoud 1983]. It is useful because, in its principles if not in its detail, much is still valid a decade later.)

Where perhaps the problems were (and are) still felt most, however, was in the physical transfer of information (typically data and program files) from machine to machine. There is no point now in rehearsing the histories of punched cards – standard physically but with incompatible encodings – or of magnetic tapes, but they are mentioned to show that these histories are still repeating themselves in other contexts. When users have wrestled with, and if lucky come to terms with, one lot of incompatibilities, along comes a new medium, displaying the same kinds of old problems.

In the early 1980s **D. Blyth** and **R. A. Starling** produced a report [Blyth and Starling 1984] describing work carried out at the National Computing Centre in Manchester, as part of a project funded by the Electronics and Avionics Requirements Board of the UK Department of Trade and Industry. The report described the authors' experience in producing and using a standardsconforming interchange tool to support interchange of files between different microcomputer systems on flexible diskettes. There follow some extracts, relating to the diskettes rather than their interchange tool, and the diskette standards of the day. The age of the report is revealed by the sizes of diskette discussed, but the issues raised are as valid in the 1990s as they were in the previous decade; the statement that opens the abstract, "incompatibilities amongst floppy disks often make them difficult to use for information interchange", could have been written in 1992. Editorial commentary in what follows is italicized and indented.

Information interchange using flexible diskettes

A few sentences into the introduction, the authors embark on the problems that flexible disk users faced:

Flexible disks are so widely used that there have arisen differing and incompatible disk types. To appreciate the variety one need only list the various characteristics of disks themselves:

Size – 8 in, 5.25 in, and more recently several sub5.25 in types.

Singlesided or doublesided.

Sector boundaries marked by index holes (hardsectored) or by special recording patterns (softsectored).

Various methods of recording leading to varying recording densities.

Varying numbers of tracks per side, sectors per track and bytes per sector.

These differing characteristics are not all combined orthogonally (thank goodness!). Nevertheless there are about two dozen different types of disk available from major media manufacturers in the current UK market. When one considers in addition that different operating systems organize disk filestores in different ways, then the full scale of diversity is readily apparent.

Variety is the spice of life, but it is the bane of efficiency. As a result of the variety of flexible disks, it is often difficult if not impossible to use them for information interchange. The obvious and only remedy is standardization.

Though the problems with the 3.5 in (90 mm) diskettes of the 1990s may not be quite the same, many users of them would still add a fervent "amen!" to the sentiments in the first sentence of the last paragraph quoted.

The authors then go on to discuss the standards of the day, the design of their interchange tool, and the problems they encountered. They end with a discussion of the deficiencies of those standards, for example castigating the error handling procedures specified in one of them as "unworkable".

The conclusions of the report are still worth quoting in full:

Most flexible disk use is on small systems which are also likely to have straightforward disk control architectures. The authors see no reason why it should not be possible to implement standards-conforming disk interchange capabilities on most of these systems. Provided that a minimal interchange system is all that is required, an interchange utility can be made effectively portable across a wide range of small machines.

The source code size of the authors' implementation (about 1000 lines of Pascal) demonstrates that, by the standards of the IT industry, the cost of conformant implementations can be remarkably modest. Most system manufacturers could supply such utilities without undue difficulty or cost.

At present few users are aware of flexible disk standards. Many accept incompatibility almost with resignation. Often the high cost of ad hoc conversions is borne with minimal protest. A standardsconforming disk interchange package is very cheap to implement. The time is long overdue when such products should be plentiful in the marketplace.

In the 1990s there are of course interchange packages available – at a cost to the user, naturally – and some packages do claim to support a variety of formats: the acceptance by Apple Computer in 1991 that their Macintosh systems had to recognize the existence of an IBM-compatible world outside was a considerable step forward for many users. Yet the limitations are still severe and the problems still considerable. Since these tend to arise not just from the physical media but their combination with encodings and the use made of them by software, this will not be pursued further in this section.

The examples of flexible diskettes shows that often there are good technical reasons for options in standards or, in this case, multiple standards. Multiple standards can easily arise with an advance in technology: while the new is supplanting the old, both necessarily coexist, and the old may take a long time to die out. By the beginning of the 1990s the dominant diskette size had become 3.5 in (90 mm), just emerging at the time the extracts quoted above were being written, and (of particular interest) with two main flavours, double-density (DD) and high-density. Yet the lessons of the past had still not been learned, the mistakes were still being repeated.

Three papers at the 1989 INSITS conference brought out some of the problems [Schroeder 1990, Thiel 1990, Harcken 1990]. A paragraph by Schroeder is particularly damning:

> A conformance test according to the existing standards could lead to results which make no sense: an excellent diskette can be found to be "not in conformance" if one of the unimportant dimensions is just out of the tolerance range. On the other hand, a diskette with poor performance characteristics may be completely in conformance.

Which, put another way, means that the standards are not addressing the issues that really matter to the user; Schroeder remarks that of a total of 443 (four hundred and forty-three) parameters to be tested for conformance, 102 refer to dimensional requirements.

The transition between 5.25 in (130 mm) and 3.5 in disks was clearcut – a disk of one size would not fit the drive for the other. Here there was every likelihood that users would be likely, through accident or ignorance, to try to use 3.5 in disks in drives that were not designed to cope with them. It is hardly being wise after the event to think that an obvious user requirement for standards would be that they would ensure some kind safeguard for users against that kind of problem. Yet, as the paper by Thiel in the same sequence indicates, they offer the user no such protection, as huge numbers of users worldwide have found to their cost.

Finally, we return to the question of hardware performance, mentioned in the opening passages of this section. This was a question discussed in a popular article written in the mid 1980s by **Brian Meek**. What follows is an abridged version of this article [Meek 1986] as originally written, adapted to the purposes of this book and with some necessary updating.

Performance statistics and standards

In the modern world we are bombarded by statistics – by politicians and political pollsters, by economists, by weather experts, by television companies, by sports pundits, and above all by advertisers. Sometimes it seems that almost every issue on which we might be expected to hold an opinion can only be decided after considering an exhaustive barrage of statistics from proponents of one view or another.

Yet we all know that statistics never tell the whole story. Value does not reside only in that which can be measured, whether in terms of experimental data, which is all some scientists regard as useful, or in terms of money, which is all that seems to interest some politicians.

The reason that the subject listed lend themselves to this kind of elaborate statistical treatment is of course that they are very complex and data-rich; which also helps, in part though not wholly, to explain why the statistics do not (and cannot) tell the whole story. Modern computer systems are also very complex, and data-rich as far as their performance is concerned. Similar arguments apply to them.

It is this which is at the root of an argument that you often hear advanced: that statistics of performance of computer systems are unreliable, misleading and a general waste of time. No-one, it would appear, trusts benchmarks, of which I recall Stan Kelly-Bootle's marvellous description in his definition of *mendacity sequence* – "The basic sequence, in ascending order, is: lies; damn lies; statistics; benchmarks; delivery promises; DP dictionary entries" [Kelly-Bootle 1981]. In the standards field, this attitude appears in the form of claims that performance requirements are not the concern of standards, and to try to put them in is unthinkable.

I wish to argue that this view is mistaken. Statistics do not tell you everything, but they do tell you something. They may be misleading, in isolation, but the answer is not to take them in isolation – and to take the ones that are relevant to you. People flock to see particular athletes perform or particular football teams play, not necessarily because they will always be successful but because their performance record suggests that they may, and anyway indicates a level of skill that is likely to be worth watching. When planning a holiday, it does help to know that in one place there is a mean temperature (celsius) of zero and a mean wind speed of force six, whereas somewhere else the temperature (fahrenheit) and humidity are both usually in the nineties.

So with performance measures for computing products. However useful or not they may be as indicators, people are interested in them just as are interested in performance measures of the weather at a famous Costa del Somewhere resort or a tennis-star's victories. And, since the computing products are manufactured rather than natural, it is not unreasonable for potential purchasers, who are going to part with their money, to look for performance requirements in standards. They can accept that a week in the famous resort may provide weather like some grim British industrial port during a bleak autumn, or that the tennis star's performance they have paid to see could have been matched by a Costa del Somewhere barman, because the player is off form or not completely fit; however, quite reasonably they expect greater assurance of value for money, in terms of performance, when they buy a gigaflop vector processor or a PC database package.

Despite all the moans about benchmarks, people use them. Even suppliers quote them, when they look good, in between assuring us that they don't mean anything, when they aren't so favourable. Not that I am in favour of putting benchmarks, as commonly supplied to date, into a standard. A benchmark, if specified in advance, allows the designer to tune "the system" (whether it is anything from a compiler on a micro to a multiprocessor network) to cope with it. The tennis equivalent to a benchmark would be a player who knew in advance the characteristics of every stroke the opponent would play, in predictable order. The results would not be meaningless, but they would be artificial, and of very limited value.

Of course, I can see the difficulties in putting performance requirements into standards given the present state of the art. What I refuse to accept is that buyers of a standard-conforming IT product should forever be deprived of this kind of benefit from standard conformance. It is something which anyone buying a standard-conforming product should have a right to expect.

In the past, the few of us who were saying such things were very much lone voices lamenting in the wilderness. However, there seems now to have been some change in the climate – or at least in the weather. This began with talk of "functional" standards or "procurement" standards, the terms which, like so much in this trade, seemed to be used in a fairly casual, handwaving way.

Functional standards, by the beginning of the 1990s, had advanced to functional profiles, which specify which options to invoke of those allowed by the technical standards, in order to obtain the necessary compatibility and interfacing, and applied primarily in the OSI area.

Mention of options leads me to remark in passing that the more options there are in a standard, the less of a standard it is. I'd like to know how many options appear in standards only to satisfy conflicting commercial interests of vendors rather than to meet genuine variations in user requirements. Far more than is generally admitted, I suspect.

I would like to see the concept of functional standards extended to be used for secondary standards defining the complete range of additional requirements upon products which, to perform a given function or task for the end user, have to conform not just to one but to several technical standards. These would include performance requirements, and safety requirements including error protection and recovery if the base standards were not adequate in that respect, as well as coping with the inadequacies caused by the presence of options.

The term "procurement standard" seems in the early 1990s to have dropped out of general circulation. I should like to see it revived, and applied to single standards for products which specify all the necessary requirements for products – standards good enough to use on their own as a basis for a purchase. I should like to see language standards to be of this kind, so that if you buy a compiler for language X to run on machine Y, standard conformance will guarantee to you that it will run to at least an assured minimum level of safety and performance, possibly dependent on your particular configuration of machine Y. However, it could equally apply to many applications such as database products, spreadsheets and word processors, and of course hardware.

Incidentally, I don't like the term procurement *version* standards, mainly because to me "version" smells of "options" with an implication that there are other versions than procurement versions. Certain kinds of technical standards, which specify properties of products rather than the products themselves (such as interfacing requirements) are necessarily never going to be procurement standards on their own, which is where the functional standards should come in. But where standards specify identifiable products, then they should be procurement standards, full stop. **No** "versions".

It will be seen that, with this philosophy, all functional standards should *ipso facto* be procurement standards in this sense.

I fully accept that this happy state of affairs cannot be brought about overnight. There are various ways of bringing performance requirements into standards, and for any of them, performance measures will need to be specified. And for anything as complex as a computer system, or even a spreadsheet or a language compiler, a single measure is unlikely to be adequate, as those beguiled in the past by Atlas units and the like well know. Any child with a pack of "trump cards" knows that there is more than one measure you can use for cars, and that on some the family runabout will beat the Rolls Royces and the Porsches.

What matters is what you need it for. To return to another sporting analogy, golf is mainly an individual game whose statistical ratings of players are measured by success in stroke play tournaments (and in terms of money, which must be indicative of something). Nevertheless, when it comes to team contests, selectors, even if bound by the rules to select mostly top-rated players, usually try to include some reliable match play golfers regardless of what the ratings say. Another sporting metaphor is "horses for courses".

This brings to mind the view, sometimes expressed, that standards should not specify performance requirements directly, but demand that suppliers supply performance information with their documentation – which courses they will guarantee the performance of their horses on, if you like. I don't think this goes far enough, but it is better than nothing. Given the present state of the art, I'd be happy enough with that as a start, provided it is recognized that "a start" is all it is.

Furthermore, if such an approach were to be used, the nature of the information would have to be specified in the standard, as precisely as possible. Leaving the choice of criteria to the supplier would be hopeless. To use the weather analogy again, I seem to recall a forecaster being taken to task for predicting "bright intervals" when in fact it poured with rain all day; the defence was that the bright intervals had occurred – but in the middle of the night.

Another example is even more to the point. In the UK in the 1980s, a British Rail (BR) advertising campaign used black and red dots to indicate trains how many trains ran "on time" or not. This "performance statement" by BR was based on their "standard" definition of "on time" as "no more than five minutes late" – which may satisfy intercity travellers but not the regular short-haul commuters – and was based on trains, not on passenger journeys. That is, a short mid-morning cross-country service "on time" cancelled out a main line 12-coach evening commuter service, carrying hundreds of passengers, being half an hour or more late, as far as their "performance figures" were concerned.

I frankly doubt if supplier-chosen performance data for computer systems would be less misleading, and I am sure there would be more scope for them to be rendered less obviously ridiculous. Furthermore, if choice of criteria were left optional, it would be that much more difficult for validation services to provide independent assessment of conformance – a vital requirement.

Suppliers may still argue against performance requirements in standards, on the basis that any criteria will be "unfair" on someone. But provided the criteria relate directly to user needs and are independently verifiable, I do not see they have a case. Anyway, such criteria in standards are coming, let there be no question about that. It is now a matter of when, not whether. My advice to any who are worried about this is to forget about fighting a rearguard action against performance requirements or any other "procurement" criteria in standards, but to do the research necessary, or sponsor others to do it, to ensure that the criteria are fair and reasonable.

The time is coming when such requirements are going to be in standards: it is in suppliers' as well as purchasers' interests to ensure that the best available are adequate, to avoid the risk that the best available will be used whether they are adequate or not. Some of us have worked for a long time to get to the present level of acceptance to the idea of "procurement" standards. We are not going to give up now.

The mention in that contribution of functional profiles in OSI brings us naturally to the next section, which deals with the interconnection and communications aspects. We can see already, however, that even in the huge OSI standardization programme, much hailed (and with some justice) as a "new approach" and "the future way" in IT standardization, the lessons about options were still not learned, and the mistakes of the past were repeated yet again.

Nevertheless, performance measuring is coming. In hardware media, "Japanese diskette standards, which are based on ISO standards, describe also test methods and requirements for durability and stress" [Schroeder 1990]. In communications too, performance is being monitored [Pattinson and Strachan 1990]. Users must hope that this trend will steadily extend into all areas – indeed not just hope, but work actively towards it.

References

Standards and standards body documents

ANSI X4.23:1982 Office machines and supplies – alphanumeric machines – keyboard arrangements

ANSI/IEEE Std 754:1985 Standard for binary floating-point arithmetic

BS 2481 Part 1:1982 Typewriters, specification for keyboard arrangements

BS 4822:1980 Keyboard arrangements of the graphic characters of the United Kingdom 7-bit data code for data processing (UK equivalent to ISO 2530:1975)

CCITT E.161 Arrangement of figures, letters and symbols on rotary dials and push-button telephone sets, CCITT 1988 Recommendations

ISO 2530:1975 Keyboard for international information processing using the ISO 7-bit coded character set – alphanumeric area

ISO 6937:1992 Coded graphic character set for text communication – Latin alphabet, 2nd edn.

ISO 8884:1989 Keyboards for multiple Latin alphabet languages: layout and operation

ISO/IEC 9241-4 Ergonomic requirements for office work with video display terminals – Part 4: keyboard requirements (draft, March 1992)

ISO/IEC 9995 Keyboard layouts for text and office systems (due for publication in 1992)

ISO/IEC JTC1 CD 10967 Language independent arithmetic, Part 1 (draft, 1991)

Other references

[Berg and Schumny 1990] *see general bibliography*

[Blyth and Starling 1984] BLYTH, D. and STARLING R.A., Information interchange using standardsconforming flexible disks, internal report, National Computing Centre, Manchester

[Harcken 1990] HARCKEN, H., Certification of reference diskettes, in [Berg and Schumny 1990], pp 375-382

[Hill and Meek 1980] *see general bibliography*

[Kahan 1992] KAHAN, W., Analysis and refutation of the LCAS, *Sigplan Notices of the ACM*, Vol 27, No. 1, pp 61-74

[Kelly-Bootle 1981] KELLY-BOOTLE, S., The devil's DP dictionary, McGraw-Hill, New York

[Meek 1986] MEEK, B.L., So what's the score?, *Computer Weekly*, 31 July 1986

[Nicoud 1983] NICOUD, J.-D., Expectations of standardization, in MASON, R.E.A. (ed.), *Information Processing 83, Proceeding of the IFIP World Congress, Paris 1983*, North-Holland, Amsterdam

[Pattinson and Strachan 1990] PATTINSON, C., and STRACHAN, R.M., The performance monitoring of computer communications systems, in [Berg and Schumny 1990], pp 323-335

[Payne, Schaffert and Wichmann 1990] PAYNE, M., SHAFFERT, C. and WICHMANN, B., A proposal for a language compatible arithmetic standard, *Sigplan Notices of the ACM*, Vol 25, No 1, pp 59-86

[Schroeder 1990] SCHROEDER, H.J., Conformance tests for magnetic media – a rational task or a hazardous venture?, in [Berg and Schumny 1990], pp 361-366

[Thiel 1990] THIEL, A., Quality of standards – a weak point of flexible disk standards demonstrated by an example, in [Berg and Schumny 1990] pp 367-374

4 User needs in networking and systems intercommunication standards

The basic need of users for networking standards is that they should define products which will allow any systems conforming to these standards to communicate with each other easily and consistently.

By "communicate" is meant that it should provide for:

exchanging data files;

exchanging mail;

provide access to one system from another for both batch and interactive working;

enable program to program links.

Currently the international networking and communications standards are collectively known as Open Systems Interconnection or simply as OSI. These standards are recognized worldwide, and there are some governments and large organizations which insist that all IT communications products conform to the OSI standards wherever appropriate ones exist.

The problem lies with the complexity of communications and the flexibility of base standards. Base standards currently allow for many options at each level. This means that it is impossible, or at least impracticable, to produce a system which conforms to the whole of the OSI standards.

This has led to the creation of *functional profiles* which link a number of standards together such that products conforming to a particular profile will do certain tasks in a uniform and unambiguous way. Thus a functional profile can be used as a part of a systems specification, whereas a base standard can rarely be used in this way.

There are some points which are made more than one in these papers. That is no bad thing in a subject as complex as this. By the end of this section, oft repeated comments may have created an important impression.

The first contribution in this section, by **Cliff Evans** of Kodak Ltd in the UK, was originally prepared as a paper for a computer conference in March 1991. It has been revised for the purpose of this book. It examines the concept of "open systems", in particular OSI, from the viewpoint of the user.

Open systems – straitjacket or freedom?

Introduction

"Open systems" for Information Technology (IT) is a much talked about, and a much misunderstood concept. We read in the press about European Council and UK Government pronouncements encouraging the use of open systems in industry and commerce, and in the same journal, papers attacking open systems as being useless or non-existent. Some eminent computer consultants regard the open systems concept as a cure for all IT ills, while others dismiss it as a myth. Some regard the concept as being nothing more than an expensive straitjacket which limits their freedom of choice, while to others it provides the flexibility which enables them to control their changing IT environment.

This is not a full treatise on open systems, but rather an introductory paper concentrating on the problem of whether open systems will be of benefit to you and to your company, and whether you should enquire further. The paper assumes little or no prior knowledge of open systems, or of IT standards. It assumes that the reader knows what a computer is, and that he/she will have used one for their work.

What do we mean by "open systems"?

A generally accepted definition of *open systems* is "IT systems that are 'vendor independent' in some, or all, aspects". By "vendor independent systems" is meant IT systems that consist of components from several vendors, chosen for their suitability for the job they have to do, and designed and produced according to international standards that enable them to interwork with the other components in the system, irrespective of their origin.

The components of an open system include the "five Is":

Interconnection (communications)

Interchangeability (including portability)

Interworking

Interface (human and systems)

International standards (ISO)

We can now enlarge our formal definition of an open system to mean:

> *A computer system designed to an International Standard, functioning compatibly with any product designed to that standard.*

From this definition it follows that, in an open system, elements are not constrained to working within a single configuration; instead, they may be removed and replaced as business needs grow and information can be exchanged between, and be used by, different parts of the system.

This leads us to one of the primary advantages of open systems, ie that open systems allow information resources to be fully exploited by building flexibility into the IT infrastructure.

What are the advantages of open systems?

Many companies and organizations need *flexibility* in IT. Many companies now work in a multivendor computing environment. Because of this it is essential that the various components of that environment are capable of working together. No one vendor can, or is ever likely to, satisfy all computing needs, however much the salesmen try to convince us that this is so. The only proviso for attaining this desired flexibility is that all components should conform to relevant open systems standards.

So what are the advantages, other than the somewhat vague concept of flexibility? I see the main advantages of open systems as:

the ability to select the best system for a particular job, independent of source;

the ability to mix and match components in a system for best functionality, and savings in cost;

there is reduced obsolescence – the old can often work with the new;

your purchasing department has a greater ability to "second source";

you have the ability to interface with other consenting systems which comply with open systems principles;

again, flexibility – the ability to change course with minimum resource impact;

the possibility of the portability of systems between different hardware platforms;

the integration of electronic mail facilities across different system platforms;

the ability to access and transfer complex documents and information in editable/printable form between different systems;

lastly, and by no means least, "open systems" has the backing of major suppliers and users, and governments including the US and the EC. That means suppliers cannot afford to ignore it.

But, you may rightly say, are there any disadvantages? Does not this glowing list of advantages show the author's prejudice? The answer to both questions is *YES!*

There are some disadvantages which we cannot ignore. These include the following.

The international standards on which open systems rely are not yet complete. This means that suppliers have to leave (sometimes large) gaps in their open systems product range, or try to second guess what the future standards might be. This is further complicated by the fact that both the technology and the standards are still changing, but more of that later in the next part. This means that open systems products are not as widely available as they need to be.

Following on from this, there is the problem of the complex and slow way in which IT standards are produced. The means of evolving IT standards are too slow to cope with a rapidly evolving technology!

There are still widely used and accepted proprietary systems in use which users are reluctant to relinquish. It is unlikely that many of these systems will eventually become an international standard, or that they can migrate to one. Hence the problem of migration from a proprietary system to an open system is a often significant deterrent.

Products made to the open systems specification are often more expensive than proprietary products. Of course, there are eventual savings (often substantial) to be made, but how do you convince the finance department of the business case for open systems?

Lastly – education! To gain real benefit, the concept of open systems has to be built into a company's IT strategy. That means there is a need to educate management (both IT management and general management) at all levels about open systems... but they don't have the time, and don't see the need to spend what time they have on this. It is a vicious circle! This can lead to a lack of organizational vision, where the concepts and the IT strategy that goes with the concepts are driven from the bottom up, rather than from the top down.

I said several times that "open systems" is based on international IT standards... so what are they, and why should you bother?

Why be involved with IT standards?

Open systems are based on international IT standards. To understand open systems concepts one needs some understanding of the underlying standards on which they are based. If you are going to propose and implement an open systems IT strategy, or even if you are presenting a case for this to your company, you have to know something about the underlying structure of open systems, and that means knowing about IT standards.

Further, to understand how open systems will evolve in the future one has to be aware of which IT standards are being prepared, what their timescale is, and what effect they are likely to have on the future development of open systems. This can be important as you evolve your strategy.

Many companies include some IT component in their products. Because a large part of the IT market is requiring IT products which conform to open systems concepts, it is important that your company's IT products are developed in conformity with relevant international IT standards, otherwise a large part of the potential market will be closed to them. Users require products which can fit into their existing IT structure. If this IT structure is based on proprietary products, then the market is closely targeted, but if the IT structure is based on open systems (as large sections of the market are), then conformance to open systems standards becomes essential.

If you are a "user" you could be dominated by supplier interests. The main thrust of the development of IT standards is provided by suppliers of IT products. Unless the "user voice" is heard, the users may get products which are less useful to them than if they had spoken at the right time. In general, suppliers welcome the user view.

There are two basic types of IT standards, "base" standards and "functional" standards. Base standards contain a wide variety of options, and cover the detailed technology within the standard. Functional standards are standards with the options removed, but designed to work with other linking standards to provide a specification for products to do a real job.

Functional standards are now being created from the base standards. There are a number of international standards bodies (e.g. EWOS, AWOS and PAGODA) which are almost solely concerned with developing functional standards. It is products conforming to the functional standards which users will use. That is where the user voice is most required.

International IT standards exist in whole or in part in many areas including:

>   data, including office systems;

>   communications (OSI);

>   security;

human-computer interface;

system development;

open applications.

International standards do not currently exist for operating systems. Unix is still a proprietary standard, and as such cannot, in my opinion, yet be regarded as a true part of open systems. However, a standard is being developed for an operating systems interface. This standard is known as Posix. There are already several operating systems on the market which are Posix-compliant, including several versions of Unix. It is possible to port software between Posix-compliant systems. *[Posix is dealt with in more detail in Section 6 – Eds.]*

What to watch out for

There are traps for the unwary approaching a path to open systems. The particular traps you might encounter depend on your circumstances. However, I give you below a non-exclusive guide to some of them. User beware!

Security. Because the international standards are public knowledge, systems security can no longer rely on proprietary quirks to protect open systems. Security standards are evolving, but a comprehensive security policy needs to be agreed in your company to make your systems "open, but secure".

Standards. The international IT standards for open systems are still evolving. While many of them are complete, and in place with products on the market, there are gaps. You will need to agree how to cover your particular gaps.

Proprietary, or de facto, standards. There are many proprietary standards with products on the market. Some salesmen claim they are true international standards, when they are not. We need to know the difference, and when to use these "industry" or "de facto" standards because they are likely to become true standards, or because there is nothing better available in international standards.

Cultural and legal differences. There are differences between USA, Europe, Japan, Australia, and many other countries in the way things are done – for example PTT regulations, data protection, computer misuse regulations, etc.

Standard operating systems. Many people in the IT industry recognize Unix and TCP/IP as international standards. I have mentioned this before, and it needs repeating. There are many versions of Unix. It has been estimated that there are over 250 differences between the different major implementations of Unix. I personally have not counted them, but until Unix or some other operating system is accepted by the international standards organizations as a standard, it remains a proprietary standard, and therefore not a full part of open systems. It may be necessary to use Unix to fill a gap in your open systems strategy, or for other reasons applying to the choice of any suitable operating system.

However, the Posix standard discussed in the previous section opens up a way for making many operating systems "open" in so far as software designed to run under Posix can run under any Posix compliant system.

TCP/IP. TCP/IP is not an international standard. It has one advantage over OSI in that there are currently (i.e. in 1992) more products available for TCP/IP than for OSI. Also, an increasing number of products are available supporting both TCP/IP and OSI. The future is a little unclear. TCP/IP has some inherent limitations which in the long term may force a change towards TCP/IP becoming more like OSI. My view is that OSI will eventually become the accepted standard, but the two protocols will coexist for many years to come – or may eventually merge.

A question answered

Open systems – straitjacket or freedom? Which is it?

As in so many questions, the answer lies in where you stand. If you have an IT infrastructure based totally on, say, IBM systems, then open systems could be irrelevant to you, and the answer could be "straitjacket". If you have an IT infrastructure based on a multivendor environment, then open systems could spell "freedom". I hope this paper has presented some of the facts and opinions which can help you to sort out the answer for your particular situation. Like the answer to "life, the universe and everything" the answer may be "42". You have to understand the question to get to a meaningful answer.

Where should an open systems policy apply in your company?

The easy answer is "everywhere", but this may be impracticable. Where well-defined standards exist, and products are available from them, then these should be used. Where they do not exist, you will have to define a policy, taking account of the problem areas discussed in this paper.

The question needs to be asked for any new system and equipment as to whether it needs to conform to the requirements of open systems. This does not only apply to obvious IT equipment, but to equipment with embedded IT components in it, e.g. data gathering instruments which may be connected to a local area network. We also have to face the problems of transition, i.e. how do we use both open systems, and systems which are already in place.

This an area for much discussion, and must depend on the special circumstances in your company.

In practical terms, you must decide whether your company needs an open systems strategy, and where such a strategy should apply. You will have a big job to educate all relevant people, to produce your strategy, then to sell it to those who matter in your company.

Good luck!

The second paper in this section, by **Peter Judge**, an IT consultant and author in the UK, looks more closely at OSI standards from a user viewpoint. This paper provides a brief guide through the maze of OSI standards and the processes which produce them. Some of the material duplicates other parts of this book, but this has been left, so as not to spoil continuity, and to provide a useful overview in one place.

Where do OSI standards come from?

"If a committee tried to design a horse, it would create a camel" – anyone who has served or suffered on a committee will know the truth of that. But in the IT industry, it seems things can go differently. OSI communications standards are famous for being designed by committees, but much of the industry accepts them as useful workhorses, with a long working life ahead of them.

True, some people are reluctant to accept them, arguing that OSI standards are as slow and ugly as camels. True, other protocols exist which do many of today's jobs quicker and cheaper. OSI has made much slower progress in the market than expected, but a majority in the IT industry still pays at least lip service to OSI and believes in its eventual success.

How did this come about? In an open systems world, suppliers must work to agreed standards, and those standards have to come from somewhere. A lot of the ferment in the industry right now is a debate about where and how those standards should be set, but at the moment, the only way we know to agree a standard is in some kind of industry group.

Since the OSI programme has produced a range of standards that are accepted, at least in principle, let's look at where those standards came from. In particular, let's look at the new structures that are evolving to keep the standards process moving. As the industry moves towards standards, this kind of process will be more and more pronounced.

ISO is the body in charge of it all. Its policy is decided by representatives from more than 70 national standards bodies. These are mainly from the developed world, but with observers from the developing countries as well. Standards are developed in national bodies and passed to ISO for completion, or developed by ISO committees, made up of representatives chosen by national bodies.

When it comes to IT standards, however, things get more complex. Other bodies are involved and, as it turns out, much of the OSI portfolio comes from outside the normal ISO structure.

The International Electrotechnical Commission (IEC), an industry body, has worked on IT standards, but joined forces with ISO in 1960. The joint technical committee in charge of all IT standards is now known as ISO/IEC JTC1.

Among the standards set within ISO/IEC are the basic OSI model, and services within it such as FTAM (file transfer access and management).

The Institute of Electrical and Electronic Engineers (IEEE) had teams working on networking standards in its 802 Committee. The American standards body, ANSI, decided to pass that work straight on to ISO, making 802 an Accredited Standards Committee (ASC) of ANSI. That is where the ISO LAN standards came from, including 802.3 (Ethernet) and 802.5 (token ring).

Another body ISO "teams up" with is the International Telephone and Telegraph Consultative Committee (CCITT). CCITT is made up of national telecommunications authorities. For most countries the service provider (PTT) is the member but, since BT is a private company, the British member is the Department of Trade and Industry (DTI). A European subset of CCITT meets, under the name of CEPT, agreeing requirements for equipment to connect to networks across Europe.

CCITT has clear goals and, since its members benefit directly from its work, it works quickly. It also helps that it publishes voluntary "recommendations" not "standards". Where ISO needs a unanimous decision, CCITT can accept a majority vote. The recommendations are published every four years in "coloured books", a different colour distinguishing each edition (blue for 1988).

CCITT adopted the OSI model, and worked to fill in the standards which telecommunications providers needed. X.25 wide area networking was one success, and application services including X.400 electronic mail and X.500 directory services have followed. ISO adopted X.25, and abandoned its own work on electronic mail, adopting X.400 unchanged.

CCITT has a liaison status in ISO, as do other groups, including the European Computer Manufacturers' Association (ECMA). Within OSI, ECMA came up with the ODA standards which allow electronic mail documents to be sent in intelligible forms, suitable for editing and processing.

A striking feature of the bodies with liaisons to ISO is their focus. CCITT addresses the needs of telecommunications providers, and ECMA supports manufacturers. Other groups cover geographic regions.

This is a crucial shift in emphasis in standards. With the spread of multinationals, and business practices becoming more aligned, there is less need for "national" standards than ever before. Some multinationals have more brute economic power than many countries – let alone their influence over their specialized business area.

Suppose DEC wanted to contribute to document format standards. Which country's standards body should it go through: ANSI in the US, where it is headquartered, or AFNOR, the standards body of France, where it has its networking centre?

There is a trend to pooling all the effort on particular standards together, regardless of geography. Where this has been hard to do within the standards body, or where the needs of particular groups have been left out, pressure groups have formed at an ever increasing rate.

The MAP/TOP movement began in the early 1980s when General Motors decided it needed OSI protocols right now to link its factory equipment. Other manufacturers joined in (now mainly in the automotive industry).

Specialist groups most often select from the options in the OSI portfolio, creating their own "profile", sometimes a profile of one particular standard. More rarely, they need to create their own specialized protocols. The MAP/TOP movement did both, and now the World Federation of MAP/TOP User Groups (WFMTUG) maintains the specialized protocol (manufacturing message service, MMS) and the profiles. MAP is not dead, by the way, though the recession in manufacturing isn't helping it.

The Network Management Forum, formed in 1988, was the first body formed outside ISO by suppliers to help progress the work on one particular OSI standard, in this case network management. After initial fears that it would try to influence the OSI work unduly, it settled into highly regarded work, essentially creating a profile ("implementation specification") of the management standards, and feeding input into the ISO standards process. Recognizing the success of non-OSI standards, it has shifted its emphasis considerably towards multi-protocol networking.

The X.400 Application Programming Interface Association (APIA) was formed in January 1989 to develop practical interfaces to message handling systems, based on X.400, to aid developers in making portable products which linked to other services such as electronic data interchange (EDI).

The SQL Access Group is focused on the Structured Query Language standard, and is working, again on APIs, to make practical client/server database systems in which different suppliers' products can be integrated.

In 1991, the Open Document Architecture Consortium (ODAC) formed around the ODA standards. ODAC intends to go further than the other "specific service" groups, and make and sell working code. Essentially its aim is the same – to make a standard more usable by vendors.

All these groups also work on testing: a conformance test is now an accepted part of every standard – how else would you be able to tell if products meet the standard? A structure of specialist groups exists, dedicated to making sure that tests are universally applicable and, for instance, a Chinese user will accept an OSI conformance certificate issued in Britain. OSTC and ETCOM are the European bodies involved.

In all this, the user interest might seem to be left out, but "user power" has been one of the big stories of the last few years. In 1988, Bryan Wood of Sema Group, then chairman of the UK committee in BSI corresponding to SC21 (upper levels of OSI) in JTC1, spoke at a London conference of the difficulty of getting users involved in OSI. By 1991, the user involvement was getting noticeable – but, again, not always through the traditional channels.

One of users' biggest needs is for profiles. Confidence in OSI stumbles if two conformant products fail to work together – and that is exactly what happens if you select two products which use different options from within the standards.

The most important profiles are undoubtedly the government OSI profiles (GOSIPs). The UK central government buys some £2 billion of information systems each year, and that has to conform to OSI and other standards. An EC Directive demands it, quite apart from the pro-OSI stance of the DTI and the Government Centre for Information Systems (CCTA), the UK Treasury department which advises government agencies on IT. A European version called the European Procurement Handbook for Open Systems (EPHOS) has been developed by the EC and launched in 1992.

The CCTA is the source of the UK GOSIP. In the US, a somewhat similar body, the National Institute of Standards and Technology (NIST), defines the US GOSIP. Suppliers who want access to the largest single market sector toe the line – and users won't lose by reading the manuals, and even using the GOSIP specifications when issuing tenders.

The GOSIPs are "procurement" profiles, tailored for users buying systems. ISO, meanwhile, is working on its own "international standardized profiles" (ISPs), in a Special Group on Functional Standards (SGFS). The groups submitting are, again, outside the national standards bodies. They include the World Federation of MAP/TOP User Groups (WFMTUG) and three regional workshops: the European Workshop on Open Systems (EWOS), the US-based OSI Implementors' Workshop (OIW) and the Asia and Oceania Workshop (AOW).

EWOS' profiles are also used as European standards. The group is assisted by the European Telecommunications Standards Institute (ETSI).

For completeness, it needs to be said that ETSI is one of three European standards bodies, along with CEN and CENELEC which are, roughly, the European subsets of ISO and IEC respectively. ETSI covers standards work in the field of telecommunications, and also assists CEPT (as astute readers would expect!).

A final and utterly fundamental thing that users would like to have is assurance that products will work together. Of course that is what OSI promised originally, but it has turned out to be a more complex game than that.

Two long established supplier-led bodies (and possibly three) are working to offer just that, with interoperability brands. The Corporation for Open Systems (COS) in the US has been promoting its COSmark brand (so far three products branded) while in Europe, Standards Promotion and Application Group (SPAG) has completed a pilot study for its Process to Support Interoperability (PSI) brand, and launched a brand for X.400 messaging products.

SPAG and COS have been involved in many of the other initiatives mentioned above. SPAG in particular sees itself as a catalyst, starting work and handing it on if more qualified groups emerge.

The two branding schemes have fundamental differences, too complex to cover here. Both are in their infancy, but they differ greatly from conformance testing. Conformance testing, essential in product development, confirms that the product meets standards, but that is only incidental to the user. Interoperability branding offers an assurance that the product will work with other branded products.

The third group waiting in the wings is X/Open, said to be "considering" an interoperability brand, possibly developed in collaboration with one of the other groups. X/Open is certainly the most visible supplier group in open systems, having set itself up as a broker of information about user needs, running the "Xtra" annual market research programme. Starting from the (Unix-based) "portability" side of open systems, it has moved to include OSI.

Lastly, what happens to the national standards bodies, as IT standards work shifts to vertical and regional groups? Britain's own BSI has seen the change and responded with DISC ("Delivering Information Solutions to Customers"). DISC now manages the UK's contribution to international IT standards, and seems likely to focus on local user needs. *[See Section 10 – Eds.]*

In conclusion, whether OSI standards are horses or camels, there is no doubt that their source is a hydra, a mythical beast which sprouts new heads at every challenge. OSI is the most developed part of open systems standards, and yet its committees are still changing rapidly.

The main reasons are the continuing changes in the economic situation of the IT industry, the rapid development of technology, and the changing political structure of the world. OSI in itself is not the most thrilling topic, but the creative process that spawned it is compelling.

Several of the topics covered in that contribution will be encountered again, including EDI, ODA and X.400 in Section 5. Extracts from two major "Framework" documents by EWOS and DISC will be found in Section 10.

The third contribution to this section addresses the business case for using OSI. It is by **Dr Harald Nottebohm** of Hoechst AG in Germany and chairman of the Technical Committee of OSITOP, which he helped to form. Very few finance departments will accede to a request to pay for the change to OSI unless there are some very real advantages to be gained; this contribution puts the case for OSI in the light of business requirements.

The business case for using OSI

Contents

Analysing business processes, we observe that many parts of their underlying chains of actions are not supported by information systems in a continuous way. This is also more true if those processes include two or more independent organizations. If we expect a better support of such an "externalization" of business by IT applications in the future, an infrastructure of communication has to be realized which can be implemented and used as easily as nowadays telephone and fax, and which is capable of linking heterogeneous computer systems.

For reasons of economy and universality only internationally approved standards should be the basis of such a structure. All relevant parties must be involved in the creation of these standards. For communication these are the OSI protocols. Among them the X.400 and FTAM standards are especially suited for the transmission of business data and business documents based on the EDIFACT and ODA/ODIF standards.

The business benefits of applying these standards will be derived from their ability to make easier links between IT applications including the integration of telematic services, thus reducing the number of breaks in media and manual labour. It will be possible to support and accelerate complete business processes across heterogeneous systems.

Access to market information will be improved and operations closer to the customer will be possible. Business cooperations and strategic partnerships will be made easier and more effective. Furthermore, cost reductions are to be expected in network management and for communication hardware and software.

Communication as a factor of competition

The computerization of business

Business processes in all modern organizations are supported by information systems. However, there are considerable differences in the extent of support, i.e. inasmuch as all processes of defined business activities are completely and continuously covered (Figure 4.1).

In view of the piles of paper in our offices I have my doubts here. Let me add two more aspects. Present information applications mostly have a lengthy history; and second, a business process may need numerous activities across many organizational units within and outside of its own organization. Such a process may be the timely shipment of a product, specified by the customer, of guaranteed quality. Equipping our employees with devices connected to a common network – terminals, PCs, or workstations – is not enough. Much

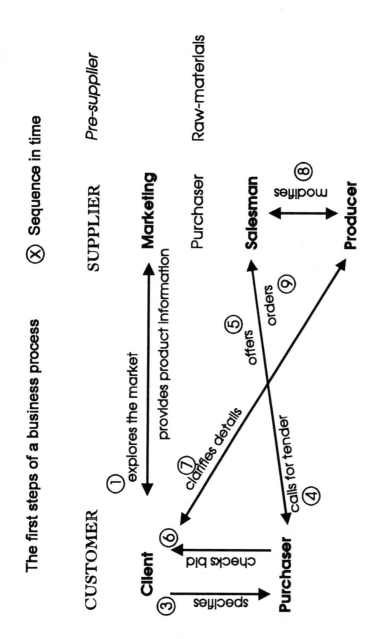

Figure 4.1 *The informatization of business*

more must be added before information systems are capable of effectively supporting all people involved in a business process: from unification of notions, over access to all consistent data under a unified user interface, to clearly defined further interfaces.

This list underlines that – irrelevant of the mass of existing IT applications – we have to go a long way, a very long way, before the full potential of consistent computerization of business is reached.

The aspect of time

One of the most important motivators for pushing computerization is the competitive factor "time". Only he who cares for the availability of the right information at the right time, at the right location, and in the right form is able to act and react in the market in a fast and competent manner. An additional trend is that for reasons of cost savings many organizations tend to reduce their stocks as far as possible or even totally like in the case of the automotive industry with their "just-in-time" shipments.

Competition moves to the axis of time. To "get faster", work has to be done in parallel. A prerequisite for parallelization is digitization and use of information technology. Only information and communication systems of adequate capabilities can provide the needed information in demanded time and quality. It is important that also functions which are not formalized are integrated and likewise supported by the system.

The role of communication

Here we have the buzzword "communication". One of the jobs of communication is to transport information to the right locations. As long as people work at terminals which have access to the same application, e.g. on a host computer, there seem to be no special problems: the application cares for access to consistent data. But as soon as the business process calls for functions which are not formalized, normally additional communication services, like telephone or fax or even electronic mail, must be used without these being properly integrated in the process.

For example, for a complete integration a person would be able to write a report using his local system, add original data from a host and other sources, then send it to another person to complete the data (Figure 4.2).

The recipient may extract and modify a part of the report and send it immediately together with a comment to a third person for use in his part of the process, all without any breaks in media.

Communication will be all the more a problem if people work with different applications on different systems. The more we try to computerize entire business processes the more we shall encounter necessities of this kind. This is especially true in cases where more than one organization cooperates in a common business process, as shown above in the case of "just-in-time" shipment.

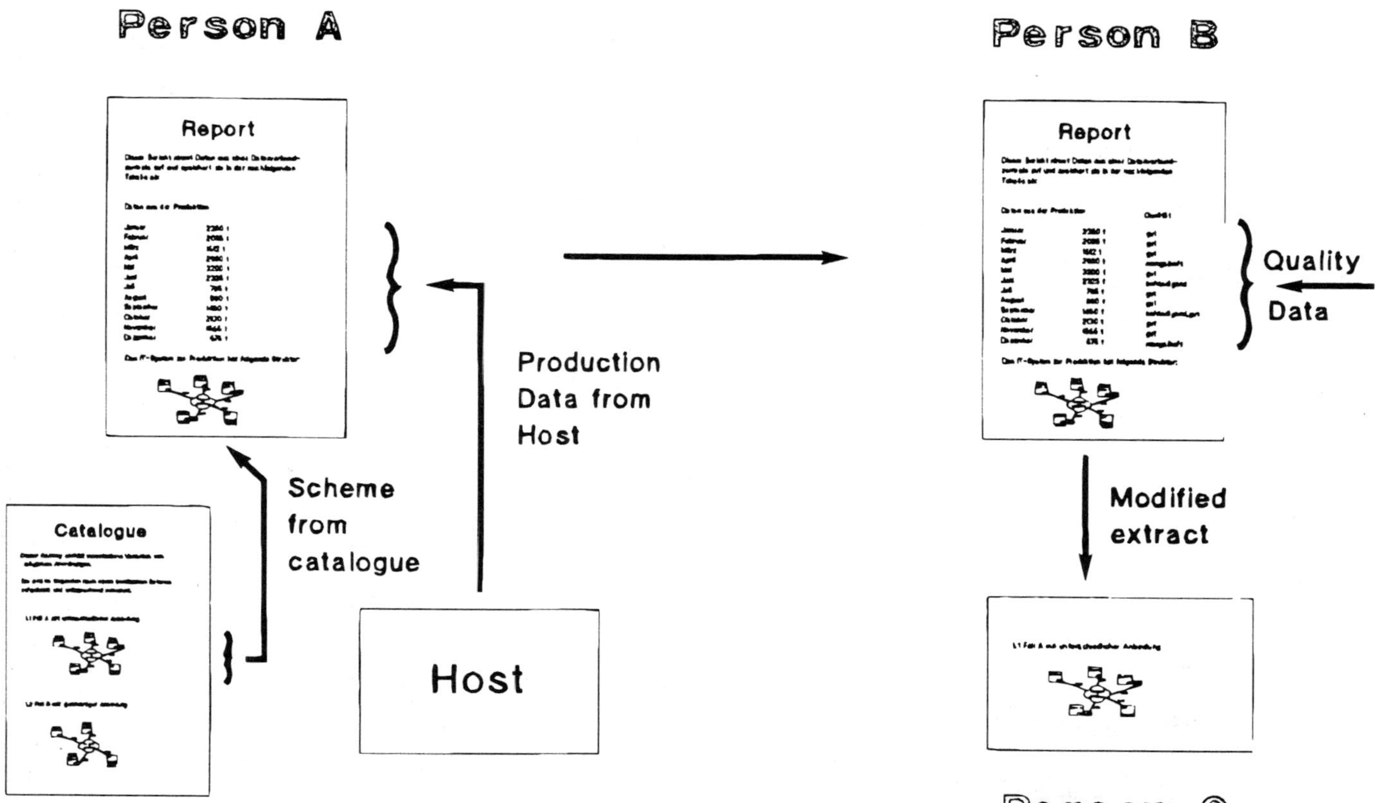

Figure 4.2 *Complete Integration*

Figure 4.3 *Interfaces and transmission protocols*

Almost all the above communication problems may be solved in one way or another. It takes the definition of suitable interfaces and transmission protocols. This is a common praxis. However, it is here also that the factor of time plays a more and more important role. Just imagine having to negotiate interfaces and transmission protocols prior to a telephone call or prior to sending a fax to a business partner (Figure 4.3).

In other words: our present way of implementing communication links to support computerization will not meet future demand. We shall have to look for new and more powerful methods.

The problem of heterogeneity

Inter-enterprise

We shall have to admit the fact that the process of computerization in an organization – at least in a larger one – will not evolve in a manner well defined among the different units and on fairly compatible systems. There is too great a pressure in the different organizational units to produce fast individual solutions – mostly PC based – which help to rationalize or support the activities in the unit (Figure 4.4).

A corporate IT strategy based on standards may limit the number of different hardware and software types and may guarantee a minimum of compatibility. However, standardization in many fields touched here is not yet mature

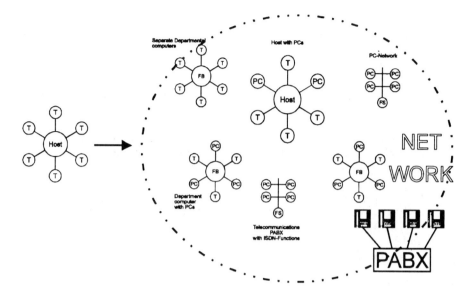

Figure 4.4 *Development of informatics systems: from central system to different subsystems in a common network*

enough to enable post integration of the various existing systems in the organization. Moreover, most of the older applications are not suitably structured to allow the implementation of needed interfaces.

Intra-enterprise

According to what has been said before it appears all the more difficult to imagine that systems of different organizations, e.g. those of customer and supplier, are supposed to cooperate. In the case of a long-existing customer-supplier relationship, individual solutions may be found and implemented; however, fast reactions in a changing and fiercely contested market are surely not possible by these means.

We just have to accept that in our environment we encounter a landscape of heterogeneous and widely incompatible IT systems. What can be done? The only answer is: we need standardized interfaces, well knowing that the effort of adapting our existing systems to meet new standardized specifications is very high. Therefore such an adaptation can only be justified if we may trust that the standards we turn to are stable on a long-term basis and that they are upwards compatible in the course of technical progress.

The only universal solution

Internationally approved standards

Long-term stability of standards can only be warranted for standards which have been developed and approved under the control of an international process with participation of all related parties. So-called "de facto" industry standards do not belong to this category notwithstanding their usefulness within their limited scope.

To solve the above problems we need, from the beginning, standards in three fields:

for the presentation of messages intended to exchange business data, the EDIFACT (Electronic Data Interchange for Administration, Commerce and Transport) standard;

for the exchange of documents containing text and graphics, including an option enabling the recipient to revise the document, the ODA/ODIF standard; andfor the transport of these messages and documents, OSI communication protocols defined by ISO or recommended by CCITT.

EDIFACT

EDIFACT defines business documents, e.g. an invoice as an example of many more "message types" (Figure 4.5).

Standardized "data segments" and "data elements" define the various components of the invoice. All segments and elements will be transmitted serially using denominators and separators according to the EDIFACT syntax. A recipient's converter turns the data file into a form which can be understood by the proprietary in-house application. The market offers programmable EDIFACT converters. Programming and adapting still take a considerable effort; some ready-made standard software from the market offer built-in EDIFACT interfaces.

ODA/ODIF

The ISO standard ODA (Office Document Architecture) defines how an editor is supposed to present a document in a universal way (Figure 4.6).

The presentation describes the arrangement of the content elements – text, graphics, images and in future sound, too – both logically, i.e. in terms of chapters, sections, paragraphs, and physically, i.e. its lay-out in terms of pages, columns, frames, etc.

The ODIF (Office Document Interchange Format) standard defines how content data and structural data shall be transmitted. Though genuine ODA editors are not yet available when this is written (1992), the ODIF standard may be used to convert suitable subsets of structural data to achieve document exchange in revisable form between different word processing systems as they are widely used today.

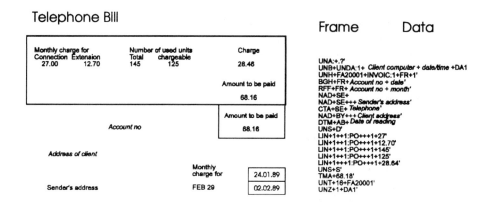

Figure 4.5 *The EDIFACT standard*

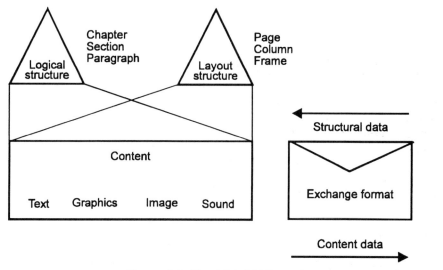

Figure 4.6 *The ODA/ODIF standard*

OSI

Modern OSI protocols are well adapted to support the transport of EDIFACT messages and documents (Figure 4.7).

The standards of the X.400 series for message handling have been amended by the so-called Pedi-protocol X.435 specifically to support EDI applications. Pedi defines an X.400 content type for the exchange of business documents not only in the EDIFACT format but also according to ANSI X12 or UNTD1 or other types, e.g. an accompanying text for comment or a technical drawing.

Pedi supports the following essential functions, among others:

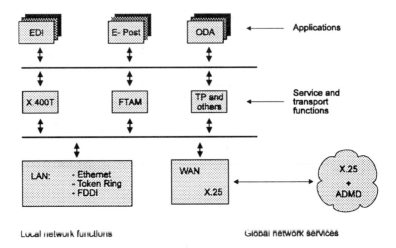

Figure 4.7 *OSI as transport backbone*

Automatic notifications inform the originator if the recipient took the responsibility for the message, passed it on to somebody else or refused it. This concept is primarily conceived for larger organizations with complex structures. A central office (or system) receives all messages and forwards them to the responsible ones according to certain criteria.

The different content parts of an EDI message may be forwarded to different units, e.g. the EDIFACT part of an order to the sales department, the attached drawing to the engineering office.

Another option of Pedi allows the user to define an external mailbox – e.g. that of a service provider. In this case the system of the service user does not have to be on-line all around the clock so that he can use a PC.

For this purpose the Pedi protocol defines services of the external mailbox which allows forwarding of the message with an automatic acknowledgement dependent on certain criteria, e.g. the identification of the originator or the type of attached document.

As with many service elements in base standards, most service elements of the Pedi protocol are optional. Which of them will be implemented has to be defined in a so-called "profile" (Figure 4.8).

Profile definition is done in EWOS, which tries to harmonize them in cooperation with corresponding workshops in the US (NIST) and in the Far East and Australia (AOW). The definition of profiles should not be left to vendor experts alone. Needed is an initiative of users across different business sectors. Within our OSITOP Business Communication Project we will take such an initiative

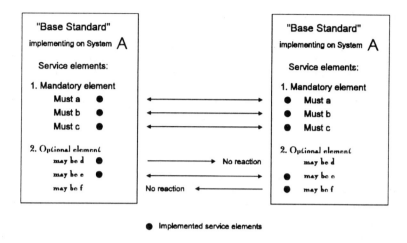

Figure 4.8 *Definitions of profiles*

together with SPAG. SPAG intends to guide the project by a "Process to Secure Interoperability" (PSI), launched in 1992. The implemented software will receive a quality mark by SPAG which guarantees not only conformity to standards but also interoperability across different systems including help in case of complications afterwards.

X.400 in its present version of 1988 offers some features of security which are indispensable in business communication. For instance, the protocols make sure that the originator is always identified, that only the intended recipient can receive the message, that he cannot repudiate it, that data integrity during transport will be maintained, and that the data will be kept confidential at request. Here too the corresponding profile has not been defined yet.

Based on the standard X.500 a distributed global directory system can be realized which renders the X.400 address of a potential recipient. It should be emphasized here that it does not take such directory services to make good use of X.400 systems. He who wants to be reached over X.400 will certainly take care of making his X.400 address known using the conventional ways of doing so.

Another transport mechanism aside from X.400 is FTAM (File Transfer, Access and Management). The differences will be explained below.

It is not intended to touch other interesting OSI standards here since corresponding products will not be available before the mid 1990s. Of great value for further applications will certainly be TP (Transaction Processing) and RDA (Remote Database Access).

Synchronous and asynchronous transmission

With X.400 and FTAM we have two standardized transport mechanisms which may be used by the originator – either a person or a machine – to send any messages, documents or data files to a recipient. In addition, FTAM enables the recipient to fetch such a message from the distant system. This is possible as FTAM establishes a link from system to system prior to any transmission. Outbound and inbound transmission occur almost at the same time: we call this "synchronous transmission".

In contrast, X.400 uses a "store and forward" mechanism. The originator can send his message at any time independent of the recipient's system status, i.e. whether or not it is ready for receiving. Intermediate transport systems called "Message Transfer Agents" care for one or more intermediate storage until the message at last is forwarded. We call this form of transmission "asynchronous". Most public PTTs are currently offering or implementing such transfer services, called ADMD services (ADMD = Administration Management Domain).

This decoupled type of transmission requires less readiness of systems for receiving messages, one of the reasons for the corresponding definitions of X.400. However, there is no guarantee at present within what time frame messages will be delivered.

The immediate delivery by synchronous transmission caused the banks to choose FTAM for the transmission of EDI messages. On the other hand FTAM neither possesses the security features of X.400 (1988) nor the additional functions of the Pedi protocol. Also, according to my knowledge, appropriate ADMD services are not intended, which means that business partners will have to implement their exact system addresses bilaterally before they can exchange EDI messages. Some banks have therefore begun to think again about the choice of transport mechanism best suited for EDI. Perhaps time problems may be solved by an "express service", as with ordinary mail, for higher fees.

Paths to implementations

We have to start out from our currently implemented proprietary systems, with their vendor-specific communication protocols. Links are made by using "gateways" as interpreters. In most cases only access from terminals of system A to applications in system B are supported (Figure 4.9).

For this purpose terminal A requires an emulation for access to B. Emulations of this kind, especially for access to IBM mainframe applications, are offered by most of the other system suppliers. The reverse path is either not possible or very cumbersome and expensive, e.g. access from IBM terminals to an application on another system.

For file transfer functions a gateway plus software products on both systems are generally needed (Figure 4.10).This is all the more the case for higher functions like transaction processing.

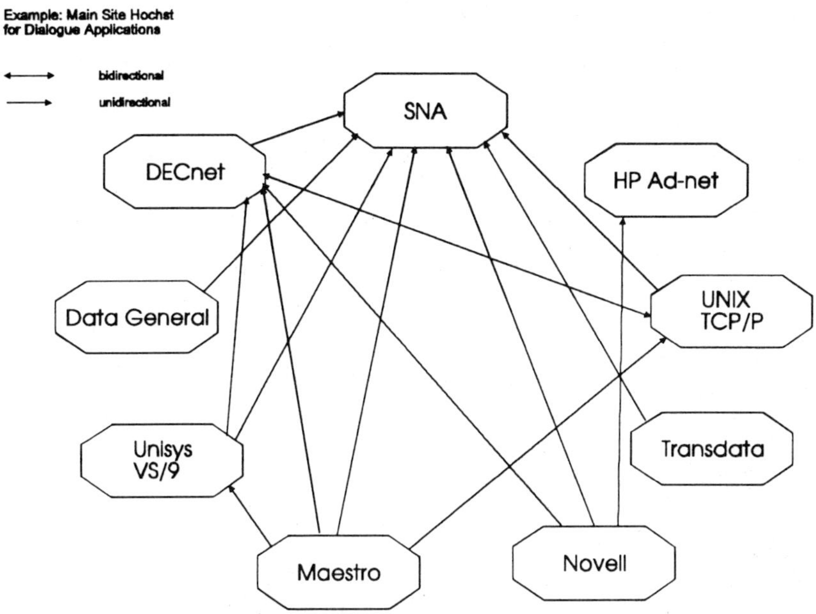

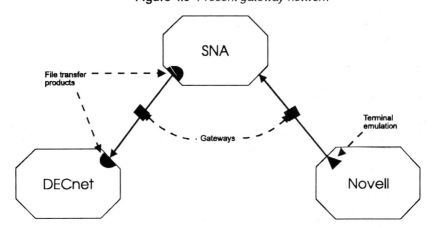

Figure 4.9 *Present gateway network*

Figure 4.10 *Problems of gateway solutions*

Effort and costs for the development of such products and for perpetually adapting them to new versions of operating systems increase with the required functionality. Only by standardizing the appropriate communication interfaces within the operating systems can the problem be solved economically and for long-term.

In other words, vendors have to redesign their present communication software according to OSI conformant standards. Nearly all vendors are doing this, e.g. Digital with DECnet Phase V or IBM who offers OSI communication parallel to SNA. The way to completion is tedious and progress stepwise. It is important to follow a clearly stated strategy avoiding being lured into side roads by seemingly less troublesome or cheaper solutions, thus losing sight of the goal.

Considering short-term availability of OSI products we can begin with synchronous and asynchronous transfer functions. Thus we can start to build up the infrastructure we require for business communication. Terminal access – as described above – is not included. It would mean use of the standard VTP (Virtual Terminal Protocol). For security reasons its use across enterprises is not advisable. To realize functions of this kind, eventually supported by search tree mechanisms, the model of the standard "videotext" could be applied.

Another important requirement discussed previously is the integration of telematic services. A first step can be taken by an "Electronic Post Office" (Figure 4.11).

One of its functions will be the transfer of X.400 messages into the public telex/teletext and fax network. Also vice versa in the future, suitable addressing conventions need to be agreed upon. Forwarding inbound fax documents is supported by the standard X.400 but profiles and products are still missing. The electronic post office is also the interface for all electronic inter-enterprise business data interchange. In this function it is best suited to support the necessary security measures. Last but not least, it allows manual forwarding of those messages which are not addressed correctly or where the address is not specified in detail.

Competitive edge

Better support of business

At the beginning we noted that we need a powerful communication infrastructure to be able to realize a consistent computerization supporting all relevant business processes. It is obvious that important – if not the most important – competitive advantages will result from this possibility.

As a main advantage we will be in the position to accelerate our business processes considerably. There are numerous contributions: no more delays in mailing, possibility of working in parallel, no manual work and no errors for overcoming breaks in media, less time for getting access to information, and less necessity of "readaptation" by avoiding breaks in work-flow. Also, specific work processes will allow more flexibility, allowing better adaptation to changing requirements of customers. Together with better and faster information about what's happening in the market, this flexibility will bring us closer to the customer – an often-heard phrase.

Better communication will make cooperative activities and strategic partnerships more effective, not to mention mergers and acquisitions. Here the incompatibility of computer systems may be a severe obstacle and can make such a project uneconomical.

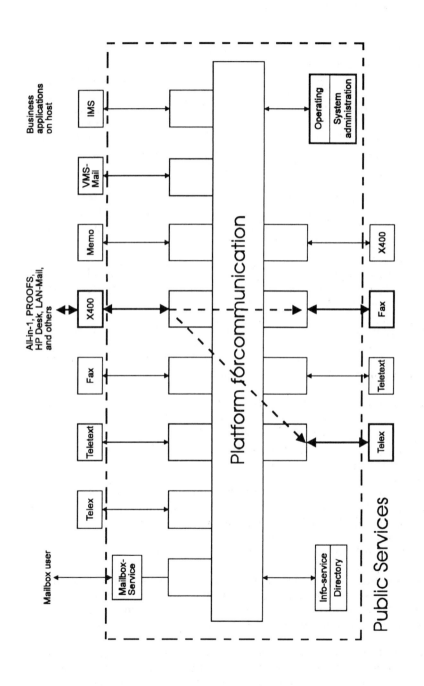

Figure 4.11 *Electronic Post Office*

In the following subsections some more aspects of benefits will be discussed.

Reduced network management

If we continue to use gateways for internetworking, we shall need more and more complex network management. If for instance somebody said in the past "I have IBM in the commercial field and Digital in the technical and research environment and linking these systems is no problem for me" he will nevertheless encounter new challenges. He will not be able to prevent users installing PC networks under, for example Novell, or the spread of Unix systems. It is also not of much help if the Unix world seems to be intact by TCP/IP. Neither will he find an open ear of his management if he requests a complete exchange of the Siemens computer systems for a new acquisition from IBM.

Additional links will inevitably be required. Users will not be content with any technical links but will require more quality, among them the certainty that the documents are transmitted with all attributes, including the use of public telematic services without breaks in media.

Continuation of the present state of the art will result in a chaos of individual gateway solutions. Planning, implementing, testing and operating them will carry the cost of increased manpower. A unification in this field will lead to tangible cost reductions, notwithstanding the fact that experts in this field are rare and expensive. In detail we expect that the workload for planning and testing new installations will be reduced, that additional requirements can be met faster, that trouble-shooting will be easier, that changes can be made with less effort, and that there will be fewer adaptations to new software releases.

Work is going on to standardize methods and tools for network management, so in the long term greater efficiency and corresponding cost savings are to be expected. The large number of different network architectures which have to be supported at present will diminish, thus reducing their management workload.

To evaluate potential cost savings, Hoechst AG has started a project together with Prof. Kônig of the University of Frankfurt-am-Main: *Informatics in economics*. Results will be published in due course.

Faster links to new customers

Imagine you are a producer of drugstore articles. A wholesaler who has not yet bought your products wants to order from you using EDIFACT; he declares that he is able to follow the EDIFACT conventions normally used in this business sector. As you are used to in such cases, you ask your communications expert to check the technical possibilities of a link. Your expert remembers his last case, the contract with his service provider, the information to be entered into his system, ordering, implementing and testing of the communication software with all the necessary adaptations of parameters and procedures.

At last he contacts his technical partner at the wholesaler – who laughs at him. He is told that the purchaser had already sent the order to a competitor without any problems, using his X.400 address, and that they had already received an acknowledgement in the same way. Moreover they had electronic access to the supplier's catalogue and started to copy the articles of interest into their own catalogue, as a matter of course also electronically without having to retype the text.

The great advantage is that – at least in the field of communications – no individual technical agreements are necessary; additional hardware and software is not required, neither test of communication links nor pilots. In other words, there are no longer any delays in establishing a new communications link.

Usage of new possibilities

With the example above we already touch new possibilities: document exchange in "revisable" form. It would make coordination much easier and more "transparent" in drafting contracts or complex calls for tender, and also for comparison of bids. Above all it would make these processes faster, a fact which is getting more and more important in future business. Also, documents in their final version may be attached to EDIFACT messages, as mentioned above.

Of course, starting into this new world we shall have to face not only problems of technical solutions but also the problem of critical mass. Only after many of our business partners can be reached by using the new communication facilities will the benefits be tangible.

But why not convert EDIFACT messages automatically into readable documents and send them together with other documents using fax or postal mail to our partners? An electronic post office should have this capability. It should also be capable of forwarding inbound fax messages to graphical workstations so that they, or part of them, could be inserted into compound documents.

Restrictions

Why don't we realize such a useful communication infrastructure right away? Many still consider this utopian.

The first argument is that standardization has not progressed far enough. Of course this is always true, because standardization is a continuous process which inevitably follows new technical possibilities after a delay. However, today the standards most needed for business communication exist, as discussed in great detail above, i.e. X.400 and FTAM.

What about products? The *OSI products report* published on behalf of the Department of Trade and Industry in the UK lists more than 400 OSI products. X.400 products according to the 1984 standard are widely offered for almost all platforms so that first migration steps can be taken. This offers the chance slowly to acquire the necessary know-how to manage heterogeneous networks across enterprises. As soon as we have become familiar with this new technique new products according to the standards X.400 (1988) will be on the market. Many suppliers are currently developing them.

When it comes to defining functional profiles, involvement of users is required. As emphasized above, there is a strong necessity to come to an agreement which covers many business sectors. Participating in OSITOP's Business Communication Project is an outstanding opportunity to acquire know-how and to effect coordination across sectors.

What is the commitment of vendors? Do they resist in secret in fear of tougher competition in standardized areas? One or the other behaviour seems to show this. However, I believe that farsighted vendors recognize the chance that lies in the creation of a unified communication infrastructure: it is a platform which can open new markets. The challenge of computerization of business cannot currently be met, for want of a suitable infrastructure. Corresponding innovations and investments are not made. Therefore the solution of the communication problem will eliminate a substantial impediment for investments.

What is the attitude of the users? Are they dedicated to creating such an infrastructure, or aren't they, rather, fascinated by the abundance of new technologies the computer sector presents in regular succession? When at last the users perceive the difference between wish and reality, they will become aware of the fact that something is wrong. Often they have to go a long way to recognize that they should abandon their passive attitude and take an active role in influencing vendors in their interest. They are aware of this weakness. The consequence is to cooperate with others to bring things forward.

Summary

Only a communications infrastructure which is based on mutual development efforts of all IT vendors, and which is accepted by the user community, will have the power to ensure problem-free and flexible transport of business data.

This process which has been going on for quite some time and has matured must be accelerated, and it will be necessary to avoid the process being slowed down again and again by vendors following their own marketing strategies. This can only be achieved by users gaining a clear perception of what is going on, and are not shy of using their buying power in order to reach the goal.

There have been some encouraging examples, like the user-driven MAP development and the User Alliance for Open Systems initiative in the USA, to show how users can act to bring about success. I hope that OSITOP will be able to set a similar milestone with its Business Communication Project, by setting up a future-oriented communications infrastructure in a faster way than would be possible for single companies.

This section has provided a brief insight into standards associated with OSI and open systems, standards which are important to all – users, vendors, everyone.

The vendors have an interest in this: their continuing existence depends on it. Users must take an interest and an active part in the appropriate areas of IT standards. They must learn to manage change in IT before it manages them; an understanding of the importance of IT standards is an essential part of this process.

As already remarked, several of the particular topics mentioned in this section will come up again, often in greater detail, in later sections. This begins in the next section, which is on the vital area of data interchange – from single characters up to complete formatted documents – and perhaps beyond.

5

User needs in data interchange standards

The provision of powerful and inexpensive communication technology has influenced the fast development of many distributed information processing applications. International user agreements for standardized information and data interchange formats are the main prerequisite for many distributed applications providing open communication and information interchange. This is the subject of this section, which has been prepared with the assistance as technical editor of **Dr Borka Jerman-Blažič** of the Institut Jožef Stefan at Ljubljana, Slovenia.

Standardized information interchange formats create a common understanding between the originator and the recipient of the communication about the information being interchanged. This means that recipients can understand and interpret the information received, and furthermore can use the information for tasks to be performed, or to trigger other actions. Depending on the application area within which the information interchange takes place, the tasks triggered or performed could be quite different. In the area of computer integrated manufacturing (CIM) the information received can influence the control of the manufacturing process, in the office environment the received information can trigger different information and storage mechanisms, further processing, preparing new documents, etc.

One of the most important application areas for information interchange is the electronic distribution of documents of different kinds. Here *document* is understood in the most general sense already encountered in Section 2, as a structured amount of information intended for human perception and/or computer processing, that can be interchanged as a unit between users and/or systems. Documents may contain information of different kinds: built of characters, raster images, graphics composed of geometric elements, moving images, and music or other sound data.

Basic elements in data interchange are *characters*, distinct symbols in some alphabet or similar repertoire of symbols. Communication between human beings or computers is in general by use of languages. Information is conveyed by means of words, sentences, etc., which, when written, consist of characters. When these are to be interchanged or processed in an IT system, they need to be coded. A *character* in the interchange process is understood as a member of a set of elements used for the organization, control and representation of data. Standardized coded character sets are used to provide unambiguous rules for one-to-one relationship between the characters of the set and the codes assigned to them.

Unfortunately, electronic data interchange is still inhibited by limited standards. The extended communication facilities of the 1990s mean that sender and recipient usually have different systems for electronic mail, different document processing facilities, terminal equipment supporting different coded characters, different systems for exchange of structured information, etc. The document and data interchange in such situation is restricted to open interchange of content-only representation of the document, e.g. by use of facsimile or ASCII encoded data. (ASCII, the American Standard Code for Information Interchange, is the national US variant of ISO 646, and, thanks to the dominance of US manufacturers during the growth of the IT industry, is still the only character coding standard close to universal acceptance despite its limited repertoire.)

This section discusses the user needs for standards in provision of mechanisms and techniques for "open data interchange". It covers the problem of use of character sets in data interchange, the problems of standard document architecture to be used in office automation, and the problems of an open electronic exchange of structured information. The first contribution, by **Borka Jerman-Blažič**, deals with the developments in coded character set standards in relation to computer communication during the late 1980s and early 1990s. Special attention is paid to the techniques provided for use of international standard character sets in higher level communications protocols which are intended to carry different computer applications, i.e. text, software, images, applications etc.

Character handling and computer communication

Introduction

Character handling is the topic most intimately intertwined with textual presentation of information. A character is a graphical unit used for representation of words and other language elements. Human beings communicate with information processing systems by issuing and receiving commands, data and reports. The dialogue is always based on written (textual) presentation of information. The presentation of the text is based on human natural language and in a form which is not ambiguous either to the computer system or to the user.

Computer systems communicate via programs which are written in particular programming languages. A program is built from basic elements called either *characters* or *basic symbols*. To be suitable for interchange, these must be transformed into sequences of coded characters that both systems can understand.

It could be said that character handling is closely related to many areas of information processing and interchange, among them:

representation of data elements;

programming languages;

text and office systems;

databases;

interfaces for application portability;

computer graphics;

labelling and file structure;

computer networks.

But character sets and their standardized codes have special treatment in the field of computer communication and networking. In recent years, up to the early 1990s when this is being written, we have been witnessing increasing demand on the international market for computer facilities to support interchange of information represented in character sets that do not belong to the English language. Today, a requirement for multilingual information processing and for internationalization of information technology is present in many parts of the world. Users and manufacturers expect that provision of technical solutions for information interchange in an multilingual environment will follow within the framework of the Reference Model for Open Systems Interconnection. The identification of a variety of character set repertoires used in different scripts is a part of the presentation level of the Reference Model for Open Systems Interconnection, the ISO 7498 document. In particular, the standardization of character set codes and their repertoires is a working task of the Technical Committee ISO/IEC JTC1/SC2. This technical committee develops the all elementary tools for expressing everything dependent on languages and scripts.

In this contribution, the existing coding systems developed within JTC1/SC2 will be presented. Their merits and deficiencies, in view of the international needs for information interchange in a multilingual environment, will be discussed.

The new coding system, recently developed, providing the largest repertoire of characters to date (1992), will also be discussed, as will the additional features in the presentation level for handling the characters encoded in accordance with the new system, that are required in view of the user need for efficient processing and information interchange. The proposed solutions are expected to solve some of the accumulated problems in the field of character handling in a multilingual and multimedia computer environment.

The terminology in this text is that of ISO standards in the field. A *character* should be understood as a member of a set of elements used for organization, control or representation of data. Where clear from the context, *character* means "graphic character". A *graphic symbol* is the visual representation of a graphic character. A *code table* is used for human comprehension and for representation of the relation between a group of characters represented by their graphical symbols and their coded forms. The subject of the international standards for coded character sets is the definition of the code for particular character represented by its graphical symbol and not the possible forms of writing and printing known as "fonts", which is the subject of other types of international standards.

The existing coding systems

The first seven-bit standard code for information interchange

By definition, a code is the rule of correspondence between the information to be represented and its associated binary configuration, each information item corresponding to a one-bit combination. A code may be defined in a wide variety of different ways since in principle it does not matter which set of *n* bits corresponds to which character. However, certain practical considerations give rise to the following simple rules for deriving a code:

>   The code must be as efficient as possible.

>   The code must include a representation of the decimal numerals, in such a way as to aid their recognition and facilitate arithmetic operations upon them.

>   The representation of letters must be chosen so as to facilitate sorting operations (collating sequences).

>   Although the code essentially defines the interpretation to be given to the groups of *n* bits representing each of the characters, it is useful to have additional application-specific codes. A transmission mode using this type of code is said to be *code-transparent*.

The first widely used code for information transmission and interchange was the Baudot code, referred to as a five level telegraphic code, International alphabet No. 2, or the CCITT Alphabet No. 2 [Macchi, Guilbert *et al.* 1985]. This code, designed and used universally for the switched telegraph network (telex), is a five-bit code which allows the appearance of 60 separate combinations. The five-bit telex code introduced the concept of bit pattern, or bit combination. Increasing use of electronic methods necessitated the adoption of a richer code which enabled, among other things, the representation of the capital and small letter of English alphabet and which had to serve the areas of application where data interchange was of primary importance. Thus ASCII (American Standard Code for Information Interchange) saw the light in 1963. ASCII was designed by its structure to serve for storage and transmission of data. The coding of the digits and letters in ISO 646 facilitates collating operations and calculations. Their consecutive allocation minimizes the number of distinguishing binary elements. Capital and small letters differ only in the sixth bit. The first two columns of the code table shown in Figure 5.1 are reserved for control functions.

b4 b3 b2 b1		b7 0 / b6 0 / b5 0 → 0	b7 0 / b6 0 / b5 1 → 1	b7 0 / b6 1 / b5 0 → 2	b7 0 / b6 1 / b5 1 → 3	b7 1 / b6 0 / b5 0 → 4	b7 1 / b6 0 / b5 1 → 5	b7 1 / b6 1 / b5 0 → 6	b7 1 / b6 1 / b5 1 → 7
0 0 0 0	0			SP	0	②	P	②	p
0 0 0 1	1			!	1	A	Q	a	q
0 0 1 0	2			"	2	B	R	b	r
0 0 1 1	3			# / £	3	C	S	c	s
0 1 0 0	4			¤ / $	4	D	T	d	t
0 1 0 1	5			%	5	E	U	e	u
0 1 1 0	6		'	&	6	F	V	f	v
0 1 1 1	7			'	7	G	W	g	w
1 0 0 0	8			(	8	H	X	h	x
1 0 0 1	9			)	9	I	Y	i	y
1 0 1 0	10			*	:	J	Z	j	z
1 0 1 1	11			+	;	K	②	k	②
1 1 0 0	12			,	<	L	②	l	②
1 1 0 1	13			-	=	M	②	m	②
1 1 1 0	14			.	>	N	②	n	②
1 1 1 1	15			/	?	O	_	o	DEL

CO Set

Figure 5.1 *IRV version of ISO 646*

Extension of the coded character set

ASCII was widely accepted because of its efficiency and because it allows appearance of 128 characters, small and capital letters of the Latin alphabet as well as other useful symbols. Therefore, it deserved an international status which was later achieved under the responsibility of ISO. Traditionally, the information processing world was an English-speaking world. The proliferation of computer and communication technology changed the situation dramatically. The access to this world is no longer reserved to an English-speaking intellectual elite. Large group of users channelled through their national bodies the requirements relevant to the internationalization of information technology. On the basis of their requirements ISO has approved the document based on the original ASCII code table with several options in the code table. Allocating characters to these optional positions resulted in national versions of the seven-bit standard code. With rules defined in ISO 646, from 1968 it become possible to code texts in Danish, Swedish, Slovene, Serbocroat and Czech, at the price of losing six special characters in the code. As a consequence of that extension, the principle of unique code-character correspondence was lost. National versions of the seven-bit character set codes to be used with escape sequences are registered in the International Register of Coded Character Sets according to the registration procedure defined in ISO 2375.

The extension technique itself is standardized in another ISO document, i.e. ISO 2022, *ISO 7-bit and 8-bit coded character set code extension techniques*. The document presents a review of the salient structure of the seven-bit code and various means of extending the control functions and graphic sets of the seven-bit code. It also describes structures and techniques to construct and formalize other codes related to the seven-bit code. These related codes are defined so as to allow application dependent usage of the code without preventing the interchangeability of the data employing them.

Solutions designed in ISO 2022 enable the extension of the seven-bit codes, while remaining in a seven-bit environment. The elements of code extension are: the C0 set (a set of 32 control characters), the C1 set (an additional set of 32 control functions), the G0 set (a set of 94 graphic characters) and the G1, G2, and G3 sets (additional sets of 94 graphic characters). The code extension characters present in ISO 646 and used in ISO 2202 are: *ESC* (escape), *SO* (shift-out) and *SI* (shift-in). In addition, for use in a seven-bit environment ISO 2202 defines other shift functions which are not a part of ISO 646. They are: *LS2* (locking shift two), *LS3* (locking shift three), *SS2* (single shift two), *SS3* (single shift three).

The designation of the character or the whole character set may be done by application of escape sequences or shift functions. In the process of data interchange, each time the *ESCAPE* sequence or a *SHIFT* function is detected, the recipient of the data changes the state and a different code set is accessed. The shift functions *SO*, *LS2* or *LS3* each invoke an additional set of 94 graphic characters, i.e. the set G1, G2 or G3. Such a set replaces the current G0 set. The shift function *SI* invokes the graphic characters of the G0 set that are to replace the graphic characters of the additional set. The single-shift functions *SS2* and *SS3* are used exclusively for extension of the graphic set, *SS2* invokes one character from the last designed G2 set, *SS3* invokes one character from the last designed G3 set. The extension technique of ISO 2022 in seven-bit environments is represented in Figure 5.2.

The extension technique of ISO 2022 is not restricted to seven-bit coded character sets; later, by defining new *ESCAPE* sequences and shift functions in the set of control characters, eight-bit coded character sets were included. The

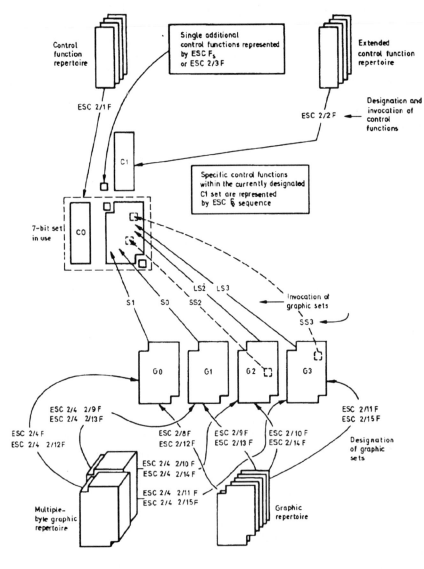

Figure 5.2 *Code extension in a seven-bit environment according to ISO 2022*

possibilities of coding characters according to ISO 2022 were extended to an almost unlimited number of characters. The extension technique of ISO 2202 in a eight-bit environment is presented in Figure 5.3.

The extension technique of ISO 2022 has not solved the requirements for easy multilingual communication because it suffers from many deficiencies. Wide practical use has never been achieved as coding according to that encoding technique requires a finite state machine with very many states.

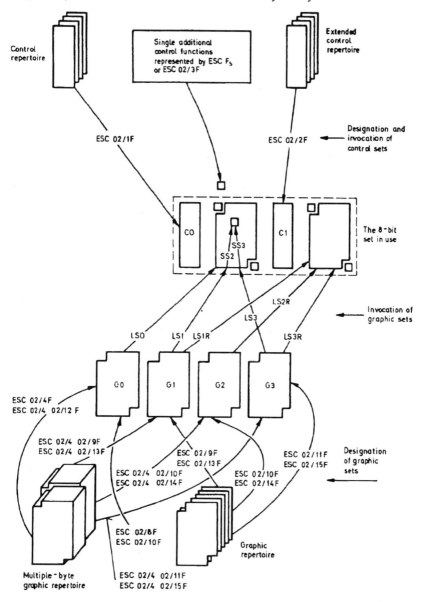

Figure 5.3 *Code extension in an eight-bit environment according to ISO 2022*

Standard eight-bit codes

After the advent of hardware with eight-bit facilities, partial solutions for some of the problems related to the complex extension technique seems to be soluble. In the course of the development of eight-bit codes the following principles were followed:

> optimize text communication in an eight-bit environment (in the case of a service like videotex or teletex the eight-bit code is used as a fixed attribute of the service and only one terminal interface is required);

> avoid the use of locking shift functions (in the case when a repertoire of more than 128 characters is in use);

> avoid duplicate coded representation of the same graphic character;

> permit start of a text communication without complicated designing and invoking procedures;

> avoid the construction of accented letters for non-Latin and Latin alphabets.

The approach implemented in the first international standard eight-bit character set code, i.e. ISO 6937, was the definition of simple and composite characters. ISO 646 allows creation of composite graphic characters by the use of the control characters *BACKSPACE* and/or *CARRIAGE RETURN*. The processing and imaging of this type of character may cause some problems, therefore in the case of composite characters an agreement between sender and recipient is always needed. The principle applied in ISO 6937 was the composition of characters by combination of "non-spacing" with "spacing" characters. The spacing characters are the letters of the Latin alphabet, numerals, punctuation marks, and the non-spacing characters are the accents. The accents are located in a column in the right hand side of the code table. The code table of ISO 6937 is presented in Figure 5.4. Arbitrary composite graphic characters are not allowed. The number of characters which may be represented by that technique exceeds the number of characters present in the code table. ISO 6937 is in fact a multipart standard with a repertoire of 333 graphic characters allowing representation of text written in the languages spoken in North America, South America and Europe that use the Latin alphabet.

The technique of having in the same stream some graphic characters coded with one octet and others with two octets is inappropriate for data processing. Programming languages and programs have significantly easier processing if each of the characters occupies exactly one eight-bit byte. Received data coded according to ISO 6937 have to be stored in an internal representation different from the external. After that, the received data has to be re-sorted to an internal mapping, otherwise the hardware of the present day octet machines cannot be used efficiently. As an example, the problem of visual editing or forms-oriented

				b8	0	0	0	0	0	0	0	0	1	1	1	1	1	1	1	1
				b7	0	0	0	0	1	1	1	1	0	0	0	0	1	1	1	1
				b6	0	0	1	1	0	0	1	1	0	0	1	1	0	0	1	1
				b5	0	1	0	1	0	1	0	1	0	1	0	1	0	1	0	1
b4	b3	b2	b1		00	01	02	03	04	05	06	07	08	09	10	11	12	13	14	15
0	0	0	0	00				0	∂	P	`	p				°	See 4.3.4	—	Ω	K
0	0	0	1	01			!	1	A	Q	a	q			i	±	`	¹	Æ	æ
0	0	1	0	02			"	2	B	R	b	r			¢	²	´	®	Đ	đ
0	0	1	1	03			#	3	C	S	c	s			£	³	^	©	ª	ð
0	1	0	0	04			¤	4	D	T	d	t			$	×	~	™	Ħ	ħ
0	1	0	1	05			%	5	E	U	e	u			¥	µ	¯	♪		¬
0	1	1	0	06			&	6	F	V	f	v			See 4.33	¶	˘	See 4.3.4	IJ	ij
0	1	1	1	07			'	7	G	W	g	w			§	·	˙	See 4.3.4	Ŀ	ŀ
1	0	0	0	08			(	8	H	X	h	x			See 4.33	÷	¨	See 4.3.4	Ł	ł
1	0	0	1	09			)	9	I	Y	i	y			'	'	See 4.3.4	See 4.3.4	Ø	ø
1	0	1	0	10			*	:	J	Z	j	z			"	"	˚	See 4.3.4	Œ	œ
1	0	1	1	11			+	;	K	[	k	{			«	»	¸	See 4.3.4	º	ß
1	1	0	0	12			,	<	L	\	l	|			←	¼	_	⅛	Þ	þ
1	1	0	1	13			-	=	M	]	m	}			↑	½	˝	⅜	Ŧ	ŧ
1	1	1	0	14			.	>	N	^	n	~			→	¾	˛	⅝	Ŋ	ŋ
1	1	1	1	15			/	?	O	_	o				↓	¿	ˇ	⅞	ʼn	

Figure 5.4 *Code table of ISO 6937-1*

entry software may be considered. The majority of existing systems have been developed with the implicit assumption that each screen position corresponds to one character which is stored in one eight-bit byte. The underlying strategy for positioning the cursor and updating the screen would also need to be changed to accommodate variable length coding. Another example which may cause trouble is the field length. How many characters will fit in a field depends on which characters they are, e.g. a form is displayed to the user with instructions that read "Enter last name, up to 12 characters". Whether 12 characters will actually fit in a database record which includes that field depends on which characters they are. User instructions for filling fields of limited length cannot be precise. The following conclusion may be drawn from this discussion: only coded character sets that are unmixed and unshifted, not permitting the use of *BACKSPACE*, are acceptable, otherwise strict and complex rules are required to ensure a unique representation.

As a reply to these objections and remarks, a new eight-bit code was developed within ISO in 1985, again with a US origin, the so-called "eight-bit ASCII" or ISO 8859. ISO 8859 was developed for unique single octet representation of

b8 b7 b6 b5 → b4 b3 b2 b1 ↓	00	01	02	03	04	05	06	07	08	09	10	11	12	13	14	15
0000 00			SP	0	@	P	`	p			NBSP	°	À	Ð	à	ð
0001 01			!	1	A	Q	a	q			¡	±	Á	Ñ	á	ñ
0010 02			"	2	B	R	b	r			¢	²	Â	Ò	â	ò
0011 03			#	3	C	S	c	s			£	³	Ã	Ó	ã	ó
0100 04			$	4	D	T	d	t			¤	´	Ä	Ô	ä	ô
0101 05			%	5	E	U	e	u			¥	µ	Å	Õ	å	õ
0110 06			&	6	F	V	f	v			¦	¶	Æ	Ö	æ	ö
0111 07			'	7	G	W	g	w			§	·	Ç	×	ç	÷
1000 08			(	8	H	X	h	x			¨	¸	È	Ø	è	ø
1001 09			)	9	I	Y	i	y			©	¹	É	Ù	é	ù
1010 10			*	:	J	Z	j	z			ª	º	Ê	Ú	ê	ú
1011 11			+	;	K	[	k	{			«	»	Ë	Û	ë	û
1100 12			,	<	L	\	l	|			¬	¼	Ì	Ü	ì	ü
1101 13			–	=	M	]	m	}			SHY	½	Í	Ý	í	ý
1110 14			.	>	N	^	n	~			®	¾	Î	Þ	î	þ
1111 15			/	?	O	_	o				¯	¿	Ï	ß	ï	ÿ

Figure 5.5 *Code table of ISO 8859-1*

graphics character sets. It is a multipart standard document. Each of the eight parts of ISO 8859 defines a character set consisting of 191 graphic characters. The 95 characters in the left part of the code table are the same as the set of characters of ISO 646, and the 96 characters in the right part of the code table and cater for the scripts of a particular region of the world, serving the needs of the following group of languages: Europe: West, Middle, North, and South; Cyrillic; Greek; Arabic; Hebrew. The first two code tables of ISO 8859 (part 1 and part 2) are presented in Figures 5.5 and 5.6.

The character set of part 1 includes accented letters and other alphabetic characters required to represent text in the major languages of North America, South America and Western Europe, viz. Danish, Dutch, English, Faeroese, Finnish, French, Frisian, German, Icelandic, Irish, Italian, Norwegian, Portuguese, Spanish and Swedish.

The character set of part 2 is suitable for English and German, and some of the Eastern European languages that use the Latin alphabet, viz. Albanian, Czech, Hungarian, Polish, Romanian, Serbocroat, Slovak and Slovene.

b8				0	0	0	0	0	0	0	0	1	1	1	1	1	1	1	1
b7				0	0	0	0	1	1	1	1	0	0	0	0	1	1	1	1
b6				0	0	1	1	0	0	1	1	0	0	1	1	0	0	1	1
b5				0	1	0	1	0	1	0	1	0	1	0	1	0	1	0	1
b4	b3	b2	b1	00	01	02	03	04	05	06	07	08	09	10	11	12	13	14	15
0	0	0	0	00			SP	0	ә	P	`	p			NBSP	°	Ŕ	Đ	ŕ	đ
0	0	0	1	01			!	1	A	Q	a	q			Ą	˛	Á	Ń	á	ń
0	0	1	0	02			"	2	B	R	b	r			˘	˛	Â	Ň	â	ň
0	0	1	1	03			#	3	C	S	c	s			ł	ł	Ă	Ó	ă	ó
0	1	0	0	04			$	4	D	T	d	t			¤	´	Ä	Ô	ä	ô
0	1	0	1	05			%	5	E	U	e	u			Ľ	ľ	Ĺ	Ő	ĺ	ő
0	1	1	0	06			&	6	F	V	f	v			Ś	ś	Ć	Ö	ć	ö
0	1	1	1	07			'	7	G	W	g	w			§	ˇ	Ç	×	ç	÷
1	0	0	0	08			(	8	H	X	h	x			¨	¸	Č	Ř	č	ř
1	0	0	1	09			)	9	I	Y	i	y			Š	š	É	Ů	é	ů
1	0	1	0	10			*	:	J	Z	j	z			Ş	ş	Ę	Ú	ę	ú
1	0	1	1	11			+	;	K	[	k	{			Ť	ť	Ë	Ű	ë	ű
1	1	0	0	12			,	<	L	\	l	|			Ź	ź	Ě	Ü	ě	ü
1	1	0	1	13			–	=	M	]	m	}			SHY	˝	Í	Ý	í	ý
1	1	1	0	14			.	>	N	^	n	~			Ž	ž	Î	Ţ	î	ţ
1	1	1	1	15			/	?	O	_	o				Ż	ż	Ď	ß	ď	˙

Figure 5.6 *Code table of ISO 8859-2*

The encoding rules of ISO 8859 are unique only in a limited sense. Where graphic characters from different regions or for different applications (e.g. when a publishing graphic character set is needed) are to be used simultaneously, then the switching technique from ISO 2022 is unavoidable. Other approaches for extension of the character repertoire which limits the complexity of coding according to ISO 2022 have been designed. The structure and the application of rules for extension of eight-bit codings are defined in ISO 4873. These rules define the use of the eight-bit codings – both ISO 6937 and ISO 8859 (only one part at a time) – as a first level of application which forbid any extensions of the character set. The second and the third levels of the application comprises extensions to supplementary graphic character sets which are used as a 96 character set in the right hand side of the code table only. They are taken from ISO 8859 parts (the right hand side of the code table) or as separate character code sets defined in ISO/IEC DIS 10367. Additional control functions for text communication (i.e. identification of the graphic subrepertoire and representation of the text) are defined in ISO/IEC DIS 10568.

In the early 1990s IBM introduced a new eight-bit code for IBM PC compatible devices. The IBM PC is a versatile computing device with ubiquitous use but when connected to other computer equipment (e.g. different IBM machines) requires a translation in the interchange of data due to its specific code. In the interest of compatibility with existing implementations, and required connectivity, IBM decided to use the character set of the ECMA-94/1 standard and to allocate the characters in the new IBM PC eight-bit code in an almost identical way as ISO 6937-6, now identified as a part of the DIS 10367 supplemental coded character sets to be used with ISO 6937 and ISO 8859, together with the extension techniques defined in ISO 4873 and the control functions for text representation defined in ISO 10568.

Accommodation of the existing coding methods in higher layer protocols

The entire presentation layer and the associated standard documents are dedicated to solution of the communication problems of two application layer entities which use different concrete syntaxes. The abstract syntax enables the definition of an application layer data structure independent of its representation. The presentation layer provides the transformation between the syntaxes of the application layer entities and the common syntax needed for communication. The transformation is performed inside the open system and the other open systems are not aware of it. In the presentation layer one service/protocol may support an arbitrary large number of syntaxes defined independently of the protocol. An abstract syntax is defined as a collection of data values with associated meaning regardless of any specification of how they are represented in binary octets. A transfer syntax is a set of rules, associated with an abstract syntax, for presentation of user information submitted to the presentation service in octets. A presentation context becomes defined by negotiation of a particular transfer syntax that is to be associated with a given abstract syntax. The transfer syntax is intended to be derivable automatically from the abstract syntax by means of encoding rules. In fact, a set of encoding rules, termed "the Basic Encoding Rules", is defined in the presentation layer documents. Application of these encoding rules produces a transfer syntax for specified values of types of data. It is implicit that these encoding rules are also used for decoding in the receiving open system for identification of the data values being transferred. By encoding in the context of ASN.1 (ISO 8824:1987) it is assumed the complete sequence of octets is used to represent the data values. The encoding rules are applied at the time of communication (by the presentation service provider) when a presentation context implies their use.

The Basic Encoding Rules for ASN.1 (ISO 8825:1987) govern the presentation of information as data elements, each representing a value of some datatype. Every data element, i.e. encoding in ASN.1, is made up of the same three components: the identifier, the length, and data contents. The contents can itself comprise one or more data elements: this possibility of nesting allows arbitrary nested data to be represented. The identifier (type) distinguishes one type of data element from another and governs the interpretation of the contents. In

ASN.1 four classes of datatypes are distinguished by means of the identifier: universal, application-wide, context-specific and private use. Universal types are generally useful, application independent types. Application-wide types are more specialized. They are defined in other CCITT or ISO documents. Context-specific types are used in a limited context and their identifiers are assigned in such a way to be distinct only within that limited context. The "private use" types are reserved, as the name implies, for private use, outside of CCITT or ISO standards, and their use is discouraged in general because they limit the open interworking of systems. The contents octets encode the data value. The types of data value are: Integer, Boolean, Bit String, Octet String Value, Sequence Value and Set Value. When a character set string is specified, then this is done by direct reference to an enumerating table (NumericString and PrintableString), and the value of the octet string is one of the following:

an IA5String (Characters from the International Version of Alphabet No. 5 or ISO 646 IRV);

a TeletexString, a T.61 String or ISO 6937 (1/2) String;

a VideotexString, a T.100 String or ISO 6937 (1/2) String;

a VisibleString;

a GraphicString;

a Generalized Time according to ISO 2014, ISO 3307 and ISO 4031.

The octet string of ASN.1 contains the octets specified in ISO 2022 for encodings in an eight-bit environment and the escape sequence and character codings registered in accordance with ISO 2375. The relevant escape sequences used for definition of the character set type are specified in ISO 8824.

Abstract syntaxes under development, or already published, by ISO/CCITT have adopted various different ways for identification of the character repertoire and the basic encoding rules. For example, in ODA/ODIF a CharacterString text body is an OctetString. An attribute item preceding it contains an ISO 2022 sequence for identification of the repertoire. Advance warning of the repertoire is envisaged at the start of the document in another attribute item; MHS/MOTIS abstract syntax is similar. In Virtual Terminal, various alternative character repertoires may be identified again by ISO 2022 escape sequences. With each repertoire an integer is associated which is treated as a local identifier. A character-string is carried in an OctetString in which the first octet is the local identifier integer. FTAM conforms strictly to the original ASN.1 and suffers the overhead of escape sequences in the basic encoding, in every instance of data item specified to be a GraphicString or GeneralString.

The new coding system

Multiple-octet code developed by ISO

The existing coding systems provided in ISO 6937 or ISO 8859 and the code extension technique of ISO 2022 suffer from many deficiencies. The major ones identified are:

no facilities for large character sets required in a multilingual environment;

no stable coding of characters (i.e. the same graphic character or the same command may have more than one code);

different coding techniques;

variable length coding specially if more than 191 characters are required;

no application in the world of ideographic alphabets;

the encoding mechanisms do not distinguish properly between "coded character set" and "character repertoire";

small repertoire even for Europe.

The requirements for a multilingual information interchange with a fixed stable coding and one to one relationship between a code element and a displayed shape were expected to be met in the new coding system developed by ISO. It was assumed that the new code will enjoy universal acceptance in the information processing world and in the information interchange similar to that of seven-bit ASCII or ISO 646 IRV. For that reason, a special ISO number has been assigned to the standard document, ISO 10646, as firmly anticipating this coding system to be a general solution for the internationalization of the world market of information technology.

The goals followed in the design process of the ISO 10646 project can be summarized as follows:

provide a code for every graphic character of the world scripts;

ensure interworking with other standards and interoperability with other systems;

facilitate migration through natural extension to existing character handling systems;

provide a higher degree of transparency to make product development easier to native language speakers;

provide smooth migration path for implementors.

The current (1991) version of DIS 10646, also named Universal Code Character Set (UCS in the text that follows), is regarded as a single entity. It consists of 256 groups of 256 planes. Each plane contains 256 rows with each row containing 256 cells. Each character is coded in a cell. The potential capacity of such a coding system is vast, since four octets per character provide enough code positions for all characters belonging to the scripts of the world that are currently of economic and cultural significance. The current version of DIS 10646 for a multiple-octet code is considered as a new coding system in itself and not as a further generalization of ISO 2022.

The most important value of the new coding technique is the expected software simplification when the application of this technique is compared to the existing ones. All characters are to be coded with same number of octets and provision of enough positions in the code for every potentially usable character, graphic or control is guaranteed. The larger number of bits used is outweighed by the simplification of the new software to be developed, and provision is made for compaction and padding of some limited sets of characters. For practical reasons, more limited and simplified forms of the code in practical implementations are envisaged in the document.

Some of the coded graphical symbols exist in more than one place in the code table but they are coded as unique members of particular character set (for example letter A in Latin or letter A in Cyrillic is a unique member of the character set of the corresponding alphabet).

The eight-bit n-octet code table is an array of n dimensions. An element position of the array is represented by an ordered set of n coordinates, each of which has an integral value from 0 to 255. The value of the coordinate is a value of the corresponding octet seen as a binary number. Octets are numbered from the most significant side as $n-1, n-2,..., 1$ and 0. In DIS 10646, octet 3 is a "group" octet (for system use, the value depending on the system and the application), octet 2 is a "plane", octet 1 is a "row" and octet 0 is a "cell" or position. The structure of the code is presented in Figure 5.7.

DIS 10646 defines 256 planes of characters. The first usable plane is termed the basic multilingual plane. The graphic characters are located in the four quadrants within this plane. The control characters (not defined in the code, but rules for use of the control characters encoding as specified in ISO 6429 are a part of the document) are to be located outside these four quadrants. Each control function, i.e. control character, is padded by *PAD* (decimal octet value 128) octets to the nearest character boundary. This has as a consequence that the body of a usual control sequence is not changed and the existing control sequence parsers (such as those in communication subsystems) can continue to understand and interpret control functions correctly.

For compatibility with existing eight-bit facilities, character codes wherein any octet has a decimal value in the range 0 to 31 or 127 to 159 is not used. This allows the common C0 and C1 control character set codes and related sequences to be used in combination with the UCS without needing to know that it is a multiple-octet code. The graphic characters are restricted to four quadrants within any given plane of UCS.

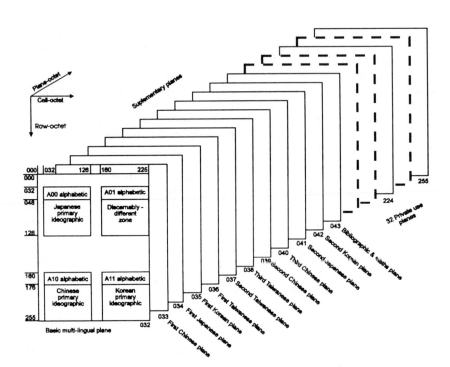

Figure 5.7 *The structure of the multiple-octet code*

The basic multilingual plane (see Figure 5.8) includes the characters of all the alphabetic scripts of the world, including Eastern European Latin, Western European Latin, Greek, Cyrillic, Arabic, Hebrew, Kana, Armenian, Georgian, Devanagri, Thai, Mongolian, and APL characters as well as various symbols. In addition, up to 7680 positions for characters with restricted use are allocated in the fourth quadrant, for various presentation forms (such as Arabic ligatures), or for dynamically redefinable character sets (DRCS) or for private use characters.

Asian "ideographic" characters (Japanese Kanji, Chinese Hanzi and Korean Hangul and Hanja) are allocated in the three quadrants of other planes in Group 032 as distinct characters. Every character set from East Asian part of the world is provide by an official authority from the country concerned.

The basic multilingual plane provides the characters needed for general use by all the countries of the world that use alphabetic scripts. Subsequent planes are regarded as supplementary planes for accommodation of graphic characters which cannot be fitted into the first plane.

The allocation of the graphic characters is arranged according to some recognizable character classification based on the increasing order of the complexity in use. There are eight recognizable classes of characters:

simple graphic characters that are used on their own, numerals, symbols and letters of many alphabetic scripts such as Roman, Cyrillic, Greek;

letters with accents or other diacritical marks or umlauts, (the smalls and the capitals);

ideographic characters used in the Chinese, Japanese, Korean and Taiwanese scripts;

characters of the Semitic scripts, Arabic, Hebrew, Moldavian and Syrian;

characters of the Indian scripts (including vowels and ligatures);

symbols used in general text and in mathematical and technical work;

numerals (Arabic, Indian and Semitic);

special symbols for bibliographic use.

Particular allocation of the scripts is presented in Figure 5.8.

On the whole, the first basic multilingual plane provides areas for accommodation of 6112 non-ideographic characters. The structure of the code enables very easy migration to and coexistence of the existing and forthcoming systems. For the alphabetic scripts the general principle of alphabetic ordering of the characters is followed. Where the script has small and capital letters, these are arranged in pairs. For those scripts for which there is a relevant part of ISO 8859, this general principle has been over-ridden by copying the sequence of the subsets of letters of that standard. This arrangement enables very easy conversion between ISO 8859 and the multiple octet code and an efficient compaction. The UCS defines several compaction methods:

one octet per character;

two octets per character;

three octets per character;

four octets per character;

dynamic (variable length).

In the first four compaction methods, number of octets per character is not subject to adjustment within text data (or a character coded data element). It is not required to support all the compaction methods. For applications where dynamic compaction is warranted, a fifth compaction method is defined that allows operating in specified one-, two-, three-, or four-octet representations

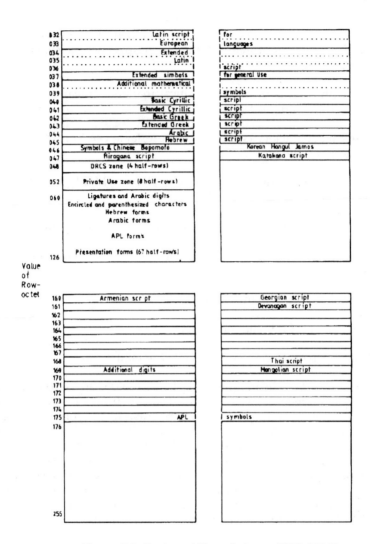

Figure 5.8 *Basic multilingual plane of ISO 10646*

(the assumed high-order octets of each character are dynamically specified within a character coded data element). The left-hand half of the one-octet representation is always ASCII by definition. This allows ISO 8859-like one-octet forms for several scripts to be provided.

A new control character, *SGCI* (Single Graphic Character Introducer) can be used to introduce a single character. The code specifies two levels of extension to determine whether *SGCI* is allowed or not. Processing level 1 (where no code extension is allowed) is designed for those applications where a fixed number of bits par character is important (such as for programming languages). The extension level (where code extensions are permitted) permits characters not otherwise accessible with the current compaction method, by use of *SGCI*. In any conforming use the code extension level must be identified.

Implementation designs of DIS 10646 are based on requirements for the target markets and thus design decisions depend on the analysis of each developer or manufacturer. The design of UCS allows selection of options by defining profiles. The conformance requirements are also defined with options. In order to claim conformance, it is not required to implement all the options but the choice of option must be declared by documentation. (For example, a UCS conforming terminal device may understand only the two-octet compaction method and the Full Latin and Greek subsets, and not have *SGCI*.)

The appearance of UNICODE

It seems that the history of eight-bit character set codes (ISO 6937 vs ISO 8859) is now being repeated at the start of the 1990s, but in the multiple-octet character set version. In parallel with ISO 10646, a consortium of manufacturers and users started the development of a two-octet multilingual character set code. The Unicode Consortium was formed in 1990 to bring Unicode (i.e. the two-byte code developed by the consortium, see [Unicode 1990]) to the world under the sponsorship of a multicorporate, multinational, non-profit organization with open membership, Unicode Inc.

Unicode was developed with a scope to meet the need for a simple multilingual character standard in information processing systems. Many of the information professionals from various companies shared the common frustration in dealing with the incompleteness and complexity of multilingual character code standards developed by ISO or CCITT. Therefore, they decided to develop a two-byte code based on use of ASCII in order to help them to exchange multilingual data by making text processes easier and more efficient to implement. That was the scope of the Unicode project, i.e.

elimination of the special-case systems and complex application codes currently used to deal with multilingual character encoding standards; and

provision of a large range of characters available to meet the requirements of professional quality typesetting and desktop publishing in a multilingual environment.

The efforts and the intentions of Unicode consortium to provide a de facto international standard, with the expectation that it would be widely accepted, were based on the following assumptions:

provide completeness, meaning that all scripts in common use would fit within a code using sixteen bits;

provide efficiency, meaning that the useful model is a text composed of a sequence of fixed-width characters, because it is simple for parsing, identifying of characters and does not implies maintaining states and looking for special escape sequences;

provide uniformity, meaning that efficient sorting, searching and editing is possible only with a fixed character code size and that methods of compression cannot be a part of the character encoding.

The Unicode project was adopted by the Unicode Technical Committee in 1989 and the first draft of the code appeared in 1990.

Unicode characters are fixed 16-bit identifiers, representing primarily, but not exclusively, the letters, punctuation and other signs that compose natural language text, including mathematical, scientific and other characters used in technical documentation assuming that characters reside only in the machine, as strings in memory or on disk. In contrast to that, rendition of characters and glyphs which appear on the screen or paper are treated as a particular representation of one or more stored characters. A repertoire of glyphs comprises a font. For that reason each character in Unicode has one code regardless of the language using it or the font rendering it. When exceptions are made to match usage in other standards, Unicode specifies a preferred encoding for each character in question. The number of different characters coded in Unicode is 65536, which is assumed to be a sufficient number for representation of all characters the world will use today or in future.

All characters in the code plane are equally accessible. The arrangement of the codes and the allocation of the characters has no major consequences for currnt information processing systems because the characters are grouped according to linguistic and functional categories, i.e.

the first 256 codes follow precisely the arrangement of ISO 646 and ISO 8859-1;

character codes unique to any given language are grouped together in standard order;

codes that represent letters, punctuation, symbols and diacritics shared by multiple languages are grouped together;

Asian language ideographic characters (Chinese / Japanese / Korean) are grouped by frequency of occurrence;

Chinese, Japanese and Korean punctuation marks used in common are grouped together as well as their phonetic symbols;

it is presumed that actions have to be invoked by the program or application and not by the control character of the code, and for that reason the C0 character set of ISO 646 is retained only for compatibility with ASCII;

floating diacriticals are treated as separate non-spacing characters, because they are to be rendered by font software;

a subset is designed for "private use"; characters in this range are not standard and can be implemented only under private arrangements.

An application may be considered Unicode conformant if it supports independent fixed-width 16-bit characters and uses Unicode code-points to represent Unicode defined characters. Code conversion from other standards to Unicode is considered conformant if the matching table produces accurate conversion in both directions. Conversion between text coded with Unicode and other character codes must be done by explicit table-matching processes. Unicode does not guarantee bit-for-bit compatibility with other codes, even though accurate convertibility is guaranteed between Unicode and other widely accepted international standards. Text coded with Unicode may be compressed for storage or transmission like any other binary data, but no preferred compression algorithm is specified in the Unicode document and no guarantees are given for bit-to-bit identity in compressed format.

UCS versus Unicode

The essential requirement of users as well as of manufacturers regarding character sets is very simple. They just want to be able to deal with all Western and Eastern European languages plus East and Middle East languages in the easiest and simplest possible way, and at the lowest possible cost.

Both projects, ISO 10646 and Unicode, initiated to satisfy these essential requirements, are results of tremendous effort and a lot of work performed from both groups of developers, one being strictly commercial, the other being more aligned on compromises that require a full consensus based on precise procedural rules. The result of these efforts lead to two different directions in implementation and use of the codes. As a consequence of that, the essential requirement of users and manufacturers for a simple solution is not satisfied, and because of that the same burden of work regarding character set codes that has affected the whole field of information processing since its very beginning is expected to continue in the future.

The existence of two different multiple-octet codes may again cause problems with code conversion, which means additional investment for development, testing and maintenance of conversion software, waste of human and other resources, performance and other memory penalties (extra overhead), overload of communication lines, customer dissatisfaction which could result in the creation of local solutions, etc.

Fortunately, both sides involved in the development of the new coding system were aware of these problems, and some ideas emerged, which seemed to be acceptable to both sides. A proposal for merging DIS 10646 and Unicode was prepared by an ad hoc group of experts. This proposal resulted after JTC1/SC2 received some papers from members who had voted against progressing the status of DIS 10646 from a draft to a full ISO standard. These papers proposed solutions to meet the requirements of the ISO members, and how to arrive at a consensus for approval.

The Unicode consortium members had a look over the proposal and decided to support the merger of the two proposed character set standards, resulting in a single international standard. The technical solutions in the merger proposal can be summarized as follows:

> The "C0" and "C1" restriction in the encoding of ISO 10646, would be removed, providing flexibility and encoding of more graphic characters in the basic multilingual plane. This was justified by the need for allocating more characters in the basic multilingual plane and by the fact that C0 and C1 restrictions are relevant only to the handling of character data one octet at a time in the existing seven-bit and eight-bit character-based communications and terminal protocols. Besides that, UCS encoded characters, which require interpretation of full eight-bit octets, meaning that they cannot be transmitted through seven-bit communication lines without the use of higher layer protocols.

> An international common repertoire of unified Chinese, Japanese and Korean ideographs would be created and this set of ideographs encoded into the basic multilingual plane of UCS. This was justified by the requirement for interworking and processing efficiency. The conversion of national standards to and from a single unified encoding of ideographic characters in UCS was expected to be much more preferable to the national bodies concerned than direct encoding of national standards on separate planes.

> Use of non-spacing marks or diacritics would be allowed in the code. This was justified by provision of compatibility and support of many scripts together with bibliographic standards. The rules for interaction of sequences of non-spacing marks was expected to be specified in an additional annex of the standard.

> The merger of DIS 10646 and Unicode would be defined as a four-octet code, meaning that other needs for encoding large numbers of ligatures, character variants, or other entities which may not all fit within the basic multilingual plane would be satisfied in a standard way, i.e. as a part of the international standard. (Some issues regarding the actual character values and the default coding are not still defined and are expected to be reworked.)

> Space for presentation forms would be allocated in additional planes of the structure, which means that a drastic reduction or elimination of the presentation forms in the basic multilingual plane has to be done. The large number of ligatures, stylistic or glyphic variants are expected to be coded in the additional planes of UCS, keeping them separate for use by rendering systems or font engines.

The repertoires of DIS 10646 and Unicode would be combined into a merged code which would be derived from a superset composed of the union of both repertoires.

The compaction methods would be simplified and a multipart standard with several annexes established.

The proposal was agreed on at working group level in JTC1/SC2 and is now (1992) out for voting as a second DIS. The proposal is defined as a multipart standard. The first part defines the architecture of the code and the basic multilingual plane. Other parts will be defined later. The new code specifies two modes of use, i.e. the four-octet canonical form of the UCS and the two-octet basic multilingual plane, and the coded representations of the control functions are specified too. A new feature in the code is the definition of the UCS transformation format (UTF) in Annex F. The UTF method transforms the coded representation of graphic characters of UCS into a form that does not use octet values specified in ISO 2022 as coded representation of C0, *SPACE*, *DEL* or C1 characters. Transformed coded characters with the UTF algorithm can be used for transmitting text data through communication systems that are sensitive to the octet values of the C0 and C1 sets.

The compromise proposal of the second DIS incorporates the best features of Unicode and ISO 10646 and discards the bad ones. By further development of the DIS an optimal solution may be expected to cover the needs for information interchange and data processing of all contemporary used alphabetic and ideographic writing systems and basic technical symbols in a clear, efficient, and non-wasteful manner, guaranteeing at the same time minimal disruption for the conversion path from existing hardware and software applications.

The multiple-octet code and communication protocols

The merging of DIS 10646 and Unicode requires resolution of several technical issues. The most relevant to data interchange is the use of C0 and C1 code space for graphic characters. A graphic character in the C0 space (spaces between 0 and 31 and 127) is interpreted by an existing transport protocol as a control character. Many transport protocols (for example the electronic mail SMTP) can behave unpredictably when dealing with UCS octets with the same contents as C0 control characters (for example a termination of the SMTP session could happen prematurely).

The situation with C1 is slightly different because transport protocols could be relied upon never to strip the high order bit from an octet and not to interpret the resulting character as a control sequence. In that case the C1 space could be used for graphic characters. See [van Wingen 1990] for a fuller discussion of character coding and network protocols.

However, another way of interpreting the compromise proposal could be that it expands the current ISO 2022 scheme from being only one (seven-bit or eight-bit) byte to also being two and four octets as well. With this view, each character in current standards can be thought of being coded in one, two, or four octets, depending on the form of coding. When a single octet standard is represented in this expanded two or four-octet form, the high order, most significant, octets are zero (corresponding to the *NULL* character when viewed in one-octet form). Thus the C0 and C1 control characters are preserved and can be used in this expanded form with each C0 (eight-bit) bit combination being represented in two octets with first octet zero. With this approach, only 65 of the 65536 positions in the code space are used for coding control functions, which is less than 0.1%, compared to the first DIS 10646 which used 44% for coding control functions.

The adoption of such a type of coding in UCS requires a definition of a standardized announcer for switching from one-octet to two- or four-octet forms. The standardized announcer then becomes an essential control function in the interchange of data between hosts, terminals and printers and between modems and terminal concentrators. Announcers are needed also to flag data, whether interchanged on communication lines or as complete files. In order for an announcer mechanism to become a part of the standard it has to meet the following requirements:

> The announcer mechanism must distinguish the following three types of interchange data:
>
> – UCS two-octet data;
>
> – UCS four octet data;
>
> – existing one-octet and variable octet coded character sets (including ANSI C multi-octet, and ISO 2022 one-octet and multi-octet sets, EUC etc.).
>
> The announcer mechanism must be unambiguously interpretable in all three forms (one-octet, two-octet and four-octet forms).
>
> The announcer mechanism must specially flag "Little Endian" data.

An announcer must occur at the boundary of a one-octet, two-octet or four-octet character, not in the middle. Thus the sender must know which form the data is currently used (one-, two- or four-octet) when inserting the announcer. In the case when switching is done from one-octet to two- or four-octet, then a way for the data stream to be switched back to the default one-octet data form of current system (i.e. to current character sets conforming to ISO 2022, including UCS) is needed too.

Such announcers could also be used as a check in opening a file by a program that was in the anticipated form. It could also be used for dynamic conversion from one or more forms to the desired forms, depending on the design of the system run-time (it is assumed to vary between different programming languages).

In closed systems, the use of the announcer has to be optional. However, if such a system interchanges its data with other systems, it must use the announcer, whether the interchange is through files or communication lines. The use of an announcer is vital also for terminals, since terminals are produced by different vendors from those producing the concentrators, modems, hosts etc.

It is envisaged that the merged UCS standard will contain an informative annex which will recommend how to perform a mapping on UCS data so that its two- and four-octet forms are not confused with the existing C0 and C1 control characters. One idea is to map the new UCS graphic characters away from the area consisting of hex 00...1F (C0), *SPACE* (hex 20), *and DEL* (hex 7F). A mapping of this kind makes it possible to transform UCS data into a form that can be correctly handled by existing hardware and software equipment (one byte) that are sensitive to these values. It is also envisaged that a statement will be included in the annex specifying the octets which will serve as a synchronization sequence. Such a sequence can be sent in cases when the sender is not sure what form the communication line is in, and/or is not sure where the character boundaries are. The annex will also have to contain an identification of the algorithm for "byte stuffing", to enable *XOFF* (*DC1* = hex 11) and *XON* (*DC3* = hex 13) to be used correctly for flow control over asynchronous, full duplex, serial communication lines.

The use of the merged UCS in higher layer protocols requires an additional extension of ASN.1. This extension should allow a separation of the abstract syntax from the identification of the character repertoires to be used within it. This enables the applications in the application layer such as FTAM or MOTIS to be adopted and used with any required character repertoire, whether UCS, or national character sets for national or region related use, i.e. in China, Japan, Greece, Eastern or Central Europe etc. The declaration of the character repertoires is then independent and does not influence the further development and publication of the abstract syntax, as well as the development of the supporting applications. Changes and additions to the list of supported repertoires can easily be made when the need arises. The local identification may take the form of an ASN.1 tag or some other already specified forms such as an "attribute", an octet in a predefined position (an announcer for example) or in the declaration statements.

The LocalString scheme and the related new generic types in ASN.1 permit an abstract syntax to identify a number of character set repertoires. The new ASN.1 generic types are recognized as:

> IdentificationCharacterData, in which the first octet is used as a local identifier to indicate one of the character set repertoires that this particular instance of interchange is using;

> CharacterSetRepertoireMap, in which the mapping of the particular global character set repertoire identifiers to the local identifiers in the range *0..255* are to be used in the particular instance of data interchange.

Each character set repertoire is made up either of a specified G0 and G1 graphic character set, and possibly G2 and G3 and C0 and C1 control function sets structured according to ISO 2022, or else of a UCS announcer indicating that the data is in two- or four-octet form of UCS.

The LocalString scheme is intended to be used with negotiation protocols and in a protocol with prior agreement. The suggested method is the following. In the protocol with character set repertoire negotiation, the initiating entity passes an instance of the CharacterSetRegisterMap type, including the associated local identifier. The recipient entity responds with another instance of the CharacterSetRepertoireMap type, eliminating the global character repertoire identifiers it does not understand. The recipient can either change the local identifier values to ones more convenient to it or can leave them as the sender suggested, depending on implementation of the recipient entity. Then the character strings are passed in both directions using the IdentifiedCharacter-Data with the first octet containing the local character set repertoire identifier.

In a protocol with prior agreement on the character set repertoires, such as a data file, an instance of the CharacterSetRepertoireMap is included in the beginning of the interchange such as in the file header. Subsequent instances of character data are then represented using the IdentifiedCharacterData type, with the first octet containing the local character set repertoire identifier.

Several alternatives were suggested for the specification of the GlobalCharacterSet Repertoire Identifier based on different items, i.e. registration number values, character set standards, object identifier, designating escape sequences, announcers etc. The decision is not easy because object identifiers for combined control and graphic character sets are not considered useful especially if the high dependence of the control characters from particular application is considered.

Conclusion

The problem and the associated solutions for character handling are especially important for applications supporting various alternative languages and scripts and therefore are most relevant for the international market. The latest technical solutions and improvements in the development of standard character sets for multilingual environments are intended to provide efficient implementations and inexpensive software support to new scripts and to the multilingual processing environment.

Multilingual processing for all scripts envisaged in the latest version of the merged UCS is much more complex than for the single-language, single script processing and communication that predominates now. The problems of handling issues such as searching, sorting, rendering and messaging or interchange of data cannot be handled simply by copying the techniques and methods applied in existing software and hardware. Dealing with large character sets requires significant changes in software design and interfaces.

It is hard to imagine that a multilingual system with an implementation of full UCS will be workable unless its script-specific parts (font resources, rendering rules, line formatting, etc.) are implemented in a modular way in similar manner to the applied language-specific expertise (for sorting, spell-checking, morphological analysis). The base products which will appear on the market can be expected to be very generic and to contain inbuilt intelligence. This part of the product has to be smart enough to "ask for help" from script-specific expert modules whenever a need to render or process "unusual" characters appears. Where and how the "ask for help" will be addressed will depend on the system design. It could be imagined that the script specific module will be loaded when needed by the system or by the service provider via the network. In so flexible a model of a system, the notion of the set of scripts supported by a given multilingual system becomes dynamically unpredictable. The conformance clause of the forthcoming UCS has to be tailored to support such a model.

For centuries paper documents have formed the basis of commercial transactions. From invitations to tender to final payments, numerous documents are exchanged between trading partners. In the modern world, in most cases these commercial documents are now processed electronically, then put into envelopes and sent by post. Prepared at the speed of light, they are dispatched over one million times more slowly. Electronic data interchange (EDI) looks like the solution to the problem of speeding up the "paper mountain" transfer. EDI is carried out either from computer to computer, through the exchange of magnetic media, or via telecommunication networks (the term EDI has become commonly to mean this second method). There are different standards defined within different standardization bodies for exchange of documents via EDI. Some are defined as EDI standards, others as exchange protocols, interchange formats etc.; in any case, they support the exchange of meaningful data between different information systems.

The next contribution, by **Dr Jordi Farrés** of the European Space Research Institute at Frascati, Italy, discusses three basic functional requirements for information interchange between information systems, and analyses some common exchange formats.

Electronic exchange of structured information: the requirements

Introduction

All companies and administrative bodies with large information systems come to a point where typing/printing all the information arriving or leaving their domain is no longer feasible. Time delays, lost of accuracy and waste of resources force them to the electronic exchange of information from one computer system to another.

The solution to this problem is generally known as EDI (Electronic Data Interchange); however, specific connotations of the term restrict the meaning of EDI to a precise understanding, that of EDI standards [Emmelhainz 1990]. For this reason, we shall avoid using the term EDI in a general context.

Information systems address, traditionally, the storing, processing, retrieval and publishing of data. To these functions, we wish to add the electronic exchange of data.

Because exchanged data belongs to an information system, we expect exchanged data to be stored, processed, retrieved and published by the receiver, as well as by the sender. This is our basic functional requirement.

Most problems arise from the concurrence of all these functionalities for the same set of data in a sophisticated exchange protocol.

This paper begins by presenting the functional requirements which a user, thought of as an information system, may demand. Some cases are then studied, showing how each requirement can be easily satisfied by a different exchange protocol; and how EDI standards, SGML and multilayered standards can cope with several functionalities. In the last section, functional requirements and some of the cases are subject to a syntactical and semantic analysis. This helps to compare different requirements and solutions.

Retrieval, publishing and exchange

Information systems perform the storing, processing, retrieval and publishing of data. These operations determine the way in which information is structured in an information system, and they also determine the minimum structure of the data which is sent to such a system.

Without loss of generality we can ignore the processing of data. Data sent to be processed in a remote computer system can be thought to be stored first and then retrieved for processing, so that requirements on the structure of the data are always due to the retrieval operation[1].

In fact, this is actually happening in most of the cases since, by definition, we are interested in the exchange of information between different computer domains, and not teleprocessing. Also, the fact of storing some data does not, on its own, impose any requirement on the structure of the data.

---

[1]   In fact, this is actually happening in most of the cases since, by definition, we are interested in the exchange of information between different computer domains, and not teleprocessing.

At this point, we can say that the three functions of interest are:

> data retrieval;

> document publishing;

> information exchange.

In one sentence, our functional requirements are:

We should be able to retrieve the data of interest using the appropriate query language, publish/preview the same data in form of a document and exchange it with other computer domains.

Additionally, the nature of the data supported (text, drawings, pictures, signatures, formatted data, ...), the query language used (SQL, full-text indexation, procedural, ...) and the services provided by the exchange protocol (delivery, confidentiality, security, handling of responsibility, ...) should be as general as possible.

Partial solutions

General practice shows all these three functions to be well-known problems, with a good theoretical background and efficient software solutions.

> **Information retrieval** requirements are usually satisfied by database management systems.

> **Document publishing** requirements are conveniently satisfied by publishing systems.

> **Information exchange** requirements are normally satisfied by standard communication protocols between different computer domains. Good examples of this are ordinary electronic mail systems.

If we combine two different kinds of requirements there are solutions still available (Figure 5.9).

> **EDI standards** provide the means for exchanging structured information for processing or, without loss of generality, for storing and retrieving in a database.

> **SGML** [ISO 8879, Goldfarb 1990, van Herwijnen 1990] has been designed for the electronic exchange of marked documents. In this sense, SGML provides the means for exchanging structured information for publishing.

> **Documental databases** implement storing and retrieval features on documents. In this sense, documental databases combine retrieval and publishing features.

EDI standards, SGML and documental databases combine features of two different kinds, but no solution seems to fill the central box in Figure 5.9, where simultaneous requirements on retrieval, publishing and exchange are encountered.

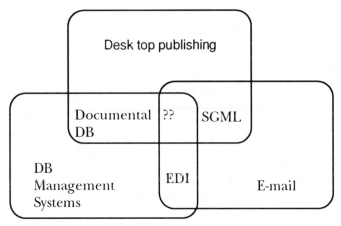

Figure 5.9 *Partial solutions*

Exchanging data for retrieval and publishing

In the following some examples of data exchange are given. They describe three different concerns: transferring database information, transferring marked documents and providing a powerful exchange protocol.

Transferring database information

Imagine we are requested to transfer records from a table such as:

```
Table Example1     ( field1 CHAR(12),
                     field2 SMALLINT,
                     field3 FLOAT,
                     field4 DATE,
                     field5 RAW(50) )
```

There are three main observations to be made:

Information in a database can be very heterogeneously coded

Data fields coded as **FLOAT, DATE, RAW** and **SMALLINT** can be exchanged as coded values in binary form or as equivalent strings of text.

In the first case the exchange protocol should allow the transfer of coded data which may be different in each occasion. This has led to the development of protocols below the OSI presentation layer such as SFDU (Standard Formatted Data Units [CCSDS 1988]) which can be parametrized by each particular coding.

Decoding all data into strings of text degrades performance in space and time. However, in cases such as **DATE**, **FLOAT** and **SMALLINT**, the transfer in textual form allows different coding formats to be used at both ends of the transmission.

In fields of type **RAW** the coding is user-defined. Translating these fields to a textual form is not a decoding as for **FLOAT** by a re-coding from arbitrary bytes to characters. In this case, transmitting the data in form of text has no advantage.

All entries in one table have the same structure

The organization of data in a table is very regular. The table in the example consists of a list of records of the form (**field1**, **field2**, ..., **field5**) where some of the fields may be omitted (with a null value).

Inter-table relations are by content

Relational databases consist of a certain number of tables. The relationships between these tables are implicitly established by their contents; i.e. the value of a certain field in a table can be used to query another table. Hence, no information about table links needs to be exchanged.

Transferring documents

Imagine we are requested to transfer a compound document with text and graphics as follows:

```
<doc>       <author>        Name of the author
            <title>         Title of the document
<section>   <title>Introduction
            <paragraph> ...
            <list> <item>    ...
            ...
<section>   <title> Example
            ...
            <drawing type="raster" file="example.raster">
            ...
```

There are three main observations to be made:

Information is homogeneously coded

Unlike information in a database, all contents of a document are expressed in text and, occasionally, using a few graphic/image standards for figures. This results in a fixed and small set of coding standards; in the example ASCII and **raster** are enough.

Document structure is recursively defined

The components of a document are structured following precise syntactical rules. For instance, a **title** should appear at the beginning of a **section**, an **item** in a **list** can also be a **list** but not a **drawing**, each **paragraph** should belong to a **section**, etc.

Most document marking standards define a set of marks to be embedded among the text, and some syntactical rules defining their correct usage, e.g. GML [IBM 1989] and TeX [Knuth 1986]. SGML allows marks and syntactical rules to be defined by the user.

When exchanging documents electronically the syntactical rules should be known to the receiver so that incoming documents can pass a conformance checker. In the case of SGML, documents must be exchanged with their self-description, i.e. the user-defined syntactical rules. Even for very simple documents, syntactical rules can be recursively defined either directly, e.g. lists which can contain other lists, or indirectly, e.g. paragraphs may contain footnotes whose text is divided in paragraphs.

Relationships between components are explicit

The relationship between the components of a document are mainly those of sequence and inclusion corresponding to the relative position of the components in the document. Additionally, cross-references add extra links between two components in a document or between different documents.

Exchange standards should take explicit care of this information.

Providing an exchange protocol

Imagine we are dealing with the creation and management of minutes of meetings. The overall process works as follows:

> *The process for the creation of the minutes of a meeting starts with the invitations sent by the organizer to all invitees describing the subject, place and date of the meeting. After confirmation from the participants the meeting is set on schedule. When the meeting takes place, the organizer writes up the list of matters discussed and a list of the actions to be taken on each matter. This document is distributed to the participants in the meeting and other interested persons, and it is left available to all staff for consultation. Specific signed messages notify the relevant responsible staff of the actions agreed. Finally, after completion, a short report from each responsible person summarizes the outcome of each action.*

There are some observations to be made:

Defining an exchange format is not enough

Both the exchange of database information and documents addressed specific format (syntactical) requirements for the data being exchanged. On the other hand, in the case of the minutes of a meeting, we are mainly concerned with the interaction between the participants in the process rather than with the format (syntactical structure) of the minutes document.

The complexity in the protocol for the creation and control of minutes of meetings shows that simple delivery facilities have to be improved with some more services, e.g. common electronic mail services such as forwarding, issue of acknowledgements and replying, and some known EDI services such as authentication of signatures and handling of responsibility.

Specific application protocols, such as that described for minutes, may require ad hoc services like notifying to the organizer that some of those invited never replied, generating warning messages if an action report falls behind schedule, etc. Contrary to common electronic mail or EDI services, ad hoc services do not refer to the sending of a message but to events at the application level.

The exchange protocol may depend on the contents of the messages

When a document is sent, the information relevant to the communication is normally encapsulated in an envelope or header, even if some of that information is also present in the document, e.g. the list of participants is part of the contents of the minutes of a meeting and it is duplicated in the envelope for distribution.

If an exchange protocol includes services at the application level, these services frequently depend on the message contents. For example, issuing warnings for action reports falling behind schedule is a service which needs to know the deadline of each action; however, action deadlines are content information which we do not expect to find in the envelope.

We shall use the term *logical envelope* for the set of all the information relevant to some protocol service, regardless of its physical inclusion in an envelope or header.

Combining requirements

The creation and control of minutes is an example of combined requirements. Minutes as well as action reports are documents and users should be able to publish/preview them as such. At the same time, the same information needs to be searched and retrieved by all staff. Finally, part of this information can affect the exchange protocol managing these documents.

The representation of the minutes of a meeting must be such that the same data can be "read" as a set of records in a database, as a marked document and as a pair *logical envelope + body*, where the logical envelope governs an exchange protocol.

Analysis of requirements

Finding a solution for the concurrent three kinds of requirements is not a simple task. In the following, we split the syntactical from the semantic aspects of each functional requirement, so that all syntactical – or semantic – aspects can be compared among themselves. This method of analysis is described in [Farrés 1992] and, in this context, has the purpose of finding a general exchange format which could be used when all requirements are combined.

Syntactical analysis

Syntactical analysis is concerned with the structural requirements introduced in the examples of last subsection. In short, exchanging database information requires a flexible coding of the information with simple composition rules, exchanging documents requires flexible composition rules with simple coding, and exchange protocols require the identification of logical envelope data.

Common standards are flexible in their aspects of interest. For instance SFDU is very flexible at the information coding level so that data files using user-defined coding can be exchanged, SGML is very flexible at the compositional level so that most document structures can be exchanged and parsed, and communication protocols such as CCITT X.400 IPM (Inter-Personal Message) stress the difference between the envelope, divided into several data fields, and the body, treated as a single unit.

EDI standards such as EDIFACT [ISO 7372, ISO 9735, Berge 1991, SITPRO 1990] provide a compromise of reasonable good coding, good compositional flexibility and explicit headers. For example, data elements in an EDIFACT message can be declared of a certain type

```
element1 a2        ; alphabetic element of length 2
element2 an..30    ; alphanumeric element of maximum length 30
```

and they can also be combined hierarchically in segments and messages with explicit reference if they are mandatory, optional or repeated.

Unfortunately, EDIFACT is not intended for sending structured documents and, in fact, its compositional flexibility does not include recursion as most documents require. Similarly, EDIFACT also falls short of coding flexibility for database fields such as **FLOAT** and **DATE** in the first example of last section.

In Figure 5.10 syntactical flexibility at the coding level is represented by the vertical axis and flexibility at the compositional level by the horizontal axis.

In this domain of *syntactical flexibility* we can say that communication envelopes require very little structure, transfer of table information may require a lot of coding flexibility, and document transfer may require a lot of compositional flexibility. SFDU, EDIFACT and SGML can be roughly displayed as in the figure. Their respective positions give an idea of the flexibility at both coding and compositional level. The question mark denotes the syntactical flexibility required to an exchange format in order to transfer data for retrieval and publishing, in the general case.

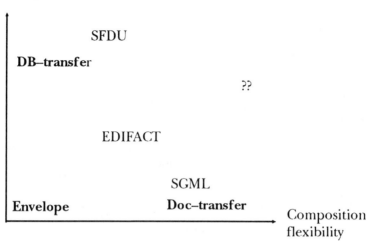

Figure 5.10 *Syntactical domain*

Semantic analysis

The semantic analysis of exchanged data leads to the division of data into *control* and *information*.

As in the case of the protocol defined for creating and controlling minutes of meetings, it is clear that an exchange protocol is not only concerned with syntax. The communication medium interprets some of the data being exchanged and provides services such as delivery and acknowledgement accordingly. Moreover, exchange protocols usually include an agreement about the interpretation of codes and tags included in messages.

Considering this, we can say that the exchanged data is divided into *control* and *information*. For example:

In an *electronic mail system* and considering the communication process, message content stands for information whereas routing data in the headers and other directives are control data, e.g. in

```
To: user1   at: NodeName
Subject: This is a message title
Here, the content starts
. . . .
.AK ;              This is a request of acknowledgement
.CC user2 ; This instructs sending a copy to user2
```

the header fields **To**, **at** and **Subject** together with directives **.AK** and **.CC** are control.

In the *exchange of documents* and considering publishing, the actual text and drawings are the information[2] whereas tags referring to the fonts, page type-setting, and sizes are control data, e.g. in

```
\begin{center} {\Large Title of the section}
\end{center}
\setlength{\pagewidth}{23cm}
\vspace{2cm}
Beginning of the section .....
```

all instructions embedded in the text control the position and the fonts of the actual text.

In an *EDIFACT message* and considering the interchange process, the data to be processed by the recipient is the information whereas the headers specifying mail-routing, recipient application and passwords are control data, e.g. in

```
UNDi UNOA:1+ Sender+ Recipient+ 010791:1200+ Reference+ Password
UNH + MRef + Type: Version: Rel: ESA + Status
INFO1 + Code + Quantity + Value
.....
UNT + 100 + MRef
UNZ + 1 + Reference
```

segments **UNB, UNN, UNT** and **UNZ** are standard EDIFACT headers for messages and interchanges.

The difference between information and control depends on the process we are considering; essentially, *control data is meaningful with respect to a computer process whereas information is not.* Sometimes the difference appears obvious, as with directives starting with a dot in electronic mail messages. However, this is not always the case, e.g. control segments in EDIFACT messages follow the same syntax as all other segments.

Moreover, some data can be considered control or not depending on its processing. For example, the deadline for an action is just information if the minutes are to be printed, displayed, etc.; however, it is control if warnings are raised by deadlines being reached.

Recalling the three functions defined earlier, we can conclude the following:

Transferring database information does not require any explicit transfer of control data, unless non-relational databases are used.

---

2   We shall ignore the amount of control associated with a printable character or a dot in a drawing

This is so because data is implicitly divided in tables for transmission, and retrieval, in relational databases, is driven by contents. In other non-relational cases, control data consists of indexing information used to organize storing and allow retrieval.

Transferring documents requires some control regarding the actual formatting of documents.

The publishing of a document depends in part on the implicit structure of the document; however, control data in form of tags or escape sequences is needed for the correct display/printing of the document.

Finally, having an exchange protocol requires messages to carry envelopes with information concerning communication services.

As already discussed, physical envelopes or headers specify services concerning the exchange of the message or group of messages they enclose, whereas logical envelopes cover all the information which affects the protocol associated with a certain application.

Arbitrary exchange standards can be classified according to the kind and amount of control they define as in Figure 5.11.

No control defined	Publishing control	Protocol control	
SGML	GML TeX	– Delivery	File transfer SFDU
		– E-mail services	X.400 IPM
		– EDI services	EDIFACT
		– Appl-protocol	Electronic Conferences

Figure 5.11 *Semantic classification*

SGML does not define any control: users must define for each kind of document the marks used, the syntactical rules applied and the meaning (semantics) of each mark. GML and TeX among many other publishing and word-processor formats control the formatting of documents. File transfer, electronic mail and EDI provide an increasing variety of protocol services related to the exchange of information.

Electronic conference packages such Vax Notes [DEC 1989] provide integrated communication services supporting the cooperative creation of documents.

Multilayer solutions

Normally, exchanges are designed in the form *envelope + body*. The envelope includes the data controlling the protocol for the transfer, and the body includes, if needed, control data for publishing and/or storing. In some cases the body part is further divided, distinguishing several inner parts which are different in nature and functionality. In all these cases we say that the exchanged message is *layered*. This situation arises because each standard covers one aspect of interest, leaving concurrent standards to handle other aspects of the exchange.

Common layered messages are formatted documents wrapped into electronic mail envelopes. Since publishing standards have been designed for the representation of device-independent formatting properties, data controlling the actual exchange of documents has to added externally using another standard, e.g. GML documents sent in X.400 envelopes. Similarly, we can also use SGML tagged documents in EDIFACT messages. In this way, we combine a high level of communication services with the ability to load and publish the transferred data.

Unfortunately, combining standards in a layered exchange can produce several problems, basically, problems of two kinds: syntactical inconsistencies and partition of control. In the first place, we can consider EDIFACT messages in which we want to include some drawings. EDIFACT commits all segments to use a limited set of characters. Therefore, no standard with a flexible encoding can be embedded in EDIFACT without explicit conversions; in particular, this concerns raster images. Furthermore, EDIFACT defines several character sets and each of them, as it is strictly defined in [SITPRO 1990], relates to a particular coding, e.g. UNOA is coded using ISO 646. This means that EDIFACT messages arriving at a computer domain with another character coding convention will not be recognized as containing text. Despite these difficulties, problems related to coding are easily fixed by adopting some appropriate conversions (re-coding).

More serious are those problems related to the partition of control in an exchange. Even using two character-based standards, wrapping EDIFACT messages inside X.400 standard IPM envelopes is not easy due to overlappings between the two control headers (see [Hill 1990] for discussion). This cannot be avoided, since EDI protocol services have to be raised above electronic mail standard services. For instance, EDI messages may require the handling of acceptance responsibility and signatures, or ordinary services addressed to groups of related messages which are not foreseen in the IPM protocol.

Application-oriented protocols are another example. In such cases, protocol control and information cannot be easily separated and frequently, protocol control as well as formatting control is spread across the whole message/document.

Case study

Consider the case of sending compound documents. Imagine we decide to design an EDIFACT message with a segment containing (or pointing to) an SGML tagged document with figures encoded in IGES (Initial Graphics Exchange Standard). This organization of the exchange provides a high level of communication services specified by EDIFACT headers, some user-defined EDIFACT segments where browsing and tracing information can be specified, SGML tags for the correct formatting of text, and IGES graphics for the correct formatting of figures.

At each layer, a standard specifies some kind of control so that we combine a rich protocol led by EDIFACT headers, retrieval/processing led by EDIFACT data segments, publishing/retrieval led by SGML tags, and publishing led by IGES.

Nevertheless, we are still far from combining retrieval, publishing and exchange on the same data. In our multilayer document control is divided so that

> different retrieval procedures act upon EDIFACT data segments, SGML text and IGES graphics;
>
> the communication protocol depends on the information kept at the EDIFACT level and ignores the inner document contents;
>
> formatting cannot be affected by data in the EDIFACT data segments.

For these reasons, information affecting several control functions needs to be repeated in all corresponding layers. For example:

> The author and title of the document appear as an EDIFACT segment for tracing, and in the SGML contents for publishing.
>
> The text in a figure appear in a IGES file for publishing, and in an SGML component for textual retrieval.
>
> The sender and recipient of the document appear in the EDIFACT headers for the transfer, and in the SGML contents for publishing.

Conclusion

The basic functions performed by most information systems determine the requirements for the electronic exchange of structured information among them.

These requirements can be classified into syntactical and semantical requirements. Among those in the first group, there are requirements regarding the flexible codification of data and the means by which that information can be structured. Basically, data to be stored and retrieved demands flexible codification mechanisms, and information to be published demands flexible structuring mechanisms.

In relation to the semantical requirements, there are requirements regarding the communication protocol itself and requirements regarding the end-processing of the information in the target domain, but these two can be closely related in application dependent protocols, as in the example of minutes of meetings. In terms of the exchanged message, data controlling the protocol (logical envelope) and data controlling the storage and publishing of the information at the target domain must be included in the message.

Although there are standards addressing each of these requirements, the combination of all of them in a single piece of information is still a problem. Some EDI standards such as EDIFACT cope with a wide range of these issues, and this may solve all the requirements of some users; however, in relatively simple cases where information has to be exchanged for publishing and retrieval, no single standard addresses all the necessary requirements. In these cases several standards have to be used simultaneously in a layered message, but then some additional problems arise, leading to the use of encodings and redundancies.

Acknowledgements

The author would like to thank his colleagues who agreed to read early drafts of this paper, the anonymous referee for his comments, and all those persons working in this enterprise who helped him in his understanding of the problem.

He is also grateful to the European Space Agency for funding this work and allowing its publication.

One of the most important application areas for open information interchange is the electronic distribution of documents of different kinds. Documents are aimed toward exchange of information for human beings and, as mentioned earlier, may contain information of different kinds: utterances in natural or artificial languages built of characters, raster images, graphics composed of geometric elements, moving images and music. Using this definition, documents are the basis of a major part of human communications as well as teaching and leisure. Documents nowadays are processed by available word and text processing systems. Incompatibilities of media and communications protocols can often be overcome with some effort, but differences among the methods of structuring stored documents pose tougher problems. The contribution which follows discusses the choices which have existed in the past for use of the interchange document methods and the requirements for better models and standards in that area. Although in its original form written in the early years of the Office Document Architecture (ODA) standardization effort, it still provides insights into the user problems ODA attempts to overcome. The author was **David Blyth** of Incord Ltd, UK, but then of the National

Computing Centre at Manchester, in collaboration with two researchers, **C.H. Choi** and **Y.J. Jiang**, at Manchester University. The paper [Blyth, Choi and Jiang 1984] has been edited and somewhat abridged for the purposes of this book. Substantial edits, and editorial commentary, are italicized and indented.

An approach to document interchange

Since the early 1980s the market for most types of text processing system has grown very rapidly. Installed equipment ranges from simple standalone office word processors to sophisticated computer typesetting systems. For each broad class of system and particularly for word processors, a wide range of systems is available from an equally wide range of suppliers.

Text processing is an important aspect of office automation. Large office systems rely heavily on network architectures and real networks contain text processing systems with dissimilar capabilities and features. Such systems require efficient and reliable document interchange facilities. In the 1980s it therefore became vital to develop text interchange standards for heterogeneous environments.

There are two components to any data interchange system. First, an effective carrier system is needed. This may be an interchange medium or a communications network. Second, a common form of representation is needed, so that information generated by one system can be properly interpreted by another.

Standards existed for various types of possible carrier system, but there were no comprehensive standards for the representation of text for interchange purposes. In practice this made interchange of electronic documents very difficult if not impossible.

ISO therefore embarked on a work programme to develop a family of standards for text interchange. A significant part of this work has been the development of an Office Document Architecture (ODA) model to provide a common framework for defining the structure and representation of texts of many kinds.

Nature of the ODA model

To define generally applicable procedures for text interchange one must be able to characterize with reasonable precision the properties of a document. For this purpose an analytic model is needed. Such a model is by no means easy to construct because of the potentially immense variety of electronic documents.

In very simple cases a piece of text may be regarded as a stream of characters. However, this model is not appropriate for all types of document. For example, a document containing diagrams cannot sensibly be regarded as a stream of characters because the diagram will need to be encoded in a different manner from the text. A naïve linear stream model cannot reflect this.

Even when a document contains only character text it may still be unhelpful to regard it as a character stream. This is true, for example, when the document contains tabular material. In this case some semantic information is embodied in the layout of the document, and to model this some form of structural representation is needed.

Finally the rendition of characters may be important – as, for example, in cases where text may be in italics for emphasis. A generally useful model must be able to accommodate rendition attributes associated with particular segments of character text within a document.

A clear distinction must be drawn between the content of a document and its presentation via any particular medium. The content of a document is unique but it may have several possible presentations. This is easily seen by considering a book printed first with a ragged right margin and then with a right-adjusted margin – differing presentation would be no defence in an action for infringement of copyright!

The meaning of a document must not be altered during interchange and the total meaning of a document may be due to the content alone, or to the combination of content and presentation. Content and presentation are, however, separate concerns. Therefore a document model has to be able to treat content and presentation separately and to represent relations between content and presentation where these contribute jointly to the meaning.

The ODA model considers a document as a set of hierarchical structures. One of these structures embodies the content of the document. The others embody possible presentations of the document.

It is important to realize that the set of structures which may describe a document is not necessarily unique. The ODA model is not to be regarded as a means of defining a canonical form for a document, rather it should be understood to define a class of structures including several or even infinitely many possible structures corresponding with any particular document. The model does not, however, define equivalence relations between document structures. In particular the set of possible structures for a particular document should not be regarded as an equivalence class.

> *At the time the original paper was written, the ODA model was at an early stage of development. A hierarchical structuring scheme had been adopted for working purposes. This abstract overall structure needed to be tested to confirm that the hierarchical form of structure was an adequate one. The model also need to be refined to capture more detail.*

A useful initial refinement was the introduction of attributes associated with the segments of text at the nodes of a hierarchy. It is useful to classify attributes according to whether they relate to content or presentation or both. The range of possible attributes is very wide. Some attributes relate to content others to presentation, still others to both. Some attributes exhibit interdependencies with each other. The effect of attributes on the meaning of a document is sometimes very subtle.

Such is the range of attributes that they are difficult to investigate in abstract. Empirical study followed by attempted generalization seemed a more productive approach. Accordingly a major objective of the prototyping project [described in the original paper – Eds] was to classify text attributes prior to further study.

Prototyping interchange systems

Development of a prototype system is a valuable way of assessing the usefulness of a system or data model. In order to maximize the benefits of prototyping it is necessary have a clear idea of the goals of the exercise. The following aims were set for this project: to attempt to discover major deficiencies in the ODA model if they existed; to attempt to produce a refinement of the model to include attributes for items of text; and to examine the scope and nature of interdependencies among text attributes and to examine their relation to the structural representation of documents.

Since resources were limited the following objectives were set: to build a demonstrable facility supporting interchange of charactercoded text documents between simple but dissimilar text processing systems running in dissimilar environments; and to engineer the required software so as to make it portable or at least readily adaptable to several kinds of machines and operating regimes.

A syntax-directed interchange system

The authors had available at the time two microcomputer systems, with text processing software, one running Wordstar under CP/M, the other running NROFF under Unix. A Wordstar/NROFF interchange utility was the simplest basis for the prototyping experiment.

Clearly, little was to be learned by constructing an ad hoc utility specific to the particular text processing tools to hand. The authors therefore attempted to implement a single, portable interchange facility which could be interfaced to each particular tool by parametrization.

Pascal compilers were available on both machines, and one of these had been validated by the British Standards Institution and was known to be a highquality implementation in close conformance with the language standard. One of the authors had also implemented in Pascal a syntax-directed editing system for programming language texts. Both Wordstar and NROFF were known to store documents in a linear form where layout is indicated by embedding control characters and formatting commands in the text. Accordingly the authors chose to adapt the syntaxdirected editor to convert linearly-stored documents into a structured interchange form. The software would be parametrized for both Wordstar and NROFF by defining separate document syntaxes. This plan offered a rapid and reasonably portable implementation.

The interchange method was straightforward. The interchange program read an input document and parsed it according to a document grammar for the particular system on which it had been produced. The output from this process was a pair of trees, one representing the content of the document, the other representing its presentation.

The tree-structured form of the document is much easier to manipulate than the original linear form. Once content and presentation trees have been generated for a document, it is quite straightforward to transform the trees prior to re-merging so as to yield a document directly readable by another system. This provided the means of interchange.

> More detail can be found in the original paper, which was a report on work which formed part of a project funded by the Electronics and Avionics Requirements Board of the Department of Trade and Industry under a research and development contract with the National Computing Centre Ltd.

In use the system proved quite robust. Several deliberately pathological test documents were devised to test the system. These contained unusual combinations of local and running attributes with variations of line width and page length. In all cases a sensible, but sometimes oddlooking, approximation could be produced on the destination system for both directions of transfer.

The conclusion was that, within the limits of its application, a syntax-driven system was a useful interchange vehicle in agreement with the ODA model, and that the prototype system could be redeveloped at relatively low cost to provide a commercial quality interchange facility.

Assessment of the ODA model

> At the time the ODA model had been under development for nearly two years. In using it as a working guide, the authors did not find any serious inconsistencies. The model lacked detail, but that was only to be expected at that stage of a standard.

> However, the model seemed to have some subtle implications for the way in which standardsconforming text processing systems need to be engineered. The authors believed that it would be straightforward to develop conformant systems based on the model, but that the software design of these systems might differ quite markedly from that of systems then in use.

> The authors also identified some areas for further study. Text exhibits great diversity, which is most evident in the large range of potential attributes of text. In the authors' view, text attributes form the fundamental basis of document structure. They believe it vital that a comprehensive classification of attributes is included in the ODA model. This should be addressed urgently since it has extensive ramifications.

Data interchange has always been complicated by differing system capabilities. This is true *a fortiori* of text interchange. Compare, for example, a word processor and a phototypesetter. There is neither prospect of, nor reason for, standardizing processor capabilities.

> *Nevertheless, the authors concluded that it is essential to have at least a standardized way of describing the capabilities of a system.*

Unless such a description is available, it will be unnecessarily complicated to determine whether a document can be suitably approximated on a system to which one may wish to transfer it.

Not only is a standardized form of description needed, it is a practical necessity to classify the capabilities of systems, preferably by a scheme based on a capability matrix. This would make for simplification. Systems could be defined as offering certain levels of capability in respect of their ability to process certain kinds of document content. Given a stratified classification of capabilities, it would be quite simple to determine the feasibility of any desired interchange.

> *Finally, the authors remarked:*

There is little systematic knowledge of the means by which documents may be approximated when transferred to systems with lesser capability than that on which they were created. In many simple cases one text attribute may be substituted for another (e.g. italics instead of slanted type). As document elaboration increases, approximations based on simple mappings become inadequate.

It is likely and even probable that no two text processors will offer identical capabilities. Approximation procedures would therefore be essential for practical interchange. Once again there was a need for discovery and classification. The approximation problem, it was concluded, was perhaps the most challenging area for future study.

Critics of the ODA standards and model, as developed since that paper was written, frequently complain that this model is applicable only for word processor documents. Considerable activity in the ODA community to produce converters between word processor formats and ODA is on the way but ODA contains enough advanced features to provide transfer of high quality documents. The contribution that follows discusses some of the areas of ODA that support flexible and high quality documents. It discusses the deficiencies in the 1988 ODA standard and suggests extensions to be provided as an answer to the user requirements for support of hyper/rich text in document interchange with ODA format. It is by **Fred Cole** and **Heather Brown** of the University of Kent at Canterbury, UK, and first appeared in *Computer Networks and ISDN Systems* [Cole and Brown 1991].

ODA extensions for quality and flexibility

Introduction

The ODA standard ISO 8613:1988 is intended to "facilitate the interchange of documents". In practice this usually means that a document is created using a word processor, converted from the representation used by the word processor into ODA, transmitted in ODA form, and then converted back to another word processor representation. Some native ODA document editors are now being built, but most converters are currently for word processors and do not use the richness of the ODA logical document structures. Thus the widely accepted advantages of structured documents are lost [André *et al.* 1989].

The SGML standard [ISO:8879:1986, Barron 1989] is also intended to facilitate the interchange of documents, but it is used differently. An SGML document is often created directly by the author (with or without the aid of a structure editor), and then transmitted to a publisher who supplies the formatting and printing conventions. Authors may be provided with SGML document styles that allow them to reap the full benefits of structured documents.

Contrary to popular belief, the logical document models supported by ODA and SGML are remarkably similar [Brown 1989]. The difference in usage is explained more by the areas in which the two standards are used than by the differences in the standards themselves. The most significant difference between the two is that SGML does not support any layout or presentation semantics whereas ODA is very rich in this respect. (The ODA deficiencies that we describe below have no counterpart in SGML because SGML does not attempt to cover the area. However, the area will be covered by the *Document Style Semantics Specification Language* (DSSSL) standard, ISO/IEC DIS 10179, when it is ready.)

ODA's layout facilities may be divided into two categories. The first category simply contains the many features for describing the desired positioning and appearance of the items in the document. Simple examples of these are the provision of the attribute *character path* to define whether text should be laid out left-to-right or right-to-left (or indeed from top-to-bottom or bottom-to-top), and the ability to specify details of character imaging such as the character font to be used and whether text is to be emphasized by underlining, blinking or image inversion. The second category is to do with providing different views of the same logical document. The most important feature that falls into this category is the separation of the logical and layout structures of a document, which allows different layout structures to be used for the same logical document.

This paper concentrates on ODA's facilities for providing flexible views of a document. It provides an overview of the facilities, identifies some deficiencies in the current version of the standard, and suggests simple extensions to increase flexibility and quality. Although the proposed extensions are designed primarily for use in native ODA editors for structured documents, they open the way for ODA to provide support for hypertext as well.

The extensions suggested are not high level features designed to provide direct support for specific features such as the automatic generation of tables of content, lists of bibliographic references, or support for specific hypertext systems. Instead they are basic facilities that can be used by a document designer to build a wide range of such high level features.

Providing different views of a logical document

This section uses a simple example to introduce the ODA facilities for flexible document views. The reader is assumed to be familiar with the basic principles of the ODA logical and layout document structures, but the example provides a brief reminder of how the generic structures guide the creation of specific document structures, and of some important attributes in the layout and presentation styles. The same example is used later in the paper to illustrate the proposed extensions.

Figures 5.12 and 5.13 show simplified versions of the generic structures that might be used for individual papers in a technical journal. Figure 5.12 shows that papers consist of a title, followed by the author's name, followed by an optional abstract, followed by one or more sections. Each section begins with a subtitle, and this is followed by a series of paragraphs or diagrams occurring in any order. Figure 5.13 shows a possible generic layout structure corresponding to the logical structure shown in Figure 5.12. This defines one page style for the first page of the paper, and a different style for all subsequent pages. (In practice, far more complex structures would be needed to cope with footnotes, appendices, running titles and so on.)

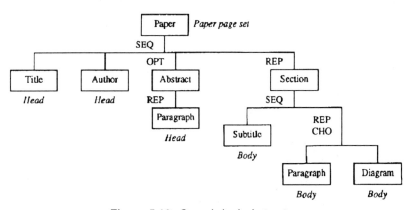

Figure 5.12 *Generic logical structure*

The items in italics show the values of three attributes that guide the document layout process. The logical **Paper** has its *layout object class* defined as **Paper page set** to indicate that each paper will be laid out in a single instance of the page set shown in Figure 5.13.

The basic logical objects in Figure 5.12 have the value of their *layout category* attribute shown, and the frames in Figure 5.13 have the value of their *permitted*

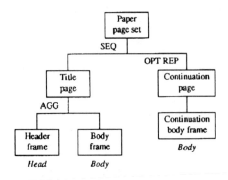

Figure 5.13 *Generic layout structure*

categories attribute shown. The layout process uses these categories to divide the contents of the document into streams, and will only place the contents of a basic logical object with a given *layout category* name into a frame with the same name given as one of its *permitted categories*. Thus, in the example, when the layout process attempts to place the contents of the **Title** it looks for a frame with **Head** as a permitted category, and therefore creates a **Title page** and places the **Title** in the **Header frame**. When it reaches the contents of the sections, however, the layout process looks for frames with **Body** as a permitted category, so it uses the **Body** frame until that is full and then creates **Continuation pages** as necessary in order to use the **Continuation body frames**.

When the layout process has finished its work, it will have created a specific layout structure that associates the content of a specific logical structure with pages, frames and blocks. Figure 5.14 shows a possible fragment of the two

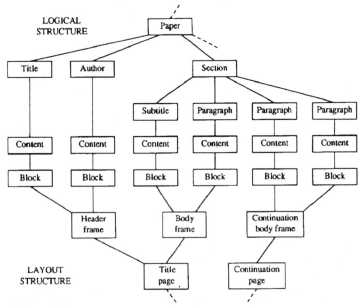

Figure 5.14 *Specific logic and layout structures*

specific structures for the beginning of a paper. The fragment assumes the paper has no abstract and that the first section begins with three paragraphs, only one of which fits onto the title page.

Although this example is very simple, it should be sufficient to show that the appearance of a specific logical document can be altered by supplying a new generic layout structure. Deleting the **Body frame** from the **Title page** in Figure 5.13, for example, would cause each paper to be laid out with only the title, author's name and abstract on the first page. (There would be no frame on the first page with **Body** as a permitted category, so the first section would have to start on a new page in a **Continuation body frame**.) Similarly, the body frames in the generic layout structure could be altered to give two-column or three-column layout.

Other radical changes to the layout can be achieved by supplying a new set of layout and presentation styles. Although the attributes in these styles apply to specific logical objects, the objects themselves (or their corresponding generic objects) contain only the identifier of the appropriate style. The styles are held separately, thus allowing a more concise document representation and the flexibility to change the styles without changing the logical structure.

The layout styles include the *layout object class* and *layout category* attributes used in the example together with further attributes governing the selection of frames and the positioning of blocks within a frame. *Same layout object* and *new layout object*, for example, specify whether the content of a logical object is to share the same frame as the content of another given object or whether it is to start a new frame. *Separation* and *offset* control the minimum spacing between adjacent blocks and between blocks and their containing frame, and the relative position of blocks is controlled by *fill order* which allows normal top-to-bottom positioning or traditional footnote positioning.

The presentation styles guide the lower-level content layout process and thus affect the appearance of content within individual blocks. For character content, for example, changing the presentation styles can alter the indentation of the first line in a block, the distance between lines, and the initial font size.

Changing the generic layoᵘ structure and the styles can thus lead to significantly different views of tʰ ame logical document. Page and margin sizes can vary, single or double column layout can be used, text can flow around diagrams, and paragraph spacing and font size can change. In particular, it is possible to cater for different "house styles" by this means and to provide different styles for interactive editing of a document and for the final printed version.

Deficiencies in the current ODA model

The partial separation of the structures and styles introduced above provides a good deal of flexibility for providing different views of a logical document. There are, however, several restrictions in the existing model. Three problem areas are listed below.

Incomplete separation of the logical and layout structures

Although the layout and presentation styles are kept separate from the main logical structure of a document, it is only possible to substitute one style for another throughout the entire document. If the original document designer did not provide different layout styles for different classes of logical object (e.g. for titles and subtitles) the one-for-one substitution cannot provide different styles for those classes of object without altering the style numbers held in the logical structures. A more flexible substitution method is needed.

Some objects in the logical structure are only present to generate items that are more concerned with the view than the logical structure. The obvious way to implement automatic numbering of sections, for example, is to begin each section with a logical object that has an appropriate content generator. However, this method makes it difficult to change to a view that does not number sections. This type of content generation should be associated with the view rather than the logical document.

Restricted attribute inheritance

The ODA mechanism for inheriting layout and presentation attributes, in spite of its complex algorithm for finding default values, is insufficient. If style identifiers are not specified for an object or its class, then they can be inherited according to a *default value list* higher up the specific logical tree. Thus styles may depend on the object class or they may be inherited according to the position of an object in the tree – but they cannot depend on both. This means that basic logical objects in, say, a section and an appendix may inherit different styles, but does not allow the paragraphs and titles within a section to inherit different styles.

A mechanism to allow style inheritance to depend on both the position in the tree and on the object class is needed.

Inability to specify selective or multiple layout

ODA does not allow a logical object to be ignored during the layout process, or to be laid out more than once. A facility to ignore objects during layout would allow outline views of complex documents to be presented and provide a facility for adding annotations that are visible during editing but do not appear on a printed copy.

If objects could be laid out more than once in a document, then multiple copies of information could be generated from the same logical object and thus avoid the problem of needing to update several objects simultaneously. The title of a chapter duplicated in a list of contents is an obvious example. It is of course necessary to be able to use different styles for each version of the object laid out.

Selective and multiple layout is useful for computer-based documents in general. It is particularly important for hypertext.

Some suggestions for improvement

Four modifications are suggested here. The first, style-tables, is fundamental to our approach to removing the deficiencies identified above. The following three modifications (generic layout content, bindings in styles, and multiple layout) depend on style-tables.

Style-tables, as described below, provide a versatile method for style inheritance, allow objects of selected classes to be ignored in parts of the document, and improve the separation between the logical and layout structures. If generic layout content and bindings in styles are also added, then it becomes possible to make the logical structure completely independent of the structures that define the view (i.e. the styles, style-tables and layout object class descriptions); the only connection needed is the references in the style-tables to the identifiers of the logical object class descriptions.

Style-tables

A style-table is a mapping from logical object classes to styles. At the simplest level, the use of style-tables eliminates the need to include style identifiers in the logical structure. A simple change of style-table could thus be used to change the view of the document without editing the logical structure.

In order to correct the limitations of ODA attribute inheritance, a new style-table can be introduced at any level in the specific logical hierarchy. The new style-table is applicable to the layout of all objects at lower levels, and can therefore make the layout and presentation of that subtree completely different from the rest of the document. Changes of style-table can be nested to any depth.

The sections below provide a definition of style-tables and explain their compatibility with the current version of ODA.

Style-table definition

A style-table is a set of style-table-elements that associate styles with logical object classes. Thus a style-table-element is a logical object class identifier, a layout style identifier and, where the logical object class identifier is for a basic object, an optional presentation style identifier. A single style-table, called the **ROOT-STYLE-TABLE**, is the "current style-table" when the layout process starts at the specific logical root. Each object is then laid out according to the style associated with its class, but any object whose class does not appear in the style-table is ignored by the layout process, as are all its subordinates.

As an example, consider the **ROOT-STYLE-TABLE** shown in Figure 5.15 (with names instead of identifiers to make the explanation easier to follow) applied to any specific structure derived from the generic logical structure in Figure 5.12. If we consider only the **ROOT-STYLE-TABLE** then all objects other than those of class **Paper, Title, Abstract** or **Paragraph** are ignored during layout, and even these are ignored if they occur as subordinates of an ignored class.

```
ROOT-STYLE-TABLE =
Paper               : LAYOUTSTYLE1
Title               : LAYOUTSTYLE2
Abstract            : LAYOUTSTYLE3
Paragraph    : LAYOUTSTYLE4, PRESENTATIONSTYLE1

LAYOUTSTYLE3 =
  styles for subordinates = PREFACE-STYLE-TABLE

PREFACE-STYLE-TABLE =
Paragraph    : LAYOUTSTYLE5, PRESENTATIONSTYLE2
```

Figure 5.15 *Style-tables and layout styles*

Thus, **Paragraph**s in the **Abstract** are laid out according to **LAYOUTSTYLE4**, but **Paragraph**s in **Section**s are ignored.

Paragraph is a basic object class and the entry in the style table indicates – if we continue to consider only the **ROOT-STYLE-TABLE** – that **Paragraph**s will have their content laid out according to **PRESENTATIONSTYLE1**. Rules for determining the values of defaultable attributes are described in the next section. **Title** is also a basic object class, but as no presentation style is given, the values of all the associated defaultable presentation attributes must be found as described in the next section.

The style-table for an object is normally inherited by all its children, but a new layout style attribute, called *styles for subordinates*, allows a new style-table to be specified for all subordinates of the object – thus defining a new environment for laying out a subtree of the document. If the value of *styles for subordinates* is **IGNORE** then all of the subordinates of the current logical object are ignored by the layout process (this is the equivalent of specifying a null style-table).

Continuing our example, but now considering the whole of Figure 5.15, we see that **LAYOUTSTYLE3** (for the **Abstract**) contains

```
styles for subordinates = PREFACE-STYLE-TABLE
```

so **PREFACE-STYLE-TABLE** is the style-table to be used for any subordinates of instances of **Abstract**. From the **PREFACE-STYLE-TABLE** we see that the **Paragraph**s in the **Abstract** will be laid out according to **LAYOUTSTYLE5** and **PRESENTATIONSTYLE2** rather than the styles given in the **ROOT-STYLE-TABLE**.

Figure 5.16 shows the final result of applying these styles to the generic logical structure of Figure 5.12, where [1] means that objects of that class are laid out according to **LAYOUTSTYLE1** etc., and [-] means that the objects are not to be laid out.

Where every logical object class is specified in the **ROOT-STYLE-TABLE** and no use is made of *styles for subordinates*, the effect is the same as in the current version of ODA, but the style identifiers have been removed from the logical

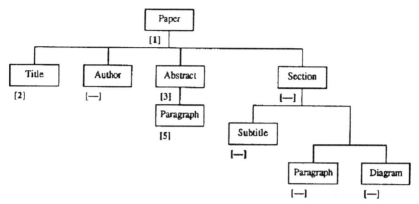

Figure 5.16 *Generic logical structure with applicable layout styles*

structures. Using the full style-tables mechanism removes the style identifiers from the logical structures, provides selective layout, and also allows different styles to be inherited according to both logical object class and position in the tree. Thus the mechanism goes a long way towards removing the deficiencies mentioned earlier.

Style-tables, defaultable attributes and compatibility with the current version of ISO 8613

Style-tables should be optional, and if a document does not contain style-tables there is no compatibility problem. If a document does contain style-tables, however, it is necessary to define how values of defaultable attributes are found when they are defined both in the styles referenced by the style-tables and elsewhere.

For the purposes of determining values of defaultable attributes, if a style (either layout or presentation) from a style-table is applied to a logical object then the style is treated as though it is the style referenced by the class of that logical object. If that class already references a style then the style referenced in the class is ignored. Apart from this change, the default mechanism is exactly the same as described in ISO 8613-2 section 5.1.2.4.

A special case is used to allow layout of a logical object in the same style as would occur if the style-table were not applied (i.e. so that the object can be selected for layout but not have its style changed). If a style-table-element references a class but the value of the reference to a layout style in it is **NULL**, then the logical objects to which it is applied are laid out, but the layout style referenced by the logical object class, if present, is used. (This has the same effect as if the style-table-element referenced the same style as the logical object class.)

As an example of this special case, if the **ROOT-STYLE-TABLE** given above contained the entry

```
Abstract : NULL
```

then the **Abstract** objects would still be laid out but the layout attributes would be determined exactly as in the current standard, with no reference to the styles in the style-table.

These modifications to the rules for determining the values of defaultable attributes have been chosen to give the greatest compatibility with the current version of the standard. One result of this choice is that use of a style-table can never over-ride values of attributes specified for a logical object, only those specified for its class. An attractive alternative is to give values obtained via style-tables the highest priority, so that the designer of the view can always control the layout and presentation. Notice that the designer of the view could still choose to accept the values specified for the logical object by setting the value of the reference to a layout style in the style-table to **NULL**.

Generic layout content

If layout is to be completely separated from the logical structure, generic content for items such as running headings should come with the definition of the view (i.e. the styles and style-tables) rather than the logical structure. The mechanism suggested for this is very similar to that currently used for the attribute *logical source.*

A set of logical object classes may be defined as part of the view, containing generic content portions and content generators giving the required headings, for example, and conforming to the same rules as *logical source.* The attribute *view source* may (optionally) be specified for a frame, its value being the identifier of one of the logical object classes of the view. Specific instances of these logical objects are created by the layout process (in the same way as for *logical source*) when it creates instances of frames with a *view source* attribute.

Bindings in styles

In order to allow facilities like automatic numbering of sections to be part of the view, rather than part of the logical structure, it is proposed that bindings may appear in the styles.

To see how this can be applied without loss of functionality, consider first the simplest case: a document with only one style-table in which the style-table references a layout style for each and every logical object class of the document. Now assume that the bindings that would normally appear in the logical object classes are transferred to the corresponding layout styles. The proposed rules for determining values for defaultable attributes mean that the functionality is now exactly the same as when the bindings were in the logical object classes (but with the added flexibility that the view can be changed, with a new set of bindings if required, by changing the styles and style-table).

If it were necessary to restrict documents to have only one style-table the usefulness of style-tables would be severely reduced, but fortunately this is not so. Suppose that more style-tables are added to the simple document considered above. If the designer ensures that each new layout style used for any particular logical object class has the same bindings as the original, then the functionality with respect to bindings remains unchanged. Allowing bindings in the styles therefore moves functionality that should rightfully be a property of the view out of the logical structure. It also, incidentally, gives more flexibility to the document designer because the bindings applicable to an object can now depend on the object's position in the document as well as on its class.

Bindings and content generators

The purpose of most bindings is to contribute, directly or indirectly, to a content generator. So a binding will only be useful (for numbering sections for example) if a logical object, with a content generator that ultimately depends on that binding, exists at the correct place in the document. This is not satisfactory because having such an object in the logical structure is at odds with the stated need to separate the logical and layout structures. It is certainly possible to ignore the logical object in views that do not use the bindings (by not referencing it in the style-tables), but such objects would have to exist, even when not used, at all places in the document where a view (even a view not yet designed) might need them.

Ideally the layout process should be able to create such logical objects when needed, or have some way of incorporating the generated content without using logical objects. Both approaches are used in the mechanism described below for implementing multiple layout, and the same mechanism can be used for incorporating this generated content.

Multiple layout

Multiple layout is not very useful unless different versions of an object can be laid out in different styles (with, perhaps, different subordinates ignored), so the extension proposed here depends on the provision of style-tables. It also allows bindings in styles to be used without having objects for that purpose in the logical structure.

To provide multiple layout it is necessary to do three things: select the object (or other content) to be laid out, select the place where it is to be laid out, and define how it should be laid out. This can be achieved with two new non-mandatory layout style attributes, *layout before* and *layout after*, which identify objects to be laid out before and after the current object. There are three different cases depending on the values of the attributes:

Case 1: The attribute value is an object identifier expression together with a style-table identifier. The object identifier expression must evaluate to a logical object identifier (the "selected logical object") or **NULL**, and the style-table identifier is optional.

In this case the selected logical object and all its subordinates are laid out as though a copy had been placed immediately before (for *layout before*) or after (for *layout after*) the current logical object in the sequence of subordinates of the superior of the current logical object. As in the layout of a reference to *view source,* a copy of the object is not actually added to the logical structure, and the *generator for subordinates* of the immediate superior in not considered to be violated. The selected object is laid out according to the style-table given in the style-table identifier (if this is **NULL** then the style-table for the current object is used).

Using this case our example may be extended to show in outline how a list of contents can be produced from the section subtitles. Suppose that **LAYOUT-STYLE3** for the **Abstract** contained

```
layout after = SUPERIOR-OBJECT, CONTENTS-STYLE-TABLE
```

where

```
CONTENTS-STYLE-TABLE =
  Paper      : LAYOUTSTYLE10
  Section    : LAYOUTSTYLE11
  Subtitle   : LAYOUTSTYLE12, PRESENTATIONSTYLE10
```

SUPERIOR-OBJECT identifies the **Paper** itself but, as the only basic objects referenced in the **CONTENTS-STYLE-TABLE** are **Subtitles**, this would cause the section subtitles to be laid out after the abstract and before the rest of the paper (as well as in their normal place at the start of each section). If the layout styles referenced in the **CONTENTS-STYLE-TABLE** contained suitable content generators and bindings, then the list of subtitles could be made into a contents page.

Case 2: The attribute value is a logical object class identifier together with a style-table identifier. The style-table identifier is again optional.

The logical object class is used to generate logical objects in the same manner as for a reference to *view source* (i.e. the same as for *logical source*) and the logical object class must conform to the same restrictions as for *logical source*. In all other respects this case is the same as case 1.

This case can be used to generate standard headings and other view specific content in the same way as *view source,* but within the logical sequence instead of the layout sequence. It can also be used to generate logical objects that use bindings from the layout styles.

Case 3: The attribute value is a string expression. This case is only applicable to basic objects.

The string that results from evaluating the expression is added to the start of the first content portion of the object (in the case of *layout before*) or to the end of the last content portion of the object (in the case of *layout after*).

This case is primarily used as a simpler way than case 2 of inserting the value derived from bindings when it is required to lay out the strings in the same style as the current logical object. It can also be used to insert simple marks, such as opening and closing quotation marks or opening and closing braces.

In all the cases the logical objects created by *layout before* and *layout after* are laid out as though they are siblings of the current logical object, they must in some respects be treated by the layout process as though they are part of the current logical object. If a value for *layout object class* is specified for the current logical object, then the required layout object is created before the evaluation of *layout before*, and both the result of *layout before* and the result of *layout after* must be laid out within that layout object. If a value for *new layout object* is specified for the current logical object, then the required layout object is created before the evaluation of *layout before*.

It is possible that these attributes should be allowed in logical object descriptions and/or logical object class descriptions, but this has not been recommended because it is not in line with the requirement to separate the logical structure from the view.

A problem with any mechanism that attempts to lay out an object more than once is that evaluation of the **CURRENT-INSTANCE** function is likely to be ambiguous. The ambiguity arises when a current instance function references the layout structure. As a logical object may now be laid out in several different layout objects the result is multivalued. One approach, yet to be investigated, uses the facility described above for associating bindings with an object via the styles, thus having different bindings in different layout versions of the same object. However, at the moment a simpler solution is recommended. A reference of this kind is always treated as though the only instance of the logical object is the one that is laid out directly, it does not reference any instances produced by application of *layout before* or *layout after*.

Towards hypertext

The layout flexibility provided by the modifications described above goes some way towards supporting the needs of hypertext. In particular, the ability to define which objects should be present in a particular view and to include the same information at different points in the document are clearly useful for supporting hypertext.

However, the single most distinctive feature of hypertext is the provision of links to allow users to navigate around the information. If ODA is to be a viable means of interchanging hypertexts, it must have some means of representing links. Current hypertext wisdom suggests that uncontrolled links lead to problems with users "getting lost in hyperspace" and that a strong hierarchical structure, together with a controlled set of non-hierarchical links, is the best way to design a hypertext. It is also generally acknowledged that links should be typed [Hypertext 1987].

As ODA already has a hierarchical structure, the main extension needed to make it into an adequate (if not ideal) means of representing and interchanging hypertexts is to add a further facility for typed links. Suggestions for extensions in this area have already been presented to the ODA standards committee [Cole and Brown 1989].

Conclusion

The ODA logical structures are rich enough to support structured documents, and the use of ODA need not and should not be limited to interchange of word processor documents. The relatively simple extensions presented in this paper are designed primarily to enable flexible and high quality document editor/formatters based directly on ODA to be built. The extensions add considerably to the quality and flexibility of the current ODA layout facilities without invalidating existing ODA documents.

ODA already has many of the facilities needed to represent hypertext. Currently it lacks a general mechanism for representing cross-references and hypertext links, but if this were added ODA could be used to interchange hypertexts as well as more conventional structured documents.

Acknowledgements

We would like to thank the Science and Engineering Research Council and British Telecom for their support of projects at the University of Kent involving ODA.

The protocols and the telecommunications means used for data interchange may have different origins and different capabilities. Data interchange can be performed via use of so-called "classical" means, i.e. magnetic media, telex, or facsimile, or by use of more sophisticated telecommunications services such as electronic mail, transaction processing or file transfer, generally put together under the heading of EDI. Which of these mechanisms is more appropriate is a question which can only be answered by the user's personal choice or defined by user requirements regarding the use to be made and the underlying applications. The final contribution in this section, by **T. Lam** and **G.C. Sudbury** of the Metropolitan Police Office in London, discusses what the authors term "the office document dilemma" – the choice between facsimile and X.400 – from the user point of view.

FAX.400? A user view of the office document dilemma

Developments in electronic messaging systems have left users who wish to exchange documents electronically with a choice between two main candidates, facsimile transmission and electronic mail.

Facsimile operates by taking a direct copy of a paper document and transferring it over the public telephone network. As well as text, the document may contain handwriting or graphics. Facsimile machines are designed in accordance with standards agreed by the International Telegraph and Telephone Committee (CCITT). Machines have been divided into four groups of which Group 3 is the current (1991) international standard. The CCITT standards for Group 3 describe the technical details required for machines to interoperate regardless of manufacturer. The standards do not however address the broader user requirements of a messaging system, notably message security and the provision of indicators to inform the user whether or not the document has been successfully transmitted to the intended recipient. Despite these short-comings, ease of use combined with relative inexpensiveness have contributed to make facsimile a very popular messaging system.

Electronic mail systems benefit from the data storage abilities and processing power gained by being computer-based. Each user is allocated a separate, password-protected "mailbox" within the system's host computer which will store incoming messages until the recipient is available to access them. Furthermore the host computer, acting as central controller, provides the confirmatory indicators to the user. Despite these advantages over standard facsimile, electronic mail has not swept the board of its brother service. This can be partly attributed to facsimile's unique ability to transmit images and paper sourced documents. It is also a result of electronic mail's proprietary evolution, the consequence of which has been systems that, despite offering broadly similar services, have problems interconnecting and interworking. Whereas most businesses and organizations have a facsimile machine which can be reached over the public telephone network by anyone who also has a facsimile machine, the electronic mail user may not even be able to communicate with colleagues within the same organization if they are connected to a different host computer. Fortunately, the current trend in the computer and telecommunications industry is towards "open systems" which allow users to buy compatible equipment from different suppliers. A communications system based on the open systems model is electronic messaging conforming to the CCITT X.400 recommendations. The X.400 standards were conceived and initially designed around a concept of secure message delivery across and between public networks. However, the facilities provided make it valid and useful as a messaging service especially for organizations with a variety of computer system suppliers. For the user, X.400 offers the prospect of combining the advantages of electronic mail with a global interconnectivity analogous to facsimile.

This paper begins by identifying the user requirements for electronic messaging systems. The subsequent sections discuss to what extent facsimile and X.400 systems meet these requirements, both at present and in the foreseeable future. Legal aspects of document transfer by the two systems, and the ability of X.400 to act as a universal interconnection medium, are also discussed.

User requirements of an electronic messaging system

General requirements

1. The functions of the transmitting equipment should make transmission a quick and straightforward procedure for the originator.

2. The messaging service should give access to as large a population of users as possible.

Information made available to originator

3. Validation that the document has been delivered to the correct destination(s).

4. Validation that the intended recipient has taken receipt of the
   document.

Services required by originator

5. Error detection and correction.

6. Only the intended recipient has access to the received document.

7. A record of the transaction is kept by the originator, including the date and time of submission together with the
   identity of the recipient.

Information made available to recipient

8. Validation of the originator.

Services required by recipient

9. A record of the transaction is kept by the recipient including
   the date and time of delivery and the identity of the originator.

10. The ability to edit a received document together with a
    means for identifying whether such editing has been per-
    formed.

Facsimile transmission

A group 3 facsimile machine operates by taking a direct copy of an original and
transmitting it over the public switched telephone network. A light sensitive
scanner reads the original, dividing the image into thousands of black and
white picture elements (pels). Effectively, each line scanned is composed of an
alternating series of black and white blocks, with each block composed of a
variable number of pels. Some machines are capable of further differentiating
between shades of grey. Depending on the grey shade and number of pels
within it, each block is given a digital code. To decrease transmission time,
blocks that are statistically more likely to occur are given the shorter codes. The
digital code stream is sent, through a modem, over the telephone network. The
receiving machine interprets the signal and recreates the image.

The CCITT recommendation T.4 states the standards to which Group 3 facsimile machines should be designed and operated. It is divided into the following sections.

Scanning track: defines direction for message area to be scanned.

Dimensions of apparatus: defines a standard resolution of 3.85 lines/mm in the vertical direction and 1728 pels along an A4 length line.

Transmission time/total coded scan line: defines the minimum and maximum times of a total coded line scan. A recommended standard of 20 ms is also defined.

Coding scheme: defines the code assigned to each length and shade of block plus a series of control codes.

Modulation and demodulation: defines the modulation, scrambler, equalization and timing signals. Generally the switched telephone network will necessitate data rates of 4800 or 2400 bps, but if leased lines or high quality switched circuits are used, data rates of 9600 bps or 7200 bps are possible.

Power transmission and power at receiver input.

In addition to complying with these standards, most Group 3 machines offer optional facilities. The British Facsimile Industry Consultative Committee classifies these optional facilities into three types:

Standard: Options which will work if both Group 3 machines are suitably equipped regardless of manufacturer.

Proprietary: Options which will work between machines of the same supplier.

Machine: Options which make operation of the machine easier or more efficient and are independent of communication.

So, how well does facsimile measure up to the user requirements identified in the previous section?

1. *The functions of the transmitting equipment should make transmission quick and straightforward for the originator.*

The CCITT recommendations do not define any services to assist the user in this area. However, several facilities are offered by manufacturers as machine options on some models. The most common facilities include:

Automatic dialling: the provision of memory capacity to store the most commonly used numbers enables one touch dialling to a single or to multiple destinations.

Store and forward: the memory may also be used to store the entire document for transmission at a later time if the called number is engaged on the first attempt.

Polling: this facility allows a central facsimile machine to dial up and collect documents from a number of remotely sited machines.

Automatic document feed: allows for the unattended transmission of long documents.

2. *The messaging service should give access to as large a population of users as possible.*

Group 3 machines are designed to operate over standard telephone lines. They are therefore relatively cheap, with prices starting at under a thousand pounds, and also simple to operate. These twin facts have contributed to produce a large user population and rapid growth, with British sales in the past two years alone (1989-91) totalling over a quarter of a million.

Group 4 machines are designed for connection to digital networks. Direct connection to data networks and, eventually, the ISDN is therefore possible. Several top of the range fax machines currently offer both Group 3 and 4 transmission. A large organization with private digital lines can therefore utilize the high-speed capabilities of such lines for internal use whilst using the public telephone network for external communications.

Group 4 products cost on average three times as much as their Group 3 counterparts. A less expensive alternative for transmission over digital networks is to purchase a Group 3 fax equipped with an RS232 port. This enables the fax to communicate with an X.25 PAD (Packet Assembler and Disassembler) as if it were a computer terminal, obviating the need for a Group 4 machine.

3. *Validation that the document has been delivered to the correct destination(s).*

The CCITT recommendations do not define a service to provide this facility. On basic machines it is therefore not possible to determine whether a document has been delivered to the correct destination or not. Faxes may be incorrectly delivered for two reasons. Either the facsimile equipment itself may mis-dial, or the telephone network, which does not have any answerback or end-to-end check, may mis-route the call.

ID confirmation is offered as a standard option on some models. On such machines, a fully automated check of the recipient's ID is made prior to releasing the message. If the wrong number is dialled a visual indicator alerts the user. Lesser equipped models, however, merely alert the user to the situation and if a speed dialler has been used it may be too late to stop the document going to the wrong destination.

4. *Validation that the intended recipient has taken receipt of the document.*

The CCITT recommendations do not define a service to provide this facility. It is not possible to confirm whether the intended recipient has seen the document. Only the proprietary option of Voice Contact Request attempts to fulfil the requirement, albeit indirectly. On machines equipped with this facility, an indicator on the receiving machine alerts the recipient that the originator wishes to speak to him after transmission of the document. This method of validation has obvious limitations.

5. *Error detection and correction.*

Until relatively recently no error correction scheme was defined by the CCITT. Since Group 3 machines transmit over standard telephone lines and relatively short line breaks can cause serious corruption, this is a major failing of facsimile transmission. It is possible to lose entire lines of text without originator or recipient knowing.

The CCITT Error Correction Mode (ECM) defines an error correction scheme which enables machines to talk error-free over standard telephone lines. Until it is fully implemented, however, error correction is a proprietary option and consequently effective only between identical machines.

As previously mentioned, communication over X.25 networks is possible for some Group 3 and all Group 4 machines. X.25 protocols incorporate error detection and correction mechanisms. They assure virtually error free transmission. X.25 access is currently expensive relative to telephone extensions.

6. *Only the intended recipient has access to the received document.*

The CCITT recommendations do not define a service to provide this facility. Since most fax machines are deliberately positioned in a central location, messages can be read or even intercepted by anyone in the vicinity.

A proprietary option is offered by some manufacturers to provide document security. Public access to a received document can be restricted by using memory models with a confidential mailbox feature. The received document is stored in memory and can be printed out only after a PIN number is entered. A few models also incorporate encryption devices at both the transmitter and receiver, which scramble the information and require the correct PIN number to be entered by the recipient to unscramble it.

The use of additional hardware is also an option. PC-fax cards allow information to be exchanged between the facsimile machine and a personal computer. A document prepared on a PC can be transmitted via the fax over the telephone network to a similar PC-fax combination. The document is received straight to the hard disk of the recipient's PC and can be printed out or viewed on screen later. Alternatively, the user may opt for a personal fax – a machine small enough, in theory, to fit unobtrusively on a desk.

> 7. *A record of the transaction is kept by the originator, including the date and time of submission together with the identity of the recipient.*

The CCITT recommendations do not define a service to provide this facility. However, most machines produce local journals which produce for each document a printout displaying the date and time a document was sent as well as the originator's and recipient's ID. However, for reasons indicated above, the called number in the log may not necessarily be the number to which the fax was actually delivered.

As a machine option on virtually all models, a mark is put on each page of the original document as an indicator to confirm it has been faxed.

> 8. *Validation of the originator.*

The CCITT recommendations do not define a service to provide this facility and there are no standard options to support it either.

As an indirect solution to the problem a proprietary option provided on some memory fax machines allows receipt only from authorized transmitters.

> 9. *A record of the transaction is kept by the recipient including the date and time of delivery and the identity of the originator.*

The CCITT recommendations do not define a service to provide this facility. As stated under heading 7, most machines produce local journals which, for each document, produce a printout which includes the date and time received as well as the originator's and recipient's ID.

For large organizations, the lack of any central journal can be overcome with the use of a faxswitch which acts as a central node to a number of local machines. All incoming documents are received by the faxswitch which gives each a unique identity with date and time of reception. The document is then passed to the machine nearest the recipient.

> 10. *The ability to edit a received document together with a means for identifying whether such editing has been performed.*

Since the output of a facsimile machine is hard copy, post-receipt editing is not possible. Long term, the hybrid technology of PC-fax offers the ability to edit faxed documents. However, at present the character recognition software, which is required to convert the encrypted light/dark code that the originator's fax machine produces to ASCII text which the recipient's PC can manipulate, is still in its infancy.

Identifying whether such editing has been performed is therefore a matter of detecting fraudulent modifications to paper documents.

X.400

The X.400 recommendations describe the technical details of a Message Handling System which can broadly be split into two parts:

The *Message Transfer Service*, which describes the technical details of a network of store and forward message exchanges. The exchanges are called *Message Transfer Agents* (MTAs). The MTAs support message transfer in an application independent manner.

The *User Service*, as the name suggests, provides the actual functionality to meet a specific user application. There can in theory be a number of User Services, each using the Message Transfer Service to achieve interconnection between originator and recipient. However, there has been only one User Service defined so far, the *Inter Personal Messaging Service* (IPMS). The IPMS is effectively the X.400 version of electronic mail.

Equipment which users actually interface with are classed as User Agents (UAs). The originator prepares messages with the assistance of the local UA, which then submits the message to its local MTA. Operating together, the MTAs in the network relay the message and deliver it to the recipient UA which then makes the message available to the recipient. Functions performed solely by the UA and not standardized as part of the Message Handling Service are classed as local functions.

So, how well does the IPMS measure up to our user requirements?

1. *The functions of the transmitting equipment should make transmission quick and straightforward for the originator.*

The way in which users interface with their equipment to prepare and send messages is defined as a local matter in the X.400 recommendations. The ease of use will therefore be a proprietary matter, though as with existing electronic mail services, a degree of computer literacy is required.

The method of addressing the intended recipient is simplified by the use of the directory services defined in the CCITT X.500 recommendations. The service relates names and aliases to unambiguous names and specific network addresses. The originator need only know the name of the recipient. The equipment will then automatically access the local directory, look up the addressing information, and insert it where appropriate.

2. *The messaging service should give access to as large a population of users as possible.*

Since the X.400 standards are relatively new, usage is low at present (1991).

British Telecom's X.400 service has currently about forty users, the bulk of which are computer manufacturers and software houses. It is estimated that it will be three to seven years, i.e. mid to late 1990s, before the number of users increases sufficiently to make X.400 commercially viable as a public service for most organizations. The potential of X.400 has been well documented, however. The market research company Ovum estimates that 150,000 computers and 500,000 PCs will be using X.400 by the end of 1994.

> 3. *Validation that the document has been delivered to the correct destination(s).*

The CCITT recommendations define Delivery Notification as an optional service element. Optional services may be selected by the user on a per-message basis or for a given period of time. It enables the originator to request that an explicit notification be returned when the document has been successfully delivered to the recipient's machine. The originator will automatically be notified if the document cannot be delivered, together with the reason why the message was not delivered.

X.400 is part of the seven layer Open Systems Interconnection model. Each layer of the model provides a service to the layer above whilst maintaining a relationship with the same layer in the system it is communicating with. X.400 protocols reside in the top two layers of the model. Any X.400 implementation will encompass the lower levels of the OSI model including the routing and addressing protocols contained in the third, or network, layer. These protocols ensure that the correct connection has been established before message transfer can take place.

> 4. *Validation that the intended recipient has taken receipt of the document.*

The CCITT recommendations define Receipt Notification as an optional service element. This enables the originator to request to be notified of the receipt by the recipient of the document. The originator can also request to be notified if the document was not received by the intended recipient.

> 5. *Error detection and correction.*

As stated above, an X.400 implementation encompasses the lower levels of the OSI model. This will include the error detection and correction protocols contained in the second, or data link layer.

> 6. *Only the intended recipient has access to the received document.*

Each user is in effect allocated an electronic "mailbox" which is protected by a password and stores incoming messages, even if the user's equipment is turned off, until they can be read.

The directory service provides further security controls, by preventing the unauthorized from using the system, and maintaining a log of the authorized users.

7. *A record of the transaction is kept by the originator, including the date and time of submission together with the identity of the recipient.*

The CCITT recommendations define Submission Time Stamp Indication as a basic service element. This enables the MTS to indicate to both the originating and recipient UA the date and time at which the message was submitted.

The X.400 1984 standards do not, however, include provision for a log or journal in which a record of transactions is kept by the originator. Such a service may be provided as a local function. If it is not, all evidence of the transaction will be lost if the originator decides to delete the document. The consequent security implications of this lack of traceability were addressed by the newer X.400 1988 standards. The enhancements incorporated in this version provide for non-repudiation of both submission and origin. The former provides proof that the message was submitted, the latter ensures that the originator cannot deny sending the message. Owing to the inevitable industry lag behind the standards-making bodies, X.400 1988 implementations are only now beginning to reach the market.

8. *Validation of the originator.*

The CCITT recommendations define Originator Indication as an optional service element. This allows the identity of the originator to be transmitted to the recipient as an encrypted electronic signature to prove that the stated origin of the message is genuine.

9. *A record of the transaction is kept by the recipient including the date and time of delivery and the identity of the originator.*

As stated above, the X.400 1984 standards do not include provision for a log or journal in which a record of transactions is kept, although such a service may be provided as a local function. The newer X.400 1988 recommendations offer non-repudiation of delivery as a service to ensure that the recipient cannot deny receiving a message.

10. *The ability to edit a received document together with a means for identifying whether such editing has been performed.*

The X.400 recommendations are concerned purely with message delivery. What the recipient decides to do with a received document is therefore considered a local matter. Consequently the X.400 standards do not identify if a document has undergone any post receipt editing. The only way of detecting whether a received document has been edited is likely to be the change of time and date received indicators.

A summary of the services offered by both facsimile transmission and an X.400 compliant product are shown in Table 5.1.

Table 5.1

Service	Facsimile	IPMS
General		
1 local functions of equipment	simple to operate	computer literacy required
2 User population	large	small at present
Originator information		
3 Validation of delivery	standard option	supported
4 Validation of receipt	not supported	supported
Originator services		
5 Error detection and correction	proprietary option	supported
6 Confidentiality	proprietary option	supported
7 Record of transaction	standard option	local function
Recipient information		
8 Validation of originator	not supported	supported
Recipient services		
9 Record of transaction	standard option	local function
10 Post receipt editing	not supported	local function

X.400 as a universal interconnection medium

An X.400 message is carried within an "envelope". The envelope contains all the information required by the MTAs to deliver the message. Since the MTAs do not "open" the envelope, the type of information contained within it is not important to the MTS. The recommendations recognize nine different types of information including standard IA5 text and Group 3 and 4 fax. A facsimile machine can thus be a UA, making it possible therefore to send a document from facsimile machine to facsimile machine or terminal to terminal over the same network.

X.400 goes further, however, by offering the ability to "convert" information types. Just like a translator who converts the language of the speaker to one which the listener can understand even though both speaker and listener already use the common mechanisms of speech to communicate, so X.400 converts the information type of the originator's UA to one which the recipient's can understand even though both already use a common network. This ability to act as an interconnection medium between various types of equipment and services is one of the major applications of an X.400 messaging system.

In practice the technology to perform conversion of information type, together with the applicable CCITT recommendations, are not mature enough for widespread implementation. This is especially true for text and fax due to the inherent difference in the nature of the two systems.

It is recommendation X.408 that specifies the algorithms which the MTS uses when converting between different types of encoded information. The conversion from fax to text is classed as "impractical". The imprecise nature of handwriting and current state of character recognition software rules out messaging in this category for the foreseeable future. The conversion from text to fax is classed in X.408 as "possible without loss of information". However, the subject is later classified as a "subsection for further study". Although technically possible therefore, the standards have yet to reach maturity.

Legal aspects

For documents received via messaging systems, only those sent by the postal service have legal status in the UK, where proof of sending is proof of delivery. Amongst electronic messaging systems, telex has some legal validity, although this is based on case law, not statute. The reason for telex's position lies in the exchange of "answer backs". These provide the originator with a printout of the recipient's telex code both before and after transmission, as an assurance that the document has been delivered to the correct place. An exchange of telex is therefore regarded as a de facto contract.

Not surprisingly, neither facsimile nor X.400 has the legal validity of telex. As previously stated, the current generation of fax machines can corrupt and lose sections of text or deliver the entire document to the wrong place without the originator ever knowing; whereas the recipient of a document sent by an X.400 1984 implementation can deliberately alter or delete it without trace.

If legal validity is required, a possible solution is the path taken by some Electronic Data Interchange (EDI) users. EDI is the automatic transfer of commercial information from one application to another within business communities and between trading partners. As has been the case, two parties who regularly transfer information may draw up a legal agreement stating that information passed between them via EDI has legal validity.

Conclusion

Organizations require confirmed, secure person-to-person messaging as part of the proper control of their business. If facsimile is going to measure up to the services incorporated in the X.400 standards the industry and its users should be pressing towards the standardization of facilities which will meet the user need for integrity in document transmission. Alternatively, organizations seeking integrity should press forward with electronic office implementation using the X.400 standard.

Given that much material will continue to be in image or paper source, organizations should also give thought to the use of X.400 as an envelope for facsimile.

Acknowledgements

The following sources were used in the preparation of this paper and are gratefully acknowledged: [BFICC 1989, Chilton and Bird 1988, Costello 1989, Day 1989, King 1989]

We have come a long way in data interchange from the days when ASCII was all there was. A long way, certainly, in terms of need; less so, perhaps, in actuality. Many of the needed standards are there, in some form, but in 1992 we are still well short of the universal acceptability which would mean that we could take it for granted that interchange will be trouble-free. There still needs to be the pressures to achieve that. Users, especially corporate users, can help, by exerting market pressures, but to achieve the aim of universality, government pressures, preferably by many governments acting in concert, will be needed. In Europe, the introduction of the Single Market by the European Community at the end of 1992 will boost EDI, while in the USA the CALS (Computer-aided Acquisition and Logistic Support) strategy of the Department of Defense (see [Smith 1990]) will provide a boost in the SGML/ODA area. The question is, will such pressures be enough to ensure that users will not, in the 21st century, still be forced too often to fall back on ASC'I?

Nor has the story of data interchange ended. Further needs are emerging in the 1990s, in the field of digital multimedia, where the user need for effective standards, universally implemented, is if anything even greater. This need has begun to be recognized. Space precludes extended coverage here, but discussion of the issues can be found in [Fox 1991] and [Newcomb, Kipp and Newcomb 1991].

From data, we now turn to what controls the processing of data: software.

References

Standards and standards body documents

CCITT T.4 Recommendations (1988) Standardization of group 3 facsimile apparatus for document transmission

CCITT X.400 Recommendations (1988) Message handling system and service overview

CCITT X.408 Recommendations (1988) Message handling systems: encoded information type conversion rules

ECMA 94/1:1986 8-bit single-byte coded graphic character sets – Latin alphabets no. 1 to no. 4, 2nd edn.

ISO 646:1983 7-bit coded character set for information interchange, 2nd edn. (3rd edn. ISO/IEC 646:1992)

ISO 2014:1976 (replaced by ISO 8601:1988)

ISO 2022:1986 ISO 7-bit and 8-bit coded character sets – coded extension techniques, 3rd edn.

ISO 2375:1985 Procedure for registration of escape sequences, 3rd edn.

ISO 3307:1975 (replaced by ISO 8601:1988)

ISO 4031:1978 (replaced by ISO 8601:1988)

ISO 4873:1986 ISO 8-bit structure and rules for implementation, 2nd edn. (3rd edn. ISO/IEC 4873:1992)

ISO 6429:1988 Specification for control functions for ISO 7-bit and 8-bit character sets

ISO 6937:1991 Coded character sets for text communication

ISO 7372:1986 Trade data elements dictionary

ISO 7498:1984 Open Systems Interconnection – basic reference model

ISO 8601:1988 Representation of dates and times

ISO 8613:1989 Office Document Architecture (ODA) and interchange format

ISO 8824:1990 Specification of Abstract Syntax Notation (ASN.1), 2nd edn.

ISO 8825:1990 Specification of basic encoding rules for Abstract Syntax Notation (ASN.1), 2nd edn.

ISO 8859:1985 8-bit single-byte coded graphic character sets (some parts published in 1987 and 1988)

ISO 8879:1986 Standard Generalized Markup Language (SGML)

ISO 9735:1988 Electronic data interchange for administration, commerce and transport (EDIFACT) – application level syntax rules (amended and reprinted 1990)

ISO/IEC 10021:1990 Message-oriented text interchange system (MOTIS)

ISO/IEC 10367:1991 Supplemental coded character sets

ISO/IEC 10568:1991 Control functions for text communication

ISO/IEC DIS 10179 (1991) Document Style Semantics and Specification Language (DSSSL)

ISO/IEC DIS 10646 (1991) Multiple octet coded character set

Other references

[André et al. 1989] ANDRE, J., FURUTA, R. and QUINT, V., Structured documents, Cambridge University Press, Cambridge

[Barron 1989] BARRON, D., Why use SGML?, *Electronic Publishing – Origination, Dissemination, and Design*, Vol 2, No 1, pp 3-24

[Berge 1991] BERGE, J., The EDIFACT standard, National Computing Centre, Manchester, and Blackwell, Oxford

[BFICC 1989] Fax Information Pack, British Facsimile Industry Consultative Committee

[Blyth, Choi and Jiang 1984] BLYTH, D., CHOI, C.H. and JIANG, Y.J., An approach to document interchange, National Computing Centre, Manchester

[Brown 1989] BROWN, H., Standards for structured documents, *Computer Journal*, Vol 32, No 6, pp 505-514

[CCSDS 1988] Standard formatted data units – structure and construction rules, edited by Consultative Committee for Space Data Systems, Blue Book CCSDS 620.0-B-1

[Chilton and Bird 1988] CHILTON, P. and BIRD, J., Text communication – the choice, NCC Publications, Manchester

[Cole and Brown 1989] COLE, F.C. and BROWN, H., ODA modifications/extensions, version 3, University of Kent, Canterbury

[Cole and Brown 1991] COLE, F.C. and BROWN, H., ODA extensions for quality and flexibility, *Computer Networks and ISDN Systems*, Vol 21, pp 221-230

[Costello 1989] COSTELLO, J., Incorporating faxes, *Communications*, August 1989

[Day 1989] DAY, M., Security: why fax lags behind telex, *Communicate*, September 1989

[DEC 1989] Guide to VAX Notes, DEC manual AA-GH98B-TE, Digital Equipment Corporation, Maynard, Massachusetts

[Emmelhainz 1990] EMMELHAINZ, M.A., Electronic data interchange: a total management guide, Van Nostrand Reinhold, New York

[Farrés 1992] FARRÉS, J., Classifying electronic data interchanges, *Computer Standards and Interfaces*, Vol 14, No 1, pp 13-21

[Fox 1991] FOX, E.A. (guest editor), special issue on digital multimedia systems, *Communications of the ACM*, Vol 34, No 4

[Goldfarb 1990] GOLDFARB, C.F., The SGML handbook, Oxford University Press, Oxford

[van Herwijnen 1990] van HERWIJNEN, E., Practical SGML, Kluwer Academic Publishers, Dordrecht, Netherlands

[Hill 1990] HILL, R., EDI and X.400 using Pedi, Technology Appraisals, Isleworth, Middlesex

[Hypertext 1987] *Hypertext 87*, Chapel Hill, North Carolina

[IBM 1989] Generalized Markup Language Starter Set user's guide, IBM Manual SH20-9186-06, International Business Machines Corporation

[King 1989] KING, W., What new technologies will facsimile embrace?, *The Office*, April 1989

[Knuth 1986] KNUTH, D., The TeXbook, Addison-Wesley, Reading, Massachusetts

[Macchi, Guilbert *et al.* 1985] MACCHI, C., GUILBERT J.F. and 17 co-authors, Tele-informatics, Elsevier Scientific Publications, Amsterdam

[Newcomb, Kipp and Newcomb 1991] NEWCOMB, S.R., KIPP, N.A., and NEWCOMB, V.T., The "Hy-Time" hypermedia/time-based document structuring language, *Communications of the ACM*, Vol 34, No 11, pp 67-83

[Smith 1990] *see general bibliography*

[SITPRO 1990] The EDIFACT service, edited by Simpler Trade Procedures Board

[Unicode 1990] UNICODE, *version 1.0*, December 1990, Unicode Inc.

[van Wingen 1990] van Wingen, J.W., Networks and coded character sets, *Computer Networks and ISDN Systems*, Vol 19, pp 275-284

6

User needs in software standards

Of all IT areas, software is perhaps the most complex as far as standardization is concerned. A short general overview of standards in or of relevance to the software area can be found in [Hall and Resnick 1991], but in the space available here it will not be possible to cover all parts in depth. It will mainly be a matter of concentrating on general principles, and using specific kinds of software as illustrations of those principles. We begin this section, therefore, with a contribution by **Brian Meek** on the problems which the nature of software presents as far as standardization is concerned. It is based on a presentation given to the SoftProd 89 seminar at Tampere, Finland in October 1989, and was published in its present form the following year [Meek 1990d].

Problems of software standardization

While all standardization efforts are likely to encounter problems, software standardization faces particular problems because of the abstract and flexible nature of software. This has a number of consequences, including pressures to include options, and difficulty in finding a stable foundation on which to begin standardization. In the case of software, stability may have to come from the establishment of standards, rather than the standards coming from the technology achieving stability.

A later paper will discuss the possible future of software standardization, in the light of the problems described here *[see Section 10 – Eds]*.

Approach

Though this paper is concerned with problems of software standardization, there are many problems that are common to all kinds of standardization – political, economic, and human problems. These will be dealt with first.

Political problems

Political problems can occur especially internationally, where one country perceives that its interest is best served by adopting a particular form of standard from a selection of possible standards, e.g. because this is believed to give that country a technical lead over others. Other countries oppose because they have a similar perception. Such attitudes ignore the fact that agreeing a worldwide standard generally benefits everyone, but though the fears on which such attitudes are based may be imaginary, the problems are real enough. They arise because of the occupational hazard of politicians (and others) that they too often think in terms only of short-term tactical advantage.

The problems get worse when national pride and "loss of face" enter the argument as well.

Economic problems

Economic problems tend to arise at the supplier level though they can arise at the customer level as well. They mainly relate to the cost of conversion to making or using products which conform to the standard, though in some areas, including IT, the cost of deciding on what the standard should be can become a factor. Again the problems can mostly be traced to short-term attitudes among those who control industry (whether privately or publicly owned) with sometimes an element of "company prestige" corresponding to "national pride" in the case of political problems.

The problems caused by short-term attitudes have come up both in this subsection and the preceding one. How to deal with such attitudes is an issue discussed in another paper [Meek 1990c] [see Section 10 – Eds].

Human problems

Human problems arise when people involved in standardization have a personal involvement in the issues. This can be observed in the attachment that some people have to particular programming languages, or a liking for a particular word processing package or a particular style of user interface. Whether a user thinks a system is user-friendly often depends as much on the user as on the system. This can make it difficult to achieve consensus. The examples cited have come from IT but can be expected to occur generally.

Problems particular to IT

This paper therefore does not spend much further time on problems such as that, which are inherent in all standardization, except where they are particularly acute in the case of software. IT standardization generally (hardware, communications etc. as well as software) share particular problems, some of them of the general kind but especially acute – mainly because of the high economic and political importance of IT – and others because of the all-pervasive and highly complex and interconnected nature of the field. Though vigorously denied by some, there is a widespread feeling that existing standards-making machinery is inadequate to cope with standards of such complexity. As far as software is concerned such problems are even greater than for other aspects of IT, because of its adaptability and expandability, which is the next question for discussion.

Soft, not hard

The special problems of software standardization stem from the very fact that it is soft and not hard. Software standards have to deal with abstract rather than concrete entities (though some make matters worse for themselves by muddling up abstractions and realizations on actual hardware). Possibilities are infinitely variable, limited only by the range of inventiveness of those concerned. So there are problems of:

> endless variety, difficult to contain and pin down in standardized form;

> abstract nature making incompatibilities less obvious than, say, a plug not fitting a socket;

> flexibility making general agreement on what is "standard practice" very difficult.

Flexibility

The flexibility of software encourages customized solutions and attitudes opposed to the idea of standardization. The apparent freedom from limitations makes it harder for people to accept that some self-discipline is desirable. Arguments against standardization are advanced such as that standards impose constraints when there is no need, that standards inhibit progress, that standards are extremely expensive to develop and implement – all based on the idea that this limits the benefits of adaptability without compensating benefits in return. For example, arguments have been made that there is no need to standardize Fourth Generation Languages because it is so easy to write in them. Similar things were said about Fortran and Cobol in the 1960s. Some of the greatest poetry has been written by poets who voluntarily constrained themselves to a standard form: Shakespeare's sonnets are an example. As for inhibiting progress, good standards actually encourage progress because they reduce the need to think about those areas, and frees energy, effort, resources and inventiveness to concentrate on new things. The best standards are those that are so taken for granted that people are hardly aware of them. (The industry would not exist at all were it not for the firm basis of previous standards on which it depends, and which those who argue against standards take for granted.)

Of course, absence of standards can also be taken for granted. Many people routinely spend time, effort and resources on dealing with incompatibilities, e.g. between word processing systems, that they take for granted though often there is no justification for them.

As for the cost of standardization, it is very expensive, but the cost of lack of standardization is enormous. The difficulty in countering this argument is that the first cost is fairly easy to estimate whereas the second is not. It is hard enough anyway, but the nature of software makes it especially so.

Options

When standardization is started, a new problem appears, though still stemming from the flexibility of software. Where agreement is hard to reach, for any of the general reasons listed earlier, it is easy – dangerously easy – to resolve disputes by inclusion of options. These can be of two kinds – supplier options or user options, and both create problems.

Supplier options

Here the supplier has a choice of paths to follow. Such options are usually included to satisfy vendor vested interests, and undermine the very concept of standards. Where the options are built into the same standard it can mean that two different products both conforming to the same standard are incompatible. Particular forms of the options concept are "levels" (i.e. subsetting or modules) and – even worse – options by omission, by things being left system defined, or system dependent (worse) or not mentioned at all (worst, because it is easy to overlook their absence). In extreme cases there can be more than one standard for the same area.

Of course, compatibility between different options or different standards can be achieved by providing automatic converters, and standards can require their presence (regrettably they do not always do so). However, this adds to the size and complexity and hence the cost of products, and there is a hidden cost in using the converters whenever they are invoked. The cost of lack of standardization is hard to estimate, and tends to be spread thinly over the user community. But it is paid for by the users over and over again. Similarly the costs of bad standards are paid by the users, over and over again – and it does not take many options to make a standard a bad standard.

An analogy from everyday life is the cost of currency conversion when moving from one standard unit of exchange to another on crossing a border. It is not simply the cost of servicing the conversions that needs to be considered – it is the human time and effort spent in having to think about it at all. When national economies were mostly self-contained and foreign travel a rarity, this was not a major problem, but in modern conditions of trade and communications in the developed world it becomes very significant. It has been estimated that the cost to the European Community alone, simply of internal currency conversions, exceeds the cost of the Common Agricultural Policy, by far the most expensive of the Community's programmes. The one cost is highly visible and has given rise to much dissension and concern; the other has long been taken for granted and is only now becoming visible as moves are proposed to do something about it.

The analogy with information technology and software is clear enough, especially since currencies are now essentially abstractions rather than physically existing in lumps of metal. Included in the analogy are the existence of vested interests who make a living, sometimes a very lucrative one, out of lack of standardization, and of course the element of national pride.

User options

On the face of it, user options are better. Any conforming product must offer the choice to the user. However, as with converters, providing the options increases the size, complexity and cost of products. Also, to balance the work improvement when users can adjust the options to their needs, there is cost to set against the benefit, when users need to collaborate. Anyone who has edited a multi-author document, even when the writers are all using the same word processor, will recognize the problems here. Converters may be provided, but however automatic they are, they still add to size, complexity and cost.

However, just as suppliers often seem to have the attitude "a standard is OK provided it is mine", so users, when an attempt is made to reduce options, will say "reducing options is fine provided my preferred options are there". User-selected options are therefore probably unavoidable; the trick is to find the right balance between flexibility and uniformity – and then convince everyone that it *is* the right balance!

There is need for a research programme into IT standardization – which the relevant authorities have partially, though not yet adequately, addressed, a point returned to below – and this is one area that needs it.

Lack of firm foundations

Another aspect of the flexibility of software is that trying to build standards on firm foundations of agreed commonality is almost impossible – to build something that will last, it is necessary to have a base of something solid, not fluid. The term "software engineering" is in common use but objectively has to be seen more as something the industry is working towards, rather than having yet fully achieved.

The word "engineering" implies standards, of various kinds – standards of professionalism, standards of quality, standard practices, the use of standard tools and components. Software engineering is not totally lacking in such standards but has to be recognized as still having some way to go before it can stand comparison with older-established engineering disciplines. In most engineering disciplines the technology stabilizes and then the standards get stabilized too. The abstract and infinitely variable nature of software suggests that it is likely to take a long time to stabilize without the standards developing along with the technology.

This may be regarded as accusing the software engineering industry of being immature, but it surely cannot be expected to be anything else. It is too young. The concern expressed here is not that it is immature but that there is not enough indication that it wishes to become mature – and that applies both to suppliers and to users. A sign of maturity is taking standards seriously, and there is so far insufficient of that.

Another sign of lack of maturity is inability to think clearly about issues and separate out different levels of abstraction. For example, those concerned with looking at datatypes from a language-independent point of view have found that people often find it difficult to distinguish clearly between an abstraction of such a language independent type (such as integer), an instantiation of such a type in a particular language, an implementation of that instantiation in an actual compiler or other language processor, and (most important) the representation of values of the type for purposes of data storage, data transmission, and character-based input/output or literal values referred to in program source text.

Levels of abstraction

It is sufficient for the purpose of this discussion to pursue the argument only for the case of textual characters, without bringing in graphics. Character sets (part, but only part, of "internationalization" of software) have been the subject of much discussion in the late 1980s, and the impression has been left of attempted dialogues between those who think of characters mostly in representation, coding, and display terms, and those that think of them at higher levels of abstraction – though not always the same one. The attempts do not seem yet to have been very successful, because perceptions are at different levels. If people are mixing up different levels then there may be some overlap – which makes matters worse because there is the impression of talking about the same thing, which is actually deceptive.

This question of identifying and separating different levels of abstraction seems to me to be crucial to many of the problems of software standardization. The OSI reference model built an edifice of seven layers, for intercommunication purposes, but the distinction which this paper is making is between different levels of abstraction all existing mostly at the application level. One problem to be faced is that existing software standards (such as for programming languages) tend to incorporate different levels of abstraction, sometimes without clearly distinguishing them. This is particularly true of character sets and data though it occurs with other data as well.

The conclusion is that there is need for research to identify clearly different levels of abstraction in terms of what standards should cover – to do for software what the OSI model did for interconnection. In a way, ISO/IEC JTC1 TSG-1, the ISO study group on interfaces for application portability, and some of the working groups of some JTC1 committees could be regarded as looking at parts of this, but is not realistic to assume that an ISO committee is an adequate, let alone very effective, research mechanism, despite the excellent work that has undoubtedly been done. Much preferable would be a properly funded research project, though retaining the ISO committee as a useful forum for the exchange of ideas and as a means of monitoring the progress of the research.

Aims

Turning finally to what the aims of software standardization should be, as remarked earlier the best standards are the ones which can be so taken for granted that people do not have to think about them. People sometimes complain that all airports worldwide, at least the international ones, are much the same. That, surely, is all to the good: it saves time and relieves worry for millions of air travellers every year. (Incidentally, like all good "standards" there is ample scope for imaginative realization, which is one reason why some airports are so much better than others.)

Staying with the theme of travel, a traveller can take a camera round the world without even having to think about whether it will be possible to buy a film for it. Similarly, an audio cassette tape can be taken, in the sure knowledge that there will be no trouble in playing it. Not all standards are that good – it is not possible to take a cassette tape recorder and be sure that it can be plugged in and used – unless of course it is a battery recorder.

A traveller taking a floppy disk, however, containing something as simple as a text document, cannot be sure that there will be a machine that can physically accept the disk at all, or if it does that it can actually read it, and that if it does that the text will appear ungarbled, and that if it does the available word processing package will accept it, and that if it does there will be no need for a major re-edit – using, of course, an unfamiliar set of commands.

Millions of hours of people's time are wasted each year because of such problems. The aim should surely be to ensure that a time will come when the following might be possible. Dr Smith is sitting at a personal computer, working on a document or a spreadsheet or a graphical image, and the telephone rings. "Drop everything, pack a suitcase for a few days, you have to go to (somewhere – Tampere, Adelaide, Montevideo, Vladivostok or wherever), your flight is booked, there will be a car to collect you in half an hour." So Dr Smith saves the piece of work she was doing onto a floppy disk, and puts it in the suitcase along with the other things (including a camera, of course!). At the destination, Tampere or Adelaide or wherever, she deals with whatever it was the panic was about, and when she finally has some time for herself before she has to leave for home, she borrows a workstation – of completely unfamiliar make. She switches it on, puts in the floppy disk, calls up the file, and carries on the piece of work she had been doing. The borrowed system has recognized what she had been doing, and her preferred user interface and set of defaults, and it has provided them – without her having to think about it.

This may sound Utopian, but there is nothing in what has been described that is not achievable now with current technology. The problem is not the technology, but persuading all concerned that it is a worthwhile goal, and that universal standards raise the level of the market for everyone, and releases large amounts of time and effort, on the part of users and suppliers alike, for more productive purposes than having to cope with incompatibilities.

With that as background, we can now proceed to consider user needs in particular areas, while recognizing that the field is too vast to cover completely, as already indicated. The instances discussed in the remainder of this section should be regarded as selected illustrations – the selection being primarily on the basis of what was readily available. Very often, the examples of user need in one application area can be found to be relevant in other areas, when translated directly or by analogy into the terms of those other environments.

Programming languages

By a good margin, the first software standards were standards for programming languages. Programming languages, at least of a primitive kind, have existed since the earliest days of computing, were the first kind of software to be developed into anything resembling modern form, and have by far the longest track record in terms of standardization. They therefore provide the largest source of experience of how well or badly user needs are served by software standards. By the same token they are a good source of evidence of attempts to see that user needs are met.

A significant amount of material in [Hill and Meek 1980], especially in the "issues" discussion in Part 2, and in the later update of that Part 2 [C&S 1983], relates to user needs and the shortcomings of the language standards of the time in that respect. The matter was certainly a live one in language standards circles in the 1980s, and remains so into the 1990s. Probably the earliest comprehensive attempt to provide a framework for users to specify their requirements was BS 6832:1987 in the UK, entitled *Method of specifying requirements for Fortran processors*. It was an example of a secondary standard, i.e. one based on an existing standard (in this case the then Fortran standard, informally known as "Fortran 77") and concerned with additional properties required of conforming products. Furthermore it was an indirect standard, in that it did not of itself place additional conformity requirements on such products.

BS 6832 appeared so long after most Fortran 77 implementations were designed and built that its direct influence was limited, and furthermore it was tied to one particular language. Nevertheless it did point the way to the kind of thing that was possible. The user concerns remained, for all languages. The next and most tangible outcome of these concerns was the establishment of an ISO working group and its subsequent production of an ISO technical report TR 10176:1991, called *Guidelines for the preparation of programming language standards*. While by no means confined to specifying user requirements, it certainly covered that aspect, as well as others. Below is reproduced a summary of the main headings and subheadings in the section of the report which lists the guidelines themselves.

Guidelines for the preparation of programming language standards

Guidelines for the form and content of standards *(The general framework; the use of character sets; error detection requirements; exception detection requirements; static detection of exceptions; recovery from non-fatal errors and exceptions; requirements on user documentation; provision of processor options; processor-defined limits.)*

Guidelines on presentation *(Terminology; presentation of source programs)*

Guidelines on processor dependence *(Completeness of definition; optional language features; management of optional language features; syntax and semantics of optional language features; predefined keywords and identifiers; definition of optional features; processor dependence in numerical processing.)*

Guidelines on conformity requirements

Guidelines on strategy *(Secondary standards; incremental standards; consistency of use of guidelines; revision compatibility.)*

Guidelines on cross-language issues *(Binding to functional standards; facilitation of binding; conformity with multi-level functional standards; mixed language programming; common elements; use of data dictionaries.)*

It can be seen that some of the guidelines definitely address common user concerns, for example error and exception detection requirements, and user documentation. There is some further discussion later in this section on the aspect of this report dealing with processor options, in relation to the question of ease of use.

Some extracts from the introduction to the Technical Report are worth quoting here:

Over the last 20 years and more (1966-1989), standards have been produced for a number of computer programming languages. Each has dealt with its own language in isolation, although to some extent the drafting committees have become more expert by learning from both the successes and the mistakes of their predecessors.

The time is now right to put together some of the experience that has been gained, in a set of guidelines, designed to ease the task of drafting committees of programming language standards....

While each language, taken as a whole, is unique, there are many individual features that are common to many, or even to most of them. While standardization should not inhibit such diversity as is essential, both in the languages and in the form of their standards, unnecessary diversity is better avoided. Unnecessary diversity leads to unnecessary confusion, unnecessary retraining, unnecessary conversion or redevelopment, and unnecessary costs. The aim of the guidelines is therefore to help to achieve standardization across languages and across their standards.

The existence of a guideline will often save a drafting committee from much discussion of detailed points all of which have been discussed previously for other languages.

Furthermore the avoidance of needless diversity between languages makes it easier for programmers to switch between one and another.

A note about diversity, which follows immediately, is also worth quoting in full, not least because of its wider applicability.

Diversity is a major problem because it uses up time and resources better devoted to the essential part, both by makers and users of standards. Building a language standard is very expensive in resources and far too much time and effort goes into "reinventing the wheel" and trying to solve again, from the beginning, the same problems that other committees have faced.

However, a software writer faced with the task of building (say) a support environment (operating system facilities, utilities, etc.) for a number of different language processors is also faced with many problems from the eventual standards. Quite apart from the essential differences between the languages, there are to begin with the variations of layout, arrangement, terminology, metalanguages, etc. Much worse, there are the variations between requirements of basically the same kind, some substantial, some slight, some subtle – compounded by needless variations in the way they are specified. This represents an immense extra burden – as does the duplication in providing different support tools for different languages performing basically the same task.

Quite a few of these remarks can be applied to other kinds of software than just programming languages.

These were not the only technical reports providing guidelines which were produced during this period: another working group produced ISO/IEC TR 10034:1990 which provided guidelines for the preparation of conformity clauses in programming language standards, and ISO TR 9547:1988, which laid down guidelines for the development and acceptability of test methods for language processors, while yet another worked on a fourth technical report providing guidelines for specifying bindings of language-independent functional standards (e.g. for graphics, or databases), which was completed in 1991 and due for final approval and publication as ISO/IEC TR 10182 a year or two later.

Before we leave the question of languages altogether, a little needs to be said about an often overlooked user need, for the standards to be specified as far as possible by the use of formal methods of definition. The following notes were prepared by **Brian Meek**, attributed because they contain personal views as well as background information.

Formal definitions

At first sight, it seems to be a contradiction in terms that it should be a user need for formal definitions to be used in standards. How are users to know if a standard meets their requirements, if it is expressed in some arcane formal notation? In the languages field it is often argued that the standards have to be "readable" by the ordinary programmer.

This overlooks several significant factors. One is that language standards are somewhat unusual in that a significant proportion of programmers are occasional programmers and not professionally trained and employed to write programs; they write programs to help them in their main work, where software to do what they need is not available off the shelf – typically though not exclusively in research environments. The vast majority of standards, however, are for professionals: such arguments do not apply to them.

Furthermore, programming languages themselves are tools for writing formal definitions. The idea that a non-professional programmer capable of mastering any of the standardized languages is not capable of learning and understanding the far simpler metalanguages for the definition of language syntax is self-evidently ludicrous – yet advanced it is, as an argument for informal, natural language definitions. Even when a formal metalanguage is used, it may not be used for all of the syntax, just for a framework, with other rules, often qualifications or constraints, added in ordinary text. (The use of such qualifications also helps to undermine the value of the formal definitions that *are* there, of course!)

One-level (BNF or Backus style) metalanguages, and two-level (van Wijngaarden style) metalanguages capable of expressing context-dependent and "infinite productions" grammars, have been known since the 1960s. Their universal use ought by now to be taken for granted – and a standard exists, at least in the UK, BS 6154:1981. Formal definitions of semantics are a different matter, since the problem of expressing semantics is of a quite different order of complexity; but even there, the Vienna Definition Method (VDM) also dates back to the same period, yet only in the late 1980s gained enough (and in some quarters reluctant) acceptance to allow work to begin on a standard. After all, if formal definitions even of syntax met with so much resistance, it is hardly surprising that work on formal semantics languished in the standards wilderness for so many years.

VDM did indeed gain a reputation for obscurity, which was only partly a consequence of the difficulty of defining semantics, the reason being that it tended to be used by people with a strong mathematical background who hence made plentiful use of mathematical symbolism. However, with all formal languages, it is relatively straightforward to generate more "readable" if less concise versions of definitions, or to generate diagrammatic representations, for example with production trees or "railroad charts" for syntax. This can be a valuable aid both for explanation to the uninitiated and for checking that the formal definition is as intended. One does not need the manifold examples of bugs in programs to be aware that a precise definition of something not intended is no better than an imprecise definition of what *was* intended!

Nevertheless, precise, formal definitions, however obscure they may appear, at least have the advantage that analytical tools can be used to check them for correctness, consistency and completeness. Which brings us to why it is that use of formal definitions is an important user requirement: it gives far greater assurance that the standard is well-defined. The problem with the use of natural language is that it is prone to ambiguity, and attempting to render it unambiguous can tend to make it just as unreadable, in a different way. That is why there is a whole profession dedicated to arguing the correct interpretation of legal documents.

Another, and perhaps even more important, benefit to users of formal definitions is that they can be used as a basis of testing the conformity of products – see for example [Appelt 1988, Appelt *et al.* 1990]. The greater rigour of such conformity testing makes the price of the use of formal methods well worth paying.

During the 1980s formal methods, usually termed, rather sloppily, "formal description techniques" or FDTs, became more widespread, for example for the definition of communications protocols for OSI as well as the ODA work just cited. However, the history of programming languages began to repeat itself, with the growth of alternative (including *standardized* alternative) notations – another instance of one part of the standards world not learning from the experiences of the past in other areas.

JTC1 did lay down rules to limit proliferation of FDTs, but in the process also met some resistance, of the kind already known in the languages field, to being *required* to use formal methods. Hence the guidelines for FDTs, as they appeared in the late 1980s, were decidedly on the timid side. Indeed, it was a developing art, but so is IT itself and this had not noticeably inhibited people from using what technology was available. There were certainly indications that some IT standardizers found the precision and certainty of formal definitions rather uncomfortable, and felt happier sheltering behind a protective shield of natural language descriptions potentially "open to interpretation".

In the long run, the use of formal methods in IT standards is bound to increase, as the technology matures and standards-making becomes more a matter of routine professionalism, with less pioneering improvization. Users can only benefit from the improvement in the quality of standards that will result.

Operating systems

During the 1960s, computers became more powerful and more complex, and other software began to join programming languages as important software features of systems: first operating systems, then database management systems, graphics and an ever-increasing range of other products and tools. Language implementations no longer ran on the raw hardware, they ran on what later became termed an operating system "platform" which in turn ran on (and controlled) the hardware platform. For a long time this distinction between platforms was not really recognized, because operating systems were hardware-specific.

During the late 1960s and the 1970s people came increasingly to recognize that standards were about portability of *people* as well as of programs, and that while language standards guaranteed some level of portability of programming skills (despite the still high proportion of aspects left as system-dependent by the standards), skills in the use of operating systems were becoming more and more important, and considerably less portable than the ability to program in Cobol or Fortran despite the existence of common fundamental principles.

The locking of operating systems into the hardware had several consequences. One was that users began to look for means of providing a standard command language, or command and response language, covering the basic operations like reading and writing files, file management, input/output, and so on. Another was that the dropping cost of hardware and the escalating cost of software (especially operating systems as they became more complex with the complexity of the machines), and "unbundling" of hardware and software, meant that the main suppliers had a vested interest in keeping their users "locked in". New systems would now not sell without an operating system to run on it, so with every new hardware platform they were forced also to supply an operating system that would run it. At the very least, they were reluctant to encourage any trends which might favour the development of a non-proprietary standard operating system.

The chequered early history of what became known as OSCRL (Operating System Command and Response Language) can be found in [Dahlstrand 1980] and [Dahlstrand 1984]; it will also be referred to again in Section 7 which follows, on the human-machine interface.

In the 1980s, the change in the climate of opinion resulting from the move towards open systems, the gradual emergence of a viable portable operating system, and sheer user necessity that a solution had to be found, resulted in a move, which became what seemed to be an irresistible tide, in favour of Unix.

That Unix became the pivot around which operating system standards turned has a number of interesting aspects. Originally designed as a tool for professional software developers, in itself and in the forms it usually came, it was hardly the obvious choice for the general run of users. Furthermore, designed for cooperative development by teams of people, in its early forms it emphasized ease of making things generally available, rather than security – hardly a feature likely to commend it in some environments. Much of the rapid spread of the famous Internet worm [ACM 1989] was attributed to its exploiting security weaknesses in various Unix implementations.

Unix would probably have emerged "because it was there", the basis of its portability in its accompanying and also portable language "C", in which it was written, and the possibility of overlaying its "kernel" with a variety of "shells". However, just as with the language Pascal a few years earlier, one factor is likely to have been a delayed effect of its widespread use in universities, especially in the USA.

Niklaus Wirth, the designer of Pascal, had a policy of making the language, and an accompanying compiler written in portable intermediate code, available at low cost to educational institutions. Computer science departments liked both the language and the price compared with the offerings at the time from the major suppliers, and used it in their programming and software engineering courses. A few years later the graduates, some of them "whizzkids" whose expertise was of importance to their companies, got to positions where they were consulted about future developments. Enough of them had a yearning for the Pascal they had been trained on, rather than the older languages in widespread use in industry, and in due course this led to a demand for a formal Pascal standard.

So with the next generation, a few years later. They in their turn had been raised on C and Unix and when they got into positions of influence that is what they asked for. It would be difficult, now, to establish for certain that this happened, either with Pascal or with Unix, on a sufficient scale to have been decisive, but it must have happened in some places some of the time, and it all helped the tide along.

So the history of Unix, and the involvement of Unix users in the move towards the standardization effort based on it, termed "Posix" because of the trademarking of the original name, is worth looking at in more detail. If there is to be anything like a standard operating system widely established in the 1990s – and there are powerful pressures, including from governments, in that direction – Posix is what it will be based on.

The contribution below is by **David Cannon** of Exeter University, UK. It consists of extracts, slightly edited, from a report which was originally prepared for the UK's Joint Network Team (JNT) for Research Councils and Universities, in September 1990. Omitted here are some of the detailed briefing about the various standards projects and committees, and the more extended coverage of the networking aspects which was, of course, what the JNT were particularly interested in.

Posix networking standardization

The IEEE Posix standardization effort has its origins in the work of /usr/group, an American-based organization whose aim is to promote the

Unix operating system. The roots of the Unix system itself go back to the late 1960s, to Bell Labs.

The origins of Unix

Ritchie and Thompson

Ken Thompson and Dennis Ritchie had been involved in the development of the Multics Operating System at Bell Labs, but when Bell pulled out of the project Thompson was left with a desire for a program development environment but nothing other than Fortran batch to fulfil the need.

Thompson decided to resolve his own problem, and thus in 1969 was born the first version of Unix, at Bell Telephone Laboratories, Murray Hill, New Jersey, on an unused DEC PDP-7. This first version was written in B, a derivative of Martin Richard's BCPL.

One of the first aims of Unix was portability, and as it was moved onto a PDP-11, Ritchie took B and refined it into C, porting first the compilers then Unix itself, which was then re-written in C. By 1973 Unix was coded entirely in C and within Bell Labs was running on a number of different machine architectures.

Bell Labs and AT&T's role

Unix went through several internal revisions at Bell before a few copies of Version 4 and then Version 5 were made available outside the company between 1973 and 1975. Version 6 was the first widely available release of Unix to be licensed by Bell in 1976, but American anti-trust regulations made it impossible for the system to be commercially exploited by its owners, and these first licences were mostly to educational institutions for minimal fees, and normally included the Unix source code!

AT&T (American Telephone and Telegraph, Bell Labs parent company) offered the first commercial version of Unix, known as the Programmer's Workbench System (or PWB/Unix) derived from Unix Version 6 in 1977. However, the Unix market did not open up until AT&T loosened its licensing terms in 1979, allowing Unix to be ported to the flood of cheap microcomputers which were beginning to appear. Unix System III was released in 1981, combining PWB/Unix with Bell's Version 7, but US government restrictions prevented this from using then current software encryption technology. After the US courts ordered the break-up of AT&T from the Bell Telephone Operating Companies, AT&T was free to try to recover commercial control of its product, and the means to this end was Unix System V, which through a series of releases from 1983 sought to incorporate most of the enhancements which had appeared in other vendors' Unix products. These features included InterProcess Communication (IPC), Streams (from Bell's Version 8) and the Transport Layer Interface (TLI).

(AT&T later established a subsidiary corporation, Unix System Laboratories, to oversee the development of Unix System V.)

The Berkeley offshoot

The ability from 1976 for educational establishments to take up Unix source licences presented an opportunity that few resisted for long: in-house versions of the system began to multiply as improvements and new features were added. Pre-eminent of these were the University of California at Berkeley versions. Early work here on PDP-11s resulted in the *vi* editor and the Ingres relational database system, together with a new user command interpreter for Unix known as the C-shell. When in 1979 Bell followed Version 7 with Unix 32V for the DEC VAX hardware range, Berkeley immediately took it and added its existing enhancements, plus virtual memory handling, resulting in a version of Unix known as Berkeley 3BSD (Berkeley Software Distribution).

The US Department of Defense soon recognized the worth of a single operating system for its research projects, and funded the establishment of the Computer Systems Research Group (CSRG) at Berkeley to produce further improvements to their version of Unix. 4.1BSD emerged, including job control and network support, and largely replaced Bell's Version 7 on College campuses, then in 1983 was followed by 4.2BSD, which improved the network facilities with Ethernet drivers and TCP/IP protocol support. Many of these enhancements were taken up by other Unix vendors as networking became a prime requirement in purchases of new computer systems.

System V Release 4

In 1990, Unix System V Release 4 became the latest move in AT&T's attempt to recover control of its wayward offspring, in conjunction with a major marketing campaign and the publication of the System V Interface Definition (SVID). The SVID, by way of offering an "industry-standard" specification of the Unix SVR4 system calls, was intended to promote application portability. Unix SVR4 took up many of the best features of other variants of Unix, combining the Network File System (NFS) architecture and the Remote File System (RFS) scheme, and including the Streams communication mechanism, file locking, etc. It also allowed agreement of Application Binary Interface (ABI) environments for the major CPU architectures, such as Intel, Motorola and Sun's SPARC, making "off the shelf" software more viable.

SVR4 conforms to the ANSI C, IEEE P1003.1, Federal Information Processing Standards (FIPS) 151-1 and XPG3 standards.

Over the following five years, AT&T's Unix Software Operation (USO) planned a development path for Unix SVR4 including improved security features (to the US Department of Defense (DoD) Orange Book B2 level) in 1991, multiprocessor support (1992), OSI Network support and distributed multiprocessor support (1993/4).

AT&T's goal of application portability was intended, of course, at making it possible for the majority of Unix applications to run on Unix System V, and therefore to make Unix SVR4 an attractive option to prospective system buyers. AT&T were largely successful in this, and Unix System V became a requirement of a significant proportion of the market.

The IEEE Posix standardization effort

It is immediately obvious from the previous discussion that Unix's aim of portability became a millstone as soon as that aim began to be achieved, and the different versions began to diverge. This trend was recognized in 1980 by a group of Unix vendors and users; they formed /usr/group in America and began the movement to standardize Unix.

/usr/group

/usr/group was founded in 1980 as a non-profit-making trade association dedicated to the promotion of Unix. In 1981 it formed the /usr/group standards committee, which had as its objective "a specification for a portable operating system ... to which a large number of applications could be easily ported". This committee produced the /usr/group standard, which was adopted by the membership in 1984. The standard was based on Unix System III, which was already being overtaken by later versions, but was nonetheless influential, being the basis for the library section of the ANSI/X3.159:1988 *Programming Language C* standard, and formed the first draft of the IEEE P1003.1 group's standard. /usr/group remained active in Unix standardization activities with its technical committees inputting to the IEEE Posix groups. In 1990 /usr/group renamed itself as UniForum.

IEEE involvement: ANSI

The /usr/group standard was timely, but inadequate in a number of ways: by the time it was published AT&T had released System V Release 2, Microsoft's Xenix had appeared, and Berkeley had produced 4.2BSD – the target had moved. Another major inadequacy was that /usr/group was not a recognized standards body, nor was it sponsored by one; its standard was recognized by the Unix market for what it was – a well meant effort by a set of Unix vendors, but without the broad base of support to be a true national or international standard.

In January 1985 IEEE (Institute of Electrical and Electronics Engineers) took up the torch to produce a national standard, using as its first draft the usr/group standard. The IEEE was well-placed for such work, having an appropriate membership structure plus a balloting mechanism acceptable to ANSI, the US National Standards Institute. Once a standard is approved by the IEEE member ballot the document has a direct route to adoption, normally without further balloting or amendment, as a US national standard by ANSI, which as a national body can then forward the work to ISO for consideration as an international standard.

The committee formed by the IEEE and charged with the task of producing the standard was denoted "P1003". It had in its terms of reference the requirement to produce an interface standard, not a Unix standard – in other words to produce a specification which was independent not only of the underlying machine hardware, but also of the base operating system. The work was given the title Posix, for Portable Operating System Interface for Computer Environments, to reflect the intention of offering a uniform environment for application programs. To underline the operating system independent claim for Posix, both DEC with its VAX/VMS system and IBM with OS/2 stated their intention of producing Posix-compliant interfaces.

In order to manage this mammoth task, the IEEE P1003 committee soon identified subsets of its work and devolved these to working groups charged with producing that part of the standard, thus the P1003.1 group produced the System Kernel Interface standard, which was approved by the IEEE for trial use in 1986 and (as amended) as the full use standard in 1988

The Posix family of standards

A wealth of working groups have submitted Project Authorization Requests (PARs) to the IEEE Technical Committee on Operating Systems (TCOS) Sponsor Executive Committee (SEC) since 1985, as more areas have come under scrutiny for standardization within Posix. At first groups were given denotations of the form 1003.nn, reflecting the link with the original P1003, but that was later abandoned when this reflected awareness that standardization efforts were already being made in these areas; rather than duplicate work, the Posix groups have joined, where possible, with other existing groups.

The ISO standardization effort

ISO was first approached by the IEEE in January 1987 with a proposal to move the Posix standardization effort into the international arena.

The evolution of the Posix international standard was entrusted to the WG15 working group of the languages subcommittee SC22, which was formed in 1987 specifically for that task. (The allocation of this work, not strictly language standardization in the conventional sense, reflected the close relationship with language environments, and with C in particular – the responsibility of SC22/WG14 – and later led to an amendment to the scope of SC22 to take this work into account.)

The procedures for the generation of an ISO standard have little regard for the status of documents offered for acceptance, apart from a limited number of cases which are submitted for "fast-tracking", usually of well-established existing standards, of recognized standards bodies, which have for some reason or another not previously achieved international status. This was not appropriate for standards still under development, and in any case it was a mechanism only just being introduced at the time. In proposals not being fast-tracked, ISO distributes the proposed standard to its member countries for comment and ballot, like any other proposal, however close it may be to technical completion.

Given this "fresh look" approach to the source documents, plus the different format conventions between ANSI and ISO documents, and the special requirements of various ISO member countries (e.g. in terms of character sets), it is almost inevitable that the ISO and ANSI standards will tend to diverge during this process. The IEEE P1003 group and the ISO WG15 group are pledged to ensure that any two Posix standards are semantically identical before the final publication of the documents, and the close relationship of the two groups together with a detailed harmonization and synchronization strategy should achieve this.

Structure of the standard

The ISO version of the Posix standard does not retain the original IEEE/ANSI P1003 numbering, and does not completely reflect the P1003 structure either, with many of the P1003 standards, for example 1003.4 (Real Time), being subsumed as addenda to the ISO equivalent of the 1003.1 base standard.

ISO currently (June 1990) expects to produce four separate Posix standards, each with a set of addenda, and having the following correspondence with the IEEE/ANSI standards:

ISO	IEEE	Name
9945-1:	1003.1	(Base Standard)
	1003.4	(Real Time)
	1003.4a	(Threads)
	1003.8	(Transparent File Access)
	1003.12	(Protocol Independent Interface)
	1003.17	(Name Space & Directory Services)
9945-2:	1003.2	(Shell Standard)
	1003.2a	(User Portability Extensions)
9945-3:	1003.7	(Administration Standard)
	1003.15	(Batch Services)
9945-4:		(Language Bindings)
	1003.16	(C Language)
	1003.5	(Ada)
	1003.9	(Fortran)

It will be immediately obvious that there is not a one-to-one relationship between ISO and IEEE/ANSI work items. This is due largely to the nature of the standardization processes within the two bodies; the IEEE identifies an area for consideration and authorizes a New Work Item (NWI) via a PAR. There is then a time-lag while WG15 is approached to request a Division of Work Item (DWI) from SC22 to accommodate the new work.

At the June 1990 meeting of WG15 in Paris a detailed synchronization mechanism was agreed to ensure that ANSI and ISO Posix standards were semantically identical. Key elements are that the chair of the IEEE TCOS SEC has authority to delay steps in the IEEE balloting process, and uses this to force synchronization with the ISO approval process: international comments on the document are fed back into the IEEE balloting process, and the resulting changes are fed into the ISO DP approval process as comments from the US national body (ANSI). Final IEEE approval is delayed until WG15 approves the appropriately revised document for registration as an ISO DIS.

Industry "standards"

While the national and international standards documents have been jumping through these procedural hoops, the user community has seen little progress. What activity there is comes from three vendor groups, each proclaiming the virtues of their own Unix "standard" offering.

X/Open

X/Open was the first vendor group to be established in 1984 by five European computer manufacturers (including ICL, Bull and Siemens) and has subsequently grown to include DEC, AT&T, Unix International and IBM amongst others.

X/Open's aim is to achieve application portability at source code level between the set of Unix-based systems offered by its members, all of whom are pledged to offer the Common Applications Environment (CAE) defined in the X/Open Portability Guide (XPG). The Portability Guide is a published document now in its fourth revision (XPG4, 1990); it is based on the AT&T SVID and conforms to the published parts of the IEEE/ISO Posix standard.

X/Open is a major contributor to many of the IEEE groups developing the Posix standard. However, X/Open is not a standards-setting organization; it is a joint initiative by members of the business community to integrate evolving standards into a common, beneficial and continuing strategy" [X/Open 1989]. This is a bold description of X/Open's approach: use international or national standards where they exist, and industry standards where they don't.

Unix International

Unix International began life as a collaboration between AT&T and Sun Microsystems when Unix SVR4 was being developed in 1987. For a while it operated under the title of the Archer group, but when the OSF was created a name more closely identifiable with the product was adopted, together with the more formal structure of corporate status. By 1990 Unix International (UI) had over 130 member companies, including CDC, Convex Computers, ICL and Santa Cruz Operation (SCO).

Unix International's product is Unix SVR4, and the body responsible for the technical development of Unix SVR4 is the AT&T Unix Software Operation (USO), so while AT&T are seen to have released control of the strategic decisions on the future of Unix, now made in committee by UI members, it still holds a tight grip on the content of the software itself, since the USO has a voice on the UI Steering Committee, advising on the viability of proposed changes.

Unix International's product is defined in the SVID and its future is plotted in the Unix System V Roadmap, in which conformance to the Posix standard is pledged (see the section above on Unix System V Release 4), together with a commitment to OSI support.

OSF

The Open Software Foundation (OSF) was founded in May 1988 when a group of major Unix licensees saw themselves being locked out of the future development of the system by the AT&T/Sun alliance. OSF was originally formed by seven companies including Apollo, DEC and IBM, with the intention of creating a product with components from the membership of OSF. Components are sought via a Request For Technology (RFT) process initiated by the OSF Executive Committee, and a selection made from the responses by a technical working group.

The base kernel module was originally to have been from IBM's Aix system, but either commercial (licence fees to AT&T) or technical (too reliant on IBM's RISC chip) reasons have led to the consideration of the Mach System kernel from Carnegie-Mellon University instead. OSF's first version of their product, OSF/1, was in 1990 yet to be released.

Like X/Open and Unix International, OSF has pledged that its product will be Posix conformant, and given the complex cross-membership of the groups (OSF provided the chair for the Unix International Multiprocessing Special Interest Group (SIG)) and their members' active interest in the Posix groups, this is not surprising.

The differences between the X/Open, Unix International and OSF products lie not in the "cake recipe" – the set of standards being evolved to define the application interfaces to the system, but in the "icing" – the extra features that aim to make one product more attractive or usable than another in certain areas. The most obvious example here is the different Graphical User Interfaces (GUIs) being proposed by the different groups: while all three offer MIT's X-Windows as the low-level management system, OSF has opted for Motif while Unix International is offering Open Look as its GUI.

As a further updating of the involvement in Posix-related activities of X/Open, Unix International (UI) and OSF, up to early 1992, we add a further contribution by **Peter Judge**. The original piece was written for the *Financial Times* [Judge 1991]; a few paragraphs explaining the various formal standards bodies for the benefit of the general reader have been omitted here, but some paragraphs referring to open systems generally have been retained for completeness, despite some overlaps with Section 4. The opportunity has also been taken for some updating.

The standard bearers

The main difference between world politics and the politics of the IT industry is that no-one gets killed in IT. IT standards, like international treaties, do not mean universal agreement, but they go a long way towards it. And, in the IT world, each new agreement is easier, as the standards-makers get closer together.

Just as in world politics, the IT industry is beset by self-seeking organizations, opinionated pressure groups and alliances, and presided over by a United Nations – in this case ISO – which is often powerless to intervene.

Standards have become the most important issue in IT: they are fundamental to open systems, so whoever sets them wields great power. Suppliers have decided to directly influence the standards that concern them, and users are forming groups to ensure their needs are met.

But users and suppliers demand more than basic standards: new areas emerge continually, and the industry needs advice on how to implement the standards. For the most part this comes from those concerned, working directly in consortia.

And that is where the conflict comes. Rival consortia present rival standards, and suppliers' interests are often served first. Standards created in this way, or by single suppliers, are called "de facto". The most important de facto standards in the emerging open systems field are variations on the Unix product from AT&T Unix Systems Laboratories.

The spread of open systems in industry began with industry specific bodies, such as the MAP initiative, which, in 1980, started defining open systems for manufacturing, to encourage suppliers to meet the needs of large users including General Motors.

Now the Government OSI Profiles (UK and US GOSIP, and the European Procurement Handbook for Open Systems, EPHOS) are far more important. With billions of IT spending, Governments can define the predominant implementations of standards. GOSIPs simply take existing OSI standards and refine them to make OSI "profiles". Profiles select from the options within a set of standards. Without profiles, suppliers can make OSI products which are not compatible with each other; when products meet a particular profile, they probably will work together.

MAP is still looked after by a world federation of MAP/TOP User Groups. The UK GOSIP is defined by the CCTA and the US version by the National Institute of Standards and Technology (NIST). ISO has recognized the importance of profiles, setting up a Special Group on Functional Standards (SGFS), whose job is to publish the agreed output of OSI workshops in Europe, Asia and America.

Other groups have appeared, working to make particular standards usable. The Network Management Forum has prompted faster ISO work on network management, while the ODA Consortium hopes to get electronic document standards such as Open Document Architecture (ODA) into the market quicker. The X.400 API Association aims to help suppliers make compatible electronic mail products according to the X.400 recommendations.

But all these deal with communications only. The industry comes closest to spilling blood over portable software. Versions of Unix are available from several suppliers, and at least two main groups are fashioning versions which they hope to establish as market leader.

Unix International is out ahead at the moment, having established the Unix version from AT&T Unix Software Laboratories (USL) in the market. The Open Software Foundation's version, OSF/1, is still not selling in volume to users, but it is included in the Digital/Microsoft/Compaq ACE initiative and the IBM/Apple joint venture.

Meanwhile OSF has established the Motif user interface, and got a good reception for its Distributed Computing Environment (DCE). DCE is actually included in the rival Atlas product from UI.

UI and OSF are not the same kind of body: UI gathers specifications from hardware suppliers to tell USL what products to make; OSF actually makes products, which it then sells to its sponsors, IBM, DEC, Hewlett-Packard and others. The two are actually quite close together, as UI's use of DCE shows. Both of them comply with international standards, including Posix and OSI.

The body which aims to pull the industry together is X/Open. Set up by suppliers, X/Open's goal is to bring together enough standards to cover all the basic functions of an open system, including Posix and OSI. X/Open calls this a common application environment (CAE) and it includes international standards, and de facto standards with wide enough support. X/Open canvasses users, in its Xtra market research, to determine what standards are required, and keeps the balance between supplier groups, such as OSF and UI.

But X/Open could face competition as other groups marshal user interest. The IT directors of several major companies, including Dupont, Eastman Kodak, McDonnell Douglas and American Airlines, meet regularly to discuss ways to influence the industry. Their actions are carried out under the banner Standards and Open Systems (SOS), although they are not a formal group. (SOS members are mainly drawn from an earlier pressure group called the User Alliance for Open Systems, which has gone quiet since its 1990 launch.) SOS has called for a quicker route to acceptance for de facto standards, and appears to be in favour of some OSF products, such as the distributed computing environment (DCE).

Possibly in response to this, the Open Implementors' Workshop (OIW) has voted to extend its work beyond OSI profiles. OIW is hosted by the influential National Institute of Standards and Technology, the source of the US GOSIP procurement standards.

OIW will now work on an Open Systems Environment (OSE), which will be based on earlier work at NIST called the Application Portability Profile (APP). APP gathered together formal standards in an attempt to produce a CAE which could act as a procurement standard for the US public sector. The OSE will attempt to fill in the gaps in APP, using de facto standards in the public domain. OSF's DCE and Motif user interface are certainly candidates. And OIW's status will give OSE a chance to try for acceptance by both the US Government and the formal standards bodies.

The likely outcome will be some form of compromise. X/Open is a voting member of the OIW management, which will help the two groups to work closely together.

It is too early to tell what the eventual outcome might be. Meanwhile, a ray of hope has appeared from another direction, in the form of the progress made by the Object Management Group (OMG), originally formed in 1989 by nine companies developing "object-oriented" products. Object orientation is a key technology for a new kind of distributed computing which has yet to be delivered to the market.

In the normal way, suppliers would be at each others' throats trying to gain market share for their own ideas. But OMG appears to have persuaded the industry to agree to one standard, for the Object Request Broker, the first piece of technology for this new paradigm. This offers the hope that, in this emerging area, incompatibilities of products will be kept to a minimum by agreement on an effective de facto, and perhaps eventually de jure, standard.

That was the view of one observer in mid-1992, as this book goes to press. Whatever happens in the 1990s, the Posix developments are likely to play a pivotal role as far as software standardization is concerned.

Despite the many more software areas deserving of coverage (databases, graphics, CASE tools...), those could easily fill the rest of the book on their own. It is now time to return to a more general issue, that of the quality of software.

The quality of software

Quality is an issue which often comes to the fore when software standards are discussed, so we end this section with some contributions related to that theme. First we have a report produced by a project under the UK's Alvey Programme of the late 1980s, carried out jointly by teams from King's College London and the Quality Assurance division of the British Standards Institution. The project was concerned with "Quality evaluation of programming language processors", but as this report shows, though directly addressing the programming language area, the results had wider applicability, by lateral transfer into other software areas. This particular report [Meek and Green 1987], which has been edited and updated for the purposes of this book, was aimed at capturing the elusive and subjective concept of "ease of use" – something often regarded as important in software, but generally regarded as being beyond the province of standards to address. The authors were **Brian Meek** and **Collette Green** of King's College London, UK. Copies of the original report and of others from the project may be obtained from the first-named author.

"Ease of use" assessment of language processors

Introduction

While "ease of use", like the similar and overworked term "user-friendliness", is often mentioned in connection with software of all kinds, including programming language processors, precise definitions are hard to come by. Measures of how "easy to use" particular processors are considered to be are even harder to come by; by its very nature, ease of use is a subjective concept, and hence difficult to quantify or measure. The objective of this report is to try to clarify what aspects of language processors contribute to ease of use, and to suggest means whereby at least some non-subjective assessment of relevant properties may be made – though it must be stressed at the outset that nothing approaching a "measure" of ease of use is attempted.

Many helpful comments were received during the course of this work, in particular from Martin Davies and K.K. Siu. We are also grateful to Peter Robinson of Cambridge, whose comments on one of the later drafts led to noticeable further improvements.

The scope of the report

It is apparent from observation that what people regard as part of "ease of use" varies subjectively from person to person, as well as how they prefer particular properties or facilities to be provided, and the order of priorities that they place upon them. At its widest, "ease of use" would seem to encompass virtually all of the "quality" areas that the project was concerned with. For example, some would regard it as including aspects like speed of compilation and execution; and indeed it is not unreasonable for some users with particular needs to say that they will find no compiler easy to use if it compiles too slowly. However, for the purposes of this report questions of processor efficiency and performance are regarded as separate (or at least separable) and hence will not be dealt with here. Some other aspects of quality, which undoubtedly have an effect on ease of use, are also distinguishable as separable concepts large enough and complex enough to be worthy of study in their own right, including error handling, exception handling, documentation and reliability. (These were the subject of separate investigation in the project and do not figure largely in this report.)

The processor and its environment

In addition, ease of use of a language processor is affected by the environment in which it is used, as well as its own intrinsic properties. Software tools such as debuggers, syntax oriented tools, libraries of procedures or modules, and integrated program development environments are examples of relevant kinds of software external to the language processor itself (specifically as defined by the language standard, or at least capable of inclusion in a language standard, see for example [ISO/IEC TR 10176, Meek 1986]).

The particular case of procedure or modules libraries is interesting because some modern programming languages have been designed and specified in such a way that facilities can be specified by modules or module libraries – including those as fundamental as input-output. These can be required by the standard to be provided, but even if this is not the case, the very design of the language virtually ensures that the capability will be there – not necessarily the case in older languages even though they may contain the concept of "procedure" in some form. Ease of use for a particular user may depend critically on the existence or otherwise of suitable, and easily invokable, module or procedure libraries.

It would be necessary to include all such "support environment" aspects in any wider study, of quality or ease of use of complete software development systems, of which language processors would form a part, but they too are mainly beyond the scope of this report. However, it should be noted that certain kinds of tools have tended to be developed outside the language processor simply because of the inadequacies of language standards and of the traditional way that language implementations have been built. It could be argued that some at least of these tools have been developed in order to make good deficiencies in the implementations themselves.

There have been, in the past, good technical reasons for this; it was not reasonable to burden 1960s or even 1970s implementations with too many additional resource requirements. Over the years, however, the importance of that factor has been steadily diminishing, and in most cases (apart perhaps from "home computer" implementations) it can be said to have almost now vanished. Regrettably, but not surprisingly, established attitudes to such matters have not changed so rapidly; however, it may be that Ada will prove to be the last major language to have its support environment designed after, rather than alongside, the language features themselves.

One resource factor which remains important is that of the human effort needed to build the implementation; but software tools, greater experience, and better techniques have helped there too.

Thus, strictly, only things like language-independent tools or cross-language tools might be considered outside the potential scope of a "processor", especially if it is recognized that a processor is best regarded as a package of facilities rather than a monolithic entity (see [Meek 1986] for further discussion of this point). Even there, it would not be impossible to imagine a standard requiring the presence of language-independent facilities; this would be a natural extension of the concept of requiring (say) graphics to be provided by a suitable binding of the (language-independent) GKS standard.

Hence we shall not altogether ignore such aspects, though recognizing things as they are rather than as they might be, and that sometimes it will make very little difference to the user if a facility is provided inside the processor or independently – e.g. a keyword / identifier / symbol indexer – they will not be given much prominence.

Properties required for ease of use

We assume, then, that we have a processor which is reliable, has good error and exception handling, and is well documented (in the senses described in other reports arising from the project) and is embedded in a suitable environment (or at least one which is not actively hostile). With that as our starting point, we consider here what further properties users might require of it to make it "easy to use".

We here come directly up against the problem recognized at the outset: that "ease of use" is subjective. This can be seen in languages themselves. One user finds APL an easy language – because of its conciseness and the powerful functions it provides – while another finds it virtually impossible, through being unable to cope with the symbolism. This second user might, however, find Cobol very easy to use, because of its pseudo-English style of expression, whereas the first will find it intolerably verbose.

It is possible to distinguish between properties which, in general, all users will regard as contributing to ease of use, and those on which opinions will differ, perhaps markedly. We can call these two groups "objectively desirable properties" and "subjectively desirable properties" respectively. We shall return to this question later, but an example of an objectively desirable property is "fast compilation speed", which it is unlikely that any user would positively dislike, while an example of a subjectively desirable property is "mouse-driven user interface", which some users find very attractive but others dislike intensely. We include among "subjectively" desirable properties some which are mutually opposed, such as the properties of "having understandable, natural-language commands" and of "having concise, abbreviated commands".

It is clear from the description and examples of subjectively desirable properties that there are potential conflicts between the requirements of different users – or even between the requirements of the same user for different applications or at different stages of development of the same application. However, the various objectively desirable properties may also mutually conflict, in practice and sometimes even to some extent in principle; for example, between "compact object code" and "high run-time security". A balance may need to be struck between what is desirable and what is achievable, and the "ease of use" balance will vary similarly, because of the different ordering of priorities of different users and of the same user in differing circumstances.

Ease of use via options

The main conclusion of this report, which we shall state immediately, is that the way to reconcile such conflicting requirements is to provide users with processor options, so that they can choose for themselves what to use for different applications and at different times, in ways which suit their particular wishes and needs. A processor which is configurable to a user's preferences is clearly more usable for that individual than one which is not. Rather than software designers or implementors providing what it is convenient for them to supply, or providing what they themselves find helpful or congenial, or having to try to anticipate the likely needs of some target group of envisaged users, they should think in terms of providing choice. There is nothing revolutionary or even very new in this idea; after all, processors for programming languages very commonly do provide user options. They vary, however, in what they provide, how they provide them, and the extent of control that a user has over them. The argument here is that the provision of options should be explicitly and consciously aimed at allowing users to select means of making processors easy to use for *them*, without their having to fit in with some preconceived view of "easy to use" which has been devised by someone else.

Of course, there is a price to be paid for such flexibility, by implementors (in terms of effort), by the system which forms the processor's environment (in terms of resources), and possibly by the users (in having to do the work to tailor the options, and indeed in having to learn what the options are and how to control them).

For implementors, the price may be worth paying because of the enhanced value and attractiveness of the product. As far as the system is concerned, modern advances in technology have made the price of flexibility much easier to pay. For users, the learning curve for mastering the array of options may be steeper than for simply learning a "take it or leave it" system, but users are the ones who ultimately reap the benefits.

Provision of options: content

The ISO/IEC technical report TR 10176:1991, *Guidelines for the preparation of language standards* gives a checklist of processor options potentially suitable for inclusion in programming language standards. The report recommends committees drafting language standards to consider such options, with a view to specifying them as requirements which a processor is to provide if it is to be standard-conforming. The report says, "the standard produced should address all that are appropriate for the language and types of processor covered".

The checklist was intended to be indicative rather than exhaustive, and was not specifically oriented towards ease of use; it was also conservative, in that it contained options commonly found in actual implementations. A full list of processor options which should be taken into account – if appropriate to the language and the nature of the implementation – when performing a quality evaluation of a language processor, has been drawn up in the course of the project and will appear as a part of a report covering quality evaluation metrics generally. However, the checklist is sufficient for the purposes of the present report, and it has interesting features in its own right, so that is the one we shall consider here. It is:

1. The handling of non-standard features.

2. The use of machine-dependent or processor-dependent features.

3. The type(s) of optimization.

4. The use of overlays.

5. The selection of debugging, profiling and trace options, including post mortem dumps.

6. The handling of errors, exceptions and warning messages.

7. The handling of array bound, overflow and similar range checking.

8. The control of output listing and pagination, including any listing of variable attributes and usage and listing of object or intermediate code.

9. Operating modes, such as execution automatically following compilation.

10. The mapping of relevant language elements (such as files or input-output channels) into corresponding elements of the host environment.

11. The use of preconnected files and their status on termination.

12. The rounding or truncation of arithmetic operations.

13. The precision and accuracy of representation and of arithmetic, as appropriate.

14. The default setting of uninitialized variables.

15. In the case where a language standard is a revision of an earlier standard, the detection within programs, and reporting, of usage incompatible with the old standard.

The first point of interest in this checklist is that, as can be seen, most proposed options relate to some extent or another to ease of use, though some only marginally if at all (such as 10 and 11 which are concerned with interfacing the processor with its environment). Since the list was based on options already commonly implemented, this shows that, at least implicitly, the need is already being acknowledged.

The second point is that some of the items in the list could be regarded as options to rectify omissions in the language itself – for example, 12, 13 and 14. Options like those could be regarded as making the language itself usable rather than making the implementation easier to use. Indeed, it could be argued that such options make matters worse by creating work for the user which the programming language designers and standardizers ought to have done. However, the blame rests not with the options themselves but with the reasons why it is found necessary to provide them; ease of use starts with the language definition itself. Though perhaps somewhat peripheral to the main arguments in this report, this does underline the point that ease of use is language-dependent as well as user-dependent.

The third point of interest is that those options listed which are very clearly "ease of use" options (such as 5 to 9 inclusive) are all in the "objectively desirable" category. This is not surprising: there is no point in putting into a list produced for guidance purposes anything that is likely to provoke adverse comments! However, as already indicated, the options listed were derived fairly directly from those already available in existing language processors. This explains why the list omits things like the presence or absence of help systems, the style of commands and responses, and so on – which are not only less common, but come more into the "subjective" category.

Again it is not surprising that it is objectively rather than subjectively desirable facilities that implementors tend to provide; however, it is noticeable that this is the kind of option that mostly gets provided, rather than options which allow choice in the mode of user interface. That the implementor determines the user interface is of course part of the "implementor knows best" tradition, which leads so many users simply to accept what they are given, and live with it. However, the very common presence of "compiler options" and the like does contain implicitly the recognition that implementors cannot, in the very nature of things, always know best.

Provision of options: presentation to the user

It can be seen from this discussion that, essentially, ease of use options come in two levels: options giving some control over what is happening at the basic, language processor level, and options over the mode of interaction between the user and the processor. This second level applies, of course, to the options themselves: the interactions which permit the options to be selected, for example by command, by menu, or by "wimp" interface. It is not difficult to see that, broadly speaking, it is the first level which contains the objectively desirable properties, and the second level which contains the subjectively desirable ones.

It is easiest to consider the question of presentation by following through the first delivery of a language processor (it does no harm here to think of it as a conventional compiler or interpreter, realized in software).

Clearly, when the processor first arrives, it should be possible to use it without having to set any options at all. Even on a large multiuser mainframe system, it should be possible for a processor to be switched on and immediately used without the need to set up options; for true ease of use, at all levels, anything else is unsatisfactory. Thus every option should come with default settings which are in place on delivery.

The selection of delivery-time defaults is inevitably to some extent arbitrary. The defaults will be chosen by the supplier to match the perceived needs of the projected market, but that should be no great cause for concern provided that the selection made has been clearly documented, and of course that it is a sensible one. For example, on first delivery of a new product, for any market, sensible default settings will be that all warning messages are enabled – users will need them during familiarization – and that standard conformance checking should be on. The sensible choice of defaults will be one of the quality aspects of a product, albeit secondary compared with the provision of the options themselves.

All these arguments apply even more strongly, of course, to a single-user system like a personal workstation.

At this point, of course, not only the options but the means of resetting the options is fixed. The facility is needed now to reset the default options to system (start-up) defaults, and various user-machine interfaces including the option-resetting interface. For example, both that interface and, say, means of obtaining help during error correcting sessions could be via a menu or by the use of action codes/command lines; these should be individually selectable. Default settings for error reporting could be reset to (say) full explanatory with additional on-screen help (for a teaching environment), through brief indicative codes, to recording in a separate file displayable in a separate window, for more professional environments.

For a multiuser system, the facility is next needed for a regular user of the processor to be able to set personal defaults, overriding the system defaults – again, at both the (first) processing level and the (second) interface level. Of course, for a personal machine this will not be necessary, but it is still needed in some way for a single-user but shared machine.

Once these personal defaults are set up, it is still necessary for the user to be able to switch easily to different settings appropriate for different applications and different stages of a project. This is the stage particularly addressed by the TR 10176 guidelines, though the report makes a number of additional points relevant to ease of use, including:

> it may well be appropriate in many cases to specify several different settings of a given option, or a hierarchy of combinations of settings;

> options may be provided, for example, as "switches" set when the processor is invoked by the user, or as "processor directives" embedded in a standard-complying program;

in some cases it will be appropriate to require the option to be provided both statically – e.g. processor option – and dynamically – e.g. processor directive or interactive session command.

More discussion of such issues was included in other reports from Alvey project SE/064; one point made was that, given that different combinations of options are likely to be in force at different stages, it is important for the current settings of options to be logged throughout, and the information to be retrievable later if needed.

A further related point made was that the release date and the current version of the processor (and perhaps the dates of compilation and run as well) should be recorded and be retrievable later if required. The reason is that a new release of the processor might affect the consequences of use of options. The idea behind both points is that the state of the processor in all relevant aspects should be recorded and the information be readily accessible to the user.

All these remarks, both from TR 10176 and from the Alvey project, of course apply to all of the kinds of option we have been talking about, not just the particular, "objectively desirable" kinds of option considered in TR 10176 and needing to be recorded in order to document the functional state of the processor. They also apply at the second, subjective level; users should be given flexibility through the ability to reconfigure the user interface, and be provided with choice rather than having to fit their requirements into a pattern dictated by the implementor.

Note also that, at both levels, the user should be able to specify default settings of options either globally or locally, at will. Thus if the default user interface is "wimp", it should be perfectly possible to change the global, user-determined default to "menu" but to retain "wimp" for some classes of interface and specify "command" for yet others.

Practical criteria

The chief lack at present is for ways for users to *choose*, rather than just take what they are given – at all levels. Though many processors offer some options, there are few around, if any, with a wide enough choice of facilities to satisfy most types of user. Given that nothing is (at present) providing what is needed, what users are faced with is choosing the best, or least bad, from what is available. As often happens, they have to compromise, and to decide overall what their priorities are.

Below we indicate some practical criteria which can be used to determine how easy it is for a particular user to use a particular product. It is not claimed to be comprehensive; the examples are simply illustrations, and are at the (first) level of facilities rather than the (second) level of presentation. (Others appeared, explicitly or implicitly, in other project reports.)

Commands

In general, users will wish for easily usable commands, though what this means depends both on personal preference and on presentation. For a text command interface users are likely to want to use words which can readily be associated with the tasks they invoke. Examples are *edit* or *ed* to enter the editor, and *help* or *H* for calling the help facility. These provide suitable mnemonics whether or not one prefers the full or the terser form.

For more complex commands, understandability is important but slows down the experienced user; and the beginner may find them not altogether a boon, since it is easier to make a typing error on a long command. This points to the need for a means of recalling, within the processor interface, the last few commands submitted, for editing and resubmission rather than retyping.

Although this may be obvious enough, most users with any length of experience of different systems will be aware of processors and related tools where these "obvious" criteria have been ignored: in editors, things like *se* or *c* to enter screen editing mode, and *rm* (remove) rather than *del* for delete are less clear and less easy to remember.

Nevertheless, what is a good mnemonic may not always be obvious. To take a very simplified example, a processor may call the successive stages of handling a conventional batch job *PASS_1*, *PASS_2* and *PASS_3*; easy enough to remember, but *COMPILE*, *LINK* and *RUN* are more expressive. In the first case, a naïve user may not know what each pass does but at least will be able to see the order in which they are performed. The second case assumes that the user knows rather more about what is happening. Each person will have a preference; the long-term answer perhaps is to allow both, but meanwhile this too becomes a selection criterion.

Of course, the next stage beyond a choice of commands or of preset abbreviations is for users to be able to specify their own abbreviations, or their own alternative commands. Among other things this benefits users whose natural languages differ from that assumed by default.

A further such potential development is on the lines described by Good [Good *et al*. 1984] where a self-adjusting user interface (in the case described, for an electronic mail system) is capable of reacting to and moulding itself to the commands submitted by the user. The particular investigation was concerned with adjusting to the immediate needs of naïve users rather than long-term needs of regular users, but significant gains in ease of use for such beginners, in a matter of minutes, were reported. An experienced user trying out a new system would probably wish, at a fairly early stage, to be able to freeze the interface or to direct it to adjust in particular ways, but the work described in that paper at least demonstrates that such an approach is feasible.

Similarly with a mouse-based interface, some users may wish for a command menu whereas others would prefer icons; again the long-term answer may be to provide both, and to allow adjustments, and also to allow mouse commands to be replaced by keyboard commands; but meanwhile it is something that some people feel so strongly about, one way or the other, that if the system does not provide choice it can become a very important selection criterion.

Error and exception diagnostics

Most users require diagnostic facilities to meet criteria such as accurate pinpointing of where the error or exception has been detected; the absence of misleading messages; the absence of extraneous (gratuitous and unwanted) messages, even though not misleading; helpful indications of what the error or exception may have been caused by. However, quite apart from the problem that what is "misleading" is to some extent subjective, some of even these apparently objectively desirable features are not totally clearcut; for example, an expert programmer may prefer just to have the accurate pinpointing, finding the "helpful indications" merely a distraction.

Again, the solution to this is the provision of a thoroughgoing set of user-controlled options, covering detection, action taken on detection, and the means and level of reporting (i.e. user interface). This is an area where some limited range of options is commonly supplied by existing language processors, though usually in terms only of a few levels of detection.

Testing and measurement

Possible ways of measuring the ease of use of a processor include:

> observed difficulties in learning to use the product;

> total time needed to learn to use the product;

> time needed to perform selected tasks;

> frequency of use of on-line help, documentation, assistance;

> success or failure in completing the selected tasks;

> efficiency with which different features are used.

There are inherent problems in performing this kind of testing. Users may, as remarked earlier, find it initially difficult to learn to use a sophisticated product, as compared with a simple-minded one; hence a processor with no options at all might score well on measures based on the first two criteria, yet do badly overall because it is too inflexible. Also, for results to be meaningful one needs a large pool of "subjects" and even then one needs to filter out subjective factors, at least to the extent that one can say "processor A seems to be easier to use than processor B for users of such-and-such a class". This, however, though difficult, time-consuming and expensive, is not totally impossible. Adaptations of the methods advocated by Gilb [Gilb 1977], or of those used by Roberts and Moran to evaluate text editors [Roberts and Moran 1983], certainly hold out some hope.

As well as observational methods, user comments, suggestions and preferences can be sought and recorded. From all these results, it might well be possible to group certain criteria together and categorize them; and similarly to categorize what particularly attracts certain classes of user. Ease of use factors which continually appear and reappear (and, of course, some are already known from the accumulated experience of the last thirty years) can be focused upon to see if they might be amenable to individual criteria or metrics, just as this project has been able to identify particular areas and concentrate upon those. To some extent, the data already exists. What is lacking is the collection and organization of the data, and subsequent checking by further observation and experiment of ideas which might emerge from such a synthesis of, or distillation from, what is in some sense already known, but not codified or classified. The growth in the 1980s of the human-machine interface area as a significant branch of computer science research demonstrates that there is potential – as well as offering ideas and techniques which could be of value. This is certainly worth exploring as an area for further research.

There is a somewhat different way of looking at the measurement problem. The difficulty in developing a general metric arises from the fact that ease of use is user-dependent, and frequently application-dependent, as well as language-dependent and system-dependent. Languages and implementations are often designed with particular classes of user or particular kinds of application in mind. Rather than attempt to allow for, smooth out or statistically average over different classes of user or application, it would be possible instead to cooperate with the inevitable and aim not for direct objective metrics but indirect methods based either on the declared design aims of the language and implementation, or on criteria which a user determines for a particular kind of application.

To measure an implementation against its declared aims, this would imply a relatively small number of expert users, following Gilb-like software metrics procedures [Gilb 1977], indicating relative weights to be attached to specific criteria (either measured, like compilation speed for a particular set of "typical programs" or assessed, like helpfulness of error messages). The implementation is then measured against this metric, using different combinations of options until the best combination of setting is reached.

For users to do their own assessment, they would effectively need a parametrized metric on similar lines so that they could provide their own weightings for given applications, and optimize the overall result by selecting the optimum setting of options. Note that, in either case, the range of "tuning" of options to give good results over a variety of requirements leads indirectly to some kind of general assessment of "ease of use" which will be less user-dependent and less application-dependent. Such an approach offers a less labour-intensive if circuitous route to a general metric than the simple frontal attack approach mentioned at the beginning of this section, albeit with some risk of distortion through unconscious selection.

Concluding remarks

The subjective nature of ease of use is inherent; it is unlikely that it will ever be possible to say, in any absolute sense, that one processor is unequivocally and in all circumstances easier to use than another, and even less likely that it would be quantifiable. Nevertheless, this does not mean that we should simply give up any attempt to define criteria for it, nor that language standardizers should flinch from the task of attempting to incorporate such criteria in standards. The guaranteed presence in conforming, validated processors of "ease of use" features would be so beneficial that standardizers should face up to the responsibility of trying to specify them; identifying at least a basic set of criteria is a worthwhile and not impossible task. What we have tried to show in this paper is not only that this is the case, but that, in particular, providing users with choice through processor options, at both the functional and the user interface level, is a feasible way for implementors to make processors easier to use and for standardizers to begin introducing ease of use requirements into standards.

That report shows that ease of use aspects usually involve not just the software per se but the user interface supplied with it. Such interfaces are often, and properly, regarded as not in the province of the software standard itself. The traditional view in the programming languages field was that this was a matter for the implementor, a view which by the end of the 1980s had been largely discredited. Since the human-computer interface area is the subject of a later section, we shall not pursue this further here, but instead turn to the more general question of user needs with respect to the quality of software products in other respects, more inherent to the software itself – things like fitness for purpose, reliability, resilience to faults, efficiency of implementation, and maintainability.

This is the area generally referred to as "quality assurance". Standards for software quality assurance came into increasing prominence during the 1980s. Though some in the user community, while not objecting to this, felt that more attention ought to have been given to standardizing the software itself, for reasons discussed earlier, quality assurance (QA) standards at least have the virtue that they can be applied, in principle at least, to all software products, whether there is a software standard or not. For large corporate users this general applicability is a very valuable feature, since once the QA standards exist there are immediate payoffs in all areas, whereas specific software standards affect only one.

The next contribution, by **Kenneth S. Johnson** of Neville-Clarke Limited, UK, discusses this issue, in relation to software development. It is based on a presentation given at the first international conference to be held in the USSR on software engineering, *Software engineering of the '90s*, held in Kiev, Ukraine, May 1991.

The application of quality assurance in a software development environment

Introduction

Within an organization which operates a quality management system to ISO 9001, there is an obligation to provide quality assurance of the product or service to ensure that the appropriate level of quality is being maintained.

Many organizations work on a project basis. This enables them to handle the development of a particular product or service to meet the specific needs of the intended customer in such a way that the appropriate resources can be concentrated on the development in hand with minimal intrusion from other activities.

During a software development project, it is essential to provide a quality assurance (QA) function if the integrity of the software product is to be maintained. This paper discusses a number of practical QA techniques and related project management topics applicable to the software development environment.

Project management

For a software development project to be successful it is essential that it is managed correctly. Successful start-up of a software project [EEA 1985] enables the ensuing activities to be managed from a position of confidence and control rather than one of struggling to retain or, worse, regain control.

Initial consideration of the project requirements should be made with as much care as is possible. This may seem obvious, but time is frequently short and the temptation to rush ahead with the more technically challenging aspects of the design has caused many a software development project to run into severe difficulties at a later stage.

A requirements review, during which the customer requirements are discussed, is a primary means of ensuring that the requirements are understood by both parties. The customer is an important participant in this review. Whether the customer is external to the organization or internal (i.e. the marketing function acting on behalf of a perceived market need, or another part of the organization) is not important, but it is important to establish the customer needs and to document them.

During a requirements review, participation from an independent person representing the QA function within the organization can be very beneficial. The independent aspect of the quality function enables a perspective to be taken of the topics under discussion which can highlight potential problems which may not be apparent when seen from the viewpoint of the project manager and other project staff.

Technical and physical constraints of the product will need to be considered at this point and, again, participation from the quality function will be of value. Typically, QA staff will have had a wide experience of a number of projects, and may be able to draw on that experience to advise project staff.

Quality management

Project planning is important and is likely to be mainly the domain of the project manager. However, the resource scheduling should take into account that there will be a number of quality-related activities to be considered. These activities are in two categories [EEA 1981]:

> quality controls; and

> quality assurance.

Quality controls are associated with the achievement of the appropriate level of quality for the product. The responsibility for this is almost entirely with the project manager and the project staff.

Quality assurance is associated with the need to carry out a number of independent activities which are designed ensure that the quality controls are effective. The responsibility for this is almost entirely with the quality manager and the quality staff.

Planning for quality

The achievement of quality in software [BS 7165:1991] relies on planning just as much as the project itself. It is vital that, whatever the software product, whether it is safety critical like a fly-by-wire system for controlling a passenger-carrying helicopter, financially critical like a spreadsheet product, or a leisure product such as a game, that the appropriate level of quality is planned. Having decided the level of quality, it can be specified in a quality plan and the achievement of the quality managed.

A quality plan, stating the quality control requirements of the software product, should be produced by the project manager who will, in turn, pass it in draft form to the quality manager for concurrence and addition of the QA related topics.

The preparation of the quality plan is primarily the responsibility of the project manager because it is a result of choosing the appropriate quality controls, but there will need also to be a choice of the appropriate QA activities to ensure that the controls are effective.

When both managers are agreed on the plan it can be issued under joint authority for action.

Resourcing the quality function

The resources available for quality related tasks on a project will depend on a number of factors. Many organizations which produce software products are small, typically 10-20 people. Such small groupings would be unlikely to have a quality department as such. However, staff can be used part-time in the QA role to great effect but they will need to receive thorough and specialized training first. In larger organizations, there will a need for full-time staff to carry out QA functions.

There will be a focal person for quality assurance; this person is the management representative in all organizations operating a quality system to ISO 9001. This person will be responsible for ensuring that the quality function is adequately staffed and trained for their duties.

The management representative is frequently given the title of quality manager although this is by no means universal. It can be a misnomer in the sense that the project manager is responsible for quality controls, an arguably more significant role where the quality of the product is concerned.

The quality manager does have overall responsibility with regard to quality assurance, and will need to allocate staff accordingly. As suggested above, this may be on a part-time basis if necessary; indeed, the quality manager role itself may be part-time in a smaller organization.

Quality assurance tasks

Quality assurance tasks may include the following:

> participation in design and other reviews;
>
> system and project audit;
>
> project monitoring;
>
> participation in testing;
>
> vendor assessment;
>
> subcontractor assessment;
>
> inspection;
>
> analysis of quality records.

All of these tasks are able in some way to affect the software development process.

Design and development

It is essential to appreciate that almost all of the activity involved in producing a software product takes place in the design and development phase. As a result of this, the quality assurance activities are almost all required during that phase.

Traditionally, in many companies producing hardware products, the QA function has been perceived as a mainly production-oriented activity. The production phase of a software product is viewed by many as the replication process. This activity is minute compared with the rest of the process which produces a deliverable software product and it may not happen at all if the product is shipped electronically as is increasingly the case.

Thus software quality assurance is carried out mainly during design and development.

It is interesting to observe that this fact has had an important effect on the hardware-producing companies which also have a significant software design and development capability. The advantages of quality assuring software have been appreciated and similar disciplines applied to the hardware design process with corresponding benefits.

Quality assurance activities during design and development

The monitoring role

Having been involved in the requirements review and the quality planning process, the QA function will be starting to carry out its main monitoring role as the design and development process begins to gain momentum.

The monitoring role has two main aspects, formal quality audit [EEA 1988] and unannounced project monitoring. Each of these techniques has its own particular value and each complements the other.

Quality auditing

Formal quality auditing is a planned activity. Each audit is programmed in advance, generally about six months before the actual audit takes place. Frequently there are two types of audit, system and project audit. System audits are planned to form part of an assessment of the complete organization and could quite easily take place at any time during the project because they are independent of work activities at that level.

Project audits are, as the name implies, specific to the project and would be planned to take place at such times as to have the maximum effectiveness.

Quality audits are designed to provide confidence that the planned level of quality is being achieved, whether on a system (organizational) level, or on a project level.

Due to the planned nature of system and project audits, the fact that they take a relatively long period of time to take place (typically, one or two days) is not a particular problem because they are planned well in advance. However, the fact that they are planned well in advance means that there is plenty of time to prepare for them and consequently the view could be taken that between audits the quality of the product could be at risk.

Quality audits are carried out by technically competent staff who are trained in the auditing role. In the UK, guidelines for the professional attribute/performance standards for software quality auditors have been published as a result of the UK Government Department of Trade and Industry initiative known as TickIT [BCS 1991].

The audit process is designed to compare the practices in the organization with the procedures published as part of the documented quality system. The auditors follow lines of technical investigation known as "audit trails" and any non-compliances found are be documented. At the conclusion of the audit, the non-compliances are reviewed at a meeting of representatives of the organization (or project) and the audit team, the appropriate corrective action is agreed and a date set for implementation.

Project monitoring

It is between audits that the effectiveness of project monitoring is at a maximum. The risk associated with formal audits in which the prior knowledge of the audit could (and often does) lead to last minute preparations is eliminated. The element of surprise and the random nature of when and where the monitoring will occur means that it is not practical to make specific preparations and the only way to ensure success is to operate to the quality system at all times.

The monitoring is done on an "unannounced" basis. This means that the QA representative who is tasked with carrying out the activity will not give advance warning before arriving in the area to be monitored.

On arrival, the QA representative will carry out a very short audit trail to establish that there are no non-compliances with the quality system. The fact that the activity took place is then documented in the quality records. If any non-compliances are found, they are recorded and corrected in the same way as for an audit.

Normally the process of project monitoring is controlled by the quality manager. The use of monitoring needs to be controlled very carefully because, being an unannounced activity, it is likely to be inconvenient for the area being monitored. This means that the time spent monitoring should be severely restricted (not more than, say, half an hour) at any one time in order to minimize the inconvenience.

Vendor and subcontractor assessment

Vendor assessment

Vendor assessment is an activity which is undertaken by the QA function on behalf of the organization to ensure that suppliers of goods and services have the capability to satisfy the purchasing requirements of the organization.

Following a successful assessment, the suppliers are added to an approved suppliers list which is kept and updated on a continuous basis.

Vendor assessment can be carried out in a number of different ways depending on the requirements.

If the supplier is already providing a product or service which has had a satisfactory history over a given period of time, it may be added to the approved suppliers list on the strength of this record.

If the supplier is new, then there are two methods of assessment. The first involves the sending of a supplier questionnaire to the proposed supplier. The questionnaire lists a number of questions relevant to the goods or services to be supplied. The questions would typically address such matters as whether the proposed supplier was registered as having a quality system, or what methods were used to ensure product quality. This type of questionnaire is most frequently used where the product to be purchased is generally available, or where the quality can be assessed on receipt. In either case, the quality of the purchased product can be monitored by the purchasing organization and further decisions made as to its use as a result of that assessment. Analysis of the replies is carried out and the potential suppliers ranked accordingly. If considered suitable after the analysis has taken place, the potential suppliers can be added to the approved suppliers list. The preparation of the supplier questionnaire and the analysis of the completed forms is carried out by the QA function, as is the maintenance of the approved suppliers list.

The second is by direct assessment of the supplier. This is done when the performance of the supplier's product or service is critical to the product of the organization. This assessment usually takes the form of a second-party quality audit.

Until comparatively recently this has been a very common practice, especially with the larger purchasers. It is now becoming less common in the UK because of the increasing number of firms becoming registered to ISO 9000/ EN 29000 series standards.

Subcontractor assessment

Assessment of potential subcontractors is normally carried out by second-party quality audit except where the potential subcontractor is registered to ISO 9000/ EN 29000 series and the scope of that registration is appropriate to the intended use of the subcontractor by the organization.

Participation in design review

The participation by QA staff in design reviews has been mentioned previously with regard to requirements reviews. Other types of design review such as system and subsystem design review can benefit from an independent participant, especially if that person is able to draw on a wide experience in design.

Participation in testing

Independent participation in testing by the QA function can be of significant value to a project. This participation can be to provide additional assistance during the test process or, as is more often the case, to act on behalf of the customer by performing acceptance tests prior to delivery.

Maintenance and analysis of quality records

Quality records include all records of design and development, verification and test. Maintenance of these records is important for future reference and analysis can provide indications of where future improvements may be found. The QA staff will have had training in statistical techniques to enable them to carry out this important task. Software metrics is an important topic which is receiving increasing attention in the academic environment and one which is increasingly being adopted by software developers because of the benefits which can accrue from techniques like failure mode and effect analysis.

Inspection

Inspection can be split into two main categories.

First, there are the traditional inspection activities associated with visual examination of products. In the case of software, the product is intangible, but may often be transported on magnetic or other media such as PROM, EPROM, optical disks etc. These media will have to be visually inspected prior to delivery to the customer and this task is carried out by the QA staff.

Second, there is a different type of inspection which may be carried out during the design and development process. This involves the inspection of items such as documentation, for example specifications, and source code. There are a number of formal methods for doing this: Fagan inspections, structured walk-throughs and code scrutiny are techniques which have been developed and are known to be beneficial. The involvement of quality assurance in these activities is not usually as cost-effective as the use of peer review. Peer involvement has the advantage of knowledge of the development project on a detailed basis. The items for inspection can be scrutinized by colleagues who are carrying out similar design activities and who are familiar with the design method requirements.

Configuration management

The application of effective configuration management to the design and development of software is essential to the achievement of quality. It could be argued that it is, in fact, the most vital element because without it there can be chaos [EEA 1983]. However, configuration management is not a QA function as such and the task of quality assurance is to ensure that the configuration management is being maintained through quality audits and monitoring.

Summary

The quality assurance element of a quality system as applied to a software development project is important in that whatever controls are needed to ensure that the delivered product meets the requirements of the customer, quality assurance can give confidence that they are being maintained.

The effective planning, execution and management of the quality assurance activities are an important discipline. The value of this discipline is becoming increasingly recognized by those responsible for software development projects of all types.

As these last contributions have indicated, a significant part of the *perception* of quality by the end user is the quality of the user interface, and it is to that important topic that we now turn, in the next section.

References

Standards and standards body documents

ANSI X3.159:1988 Programming Language C

BS 6154:1981 Method of defining syntactic metalanguage

BS 6832:1987 Method of specifying requirements for Fortran processors

BS 7165:1991 Achievement of quality in software

EN 29000 European norm corresponding to ISO 9000 (or the ISO 9000 series)

EN 29001 European norm corresponding to ISO 9001

ISO 9000:1987 Quality management and quality assurance standards – guidelines for selection and use ("ISO 9000" also used to designate the 9000 series of standards including ISO 9001, ISO 9002 etc.)

ISO 9001:1987 Quality systems – model for quality assurance in design/development, production, installation and servicing

ISO TR 9547:1988 Programming language processors – Test methods – Guide lines for their development and acceptability

ISO/IEC TR 10034:1990 Guidelines for the preparation of conformity clauses in programming language standards

ISO/IEC TR 10176:1991 Guidelines for the preparation of programming language standards

Other references

[ACM 1989] Special section on the Internet worm in *Communications of the ACM*, Vol 32, No 6, June 1989

[Appelt 1988] APPELT, W., FODA – the formal specification of ODA document structures and its use as a basis for conformance testing, *Computer Standards and Interfaces*, Vol 7, No 4, pp 377-385

[Appelt et al 1990] APPELT, W., CARR, R. and TETTEH-LARTEY, N., Conformance testing of ODA documents and ODA implementations, in [Berg and Schumny 1990], pp 299-309

[BCS 1991] TickIT guide to software quality management system construction and certification using EN29001, prepared by the British Computer Society under contract to the UK Department of Trade and Industry

[C&S 1983] Current issues in programming language standardisation, special issue of *Computers and Standards*, Vol 3, No. 2

[Dahlstrand 1980] Operating system command languages, in [Hill and Meek 1980], pp 127-137

[Dahlstrand 1984] Software portability and standards, Ellis Horwood, Chichester

[EEA 1981] Establishing a quality assurance function for software, Electronic Engineering Association

[EEA 1983] Software configuration management, Electronic Engineering Association

[EEA 1985] A guide to the successful start-up of a software project, Electronic Engineering Association

[EEA 1988] Guide to software quality audit, Electronic Engineering Association

[Gilb 1977] GILB, T., Software metrics, Winthrop,, Cambridge, Massachusetts

[Good, Whiteside *et al.* 1984] GOOD, M.D., WHITESIDE, J.A., WIXON, D.R., and JONES, S.J., Building a user-derived interface, *Communications of the ACM*, Vol 27, No 10, pp 1032-1043

[Hall and Resnick 1990] HALL, P.A.V. and RESNICK, M., Chapter 50: Standards, in [McDermid 1990]

[Hill and Meek 1980] *see general bibliography*

[Judge 1991] The standard bearers, *Financial Times*, 22 October 1991

[McDermid 1990] McDERMID, J. (ed.), Software engineer's reference book, Butterworth-Heinemann, Oxford

[Meek 1986] MEEK, B.L., Programming language standards: not language definitions, but specifications of software engineering tools, in Kugler, H.-J., Information Processing 86 (Proceedings of the tenth IFIP World Congress, Dublin), pp 301-306, North-Holland, Amsterdam

[Meek 1990c] MEEK, B.L., Changing people's attitudes: personal views, *Computer Standards and Interfaces*, Vol 10, No 1, pp 27-36, see also Section 10

[Meek 1990d] MEEK, B.L., Problems of software standardisation, *Computer Standards and Interfaces*, Vol 10, No 1, pp 39-43, see also Section 10

[Meek and Green 1987] MEEK, B.L., and GREEN, C., "Ease of use" assessment of language processors, Alvey project SE/064 Report No 1, King's College London

[Roberts and Moran 1983] ROBERTS, T.L., and MORAN, T.P., The evaluation of text editors: methodology and empirical results, *Communications of the ACM*, Vol 26, No 4, pp 265-283

[X/Open 1989] X/Open portability guide, X/Open group

7

User needs in human-machine interface standards

Into

In the first section of the book, one of the things discussed was what we meant by the word "user" when discussing user needs, and it was concluded that there are several different kinds of user, whose needs consequently differ to some extent. This is an issue that comes particularly to the fore when one is concerned with the "user interface", or "human-machine interface" (HMI) as it is commonly known, since the users we are concerned with here are certainly individual users rather than corporate users. As has been remarked, whether a system is user-friendly depends on the user as well as on the system.

Hence this section, prepared with the assistance of **Dr Ian Newman** of Loughborough University of Technology in the UK, starts by returning to the question of the "user" and what the needs of that user are. The first contribution, by **Professor Harold Thimbleby** of Stirling University in Scotland, looks at this issue. In particular, he argues that it is not good enough to require the computer user necessarily to be "computer literate".

Computer literacy and usability standards

Introduction

There is a tension between making computer systems more standardized (and hence easier to use given previous experience with other systems) and whether users should be expected to be more competent, to be computer literate. Computer literacy enables users to cope with non-standard, ad hoc, or badly designed systems; instead it should make users campaign for standardized systems that are easier to use.

Standards are a way of reducing the cost of transferring skill from one system to another. Reducing costs is a benefit at all levels: for users of systems it means that their skills are more marketable, and that they will have reduced training times in new jobs; for both user and employer, standards reduce errors, because the skills of the user transfer and because appropriate commands for one system are equally appropriate, certainly not erroneous, on another.

At one extreme, *lack of standardization* has the advantage that systems can be tailored exactly for their environment; at the same time increasing staff retention, since users (following training) are less mobile than with training on standard systems. Yet it is not obvious that non-standard tailored systems are beneficial; few software companies are technically able to produce quality solutions, and unforeseen difficulties with one-off systems may outweigh anticipated, known, problems with off-the-shelf solutions: lack of standards implies a lack of external guidance in the design process. At the other end of the scale, *enforced standardization* may stifle manufacturers' creativity, but it does ensure that end user skills are more readily transferable. In the limit, personnel officers must decide whether it is better to retain eventually demoralised staff or to be able more readily to recruit staff with higher initial skills.

Rather than standardize systems, however, we could train users in the underlying concepts. Thus users would know, for instance, that disks have to be formatted, however a particular computer system did it. It takes training to know how to use a computer, to control a word processor or to format a disk. As more businesses adopt computers for their everyday running, so there is an increasing demand for trained people to work effectively in the computerized environment. Indeed, it has almost reached the point where people cannot function at work unless they are computer literate.

Literacy

Computers are only one of many modern gadgets, and why should they be unique in being difficult to use? We don't need, and don't expect, "telephone literacy" courses – yet telephone exchanges and satellite links and so forth are terribly complex.

The point is that you can easily use complicated things when they are properly designed for you. Or again, we may have car driving lessons, but it is only the enthusiast or professional who has or even wants "car literacy" (that is, engineering) lessons. The rest of us find it quite sufficient to learn how to drive cars; we do not, and should not, need to have to learn how to fix their mechanical problems.

There was a time when the UK Government was promoting computers in schools. This was like the Victorians having a national initiative to buy every school a model railway set. You can imagine someone saying that children should know how railways work if they were to get on in the world. Children would learn all about railways from using the school layout. Of course, the Victorians never did this, and the idea seems faintly absurd. Real railways are very different from model railways – British Rail or the French SNCF are mostly in the news because of their safety record, and safety is hardly an issue that much could be learnt about from a toy layout. So, toy railways may appeal to little technologists, but they don't entirely make people "railway literate", at least not in a way that would be much use to an adult railway employee. Likewise, school computers are probably not helping anyone to be computer literate in a useful way.

Indeed, real computing (let's say as would be used for the control of a nuclear reactor) is very different from anything that can be taught at school. To give some idea of the gulf between school computing and real computing, consider another simple analogy. Suppose we have a child here playing with Lego bricks. She can make houses, she can make bridges, she can make cars. But we are not led into thinking that she will grow up to be a competent builder, bridge designer, car designer – because these things require much more careful design than can possibly be explored in Lego. You can't just make a bridge over a river by sticking plastic blocks together; it wouldn't be safe and probably wouldn't even support its own weight. Instead, of course, we see the child simply at useful play for its own sake rather than on a "building literacy" course!

This point is not so clear with computers. The trap is that real computers look rather like toy computers in a way that real bridges cannot look like Lego bridges. For example, I cannot easily tell by looking at my computer whether the programs it is running were designed by a three year old or a professional programmer. But you can tell by looking at the Forth Road Bridge that its designer knew something of bridge building, and there is no way you are going to think little Jimmy here is going to grow up to be a bridge builder just because he can make a ten inch Lego span! But we do make this mistake with computers. So we exaggerate the importance and effectiveness of so-called computer literacy. "If Jimmy can write a ten line program in Basic, why, he can get a job in pay-rolls!" Total nonsense.

Computer literacy, when it starts at school, is misplaced. Instead, think of the computer as a toy; like Lego, something that children can develop many and various skills with – the least important of which is computer literacy itself. Lego teaches manual dexterity, solid geometry, problem solving, mechanics; computers teach touch typing, drawing, music composition, writing, problem solving, even chemistry and French.

Who is responsible?

Ralph Nader's classic book *Unsafe at any speed* [Nader 1966] woke up the 1960s car industry to the fact that cars must be designed for safety. Nader strongly criticized the car industry for making intrinsically unsafe cars and blaming the driver for accidents. The driver has the accident and the driver is responsible, manufacturers argued. Of course, the car has an accident too, and very often caused it with its poor suspension or feeble brakes. Pedestrians who were "gently knocked" were killed by being slit from throat to stomach by being cut with sharp body styling. Car manufacturers argued that in any collection of accident statistics one would be bound to get some gruesome cases: arguing, again, that the dangers were not their fault! Nader's campaigning eventually made car designers take responsibility for designing cars properly – or at least he gave them a conscience in that direction, which in some cases became enshrined in standards and safety legislation.

In the 1960s people had problems with cars, whereas today people have problems with computers. In the 1960s people were told to drive more safely (to be "car literate", in fact). Today people are told to read the manual and become computer literate. Of course, if you do that the problem goes away: it makes it look like the problem is educating the users rather than the manufacturers.

With cars the real issue was not getting better driving nor making drivers "car literate". That would have been practically impossible since many designs were intrinsically unsound and could not be driven well even by highly skilled drivers. The onus – then rarely admitted – was actually on the car designers to make cars that were easy and safe to drive, and that in turn required standards: legislative and professional. Likewise the onus for better computer use is very much on the designers, not the users. When users are encouraged to become computer literate, manufacturers are making users' supposed lack of skill a scapegoat for their bad designs.

The relevance of user skill

General computer skill is not important, as will be argued by a brief digression. I once saw an old, green leather-bound pair of volumes on engines [French 1908]. Written shortly before the First World War, its author enthused about engines, or "modern power generators" as he called them. There were all sorts of engines: steam engines, gas engines, oil engines, and petrol engines. (It is interesting that this particular author saw no future in petrol engines: they were unreliable, needed hard-to-obtain fuel, needed gears – whereas steam engines were reliable, used water and easily obtained coal or wood, and didn't need gears at all. He couldn't foresee the future, of course!) But his main point was that to get on in the world – the Edwardian world of engines – one really needed to *know* about engines. Hence his two volumes told the reader everything there was to know about engines. Yet today, we have more engines around than he could have possibly imagined! I have an electric engine on my wrist – it's called a watch. I have four in my washing machine; and there are eighteen in our kitchen at this very moment (not counting the engine in the toy electric car that is in bits on the table).

In the old days, when this engine book was written, if a farm had only one oil engine it was certainly important that the farmer understood it. If it went wrong, he would clearly have to know something about engines in order to fix it. But today a farm has thousands of engines, and if one goes wrong (say, the starter motor in the farmer's car) there are many other engines to get by with. Indeed, there are so many engines and they are so well hidden that the farmer no longer thinks of engines as such, but of cars, tractors, clocks, sprays. Engines have disappeared; instead there are appliances that do useful things. So, too, has the need for engine literacy disappeared. What has happened is that "engines", so far as their users are concerned, have become standardized. An engine user no longer has to treat each sort of engine differently; they are simply started with the flick of a switch. It is important to emphasise that the technical diversity of engines, that once required a corresponding breadth in user skill, has now disappeared from the user's point of view.

Likewise, computers are beginning to disappear inside the things that they make work.

You can now get a toaster with a microchip in it. The toaster is a toaster and you don't need to be computer literate to use it! Our washing machine has one too, as has our microwave, the central heating, the car, the TV and video recorder. Indeed, to have to be computer literate to use a toaster or car is ridiculous! Instead, you might say that the toaster is toast-literate. The computer in it knows about toast (I hope) so you don't have to know about it. Only when the toaster does silly things (does it crash?) do you need to be computer literate in any sense – and, in this case, if you do have any sense you'd take it back to the shop and get one that worked properly! In terms of standards for user interfaces, the toaster conforms to toaster user interface standards.

The thrust of computer literacy, then, is misplaced. Put briefly: it is only because current computer systems are so bad that we need training to use them. Better to make the systems easier to use; far better to make the computers-as-such disappear and the users' view of them conform with what tasks they are doing! Yet the problem runs very deep, and is not so easily solved. For example, most people cannot program their video recorder, and one might suppose this is an example of a failure in computer literacy (a video recorder has a simple computer interface in it). If only users knew what they were doing, or had read the manual, or had been on a literacy course so that they could think "the right way" their problems would be solved! This is true, in a way, but it quite misses the point. It should be clear that it is true mainly in the sense that it is the more convenient solution for manufacturers to advocate rather than adopting, or even seeking, improved design standards.

Users generally have been made to feel untrained, and if they feel that way then the solution is at first sight to get trained, that is, to become computer literate. Users should not be feeling that way in the first place! When you hear that children can use video recorders, you get the strong feeling that you are old and past it – that is, you have missed out on suitable training to deal with this sort of complicated technology. But that is exactly what the manufacturers want you to think! They want you to think that the difficulty you have with their systems is your fault, not theirs. And if you have heard that children can work it, then doesn't that just confirm that it is all your fault? (Actually, it's not at all clear that children are any better at using video recorders than their parents, though they do have obvious advantages – they have more time available to play with the things, and besides, they didn't spend £500 out of their own pocket. There are indeed theoretical reasons to suppose that *not knowing* what to do – the opposite of being literate! – is an advantage. A naïve child is certainly at an advantage over an adult who thinks he knows what he is doing but is in fact wrong.)

Standards for "people literacy"

So, computer literacy – people being trained to be computer literate – is a diversion. Instead we need "people literacy" – that is, computers designed to be human-literate so that the people who use them can simply get on with their job. Yet the reality is that people do want jobs working in today's computerized environments and, sadly, for this they need to be computer trained to work effectively! Computer literacy, then, is a training for the real, rather than the ideal world. But let's not forget that it is a stop-gap, and in the long run we would be better off getting the computers up to human standards rather than reducing the humans to cope with arcane computer etiquette.

How would one get computers up to human standards? How should user interfaces be improved, standardized, to make them more usable?

This is, of course, a rhetorically posed question, with equivocal "human standards". The problem users put themselves in is that they adapt to non-standard interfaces. This has two immediate consequences, both putting the user at a disadvantage.

First, users require specific training and skills with each system that they encounter. This may increase job satisfaction momentarily, but in the long run it severely reduces mobility. If you can only get a new job with experience of (say) WordPerfect, and if you have spent months learning Word, you will be stuck. For the consumer market, such lack of standardization results in misplaced customer allegiance: users become reluctant to invest in alternative manufacturers' software.

Second, designers – not being encumbered by standards – can add and remove features at will, for secondary purposes. Systems can be implemented by cheaper, unskilled programmers. Since there are no standards to judge interactive systems for quality, it follows that designers can choose to increase market penetration deliberately (or innocently) by compromising user interface quality. Indeed, there is no requirement that individual components of a complex system have to be consistent even with each other, adhering to internal standards.

Manufacturers resist standardization. It restricts their freedom to implement in ways that suit them, for example in cheaper, more impressive, or technically easier ways. More important, it cuts against the current trend for legal protection of software systems' proprietary appearance. The current law for protection of design makes it very hard to protect conceptual ideas, and computer programs in particular. Therefore manufacturers protect their development investment by protecting what can be protected: the so-called "look-and-feel" of their products. If another company releases a product with a similar user interface, that company is potentially infringing look-and-feel. Thus, protecting normal development costs in this way works against producing standardized user interfaces, particularly since most of the modern (windows, mice, menus) style user interfaces are very much bound up with look-and-feel. Stallman and Garfinkel are leading a stand against this essentially restrictive practice [Stallman and Garfinkel 1990].

Standards and quality versus protectionism

A major problem for the entire industry is that protectionism stifles improvements: thus, even if I know a better way of doing what some manufacturer has provided, I cannot start with an improvement on their product. Indeed, from a technical point of view most user interfaces could very easily be improved. (You have only to look at the so-called macro languages of commercial spreadsheets to see that computer science seems to have passed them by.) But even if you can see what to fix, there is no opportunity to improve commercial systems because of copyright restrictions. Evidently manufacturers don't want to improve their own products, and they don't want anybody else to do any better either.

If I could legally reverse engineer a system, I could surely build a new version of it with fewer bugs. I could certainly design my program carefully rather than let it accrete *ad hoc* code over the years! (I might even be able to sell it with a decent warranty, which no commercial software has so far aspired to.)

It is time we started developing "standardized" – that is, deliberately public – user interfaces. It is now thirty years since Algol 60... where is the effort to make a similar impact in user interfaces? Imagine word processor manufacturers vying to produce, say, ISO Level 4 word processors cheaper, faster, more reliable, easier. It would generate the sort of competition that would be of great benefit to users. (This argument is developed further in [Thimbleby 1990].)

But standardization *is* a realistic goal for user interfaces. We need only look at the user interfaces provided for programmers – programming language standards – to see that standardization is perfectly possible, if not perfect. Indeed, programming languages like Cobol or Ada are fundamentally more complex than any user interface in widespread use.

Programming languages became standardized by two main routes. First, most language designers were academics with no financial stake to make a market niche, rather they intended to design a first class language; second, standards-enforcing bodies (such as the US Department of Defense that initiated Ada) recognized the advantages for programming language standards. Programming skill improves, and programmers' retraining costs are reduced (since programmers need less retraining the more Ada is required). One might ask why users don't have such a spokesman as the DoD.

Until there is some undertaking to standardize user interfaces, user interface design and usability will be a stagnant area. Both engineering and scientific progress depend on copying and improving existing designs with known performance. (The conventional paradigm is that experiments are published, claims made, and others then check the results: by repeating and trying variations.) When this is illegal nobody can systematically improve the many interrelated, design-specific features such as ease-of-use. If nobody can check up or attempt to improve designs, there will be a powerful temptation to implement systems laxly. This, in turn, will foster the impression that user interface design is easy! In short, without standards for user interfaces, manufacturers become secretive, their system implementation quality decreases, which in turn will encourage them to be increasingly secretive.

If user interface design is thought to be easy, programming language design is recognized to be hard. That is why there have been many highly motivated and successful moves to standardize languages, and hence share development efforts, improve quality, and so forth. (It is cynical to point out that programmers have a vested interest in standardized languages for advancing their own job prospects.)

If a programming language has a design or implementation error in it, everything done with it is at risk. But as computers don't tolerate errors, errors such as dividing by zero are very hard to conceal or ignore. That means that programming languages and their implementations work against an intolerant judge: whether they will work or not on a computer. User interfaces, on the other hand, work against a tolerant and powerless judge: the user. Design errors comparable in severity with dividing by zero, like irretrievably deleting a day's work "by mistake", are rarely perceived as the inevitable consequence of fundamental design faults.

User interfaces won't be standardized while users accept badly designed systems. While users accept badly designed systems, designers can get away without putting in any effort into new designs. Designers will continue to believe standardization is irrelevant – and users will continue to seek support in computer literacy courses.

The proper use of literacy to advance standards

In summary, computer literate users should not understand how to cope with badly made, one-off and non-standard systems. Instead they should use their literacy to recognize poor quality when they see it, embark on litigation, complain, and generally be as intolerant of bad design as the computers they now understand.

That contribution has made a very good case for the need for standards which will promote higher quality and easier usability in the user-computer interface area. It holds out the ideal that computers could be so integrated into products that interface issues could disappear. The next contribution also briefly discusses the need for standards, and considers arguments against standards, but concentrates on reviewing the main user interface standardization activities which are taking place, at the time (1991/92) that this book is being written. The final section examines some reasons why there has been no successful standardization effort in the human interface area up to the present and discusses the work that is being undertaken to offer users the prospect of standards that can be tailored to their requirements. The authors are **Nigel Bevan** of the National Physical Laboratory at Teddington in the UK, and **Ken Holdaway** of IBM's Entry Systems Division at Austin in Texas, USA. The text is based on material first published in *Computer Communications* [Holdaway and Bevan 1989] and in the conference proceedings *Human aspects in computing* [Bevan 1991].

User needs for user system interaction standards

Why standardize?

Ten years ago there was very little activity within the various national and international standards organizations directed towards the development of standards taking account of User System Interfaces. The industry was more concerned with standardizing the hardware, or in standardizing some parts of the software such as languages or communications protocols. Little attention was given to the human user.

However, about five years ago the scope began to expand. Various groups began to consider the impact of visual display devices on the human user. Human-Computer Interaction emerged as an important research area, and the published papers described problems with current user interfaces and suggested better ways of constructing interfaces that would increase user satisfaction and productivity [Shackel 1985]. At first these suggestions took the form of guidelines that offered advice to interface designers [Gaines and Shaw 1983]. There was no thought that this could or should be standardized.

However, within the past five years, the level of activity has increased as a result of pressure from users for standards to regulate the quality of the interface. There are two separate international standards groups, with multiple subgroups within them, both developing standards for the user interface. In addition, there are numerous national standards efforts underway – all aimed at the same target of user system interfaces.

What was the motivation that would cause so much activity within such a short amount of time? The reasons vary, but can probably be summarized into four categories.

Need for consistency

Anyone who has used several different computer terminals, or multiple applications on the same system, will recognize this need. For instance, the inconsistent use of function keys can easily lead to the frustration of deleting a file instead of saving it.

Once we learn how a system operates, it would save a great deal of time and mental anguish if other systems worked in an identical or at least similar fashion. It is routine in today's business to use terminals from several manufacturers. It would be very desirable if users could move from one system to another without having to learn or re-learn how the system operates. Proponents of a standardized interface claim it is the most effective way for consistency to be achieved.

Need for enhanced usability

The usability of a product can be defined operationally as "the effectiveness, efficiency and satisfaction with which specified users achieve specified goals in particular environments" [ISO 9241-11]. Clearly, the business community has a strong incentive to push for anything that could increase productivity while keeping employees content. Many believe that standards for the user interface are one way of achieving this. After all, if standards are based on laboratory research which has identified generally accepted techniques for creating more effective and acceptable interfaces, then conformance to the standards should result in systems which are themselves more usable and productive.

Need for assurance of the user's comfort and well-being

This is perhaps the most widely discussed reason for developing standards for the user interface. This concern started with claims of pregnancy problems caused by radiation or electromagnetic emissions from the VDT. User groups and legislators picked up on this issue and pressed for standards and laws to protect the users. At present it seems reasonable to conclude that users are not harmed by using a VDT and that statements to the contrary are not soundly based [Blackwell 1988]. However, the controversy continues. Furthermore, it has broadened into how the use of software can have an adverse impact on the well-being of the end user.

The concern is that a poorly-constructed user interface will cause stress and mental anguish to the end user. Several examples are cited as ways in which this can occur.

> The system interface takes control away from users and requires them to respond within certain time limits, thereby causing stress.

> The system interface does not adequately permit the user to recover from mistakes and try again. Nor does it help correct user errors. This leads to a reluctance by users to explore or try anything new for fear that they will do something catastrophic or "break the system". This further heightens the user's sense of stress.

> The system interface is constructed so as to intimidate the user by issuing threatening messages or inappropriate instructions. This frustrates, angers, and further increases the user's stress and dissatisfaction.

It is for these types of reason that the European directive on the minimum health and safety requirements for work with visual display screen equipment [CEC 1990] includes the operator/computer interface in its scope (see under *European display screen directive* below).

Procurement and product evaluation

When procurers of software have the task of deciding which among the tens or hundreds of products is the best one for their organization, the user interface has traditionally been difficult to specify, assess or compare. It is difficult enough to evaluate the product function – it is practically impossible to evaluate the interface without exhaustive tests [Bevan, Kirakowski and Maissel 1991].

There is an increasing belief that user interface standards could be of significant help in the procurement process. By specifying that the product must conform to Standard XXX, the procurer would like to be able to ensure that the product will provide some nominal level of consistency and usability. In addition, by using only products with a "standard interface", employers can hope to convince the using employees that there is no cause for concern relative to health and well-being.

When the potential benefits of user interface standards are appraised, this explains the ever-increasing level of activity throughout the world to develop those standards. It is believed to be a worthy goal that will yield rewards – if it can be achieved.

Is it desirable or possible?

It is comforting to think that as soon as the standards organizations have finished their work on user interfaces, all the frustrations and dissatisfactions will disappear. Professionals in the area would say that such an attitude is not only premature but very naïve. In fact, some argue that standardizing the user interface is not a desirable thing to do, even if it were possible. Their objections can be grouped into four main categories.

The basics are not known

It would seem to be easy enough to pick one of the more common user interfaces and declare it to be an international standard. But, if asked to defend your decision, you would probably be hard pressed to articulate your reasons for selecting one over another. Presumably your decision would be based on some research or measurement of user performance that supports your selection. However, such data are extremely scarce. Standards imply measurement, conformance, repeatability, and stability. The research has not yet been done that would permit us to resolve the cognitive processes associated with individual user performance into standards with such rigour and precision. This is particularly true when we know that the interface must respond to the influence of differences in culture, technology, task and environment.

Standards will inhibit advances

This statement can be made about all kinds of standards. Generally it is not true. If you can standardize the correct elements, those elements can be put together in a variety of ways that allow creativity and innovation to progress. However, in the case of user interfaces, the statement could be true.

What are the fundamental building blocks of the user interface? If you standardize the wrong ones, then you are locked into a scheme where innovation will be difficult or impossible. For example, if five years ago we had decided to standardize the user interface, we would have pre-empted many of the features we see in the advanced, object oriented, interfaces of today. We would be stuck with primarily character-based, command line, scrolling interfaces. We know that new, creative, innovative interfaces are arriving with almost every new system. Poorly framed standards must not get in the way of this new development. However, without the proper research and caution in standards construction, this is quite likely to happen.

Standards will not guarantee usable software

A full understanding of usability requires an understanding of the cognitive processes which enable users to achieve their goals effectively, efficiently and comfortably. Since we do not totally understand the cognitive processes, we do not therefore totally understand all the dimensions of usability. What makes one software design more usable than another? How much does usability depend upon the type of user, task and technology? What do we standardize – high level principles, or low level details?

If we aim our standards at high level principles we can probably find some safe ground. However, can these principles be interpreted in a practical way by interface designers so that their implementations meet the usability goals of consistency, productivity, and satisfaction? Would any two designers interpret the principles in the same way so that their interfaces were consistent?

If we try to develop our standards around low level elements, we run the risk of not finding those fundamental to the cognitive process. And even if we could, the interface designer is still faced with the task of combining those elements into an overall implementation that satisfies the usability objectives.

Standards will not provide measurable benefits

We should not standardize just for the sake of standardization, but should start with the assumption that some measurable benefits should accrue to the end users as a result of using a "standard interface". For example, let us take a trivial case. Should letters or numbers be used to designate options in a menu? Will it make a difference? What is the value of standardizing it one way or the other? Does it depend on the type of task, class of user and the technology so that different standards would be required for each application?

Standardizing, when there is no identifiable benefit, would result in interfaces which are constrained, rigid and cannot be adapted to the varying needs of the users and the marketplace.

Current standards activities

In spite of the detractors, the perceived benefits to be derived from stand-ardizing the user interface are such that several standards producing organizations are actively working in this area. In many cases they have avoided the dangers listed above by finding alternatives to the conventional style of IT standard which places explicit requirements on hardware or soft-ware. Other types of standard, which may be more appropriate when dealing with human behaviour, specify procedures (e.g. the procedure an organization follows to ensure the quality of a product, ISO 9000), or minimum levels of user performance with a product (e.g. speed and accuracy using a particular key-board, ISO 9241-4), or the method by which characteristics are measured (e.g. stress in a hot environment, ISO 7243).

Standards may also be limited in their scope. At one extreme many standards have universal applicability (e.g. codes for character sets, ISO 6937, see Section 5). However, other standards may be explicitly limited in their field of appli-cation (e.g. a keyboard layout for use with multiple Latin alphabet languages, ISO 8884, see Section 3), or may contain recommendations rather than explicit requirements (e.g. design of office tasks, ISO 9241-2).

The following information is not meant to be a complete directory of who is doing what, but it will discuss the mission, scope and status of several major groups which have efforts underway in the early 1990s.

ISO TC159/SC4/WG5: Software ergonomics and man machine dialogue

Technical Committee 159 (TC159) of ISO is responsible for standards in the area of ergonomics. Subcommittee 4 (SC4) of TC159 is responsible for the ergon-omics of human-system interaction. SC4 had previously concerned itself with task and physical issues associated with visual display terminals, but in 1985 Working Group 5 was set up to look at the ergonomics of software.

SC4 is currently planning to produce a 17-part standard (see Table 7.1). The earlier parts are already international standards.

The scope of WG5 is "Standardization in the field of human-computer interac-tion, especially dialogue interfaces, with the aim of enabling users to perform their tasks under ergonomically favourable conditions". In order to focus their efforts, and yet have a wide area of applicability, they have decided to concen-trate on activities found in the office environment.

WG5 is responsible for Parts 10-17 of the standard. Part 10 (Dialogue Prin-ciples) describes seven principles for improving the quality of dialogues. Part 11 defines usability and explains how it can be specified and measured. Part 12 contains detailed advice on the formatting and layout of screens. Part 13 explains how help and error messages should be used to give guidance to users. The remaining parts deal in detail with different forms of dialogue: menus, commands, direct manipulation, form filling, question and answer and natural language. Part 14 on menus has reached DIS stage and currently

Table 7.1 *Ergonomic standards to be adopted by CEN*

ISO 9241: Ergonomics of Visual Display Terminals	
	Status
1. General introduction	IS
2. Guidance on task requirements	IS
3. Visual display requirements	IS
4. Keyboard requirements	DIS
5. Workstation layout and postural requirements	CD
6. Environmental requirements	CD
7. Display requirements with reflections	CD
8. Requirements for displayed colours	CD
9. Requirements for non-keyboard input devices	WD
10. Dialogue principles	CD
11. Usability	CD
12. Presentation of information	WD
13. User guidance	WD
14. Menu dialogues	DIS
15. Command dialogues	WD
16. Direct manipulation dialogues	WD
17. Form filling dialogues	WD
18. Question and answer dialoges	P
19. Natural language dialogues	P

ISO/IEC JTC1/SC18/WG9, User System for Text and Office Systems	
ISO 10741 Cursor control for text editing	DIS
ISO 11580 Objects and actions	CD
ISO 11581 Icons	WD

IS = International Standard
DIS = Draft International Standard
CD=Committee Draft (circulated for national comment and vote)
WD=Working Draft (not finalized)
P= Planned

contains a combination of recommendations and requirements with a scope which is conditional on the intended tasks and users.

ISO/IEC JTC1/SC18/WG9: User system interfaces and symbols

Joint Technical Committee One (JTC1) of ISO/IEC has responsibility for standards in the area of information technology. Subcommittee 18 (SC18) is responsible for standards in document processing and related communication. Within SC18, working group 9 (WG9) is responsible for user system interfaces.

WG9 has divided its work into four areas, each with a separate subgroup:

user interface;

symbols;

voice messaging;

keyboard layout.

The user interface group is currently working on three user interface standards (Table 7.1). Cursor control specifies how the cursor moves on the screen in different modes in response to the use of cursor keys. Objects and actions specifies the essential file manipulation and editing objects and actions required in computer interfaces. This standard provides the definition of functionality for the icons specified in the standard for icons being developed in conjunction with the symbols group. The Icons standard contains principles for the design of icons, minimum requirements for icons, and the required functionality and visual appearance of a basic set of object icons.

The symbols group is working on graphic symbols used on equipment (such as copier and printer control panels). The voice messaging group is starting work on a standard for the user interface to voice messaging systems. The work on keyboards consists of developing a multipart standard to update, extend and replace existing standards for keyboard layout.

DIN (Deutsches Institut für Normung)

Germany already has a multipart standard addressing various aspects of information processing. This collective standard has the number DIN 66 234 (see Table 7.2). Part 8 of this standard, which has been approved in Germany, deals with "Principles of ergonomic dialogue design for workplaces with video display units". It consists of a statement of five high level ergonomic principles that apply to humans dealing with software. These five principles are supported by guidelines and examples that are used to explain how the principles might be interpreted and implemented. Although it gives useful guidance, the standard admits that: "At the present time there is no way of checking that particular guidelines have been adhered to since no methods of testing are known".

Much of Part 8 has been incorporated into ISO 9241-10. When ISO 9241 is complete, it will replace DIN 66 234 in Germany.

Human Factors Society – Human-Computer Interaction Committee (HFS-HCI)

In the United States, this committee operates under the auspices of the American National Standards Institute (ANSI), and is the technical advisory group for ISO TC159.

Table 7.2 *DIN 66 234: VDU Workstations*

Part	Title
1.	Character shapes
2.	Perceptibility of characters
3.	Grouping and formatting of data
4.	not used
5.	Coding of information
6.	Design of workstations
7.	Design of work environments
8.	Principles of dialogue design
9.	Measurement techniques
10.	Minimum fact sheets

The HCI group has developed a framework for how the various areas of human-computer interaction fit together. They are now working to fill in the various areas with details based on reports of laboratory research or on empirical data. Their first aim is to produce guidelines which may then be elevated to the level of a standard with explicit requirements if enough evidence can be found to warrant doing so. Each guideline is further qualified by criteria for its use – when and under what conditions the guideline is intended to be used.

So far the work has focussed on Dialogue Interaction Techniques (with particular attention to the use of Menus), User Guidance, and Output Devices and Techniques. Their work is being used by ISO TC159/SC4/WG5, which is considering it as the basis for international standards.

ANSI X3V1.9: User system interfaces and symbols

This United States group has been chartered by ANSI to develop standards in the area of text, office and publishing systems. Within X3V1, task group 9 (TG9) has the responsibility for User System Interfaces and Symbols and is the national mirror group to JTC1/SC18/WG9. TG9 is a major contributor to the work being done in the international group.

BSI PSM/39/2: Applied ergonomics – signals and controls

This UK panel has made substantial contributions to TC159/SC4. It has pioneered the user performance approach, and has produced a UK VDT standard equivalent to ISO 9241 Parts 1-5. (The UK standard will gradually be replaced by the ISO standard when this is published.)

BSI IST/18/-/9U: User interface

This group shadows the user interface topics in JTC1/SC18/WG9. It has been particularly active in developing the theoretical and experimental basis for the standardization of icons.

European Display Screen Directive

After 31 December 1992 it will be a legal requirement in Europe that visual display equipment and workplaces meet minimum ergonomic requirements, and that the software is easy to use. National legislation to implement this is required by the European Directive on the "minimum safety and health requirements for work with display screen equipment" [CEC 1990]. As a consequence, employees will be entitled to a much more carefully designed working environment.

The most important provisions of the Directive are summarized in Table 7.3. They apply to workstations including the display screen, associated equipment, the chair, table and immediate working environment, when used habitually as a significant part of normal work. (Small data screens and portable equipment are excluded.)

Standards relevant to the Directive

In some countries, legislation implementing the Directive may make reference to the forthcoming European standards to be adopted by CEN (Table 7.1). The relevant parts of ISO 9241 are indicated against the provisions of the Directive in Table 7.3. The minimum requirements of the Directive are similar, but not identical, to the requirements of the relevant parts of ISO 9241 which are given in much greater detail. It would have been simpler if the Directive had made direct reference to these parts rather than containing its own requirements. However, not all the ISO parts are complete, and the contents of ISO 9241 are agreed by experts in national standards bodies, while the contents of the Directive are approved at a political level in the European Community.

CEN TC122/WG5 is responsible for producing the European version of ISO 9241. The work is supported through a mandate from the European Commission (which is likely to be extended to include the user interface standards produced by ISO/IEC JTC1/SC18/WG9). Standards only become mandatory if they are cited in national legislation (such as legislation required by a European Directive). National legislation can only make reference to national standards, but national administrations are obliged to adopt European standards in order to reduce barriers to trade.

Interpreting the Directive

Many of the provisions cover well-established principles for the ergonomic design of visual display terminals and their workplaces, such as a clear image on the screen, a lack of reflections and a good working posture. These principles are elaborated in some detail in parts 3-9 of ISO 9241.

The provisions for the operator/computer interface have been welcomed in principle, but are phrased in such general terms that they are particularly difficult to interpret. Taken at face value the requirements that "software must be easy to use" and "the principles of software ergonomics must be applied" would exclude all but the best existing software! For example, if the Directive

Table 7.3 *Minimum requirements of the display screen directive and the relationship with standard*

	ISO 9241	
	Part	Type
EQUIPMENT		
Display screen		
– stable, clear image; adjustable brightness; easy swivel/tilt	3,8	R,U
– free of glare and reflections	7	R,G
Keyboards and other input devices		
– separate tiltable keyboard, matt surface, legible key markings	4	R,U
Workdesk		
– large low reflectance surface, document holder and adequate space	5,6	R,G
Workchair		
– adjustable in height, backrest adjustable in height and tilt	5	R,G
ENVIRONMENT		
Space		
– sufficient space to change position		R,G
Lighting		
– appropriate lighting, position prevents glare	6,7	G
Reflections and glare		
– no glare and minimum reflections	7	G
Environment		
– associated equipment should not distract attention or disturb speech	6	G
– associated equipment should not produce heat causing discomfort	6	G
– adequate level of humidity must be maintained		
OPERATOR/COMPUTER INTERFACE		
– software must be suitable for the task	2,11	G
– software must be easy to use	10-19	G
	WG9	R
– provide feedback to workers on performance	13	G
– display information in a format and pace adapted to operators	12	G

R = Requirements
G = Guidelines
U = User performance may be used to test conformance

is fully implemented, it could make use of normal operating system interfaces such as MS-DOS and Unix illegal in the office, since they do not incorporate "the principles of software ergonomics". Fortunately for MS-DOS and Unix users there are much better alternative interfaces available such as Microsoft Windows or OSF MOTIF which support most existing applications.

Software which is consistent with the standards listed in Table 7.1 should have no difficulty complying with the Directive. However, many of the parts of 9241 only contain guidelines which means that there is no objective test for conformance. This means that there can be no contractual requirement for conformance to these parts, and excludes their use in conjunction with certain legislation, e.g. that emanating from the Supplier's Directive [CEC 1988]. The whole issue of whether it is possible for ergonomic guidelines to be made requirements is currently under discussion in ISO TC159/SC4. One possible solution is that complying with the standard will include the requirement for an explanation to be provided of the reasons why any particular guidelines have not been followed.

Conclusions

Users are increasingly demanding easier to use software, but much software continues to be unnecessarily difficult to use. In the past there was no simple way for a procurer to specify what was meant by a requirement that software should be "easy to use". The advent of standards for software ergonomics and the user interface now provides specifications and guidelines which can be used in procurement and design. In Europe these standards will in some circumstances become mandatory when they are referenced to support the requirements of legislation implementing the Display Screen or Suppliers Directives.

Acknowledgements

This paper was partly supported by the Department of Trade and Industry and the Commission of the European Communities as part of ESPRIT Project 5429 MUSiC.

If both of the preceding papers are to be believed, standards in the human-computer interface area are long overdue and it might be thought to be surprising, as Thimbleby says, that we have so few when standard programming languages have been around so long. However, a closer look at what has happened in the past may help us see the present situation in a rather different light. Reference has been made in earlier discussion and in various places to the problems caused by incompatible operating systems and the attempts to do something about it. The more general work of the JTC1 study group TSG-1 has also been mentioned. **Ian Newman** was chief editor of TSG-1 and was previously involved in the operating system command language work known as OSCRL. In this closing contribution to this section, he reviews this work, to see if lessons can 'in fact' be learned from the past.

The slow start for standards – standardization and personalization

Until the middle to late 1960s there were no interactive systems and it was well into the 1970s before these became relatively commonplace. Prior to that the only people to use computers were either programmers or people entering data. Data was predominantly numbers and the "user interface" was perceived as being just to present the numbers in columns as required by the application (formatting rules did become "standardized" by a combination of custom and the vagaries of the programming language being used, e.g. Cobol, Fortran). Programmers were concentrating on their task, which was seen as writing programs and, for this, they did generate "user interface" (i.e. programming language) standards.

The only other interface that affected a significant number of people was the interface to the operating system (or executive, or director, or ...). This started as being a very small number of instructions from the user to the machine, just those needed to compile a program or to execute a program. However, as operating systems became more sophisticated, the number of possibilities increased and it became recognized that there was a separate "operating system command language" which influenced the usability of the system.

Even prior to 1970, it had been noted that some "command languages" were easier to use than others and at least one of the existing languages had been ported to a different computer to simplify the task of the users. Several activities were started in the early 1970s which were intended to prepare the way for standard command languages that would have all the advantages which are now being suggested for standard user interfaces (see, for example, the introductory article by P. Enslow in the book *Command languages*, edited by C. Unger [Unger 1975]. This work was continued in several national and international groups throughout the 1970s and into the 1980s (e.g. the BCS JCL working group [Hopper 1981], the Codasyl Group [Codasyl 1979)], ANSI X3H1 [X3H1 1982], IFIP WG2.7 [Beech 1985], ISO/IEC JTC1 SC21/WG5 OSCRL Rapporteur Group).

In this early work, two potential benefits of standardization:

> the reduction in the time, both human and system, wasted through errors; and

> the saving of time through reductions in the need for training on each system

were clearly recognized. However, two perceived problems were also identified simultaneously:

> standardization stultifies creativity and stops progress; and

> new interface hardware and interface styles are constantly emerging and standards would prevent these being used to the best advantage.

In the end it could be argued that it was the difficulties that prevailed since the standardization effort collapsed in 1988 following the transfer of the ISO OSCRL group from SC21 into the Posix working group, SC22/WG15. The alternative explanation is that the standardization failed because the suppliers saw no future in a single new Operating System Command and Response Language. They possibly felt that if a single one was to succeed then it would have to be an existing one (e.g. Posix). A further alternative is that there is an inherent resistance to a single interface. People are individuals and like to do things in different ways. For example, there are many programming languages, almost all with the same basic functionality, yet each one has its devotees and each has some types of problem for which it is particularly well suited. In the same way, it might be expected that there should be several styles for standard user interfaces depending on the experience and preferences of the user, the regularity with which the user uses the system and the tasks which the user needs to carry out. It would also be necessary to recognize that most users use several different packages (e.g. a word processor, a spreadsheet, a database, a statistics package). To minimize learning and reduce errors, the interface to all of them would need to be consistent (so that, as Thimbleby might have put it, the intuitive actions of the user were, in each case, "in tune" with the behaviour of the system).

The possibility of producing a standard which allowed users to adjust the interface to their own needs, while still keeping the benefits of easy learning and skill transfer, was one that interested the people working on command language standardization from the end of the 1970s. One aspect of the problem, the need for an application (a program or subsystem) to accommodate users with different cultural expectations (e.g. a natural language other than English, dates written in different formats) working on a variety of hardware platforms (machines plus operating systems), was a major topic of discussion during the work of ISO/IEC JTC1 TSG-1 on the requirements for Interfaces for Applications Portability (IAP). The remainder of this subsection reviews the considerations that were raised during the discussion by TSG-1 of user requirements for "internationalization" as it had been christened. Extracts from Section 6 (Internationalization) of the final report of TSG-1 [ISO/IEC JTC1 N1335] are used to illustrate the ideas that were discussed and the recommendations that were agreed.

One concern that was expressed by several of the participants related to the name for the concept. The term "internationalization" suggests that only if an application is used by people from different nations is there any need for this concept. In practice many applications have to interface with users with different cultural expectations. These expectations can involve differences in natural language (e.g. German, French, Italian) within one country, different terminology associated with different working environments (e.g. workshop, boardroom) within one company or different information processing interface experiences and preferences (e.g. WIMP, command language) in the same office. In each case the users have different *cultural* expectations. A more appropriate term for the process of producing an application which serves a group of users with different expectations would be *interculturization* (or even the clumsier, but clearer, phrase "user interface tailoring" that was originally used in the 1970s). However, it was felt that the term "internationalization" was now established since it was being used extensively in the Posix standardization work. It was, therefore, agreed that this terminology should be used for the concept despite the misleading connotations.

Once the name for the concept was determined it was possible to define the need that was being considered. In the context of the task of determining the requirements for interfaces for application portability it was agreed that there was a rapidly growing user requirement to provide culture specific user interfaces to applications. These applications needed to be ported to make their functionality available to various user communities to maximize the value of the investment involved in their production. They, therefore, needed to be written to utilize services which allowed them to separate from the application the culture dependent aspects which are not relevant to their function so that these facilities could be standardized.

The next step was to define the various functions that made up these culture dependent features. This was done by listing twenty six examples of the requirement. Although this was felt to be a fairly comprehensive list it was accepted that there would be other cultural variations that had not been explicitly recognized. Some of the examples involved differences in the natural language (Russian, French) used for messages, user input, documentation while others illustrated differences that were concerned with character sets, collating sequences and character representation (considered in more detail in section 5). Other examples, of the kind already discussed in Section 2, covered such things as date and time representations, number formats (99,999.99, 99.999,99 could represent the same number in different circumstances), representation of amounts of currency (the placing of the currency symbol varies from culture to culture), writing directions (left to right and top to bottom, right to left and top to bottom, bottom to top and left to right), postal address formats and constituent parts (significant variations here even within one culture were noted) and measurement systems (the units used for different measurements like weights, lengths etc.).

The environment in which internationalization was needed was clarified by examining the requirement from the different viewpoints of the user and the application developer. It was agreed that users wanted applications which accepted input, and provided output, in a form that was both understandable and acceptable in terms of their own culture. Applications developed for users with different natural languages and/or with different customs, need to support those local languages and customs. The objective is to satisfy this need without placing undue burdens on the application developer. Ideally the application developer should not be required to have detailed knowledge of the various cultures within which the application may be used (an internationalized application would then be capable of being used, without modification, in a predefined set of cultural environments). If this could be accomplished it would greatly simplify the task of producing working applications for such multicultural environments as airports, CERN, CEC, Belgium and Canada!

It was noted that currently, application developers must explicitly design into their products all the code that is needed to support different cultural environments. Code with similar functionality is therefore being developed repeatedly. This is a waste of designers' and programmers' effort and carries the risk of inadequate or inconsistent implementations. Also the cost of developing applications for multiple cultural environments is high and there is a tendency to produce versions of common applications that are tailored to specific cultural environments. For an individual user this has the disadvantage that, if they travel, they may find it very difficult to use the local version of their favourite software package(s), a point made by Meek in the preceding section.

The discussion also considered the requirements from several different points of view:

> presentation (output) of information suitable for a particular culture;

> input of information from a user with particular cultural preferences;

> the occurrence of information relating to more than one culture in a single document (e.g. the title of a French book appearing in the middle of an essay written in English);

> users who regularly worked in several cultures and might change their cultural requirements (possibly dependent on where they were working);

> applications that had to deal with users from many cultures but each user would expect to work with information relating to his or her culture only;

> the different ways in which an application might be implemented so that the culture dependent aspects could be separated from the culture independent aspects.

The conclusion to the discussion was that there was a need to define the facilities that were needed to support different cultural expectations for both input and output so that standards could be specified for suitable cultural support services. This task will, hopefully, be carried out by ISO/IEC JTC1 SC22 WG20 which has been explicitly formed for the purpose.

TSG-1 noted that internationalization is a topic that needs to be considered by every standardization group that defines, or specifies, information that is input by or output to, a user. It also noted that there was no possibility that an application could be specified in such a way that it could be totally independent of the cultures in which it was to be used unless the possible variations between the cultures which needed to be accommodated, could be determined in advance. Nevertheless, overall, a cautiously optimistic note was sounded which holds out some hope for improving the present chaotic situation.

In this section, among other issues the question has been raised, particularly in Bevan's contribution, of the stress which can be caused by an unsuitable user interface. This leads us into the more general issue of the safety of IT systems, and the related but distinct subject of security. These are the subjects of the next section.

References

Standards and standards body documents

[Codasyl 1979] CODASYL Common Operating Systems Command Language Committee, COSCL Journal of Development, Version 1.0

ISO 6937:1992 Coded graphic character set for text communication – Latin alphabet, 2nd edn.

ISO 7243:1989 Estimation of the heat stress on working man, based on the WGBT-index (wet bulb globe temperature)

ISO 8884:1988 Keyboards for multiple Latin-alphabet languages – layout and operation

ISO 9000:1987 Quality management and quality assurance standards – guidelines for selection and use

ISO 9241-2:1992 Ergonomic requirements for office work with video display terminals – Part 2: guidance on task requirements

ISO 9241-3:1992 Ergonomic requirements for office work with video display terminals – Part 3: visual display requirements

ISO CD 9241-11:1992 Ergonomics of visual display terminals – Part 11: guidelines on usability specification and measures

[X3H1 1982] Draft standard operating system command and response language, ANSI X3H1

Other references

[Beech 1985] BEECH, D. (ed), Concepts in User Interfaces, Springer-Verlag, Berlin

[Bevan 1991] BEVAN, N., Standards relevant to European directives for display terminals, in BULLINGER, H.-J. (ed), Human aspects in computing, Elsevier, Amsterdam

[Bevan, Kirakowski and Maissel 1991] BEVAN, N., KIRAKOWSKI, J., and MAISSEL, J., What is usability?, in BULLINGER, H.-J. (ed), Human aspects in computing, Elsevier, Amsterdam

[Blackwell 1988] BLACKWELL, C.H., Video display terminals and pregnancy: a review, *British Journal of Obstetrics and Gynaecology*, Vol 95, pp 446-453

[CEC 1988] Supplier's Directive (88/295/EEC), *Official Journal of the European Communities*, No L 127, 20/5/88

[CEC 1990] Minimum safety and health requirements for work with display screen equipment directive (90/270/EEC), *Official Journal of the European Communities*, No L 156, 21/6/90

[French 1908] FRENCH, J.W., Modern power generators (two volumes), Gresham Publishing Company

[Gaines and Shaw 1983] GAINES, B.R., and SHAW, M.L.G., Dialog engineering, in SIME, M.E., and COOMBS, M.J. (eds), Designing human-computer communication, pp 23-53, Academic Press, London

[Holdaway and Bevan 1989] HOLDAWAY, K. and BEVAN, N., User system interaction standards, *Computer Communications*, Vol 12, no 2, April 1989

[Hopper 1981] HOPPER, K. (ed), User oriented command language, Heyden on behalf of the British Computer Society, London

[Nader 1966] NADER, R., Unsafe at any speed, Pocket Books (Simon and Schuster), New York

[Shackel 1985] SHACKEL, B. (ed), Human-computer interaction – Interact '84, North-Holland, Amsterdam

[Stallman and Garfinkel 1990] STALLMAN, R. and GARFINKEL, S., Against user interface copyright, *Communications of the ACM*, Vol 33, No 11, pp 15-18

[Thimbleby 1990] THIMBLEBY, H., User interface design, ACM Press, New York

[Unger 1975] UNGER, C. (ed), Command languages, North-Holland, Amsterdam

8

User needs in safety and security standards

The safety and security aspects of information technology systems are coming under increasing scrutiny from the public at large, the legislators and the information technology community. Security is of concern with respect to:

the prevention of unauthorized access;

the prevention of virus infection or other damage; and

the maintenance of the integrity of data and service.

Safety is of concern with respect to:

the avoidance of harm caused by the systems controlled by information technology; and

the avoidance of harm caused by IT hardware.

In order for IT systems to be relied upon it is necessary for them to have an appropriate level of integrity. Integrity is required with respect to both the safety and security aspects of the functions which the systems are required to perform.

Matters of safety and security necessarily overlap with legislative requirements and hence, as we shall see, even international standards relating to these matters often have to be adapted to accord with national practices and legal requirements. Hence, unusually in this book, some parts of this section will relate to the particular implementations in one country, the UK. Nevertheless the principles are universal and this should not create major problems for readers from other countries.

This section was prepared with the assistance of **Iain H.A. Johnston** of The Centre for Software Engineering Ltd. as technical editor, and the first contribution is by Iain Johnston himself, together with his colleague **Anthony P. Wood**. Their paper discusses the concept of safety integrity and current work on the selection and achievement of necessary levels of safety integrity for control and protection systems. As will be seen, they conclude that there remain a number of aspects which standards should seek to address. The principal requirement is for the development of consistent and justifiable means of mapping the risks associated with a system to the integrity levels required of its subsystems.

Information technology and safety

Introduction

In the 1970s and 1980s the extent to which computers have been used in real-time control applications has increased enormously. In parallel with the decreasing size and increasing power of computers applications have become increasingly demanding and complex.

Microprocessors are now a common component in equipment used in all walks of life, to an extent which is not often appreciated, even by the scientist. Without the power of the computer many modern conveniences both at home and at work would not be possible, or if possible would be prohibitively expensive or would lack important functions.

In real-time control applications the use of Programmable Electronic Systems (PESs), which make use of computers and microprocessors, brings considerable advantages in flexibility and cost effectiveness over more conventionally based control systems. These "computers" may vary from large, possibly mainframe, control systems, through distributed networks of computers and Programmable Logic Controllers (PLCs), to individual microprocessor based controllers. PESs may be readily modified to implement minor changes in control requirements, they can cope with extremely complex processes and can react rapidly to a changing situation. There is the facility to store historical information for later analysis and to base control decisions on historical trends. In this way the control system can readily be used to accommodate wear in plant equipment and to monitor the symptoms of wear for maintenance purposes. Perhaps even more important the flexibility of a PES is such that it can readily be reconfigured to control completely different processes.

Most of these advantages are characteristics of the programmable component of the system, in fact a characteristic of the software.

There is increasing awareness of the role which new control strategies, made possible by the use of information technology, can play in improving levels of safety and efficiency [ACARD 1986].

The engine management systems becoming common in automobiles are based on a digital map describing the most appropriate settings for the carburettor and ignition, given the requirements of the driver. This map can be tailored to match precisely the requirements for the particular vehicle, and its state of tune, in a way which would be impossible with conventional systems. Such systems allow the compromise between efficiency, performance and environmental damage to be precisely controlled.

In many continuous processes the most appropriate action to take in the event of a failure depends not just on the current system state, but also on the events leading up to that state. The inherent ability of software to implement complex logical considerations and to access stored memory makes software an ideal mechanism for determining control actions in such circumstances. Potentially, therefore, software can provide a greater degree of safety at a lesser cost than is the case with more conventional systems.

Fly by wire systems in aircraft provide considerable gains in manoeuvrability and/or economy over conventional systems. The PES provides a mechanism by which an otherwise "unflyable" aircraft may be controlled.

Anti-lock braking systems for road vehicles are frequently based on PESs. Typically these applications could be implemented using more conventional methods. A PES based approach provides a cheaper method (usually) and allows the system to be more readily tailored to suit different types of vehicle.

Control and protection systems for the batch production of chemicals could be, and frequently are, implemented using more conventional methods. PESs provide advantages mainly in terms of cost and flexibility. There is, however, one major advantage in that a PES based approach allows for much greater flexibility in the production process and in the design of the operator interface. This is potentially a major contributor to efficient operation and to promoting safe control of the process.

From these examples it can be seen that whilst there are often alternatives to control using PESs there are many applications where they are either essential or difficult to avoid.

As PESs have become increasingly used in applications where they can affect safety so there has been an increase in concern about the potential effects of such use. Both practising engineers and academics have been working on methods and techniques which could help ensure that the increasing use of safety related PESs does not result in the occurrence of unnecessary accidents. In recent years conferences and seminars addressing the problem have become increasingly common. Governments have also acknowledged the problem [POST 1991].

There is a real, justified concern about the dangers of using PESs in safety related applications. It is important to realize, however, that the reasons for their increasing use in such applications are largely the same as the reasons for their use in other applications.

Often a PES based safety system is used to replace an earlier non PES based system either as part of a plant upgrade or in a new replacement plant. The PES based system is more up to date, more flexible and cheaper than an alternative non PES based system. Frequently the PES based system is also seen as "better" in that it can perform safety functions such as analysis of trends which were not previously possible.

In other cases a PES based system is perceived as the only practical safety system. This may be because of cost or because only a PES based system can provide the functions required.

A safety related system may deal with the control of a hazardous process or may simply provide protective actions in the event of problems arising with the system being controlled. These types of application (control or protection) are essentially different in the demands which are placed on the PES [HSE 1987]. A protection system need not be so concerned with the complexities of the algorithms required for control of the process.

The concerns about safety arise from a number of causes. With current knowledge there is no means of knowing that software is error free [Myers 1976]. There are, moreover, no "rules of thumb" (such as exist in other branches of engineering) which may be used in software development to ensure adequate margins of safety [Gilb 1977]. There are not even any generally recognized software equivalents of such basic measures or relationships as volts, amperes or Ohm's law [Bennett 1984]. Software design and implementation does not have the same mature mathematical basis as more conventional engineering.

There have been several incidents in the late 1980s and early 1990s which have given rise to increased concern about the dependence on software in life threatening applications amongst the general public. Few incidents have been directly attributable to software "failures", nevertheless air and rail crashes have been such that in several cases a control or information system which includes software has been amongst the possible causes considered [*Guardian* 1990, *New Scientist* 1991]. The number of such incidents increases all the time, as does the number of systems which rely on the correct operation of software for continued safe operation [Forester and Morrison 1990].

Applications where the consequences of a software failure could be catastrophic attract most attention from the media. Fly by wire aircraft and nuclear installation control provide examples of such "glamorous" applications on which considerable resources are expended during the design and development process to try to ensure that an acceptable level of safety is achieved. Less "glamorous" applications such as domestic equipment tend to be overlooked.

Current approaches to ensuring safety

Considerable effort has gone into the development of "Formal Methods" which attempt to rigorize the process of specifying and developing a software system in such a way that mathematics can be harnessed to prove its correctness and completeness. This is an approach favoured by many and is directed at providing the certainty that a system complies with its specification [Jones 1986].

The use of formal methods, however, is potentially costly and time consuming [IEE 1991], though this view is not necessarily taken by its proponents. More important, the task of ensuring that the formal specification correctly represents the informally expressed and perhaps unclear requirements is not addressed satisfactorily by the use of formal methods [Stokes 1991]. Many problems which arise with PESs result from incorrect or incomplete specifications, which are not recognized as such until late in the development process or till the system is in use.

Conventional specifications are written using a mixture of conventional English language and diagrams. Such specifications are notoriously incomplete, inconsistent, ambiguous and obscure. In comparison formal methods produce specifications which are precise and can be proved to be consistent and (arguably) complete. Such specifications are, however, much more difficult for a naïve user to understand, and the verification of the specification is typically left to the animation or execution of the specification to produce a prototype system which the user can study [MOD 1991a]. There is no reason to suppose that such an animation will be any more successful at ensuring a correct specification than more conventional prototyping methods.

A further problem is that formal methods are not sufficiently mature to be readily applied to many types of problem (for example real-time, concurrency) and that there are few people with the experience and training to apply them productively. It is likely that during the 1990s the situation will improve.

An alternative approach is to use techniques and tools which provide a structured development path, supported by automation, to assist the designers and programmers. Such methods attempt to divorce the designers from the more mundane and error prone development tasks, allowing them to concentrate on ensuring that the system is specified and developed in a correct and consistent way.

Quality assurance is an important contributor to the achievement of acceptable levels of safety integrity. Any safety related system must be designed and constructed to a high level of quality.

There are established schemes for achieving and confirming quality which should be applied to the design and construction of safety related systems. There are indeed standards which are either directly applicable to software, such as the military standard AQAP-13 [NATO 1981] or which are applicable to software via particular assessment guidelines [BS 5750:1987].

It is important that any quality requirements for safety related systems must not conflict with such schemes. Furthermore the requirements should make use of such schemes where appropriate. It can be regarded as a basic requirement that all aspects of a safety related system should comply with some such established quality standard [IEC 1991] and should be certified as complying by some third party body. A particularly suitable means of achieving compliance would be the provision of a Quality Assessment Schedule for BS 5750 or another generic quality standard, directed specifically at safety related software.

Many of these methods are already in use to a greater or lesser extent. CASE tools are used by some software developers [IEE 1989], formal methods are mandatory for safety critical software for the MOD [MOD 1991a] and the use of quality assurance schemes is becoming commonplace [IEE 1989]. Whilst the methods available are not the complete answer to ensuring a satisfactory level of safety they do provide a good basis for the development of safety critical software. The problems result, principally, from the immaturity and inconsistent use of the methods available and the nature of safety itself. Training can effectively overcome some these problems, provided that there is a background standard which ensures that different training courses are consistent with each other.

It is important that the need for a consistent approach is not interpreted as a need for rigid uniformity. In different circumstances and for different applications different methods and tools will be appropriate. It is unlikely that a single method will ever be appropriate, even for a single application. A carefully chosen set of tools suited to a particular application which enable the PES and its environment to be considered from differing viewpoints is likely to be the most suitable approach. Standards and guidelines should ensure that the selection process and the tools selected are consistent, not the same, over the various PES applications.

There is a particular problem with applications of a less glamorous nature. Such applications, where the risk is at a lower level, tend to be overlooked by media and technologists alike. As a result, whilst up to date development methods may be used for such applications, there is a lack of consistency with respect to the approaches taken by developers. In fact a recent study [IEE 1989] found that there was often a lack of awareness of the safety implications of a PES by its producers or users.

Relevant standards

It is important that standards, guidelines and codes of practice are introduced and used to ensure that a consistent approach is taken to the design, development and assessment of all safety related applications which involve software. Various guidelines and standards have already been developed, most of which address particular application areas, or are for use in particular companies [IEC 880:1986, EEMUA 1989, IGasE 1989, IUR 1986, MOD 1991a, Jolly and Johnson 1987, RTCA 1985].

Notable exceptions are the Health and Safety Executive (HSE) Guidelines [HSE 1987] and the IEC draft standards [IEC 1991, IEC 1992]. Whilst the HSE guidelines do address software, their main concern is with the PES within which the software operates. Nevertheless advice and checklists are provided which are useful both for planning, developing and assessing safety critical software. The guidelines are not, of course, a standard, though they do provide a means towards standardization of practices. Two important points are brought out in the HSE guidelines:

The recognition of differing levels of safety integrity (criticality), first recognized in IEC 643:1979.

The recognition of the appropriateness of applying differing levels of rigour to the development of systems or software required to have different levels of integrity.

The draft standards under development by the IEC take this further, explicitly specifying five levels of safety integrity. The IEC draft software standard [IEC 1991] presents a battery of techniques to be applied in different combinations to the design, development and assessment of software of differing levels of safety integrity. The standard is intended to be supplemented by additional standards specific to particular applications and industries. The IEC draft systems standard [IEC 1992] is of particular interest since it addresses the problem of determining the risk associated with a PES and from that risk identifying the safety integrity required of the PES and of its software. The need for such guidance is discussed below under *Risk and safety* and *Risk reduction*.

The HSE guidelines are intended to be supplemented by guidance for particular industries. The IGasE guidelines [IGasE 1989] provide guidance for the gas industry based on the HSE guidelines. The EEMUA guidelines [EEMUA 1989] provide guidance for the process industry based on the HSE guidelines.

The interim defence standards [MOD 1991a, MOD 1991b] developed by the Ministry of Defence (MOD) are mandatory for suppliers to the MOD. They deal with the particular concerns of an industry which demands extremely high standards of practice, appropriate to the high level of risk associated with many of its products and their intended operating environment. The standard 00-56 [MOD 1991b] is of particular interest since it addresses the problem of determining the risk associated with a PES and from that risk identifying the safety integrity required of the PES and of its software. The need for such guidance is discussed below as already cited. The MOD standard provides such guidance in an interim form, specifically for the defence industry.

Other standards deal, for example, with the particular problems associated with the nuclear industry [IEC 643:1979, IEC 880:1986, Jolly and Johnson 1987] and the transport industries [IUR 1986, RTCA 1985]. These do not take a common approach and further development of the standards is required to ensure that they are based on common ground and do not conflict with each other, or with other standards being developed.

The nature of safety with respect to software

There are a number of reasons why software is different from hardware:

Software does not fail through aging, all failures result from design faults.

Reliability models do exist for software but the nature of software failures means that real questions remain as to their validity and appropriateness.

The discontinuous nature of software means that small changes in inputs can result in unexpectedly large changes in output values. This means that meaningful testing is much less straightforward than for conventional analogue systems.

Any non trivial software is extremely complex and unlikely to be understood in its entirety by a single individual.

Software is deceptively easy to change and small changes can have unexpectedly far-reaching results.

Software is conceptual rather than physical, though it can be represented physically.

There are several disadvantages resulting from the programmable aspects of the PES which are particularly relevant in safety applications and which are associated with the special characteristics of software:

Changes made to software frequently introduce new faults.

There are as yet no universally applicable models on which to base predictions as to the reliability of software [Littlewood 1991].

The behaviour of the software can vary dramatically and unexpectedly for small changes in input values.

It is important to realize, also, that software on its own cannot harm anyone. Software is a conceptual, not a physical, entity which requires additional physical components to realize it. At the simplest these physical components comprise a computer and input-output devices such as keyboards and VDUs. In the context of safety the physical and software components comprise the PES [HSE 1987] which includes the sensors and actuators by which the PES reacts with the real world. It is these sensors and actuators, together with the devices and processes which they monitor and control which make the PES and its software relate to safety.

Typically a safety related PES is part of an overall system which may be composed of:

(i)   The process controlled and its associated plant.

(ii)   Operating and maintenance personnel.

(iii) Operating and maintainance procedure

(iv)   The local environment

(v)   The PES and its associated software, hardware, actuators and sensors.

(vi)   Other non safety related PESs and their associated software, hardware, actuators and sensors.

(vii) Other non PES safety and control mechanisms.

For example, an anti-lock braking system (v) is not related to safety till it is connected to a vehicle's braking system (i) and that vehicle is used in circumstances where a failure could result in an accident (iv).

Safety related software cannot therefore be considered in isolation. It must be considered in the context of the whole system within which it exists. Much of the trick involved in reasoning about such software is concerned with selecting the correct system bounds within which to consider the specification, design and assessment of the software.

Risk and safety

Safety is in essence a subjective quality, and is conditioned by the social mores prevalent at any particular time and place [Bennett 1984].

Safety cannot be absolute in most cases; it is essentially probabilistic. Risk is defined as the combination of the frequency, or probability, and the consequence of an accident [IEC 1991]; safety is concerned with the absence of or reduction of risk. For practical purposes most engineering disciplines allow systems to be constructed which are safe. This is possible as a result of the development of an understanding of the uses to which the systems are to be put and the mathematical and scientific basis for their construction [Baber 1991], together with the application of the ALARP (As Low As Reasonably Practicable) principle.

There is a wide variety of applications in which safety related PESs are currently used and are likely to be used in the future. This variety is reflected in the wide variety of potential consequences which can result if a PES malfunctions. The consequences of malfunction may vary from accidents which could directly cause death or serious injury to many people to accidents which could only cause minor injury to an individual. There is also the possibility of indirect injury, through environmental damage, and non physical effects such economic harm.

The numbers of instances of each application vary considerably. In some cases only a few examples of the PES will ever be in use. In others the PES will be in use in millions of examples of the same system. Such variety is reflected in a wide variation in the probability that a malfunction will occur, either in the controlled system or the PES.

All the different types of application need to provide an acceptable (or tolerable) level of safety. This raises the questions of what is an acceptable level of safety for an application, to what extent the PES is required to contribute to safety and how do we ensure that the PES achieves this level of contribution.

There is for most systems a tolerable risk which is the maximum risk acceptable for such a system. In fact, following the ALARP principle, there is a band above which the risk is not acceptable, below which the risk is acceptable and within which the risk must be reduced as far as is reasonably practicable [HSE 1988].

It is important to realize that the tolerable level of risk is not a fixed unchanging band, it depends on the application, its location and the people involved [HSE 1988]. It is essential that this is recognized in any generic standard addressing more than one industry.

The use of PESs in widely varying applications and application areas results in an increasing degree of commonality between the control and protection mechanisms in what were once widely diverse systems. In many industries there are well established standards and guidelines for ensuring safety when more traditional technologies are involved; for example, the use of safe and ultimate working loads in civil engineering. Such industry specific guidance is likely to be just as necessary for the use of PESs in safety related applications. It is however important that the guidance has a common basis across the different industries.

In many cases the same PESs will be used in widely varying industries and it is essential that a consistent approach is adopted in order to avoid unnecessary and unintended provision of inappropriate levels of safety. Inappropriate levels of safety may be insufficient (unacceptable or not as low as reasonably practicable) or excessive (requiring unnecessary expenditure of resource for their achievement).

Risk reduction

The principle of risk reduction is illustrated in Figure 8.1. The figure shows the reduction of risk to a level which is not unacceptable and which is as low as reasonably practicable (ALARP).

For applications where the risk must be reduced the reduction may be achieved in different ways. The selection of the means of reducing the risk is part of the design process of the system and may involve several different safety systems. A typical example is a fire detection system with automatic sprinklers. Such a system is a protection system designed to reduce the risk to personnel and goods in a building. Automatic fire detection, provided by sensors, is backed up by manually operated fire alarm points and automatically operated sprinklers are backed up by fire extinguishers and hoses. Procedures exist for evacuating the building confirming that all personnel have been evacuated and alerting the emergency services.

This example demonstrates the possibility of a number of diverse safety systems combining to provide the necessary risk reduction. Typically some of these systems may be PES based and some not. The principle is illustrated in Figure 8.2.

It is essential that any standard addressing the safety aspects of PESs deals with risk reduction. There must be clear and justifiable means of apportioning the required risk reduction to different parts of the PES (principally hardware and software). The methods proposed must be such that it is reasonable to claim that the apportionment is such as to achieve the overall reduction required.

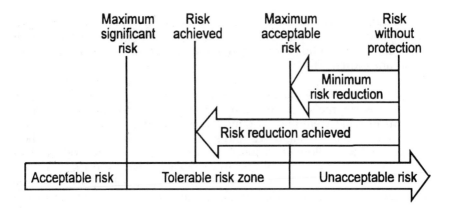

Figure 8.1 *Risk reduction and the tolerable zone*

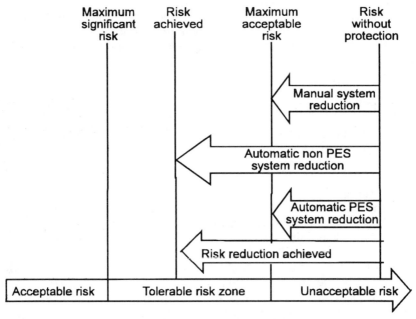

Figure 8.2 *Risk reduction by multiple systems*

There must also be clear and justifiable means of achieving the required risk reduction for each part of the system. These means must allow for differing degrees of safety integrity for both hardware and software.

Safety systems are designed to provide necessary risk reduction.

Risk and safety are not easily measurable quantities. The concept of levels has been developed [HSE 1987, IEC 1991, IEC 1992, MOD 1991a, MOD 1991b, RTCA 1985] to help with their measurement. Levels provide a quantized approach to the measurement of what is in principle a continuous quantity. The concepts of safety integrity and safety integrity levels [HSE 1987, IEC 1991, IEC 1992, MOD 1991b, MOD 1991a] have been introduced specifically to help reason about the safety required of and achieved by different PES applications. These levels of safety integrity apply to the overall safety related system and the software components of the system. They are based on the level of risk associated with the application and provide an important tool for reasoning about subjective safety requirements and achievements.

The principle of safety integrity levels is that the level of risk is identified then the appropriate level of safety integrity required of the overall system is determined. Finally the level of safety integrity required of the system components is identified. The software component can then be developed to the appropriate level of safety integrity [IEC 1992, IEC 1991, MOD 1991b, MOD 1991a]. The concept of different levels of integrity is therefore crucial to any successful standardization of approach to safety related software.

In principle then there is a need to determine the level of risk associated with an application and thus the extent of any risk reduction required. The extent of the risk reduction required must be used to determine the safety integrity required, overall. The system must then be designed to achieve that level of safety integrity.

The level of safety integrity may be achieved by single or multiple safety related systems. If multiple safety related systems are used to achieve the necessary risk reduction there is a need to determine the level of safety integrity required of each safety related system. The IEC draft systems standard [IEC 1992] and the interim defence standard [MOD 1991b] do address this but it is a poorly defined process and there is a need for it to be dealt with in detail in any standard which is to be of practical use.

The principles involved are illustrated in Figure 8.3. The shaded areas indicate the transformations for which it is particularly important that guidance is provided (see as follows).

Essential requirements

Major standards addressing the safety aspects of the use of computers in control and protection applications have been published [MOD 1991a, IEC 1991, MOD 1991b, IEC 1992]. Some of these are draft standards and others are interim standards. During the 1990s work will continue on the development of further standards and guidance documents. There are eight general requirements which emerge from the discussion in the preceding subsections which need to be addressed by the work on standards and guidance documents:

(i)   The multidisciplinary character of many major modern projects necessarily involves a diverse approach to the design, development, installation, operation and maintenance of the PESs involved. If there is no common ground within a project and between different projects inconsistencies will give rise

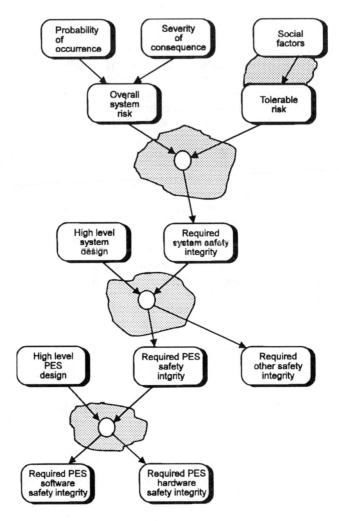

NOTE
The shaded areas indicate the transformations for which further guidance is required

Figure 8.3 *The determination of software safety integrity*

to confusion and misunderstandings which can only reduce the level of safety which can be achieved.

Standards (and guidelines and codes of practice) are required which address the safety aspects of the use of PESs in a wide variety of application areas. Standards for particular industries, applications or types of equipment are necessary. Such standards should, nevertheless, be based on common ground. The ideal is a single generic standard, or group of standards, with satellite interpretations for various industries.

(ii) Quality assurance provides an essential baseline which is necessary for any safety related PES. The provision of specific quality assurance interpretations of existing quality assurance standards for safety related systems needs to be considered.

(iii) There is a need for guidance on the selection and use of diverse and complementary methods and tools appropriate to particular applications and industries.

(iv) There is a need for standards and guidelines which recognize the need to consider differing levels of risk and therefore differing levels of safety integrity and differing levels of rigour in system and software development and assessment. The importance of this point lies in the need to avoid insufficient or excessive levels of safety.

(v) There is a need to provide for consistent approaches which allow a PES for use in different industries and types of application to be developed and assessed in such a way that work need not be unnecessarily repeated for the different industries or application areas.

(vi) There is a need to make use of and develop existing standards to ensure that they are based on common ground.

(vii) There is a need to address levels of risk and safety integrity particularly where there are a number of different possible consequences and severities of consequence associated with the application. Practical and objective means of determining the level of risk associated with an application and of using this and the tolerable risk to determine the risk reduction required of the system are needed. There is a need to address the determination of the safety integrity required of a system and the allocation of risk reduction and safety integrity between the different parts of the system or between different safety systems.

(viii) There is a need to address the achievement of specific levels of risk reduction and safety integrity and the assessment of whether the required levels have been achieved.

(ix) There is a need to recognize that the tolerable risk varies and to provide guidance on determining what is tolerable in any particular case.

There is ongoing work which addresses the means of reasoning about risk and integrity levels and their apportionment between different safety systems or different parts of the same safety system.

Satisfying the requirements

Most of the requirements just outlined express a straightforward need for specific coverage in any standards dealing with the safety aspects of PESs. The draft and interim standards from the IEC and MOD [IEC 1991, IEC 1992, MOD 1991a, MOD 1991b] already address many of the requirements.

The MOD interim standards are directed specifically at the defence industry and are intended to be compatible with the IEC draft standards. The IEC draft standards are intended to provide a single generic standard applicable across all industries, but open to specific interpretation for particular industries. This approach addresses requirement (i) in the preceding subsection.

Both the MOD and IEC standards recognize the need for quality assurance. This addresses requirement (ii) above, though no specific interpretations for safety related PESs are mentioned.

Both the MOD and IEC standards recognize the need to consider different levels of risk and safety integrity. The standards define the levels of rigour appropriate to the development of software for different levels of safety integrity. The levels of rigour appropriate to the non software elements of PESs are less well defined. Some guidance is provided by HSE [HSE 1987], EEMUA [EEMUA 1989] and IGasE [IGasE 1989]. Requirement (iv) is therefore addressed, but could be dealt with more thoroughly.

Both the MOD and IEC standards address selection of methods and tools. The IEC standards are intended to be applicable across a range of industries and provide guidance on selection from a wide range of methods and tools. The guidance is directed principally at making selections appropriate to the safety integrity level rather than the industry or application. Further guidance is therefore required to address requirement (iii) above.

The IEC standard does provide guidance on approaches intended to be used across a range of industries. There is therefore the opportunity for development and assessment of a PES to use methods and tools which are compatible with the requirements of a wide range of industries and applications. The point is not, however, addressed directly in the standard and so requirement (v) is not really addressed satisfactorily.

Both the MOD and IEC standards address the need for assessment and the approach to be taken in ensuring that the required levels of safety integrity are appropriate and have been achieved. In particular both standards require that the assessment is performed by an independent body. The MOD standard, however, only requires such assessment for the higher levels of safety integrity. The IEC standard requires a lesser degree of independence for the lower levels of safety integrity. Requirement (viii) is therefore addressed, though there is a possible lack of compatibility between the standards.

Both the MOD and IEC standards build upon existing standards and guidelines, notably quality assurance standards [BS 5750:1987, NATO 1981] and the HSE guidelines [HSE 1987]. Requirement (vi) is therefore addressed in so far as is possible within the standards themselves. There remains, however, a need for the existing guidance to be developed to support the standards.

Both the MOD and IEC standards address the determination of risk level associated with an application and the consequent safety integrity require-ments of the PES and its software. The MOD standard [MOD 1991b] makes an explicit and detailed attempt to deal with the problem in relation to the defence industry, whilst the IEC standard [IEC 1992] addresses industry more gener-ally. Nevertheless this is an area in which much further development is required if practical, objective and consistent techniques are to be used across a variety of industries. As suggested in requirement (vii) above, there is a need for further guidance in determining the risk level and tolerable risk and using these to determine the overall risk reduction and thence the overall safety integrity required. Further guidance is also required in apportioning the safety integrity between different parts of the system. It is important that the methods and tools recommended or required for this are such that they are either directly compatible with the approach outlined in the IEC and MOD standards [IEC 1992, MOD 1991b] or are such that the IEC and MOD are able to embrace the approach.

The MOD standards explicitly identify a tolerable risk level for defence appli-cations. The IEC standards implicitly recognize that different tolerable levels of risk may be appropriate to different types of application and provide some guidance on identifying the tolerable level of risk. Further guidance is needed to address the requirement (ix) of the previous subsection. Much of this guidance should be industry specific.

No system can be guaranteed to be 100% safe, particularly if it includes software. Accordingly the safety integrity requirement is an indicator of the level of safety which is appropriate for the particular application. This is not a concern peculiar to information technology or to PESs. In principle all systems which involve some element of risk implicitly or explicitly take account of this concern. The concern is essentially one of the interpretation of public opinion and social mores with respect to the risks which are tolerable in different circumstances.

In other branches of engineering "rules of thumb" identifying the practices which are acceptable in particular circumstances have been developed. A generic standard for PESs in safety applications must provide a sound basis upon which such "rules of thumb" may be developed for different areas of industry. A useful means of providing such a basis, given the wide diversity of considerations which must be taken into account, is to adopt a multidimen-sional matrix relating each consideration to a level of risk together with rules for combining these quantized levels as necessary.

The MOD and IEC standards use a two dimensional matrix of consequence and probability to the determine the risk level associated with an application. In fact any hazard is likely to be associated with a number of different possible severities of consequence, each with associated probabilities. There is a need to combine the various consequences and their probabilities for the different hazards associated with a system if a satisfactory conclusion is to be reached as to the overall level of risk associated with a system.

Hence a criticality matrix with dimensions for loss of life, injury, environmental damage, other effects on the quality of life, monetary loss and their associated probabilities may be appropriate. Rules could link the entries for each of these dimensions to take into account the social tolerability of each scale and to provide an overall quantization of the risk for each hazard. A further matrix could relate risk from different hazards to enable an overall quantization of risk associated with the application which could be mapped directly to the required safety integrity level for the overall system.

Further matrices could be used to relate required safety integrity levels to the appropriate methods for design development and assessment. The approach taken by the draft IEC standards [IEC 1991, IEC 1992] exemplifies this.

Conclusion

Whilst standards specific to particular industries, applications or equipment are necessary they must be based on common ground. If there is no such common ground inconsistencies will give rise to confusion and misunderstandings which can only reduce the level of safety which can be achieved.

Common standards must address all aspects of the use of information technology in safety related applications. The standards must also provide for variations in the amount of resource which it is appropriate to spend in different application areas and applications. In particular, the software component of the control system must be addressed in a way that enables developers, assessors and users to rely on the standard in practical day to day use.

In order for a common standard to allow for different application areas there must be a provision for a variety of approaches to design, development and assessment. These approaches should take account of the differing consequences of various types of accident. Levels of criticality (or integrity) are required which can take account of the consequences of accidents and the degree of benefit to be derived from each application.

The importance of quality as a contributor to safety must be recognized. There are established schemes for achieving and confirming quality, such as BS 5750 or AQAP-13 [NATO 1981]. Any quality requirements for safety related systems must not conflict with such schemes and should make use of them.

It is particularly important that standards adopt consistent approaches to determination and achievement of appropriate levels of safety integrity. There should be a consistent means of identifying tolerable risk, required risk reduction, system safety integrity and software safety integrity across a wide range of application areas and risk levels.

Particular needs which are not satisfactorily addressed in existing standards or guidelines are:

generic guidance on determining the appropriate tolerable risk for an application;

generic guidance for determining the required risk reduction and the equivalent system safety integrity for an application;

fuller guidance (in industry-specific standards) on the methods and tools appropriate to particular industries or types of application;

guidance on the development and assessment of multipurpose PESs in a way which avoids the need to repeat work unnecessarily for different applications;

generic guidance on apportioning safety integrity between multiple safety systems and their component parts.

It may be possible to provide at least some of this guidance using a system of multidimensional matrices, combining the approaches of the MOD and IEC.

We now turn our attention to requirements for security and resilience in an office environment. In the following contribution, **A.L. "Phil" Phillips** looks at what lack of resilience in an office system implies for its users.

Resilience of office automation systems

Introduction

As a result of a number of failures of certain high profile office automation (OA) systems it has become more accepted to consider the implications of any lack of resilience for the systems offered to general users. When distributed systems become more common it will be a problem for the managers of such systems to cope with surge effects due to localized failures and the likelihood of demand for alternative facilities at short notice. This contribution discusses the problem in the context of the types of systems that already occur (the extension to distributed systems for OA or other applications is obvious); and in the process

defines resilience, and why it is necessary;

explains how resilience is affected by a number of factors;

describes how it can be achieved by different strategies;

indicates the order of costs expected for grades of resilience; and indicates the options available and the implications of choosing to implement them at typical office sites.

Constraints

The observations are based on experience gained from several OA projects. It does not represent a complete study of all existing or proposed OA systems nor is any operational OA or automated data processing (ADP) system necessarily limited to, or likely to justify, all of the features presented in this paper. In the interests of the reader, a number of detailed technical matters have been omitted or, in one case, deferred to an annex.

Definitions

The following definitions are used, amplified by suitable adjectives where appropriate:

> *Resilience.* The ability of an OA system to continue to operate under adverse conditions to achieve an agreed level of service, which may be lower than the best achievable under normal conditions but adequate for OA based work to continue efficiently.

> *Level (grade) of service.* An agreed level of performance of one or more facilities measured by real parameters, e.g. number of packets delivered, number of staff logged on and obtaining normal service response times, number of errors or retries on a port or line per unit of time.

> *Availability.* The mean time between failures (MTBF) divided by the sum of MTBF plus the MTTR (mean time to repair (recover)): strictly, a number from 0 to 1 or expressed as a percentage.

> *Uninterrupted power supply (UPS).* A generally misleading phrase implying (absolute) continuity of power supplies. In practice it may cover such options as capacitor or battery backup (for memory), AC/AC convertors, AC/battery floated invertors, motor-generator sets and private power generation systems feeding one of the storage-invertor systems. Such systems are comparatively rare, limited in capacity, and expensive. For the purpose of this paper it will be assumed that a UPS facility will provide smooth continuity of power for a finite period.

Do we need resilience?

If we look at the non-automated office we see such things as pens, pencils, paper, files, storage of varying security levels, and a telephone. There are also books, furniture, the room and minor trivia. If one of these items fails (or is stolen or destroyed) we usually have the option to obtain quickly another or repair the failed one, e.g. sharpen the pencil. If necessary we move out to another office, similarly equipped, taking or obtaining copies of immediately relevant information from the registry, those with whom we correspond, a library, or at worst rewrite a facsimile of the original text. Resilience in this context is largely innate and only noticed by its absence at a critical moment.

When we turn to office automation, many of the features above remain as familiar objects which flow around the new facility. Often our old ways of working are ingrained over many years and it may be more efficient to continue with them for a range of activities. Particularly unlikely to be automated are initial creativity processes, short transient activities which are a few moments' work in the old but familiar manual methods, and those activities which for reasons of security, compatibility or complexity, are not amenable to an easy transfer to an automated method of working. Personal preferences obviously play an important part in determining the acceptance of OA facilities.

To make OA attractive so that it sells well the OA suppliers have had to develop extensive suites of software designed to provide facilities which the potential user can be persuaded he wants. Their presentation methods and quality have had to be improved so that a user does not need to have a computer science background to be able to use the products. In turn the hardware has become more complex to support colour graphics representations, multitasking, and extensive interaction between users, files (computer type), and communications facilities. The end result is often a very complex, sophisticated facility which includes a bewildering array of options. It may allow a dedicated, persevering user (not all systems are perfect) to undertake a very large proportion of his office tasks if these are centred on the generation, storage, analysis or dissemination of information. The poor fish is hooked! Now instead of the manual features of his office with their familiar comforting tangibility he is unwittingly faced with a glass palace full of his most treasured possessions, so to speak. This edifice can become a reality through which he treads his daily path. Before long he has become trusting of its portals and placed his faith in its continued existence. *He expects it to be there at all times and in all places* and becomes extremely dissatisfied when the illusion is broken.

Does the user *require it to be there at all times* to achieve his objectives? The answer to this question lies in the way his work is structured, the extent to which he can still share facilities with colleagues, the extent to which he can revert to less risky manual methods and the criticality of timeliness, accuracy, or throughput. Deciding upon these matters is partly up to the individual user but limitations may have been designed in by the system designer, by the user's management, or by colleagues who perhaps embraced the use of OA methods without due care.

In short, we need resilience if:

the function is operationally critical and cannot be sustained by manual methods (e.g. aircraft movements control, security and communications network management);

delays due to loss of service or performance, loss of access to information, or reduced staffing levels have increased our dependence on improved efficiency, any of which would seriously affect the effectiveness of operational facilities or associated administration, (e.g. stock control of critical items, intelligence, CCIS and to some extent key MIS);

the corporate effectiveness of the organization has (or is likely or intended to) become dependent on the use of the facility to the exclusion of other methods; this may be by user preference, or by design (e.g. for audit, security, quality or performance reasons).

With the increasing life-cycle costs of OA systems, especially the more secure versions, resilience overheads incurred just because it would be nice to have the highest possible availability cannot and should not be justified. The average IT (= OA + CAD/CAM + mainframe terminal) peripheral utilization for actual work is probably less than 10% due to over-provision, incompatibility, disillusionment of the user, inflexibility of the offered services, or downtime.

What affects resilience?

Briefly, everything! Since this is an unhelpful answer it is necessary to focus in some detail (contained in the Annex after the main text) on the matter and determine how a more constructive response can be made. If for a moment we consider the organization as a system, then any event, natural or man-made, for example bad weather, a train strike or illness may affect the working of the system. Most organizations cope with these events due to the lag between cause and effect, the number of staff and their willingness to cope with additional, unusual or exceptional circumstances and demands. Furthermore the organization has local elements of leadership, not always the management, capable of making justifiable decisions to avoid, work round or overcome temporary difficulties to achieve local or corporate objectives. Only when the importance of a function is recognized is any special preparation or alternative arrangement planned, and such plans are seldom exercised.

When we look at an OA system it is immediately apparent that, however clever or pretty the facilities provided, the average supplier has paid scant regard to the importance of resilience for his customers. The few high availability systems or multiprocessor or networked microprocessor offerings are usually oriented towards transaction processing, high throughput, or safety-critical applications. Of course, they could be used for OA, but often the software offered is mostly supplier-specific, non-OSI, non-Unix, and insecure.

To get round these deficiencies it has been necessary to specify some quite tough requirements for UK government systems, e.g. CHOTS, the MOD's

Corporate Headquarters Office Technology System (1989). Underlying that specification process there has been a preliminary task of threat assessment partly to assess the security requirements but also to determine how to prepare for contingencies. The process of threat assessment is well established and is therefore omitted from further discussion. For a specific system or site only a proportion of the potential threats may be expected to arise with any significant probability. Each system or site will contain a range of vulnerabilities to particular threats and the resulting exposure to loss of function (or information in the case of security) can be analysed.

For undertaking risk assessments a range of commercial methodologies can be obtained from the major consultancies such as those in the CSA Contingency Planning Group.

Not all of the picture is black. Existing protective measures must be taken into account; the potential for, and benefits of, fallback and recovery procedures may well reduce risk to an acceptable level. Because these may fail, it is appropriate to arrange for contingency plans for the preparation and use of backup copies of data, manual procedures and records, and the training of management and users to be disciplined in their approach to the use of OA. They need to recognize when its risks might outweigh its benefits. Such recognition skills if properly applied can help prevent major dependencies from forming, they can be used to identify the limitations of current systems and specifications, and if fed into the appropriate quarter could improve the quality of future systems.

Possible strategies for resilience

There are a number of possible strategies which depend on different approaches to achieve resilience. These include:

> *Relying on manual methods.* The use of purely manual methods may be justified where absolute security, integrity and availability are demanded, albeit at the expense of performance and image (in the public relations sense).

> *Standalone processors.* Most large organizations are well practised in providing a multitude of standalone processors suitably sourced with a range of applications software for OA or other functions. Provided that suitable constraints and precautions are taken security can be achieved and the commonality of underlying systems hardware and software can enable a ready substitution if the OA element fails. Of course, power failure may preclude local work on occasions; user laxity may reduce his protection against data loss; and intercommunication is restricted to the exchange of media, or paper and verbal means as at present.

> *Locally networked processors.* These can provide local intercommunication facilities but introduce security risks of some

significance as the sensitivity of material, the number of users, and the amount held each rise. Existing advice from security specialists tends to reflect the caution necessary as interworking increases. Loss of power and local networks affect availability and the value of further resilience measures.

Globally networked processors. These can extend the availability of intercommunication but raise the security problems. Where security is not so critical staff away from site can be given global privileges to use local resources, e.g. during site visits or in emergencies. Even in secure systems this can be done but requires a single security policy, an excellent quality of security management, and some very powerful audit facilities if any containment objectives are to be assessed.

Distributed systems. Resources are made available on demand to a user without his being concerned for his absolute location with respect to his data or the processing resource(s) he is using. The innate requirement for resilience in such systems is driving research into the problems of distributed database systems management and security, and setting the targets for current ISO OSI standardization work.

Centralized ADP systems (bureaux). The typical bureau is not geared to the support of large volume OA but can provide fairly high resilience to a limited number of users. Security can be arranged to meet the needs of specific groups though not always on the same facilities as a general user. Ultimately the provision of communications and power for the remote terminals may limit the resilience for individual users.

In short, the options are there, the restrictions arise due to cost, the need for security and related constraints, and the fact that high performance, resilient OA systems are still very much a special in the marketplace of the 1990s. Secure versions are rarer than hens' teeth.

Levels (grades) of service

It is useful to consider the provision of any facility in terms of its level(s) of service. The cost of providing the service (capital and maintenance) should be considered in conjunction with the benefits of that service if provided *and* the cost or losses incurred if that level of service is wrong (i.e. under- or over-provision, or during downtime or poor performance).

The levels of service which might be considered as options include:

(a) *No service.* This level is the baseline since no extra costs are incurred, but losses due to inability to meet corporate objectives in a timely and efficient fashion could arise.

(b) Normal working. This is the commonly accepted target level and would be met if performance and services were within the limits specified in the related specification, e.g. 95% of responses in 10 seconds, all users online performing word processing, etc.

(c) *Limited facilities for essential functions or users*. This level provides for a subset of the total services to be essential facilities for key personnel or system operational needs, e.g. duty officer, electronic mail. Since any reduction in the service for such users or functions is likely to have significant impact it may be appropriate to provide these facilities from a high resilience core element of a generally less resilient design. Another option is to enable quick reconfiguration of the system to provide resilience for such users. This approach would need to be identified as an specific operational requirement or be feasible within the general design specification.

(d) *Limited facilities for all users*. This level seeks to ensure that a finite set of services can be provided to all users possibly with reduced performance requirements over the normal service or some form of queuing for access to terminals but a normal performance when receiving service.

(e) *Resilience against specific system failures*. This level implies specific provision for failures; other levels of service might cause the supplier to propose extra equipment to meet the availability requirements but improved reliability or performance could allow him to reduce the amount of equipment provided and thereby reduce the resilience. This level may require fully or partially duplicated systems, fault-tolerant designs and extensive backup features.

(f) *Resilience against specific external risks*. Users who can justify this requirement demand confidence in the provision of a supporting service or utility (electricity, communications, water, security, etc) necessary for the continuous running of the system for part or all of the organization. This level includes the concept of UPS in their various forms, chosen normally to match the level of service required by the user. *Caution: It is possible to degrade the availability of a service if a poor quality UPS is incorporated in an otherwise resilient design.*

Order of extra costs for resilience

The following table indicates an estimate of the order of extra cost that would be incurred for increased resilience in a system.

OPTION	(a)	(b)	(c)	(d)	(e)	(f)
COST	B	C	1.05C	1.25C	1.5C-2C	D

where B equals lost benefits; C equals the cost of a system as currently specified; and D is the cost of adding one or more of a range of improvements to isolate the system from its real-world environment.

The reasoning for the numeric modifiers in (c)-(f) is as follows:

(c) Up to about 5% of users or functions are likely to be essential. Limiting total provision to only these essential users or functions is likely to lead to loss of economy of scale, perhaps doubling the cost of provision per user. Providing a full system which incorporates option (c) from the design stage would give rise to a estimated cost of 1.05C.

(d) Pareto's Rule suggests 80% of the facilities can be achieved for about 20% of the cost. The additions necessary to ensure an improved level of resilience should not be too great if the functionality remaining is limited.

(e) At the lower end it is assumed the system design accommodates redundancy and reconfiguration to meet a particular resilience strategy; at the high cost end it is assumed that significant system breakpoints are encountered, e.g. number of ports now greater than the processors originally specified could handle, so processor count goes up or model used has higher power consumption; the resulting increase in space or air-conditioning load breaks other design criteria, and so on.

(f) Consideration of this option involves a strategic rethinking of objectives and the impact of not being able to cope with certain risks. At this level of service one is looking towards diversity of siting, standby power sources, alternative communications routes or suppliers, and so on. D would need to be calculated for each site for a range of risks.

The options available for existing systems

Some existing systems could be reconfigured within their present features to provide an improvement in user protection against loss of facilities in an area by increasing the probability of finding a nearby serviceable terminal and network connection to a processor if a route fails. This would not be feasible for direct connections unless the processors were linked.

Some additional resilience could be obtained by providing keystroke recording and improving automatic backup and recovery facilities to minimize the impact of failures on a user.

A major redesign of hardware and software to create a high resilience solution is inappropriate for most projects. Some rearrangement and/or overprovision to cover essential facilities or users could be just as effective if properly planned.

Introduction of local low capacity UPS could help remove a large proportion of potential problems of noisy or intermittent supplies provided that the computers are able to make adequate use of them. The load capacity required would limit the support period to minutes rather than hours and terminals would not be protected. A major consideration would be the need for space.

Introduction of alternative power sources would in many cases prove extremely costly and subject to planning delays. Dedicated wiring would be necessary if terminals were also to be supported. A UPS would be required if the major disturbance of even a momentary outage for switching between supplies was to be avoided. Major factors in the decision would include building leases, changes of occupancy, fire and pollution risks, planning consent and the problems of obtaining support for such facilities. Resolution of these factors would involve a multiplicity of agencies or authorities even if a common policy was determined to be applicable.

Summary

This paper sets out a number of possible resilience objectives. Often the introduction of these has been limited by the judgements of the buyer on the potential costs of any greater level of resilience, e.g. dual processing or mirrored disks, etc.

Good resilience will be a key factor in generating user acceptance of a system. Experience does not justify the assumption that the suppliers will make special efforts to give the best service. The effects of changing the resilience requirements in any of a number of areas of a system and its environment are significant additional cost, additional cause for delays, and major problems with the provision of adequate acceptable space for extra hardware or power backup or power quality improvement facilities.

Major problems are likely to arise over the allocation of space to overcome the growth of dependence on electricity and OA systems.

Conclusions

The main source of disruption for a user will be the recovery of a processor after even momentary power failure. The quality of protection against this eventuality should therefore be high. It is likely that the specification for a system has placed this in the hands of the supplier.

Major improvements to the availability of power supplies by the provision of backup services may require significant investments to be made in buildings where the occupancy is tenuous. There are also problems of space and maintenance which will occur for most sites.

Recommended course of action

Suppliers should be able to provide reliability models of their system in respect of facilities for users, vital functions of the system (e.g. directory), etc. They should incorporate into the model accurate values for the MTTRs for various faults and an accurate representation of the dependencies of one part of the system or functions upon others. It is vital that systems staff have a clear understanding of these dependencies as this will be critical information for the system managers when deciding how to overcome fault conditions. When reallocating resources, a wrong decision could well make things worse.

The extent to which a particular OA system should be resilient should be obvious. Suppliers can play a part in demonstrating how to achieve a high grade of service from standard office automation products through user education, advising on good housekeeping, and the provision of support for contingency planning (which should be exercised).

An organization should press its suppliers to produce convincing demonstration and arguments for their claims to meet all resilience, fallback and recovery requirements in an acceptable, timely fashion. It may prove that the problems of recovery are best avoided, perhaps by the use of UPS so that only the most extreme circumstances result in a major outage.

Annex: Threats to the resilience of an office automation system

The following list of threats to the resilience of an office automation system is given without prejudice to their likelihood of occurrence.

Specification weaknesses. These arise where the original requirement sets down a specification which omits any, or adequate, statements for the definition of resilience expectations. A supplier may then use whatever methods and facilities to achieve his objectives to lessen cost, improve productivity of his staff or facilities, without significant reference to the unstated expectations and needs of his client. Statements in the specification could be expected to address obvious risks and to require the supplier to design to meet system mechanical, electrical, functional or performance availability or other criteria. A supplier may take a number of steps to achieve these client objectives and still not provide effective resilience if those objectives fail to demand that information held by the system is also made resilient.

Design weaknesses. The complexity of office automation applications software with its large monolithic packages, and heavy dependence on underlying support services from poorly designed operating systems may often lead to inherent obscure design weaknesses which, even if known, tend to be accepted because of the enormous cost of rectification. The common practice is to design to meet a functional objective, test, and if necessary for performance objectives, upgrade the hardware or tinker with the software bottleneck to minimize its worst effects. As a last resort internal limits may be exercised to restrain the user or number of users from causing system failure from that particular design weakness.

Implementation weaknesses. Typical problem areas are bought-in hardware and software where incipient weaknesses may not be widely known or a black box design approach is used without regard for the trade-offs already taken by the OEM or package supplier. Examples of problems in this category are prevalent in the low-cost PC clones, database management systems and query languages, presentation graphics mechanisms, file management systems, network products to mention just a few. The design weaknesses which did not present symptoms during test and early field trials will persist within the system unless and until a heavy load or unusual combination of circumstances causes sufficient trouble to make users complain in such significant volume that the supplier has to react. Often an early version of a system may be rushed to the market place to capture a niche or pre-empt a competitor. Such early versions often have a history of multiple upgrades as a patchwork of fixes and add-ons are produced to make the original look better.

Life-cycle weaknesses. A point will arise when the supplier reviews his current product design and decides to start again. The products of this new cycle may contain a wholly different set of weaknesses and often will be produced without regard to the problems of its antecedents or the user need for continuity. Resilience problems arise during use of the original, transition to the new, and unless user feedback is very strong, during use of the new system. A fundamental cause lies in the fact that designers are almost never major users of their own designs. A second cause of such problems is the extended life-cycle from design to in-use recognition of the importance of resilience and the salient weaknesses of a specific system. Professionals who point out these flaws are normally ignored by both users and suppliers on the grounds of cost, convenience or complacency.

Customer weaknesses. Many suppliers choose to give their customers lots of options to tune the parameters of their system to meet personal preferences. Inappropriate settings may be pointed out but often only an experienced systems performance specialist can achieve the optimum balance between users' preferences and the behaviour of a system. Where resilience is required at least one degree of freedom has to be constrained in order to allow the underlying system enough of its resources to provide essential protection mechanisms. Many operating and file management systems allow these to be "turned off" with dire consequences for an unwary user.

Technical weaknesses. The physical components of the system can be produced to a variety of standards, some of which are very demanding. Obvious examples are the US Mil. Spec. standards for components which have to operate under potentially very harsh conditions in space, the air, at sea or in mobile, vibrating platforms. Quality and quantity of materials used to meet these specifications are intended to improve reliability and the design and packaging is related to the adversities expected from the environment. The design process is subject to examination and effort is expended to minimize a wide range of the weaknesses mentioned above. Components for ordinary office automation on the other hand are seldom likely to receive any such scrutiny, with the result that components are obtained from much cheaper sources, are only sample tested if at all, and are likely to be substituted by a cheaper version or a simpler implementation if it reduces production costs. Where appropriate the above comments also apply to software with the added dimension that change is much less easy to control and may occur throughout the life-cycle.

Environmental risks. Even if the system has been properly specified, designed and implemented, and the users are adequately constrained to use the resulting product correctly there still remains the problems which can arise from the environment into which the system is placed. There is a very wide range of potential environmental risks which can prejudice the availability of a system. Extra care has to be taken to specify which, if any, environmental risks should be taken account of in drawing up a requirement.

Environmental risks include:

> Quality and availability of power supplies.
>
> Quality and availability of air conditioning, if required.
>
> The need for resistance to vibration, electrical noise, dust, humidity and temperature extremes.
>
> The need for resistance to acidic or alkali vapours, spillages and bacterial, fungal or biological contamination in adverse climates or locations.
>
> Electromagnetic compatibility or other exotic requirements, e.g. use in explosive atmospheres or near weapons systems.
>
> Operational factors such as mobility of the system, the user, the user's data, the nature of the task, and the timeliness of responses to a variety of tasks under a range of load conditions.
>
> The requirements for flexibility of application, growth of user population and demands, and changes in work practices.
>
> The need to permit uneventful change of the underlying technology to take advantage of developments and achieve cost or space savings.
>
> Changes in the behaviour of users, e.g. less nervous, less naive, less cautious, more devious, more demanding, more explorative of features, facilities and performance.

Changes in, or the recognition of dependence upon, trust in the system to achieve its services. These factors change the environment in which the systems managers have to operate and that may lead to more cautious procedures, overheads for backup and redundancy, and a better division of resources to reduce the risks for specific or even all users.

The above is a subjective view of the nature of threats to the resilience of OA systems and their environment. It is clear that costing estimates for the protection of a system against a range of threats can only be indicative. Each system will bring its own set of inherent risks, will face a different environment to any other system, and will be subjected to the whims and vagaries of a different cross-section of users and their needs. It is likely that a large user population such as MOD HQ staff will exhibit general qualities which can be assessed, their offices have similar features and conditions, but their expectations and needs from the system will vary widely. It is to be expected that these factors will vary, perhaps as follows:

System aspects. These will vary slowly as suppliers learn to take account of their customers' expectations and as designers realize the frailty of certain methods of design.

Users. These will increasingly experience the frustration of unresilient systems and either avoid using them or devise workaround methods to ensure their efforts are not wasted. Only major losses will cause users to generate positive and persistent demands for improved resilience.

Environmental aspects. Generally these are not expected to improve unless a major effort is taken to address them. Their broad spectrum places the task of improvement onto many different, often complacent or even hostile managements, where lack of clear initiatives and coordination will limit the scope for sustained improvements. Under these conditions only special cases are likely to justify the cost and effort of dealing with the most pressing needs and then only if solutions are achievable.

For further reading on the software security side, the CSA (Computing Services Association) in the UK, in one of its briefing notes (see Section 9), provides useful *Guidance on limiting software security risks*.

In the final paper in this section, **Ron Fiddes** addresses the issue of hardware safety with respect to office equipment, describing the history and development of IT hardware and relevant safety standards. A member since 1974 of the BSI committee which developed BS 7002, and an active participant in the work of IEC TC74 and its Working Group 8, he describes the place of BS 7002 and future developments to update and extend standards relating to IT hardware safety. The paper draws attention to the way in which safety issues have been addressed as they have been recognized, and suggests that this will continue to be the case.

Safety of information technology equipment including electrical business equipment

Introduction

There are two areas of safety in information technology, software and hardware. There is generally a good level of appreciation of software safety issues among IT specialists but the relevance and significance of hardware safety is not as well understood. The hardware issue is that of the safety of the people who come into contact with IT equipment, including business equipment. To a large extent this lack of awareness stems from the extremely good safety record of the equipment concerned. Some of the background to the achievement of this is reviewed under *The practical development of IT equipment safety.*

Hardware safety is of relevance to those having responsibility in the following information technology activities.

Equipment designers and manufacturers

Standards can provide guidance on the principles of safe design. Requirements can be set for such items as electrical insulation, flammability of constructional material used, mechanical stability, and connection to the mains.

Suppliers and vendors of IT equipment

Marketing equipment which conforms to the requirements of appropriate standards ensures that the product has a level of safety which is recognized by experts as safe for the purpose for which it is supplied. Liability in the event of an accident should thereby be minimized.

System designers and system analysts

There are ethical, professional and legal liabilities which designers of IT systems are expected to meet. The achievement of the performance requirement is the prime objective in pursuit of which insufficient consideration may be given to the safety of the hardware through lack of understanding of the risk. The provision of safe hardware requires expert knowledge. Quoting equipment which conforms to appropriate standards is an expedient way of achieving this.

Business users of IT

The introduction of information technology equipment into the place of work exposes staff to any hazards to health that such equipment may possess. Regulatory authorities in the UK expect employers to take reasonable steps to keep the workplace safe. By using equipment which conforms to the requirements of appropriate standards such reasonable steps may be met with regard to the choice and provision of information equipment.

The practical development of IT equipment safety

The early generations of computers employed thermionic valve technology which brought with it relatively high voltages (in the order of 200 V d.c.) and a lot of wasted heat. The manufacturers of those machines well knew the risks of fire and shock which careless design and production could cause. There was therefore a natural inclination to give such safety matters attention in the computer equipment they built. Even so, in those early days, the large size of those machines with the consequently large power supply current they required did cause some minor fire problems and new lessons had to be learned.

With the advent of semiconductor technology the situation changed rapidly. The voltages within the equipment fell and the heat dissipation dropped. Then the VLSI development raised the component density so that even at the reduced heat dissipation level of the individual circuits the high packing density produced significant temperatures within the equipment. Circuit tolerance to these temperatures was unreliable and fan assisted cooling was widely introduced. However, fan failure not only resulted in circuit component damage, it sometimes resulted in smoke (which could be toxic) or fire. Engineering developments overcame these problems and the importance of using materials which do not produce toxic fumes in the event of a fire is now well recognized. Also the development of circuit miniaturization has resulted in the adoption of special techniques to ensure their safety. Indeed, it can be said that as IT equipment becomes smaller and more versatile – evidence of continuing technological development – safety issues will continue to arise.

Hardware safety also relates to "electrical business equipment" such as cheque sorters, automatic enveloping machines, continuous stationery, guillotines, paper shredders and photocopiers. The speeds at which these machines operate has increased as microcomputer chip technology has been introduced in them. In some cases very significant risks of injury to the user would exist if the equipment was not suitably designed and constructed. The risks tend to be mainly in the physical injury field (cuts and bruises) in which area the UK Factories Act, the Health and Safety at Work Act, and the supervision of the Health and Safety Executive have resulted in a satisfactory, if not ideal, safety level being sustained.

From the outline above it will be evident that there is a vast amount of knowledge available concerning "good practice" in the safe manufacture, installation and use of IT equipment. Current standards distil this knowledge into a standard applicable to the technology of today. As IT equipment continues to develop, new safety issues will continue to arise.

Barriers to trade

The free movement of goods between countries depends, among other factors, on the safety requirements relating to the goods which the importing country imposes. In the case of information technology equipment there are so many safety factors which can be the subject of import control that without agreement on an international standard in this area the manufacturer would need to make different models for each country. IEC 950:1986 is such a standard. The text is the same as that of the European Standard EN 60950:1988. These texts have been developed by international experts with the object of specifying safety requirements which are acceptable internationally. The national official test houses of Europe (e.g. BSI in England, VDE in Germany etc.) have agreed to recognize one another's certification of IT equipment to any of the equivalent standards. Thus a compliance certificate for equipment obtained from the official national test house of one EC country (for example, the BSI test centre) will clear that product with regard to that standard for all EC countries.

The history of BS 7002:1989 (EN 60950:1988)

The development of this standard reflects the progressive integration of traditional and electronic business equipment as well as the growth of international trade in this area. In the 1960s business office activity employed a variety of electromechanical machines for which a safety standard was developed. The computers of those days occupied considerable space and were ensconced in their own environmentally protected rooms, serving the business but not forming part of the office itself. The safety aspects of these machines was mainly left to the designers who applied the safety principles of such relevant electrical equipment standards as they knew. This developed into the computer industry providing the principal lead in the development of a "safety standard" through the European Computer Manufacturers Association (ECMA).

IEC committee TC74 recognized the efforts of ECMA and worked with them to draw up the first computer hardware safety standard, IEC 435 *Safety of data processing equipment*, which was adopted in the UK as BS 4644:1970. Meanwhile the growth in international sourcing of office machines stimulated IEC committee TC74 to produce, in 1972, IEC 380 *Safety of electrically energized office machines*. The text of these standards were subsequently revised and were then adopted in the UK under the numbers BS 5850:1981 (replacing BS 4644) from IEC 380 second edition, and BS 6204:1982 from IEC 435 second edition (1983; the date anomaly arose from different publishing schedules).

The responsibility for these two IEC standards was with IEC Technical Committee 74 which saw the progressive technological merging of the two product areas and set out to produce a combined standard to cover them. This was published as IEC 950, *Safety of information technology equipment including electrical business equipment*. The text of this combined standard has become, with only minor changes, that of BS 7002:1989.

The USA was heavily involved in the drafting of the IEC text and their Underwriters Laboratories has adopted it for their own use as UL 1950 [Underwriters Laboratories 1989]. Canada has also adopted the text as the basis of Canadian Standard Association CAN/CSA-C22.2 No 950-M89 [CAN 1989]. Over the period of development of the standard there have been significant changes in international attitudes toward safety requirements for such equipment. In the EC a procedure for harmonizing the differences between the standards existing in the various member states was developed. In the computer area the dependence upon non-EC sources for much of the advanced technology used in those machines focused attention on the work of IEC TC74. This resulted in active EC participation in the development of the IEC standard and its adoption by the EC countries, a situation largely responsible for the success in overcoming the barriers to trade which previously existed with regard to safety.

The international involvement in the development of the IEC text on which BS 7002 is based assures that the British standard takes full account of the requirements of EC states and the other major countries who use and/or supply information technology equipment.

Scope of BS 7002

The objectives of the scope are summarized by the following extracts from the standard:

> The standard is applicable to information technology equipment, including electrical business equipment and associated equipment, with a rated voltage not exceeding 600 volts.

> The standard specifies requirements intended to ensure safety for the operator and layman who may come into contact with the equipment and, where specifically stated, for service personnel.

> This standard is intended to ensure safety of installed equipment, whether it consists of a system of interconnected units or independent units, subject to installing, operating and maintaining in the manner prescribed by the manufacturer....

> Examples of equipment which is within the scope of this standard are:

> Data and text processing equipment, personal computers, visual display units, data preparation equipment, data terminal equipment, data circuit terminating equipment, typewriters, calculators, accounting and book-keeping machines, cash registers, point of sale terminals, paper tape readers and punches, staplers, duplicators, copying machines, erasers, pencil sharpeners, documents shredding machines, magnetic tape handlers, motor operated files, dictation equipment, micrographic office equipment, monetary processing machines, electrically operated drawing machines (plotters), paper trimmers (punches, cutting machines, separators), paper jogging machines, postage machines and teleprinters.

This list is not intended to be comprehensive, and equipment that is not listed is not necessarily excluded from the scope.

The scope gives specific areas in which it either does not apply or where extra protection may be needed. The excluded area is mainly equipment which is provided to support the Information Technology system such as the air conditioning, the fire detection system, and wiring of the building.

There are other specifications for these. An interesting exception which might well be expected to be covered by the standard is

... duplicating machines, including lithographic machines, which are intended primarily for sizes larger than A3 as specified in ISO Standard 216.

Examples of situations where extra attention to safety might be needed are where the equipment is intended for use on vehicles, ships, aircraft, in locations more that 2000 metres above sea level, wet environments, in environments having high temperatures, high dust content, vibration, flammable gases, explosive or corrosive atmospheres. Extra attention to safety may be necessary for electro-medical computer equipment which is intended to be physically connected to a patient.

Overview of BS 7002

This overview is intended to give the reader a broad idea of the nature of the standard. It should not be considered to be a comprehensive review. The standard is the same text as the European standard EN 60950:1988 which is derived from IEC 950, first edition 1986. It is a single volume of 132 pages having five sections and an appendix. The coverage of these clauses is roughly as follows:

1. General

This contains the scope and definitions used in the standard. The definitions have been developed with an eye to the customary use of the terms employed, the use of similar terms in other IEC standards, and of the particular needs of translation and understanding in non-English speaking countries. Users of the standard should keep a clear idea in mind of these terms as they appear in the standard.

The difference in electrical supply system earthing and protection in different countries is recognized in the definitions for "TN power systems", "TT power systems" and "IT power systems". (In this context IT does not mean Information Technology.)

This section of the standard also gives general requirements relating to components, and marking related to safety.

2. Fundamental design requirements

Here it is stated "There shall be no energy hazard in operator access areas". The design requirements to achieve this are laid out throughout this section and tests for compliance are specified.

The standard permits the use of SELV (safe extra low voltage) circuits within the equipment. In these circuits the voltage under normal and single fault condition must not rise above 42.5 V peak of 60 V d.c.

Considerable attention is given to electrical insulation. In addition to general requirements to use suitable material which are not degraded by moisture etc., the minimum thicknesses appropriate for various voltages are prescribed in a table. This table also gives the separation distance permitted between bare conductors on printed circuit boards. There are also tables for the "creepage distance" (defined as "the shortest path between two conductive parts, or between a conductive part and the bounding surface of the equipment, measured along the surface of the insulation"). In these tables the working environment for which the equipment is designed and the ability of the component construction to withstand adverse conditions is handled by giving values for three different levels of environmental pollution.

Other subjects in this section are: safe extra low voltage (SELV) circuits, limited current circuits, provisions for protective earthing, primary power isolation, over-current and earth fault protection in primary circuits, and safety interlocks.

3. Wiring connections and supply

The power required from the electricity mains can vary from many kilowatts for a large mainframe to around 100 watts for a desktop PC, to a few watts for a peripheral unit such as a modem. For equipment to be safe it is essential that the connection to the mains supply is engineered safely. To achieve this the standard sets requirements for the size of the wiring, its insulation and method of connection to the mains supply. This includes such factors as the route taken by the wire (avoidance of sharp edges, moving parts, hot areas etc.), and anchorages to ensure that movement of the equipment or a pull on the wires does not release a wire. The provision of adequate earthing, switching and fusing is also required.

In this section of the standard reference is also made to IEC 245, *Rubber insulated cables of rated voltages up to and including 450/750 V* and IEC 227, *Polyvinyl chloride insulated cables of rated voltage up to and including 450/750 V*. This is in keeping with the practice of using other appropriate IEC standards to specify requirements when possible.

4. Physical requirements

The stability requirements are classified on the basis of the size and weight of the equipment. The object is to ensure that in the normal working environments the equipment shall not be overbalanced, fall and injure someone. The compliance tests call for the application of various forces to the sides of the equipment. A tilt test is also specified and requires that "a unit shall not overbalance when tilted to an angle of 10° from its normal upright position". Further tests relate to the stability of the unit when its doors, drawers etc. are opened to the most unfavourable position.

The enclosure in which the equipment is housed is required to be free of sharp edges, and its ventilation apertures have also to be such as to reduce the risk of fluids and harmful objects getting into the equipment. The glass front presented by monitor screens is a special area for testing. CRT screens used in monitors must pass an impact test which uses a 50 mm diameter sphere of 500 gram mass applied in a specified way. A 500 gram sphere impact test is also applied to the sides and top of enclosures. A considerable part of this section of the standard is devoted to the fire retardant properties of the enclosure both with regard to the material of which it is made and its construction.

In this section there are also requirements for drop tests for hand-held equipment, the emission of dust and toxic fumes and liquids, quality of handles, knobs, levers, and many other constructional points. Indeed, parts of this section can form a helpful guide to good design practice for a newcomer to the industry.

5. Thermal and electrical requirements

The influence of heat on the insulation materials used in the construction of the equipment is addressed here. In general the leakage current through the insulation rises and the breakdown voltage of insulation material is reduced with the rise in temperature. To remain safe under normal working conditions it is necessary for the insulation materials used to be suitable for the temperatures expected. In this section of the standard the choice of material is guided on the basis of IEC Publication 85. There is also a limit set on the temperature permitted for controls and surfaces which can be touched.

The electrical consideration is that of the leakage current which flows to earth. Such current arises from several sources and is a byproduct of the general insulation of the circuits and the filters used to limit the interference. This area of circuit design is likely to require careful attention as the new EC EMC (Electromagnetic compatibility) Directive 4 comes into operation in 1992. BS 7002 sets safety limits for the earth leakage current and specifies the conditions under which it should be measured.

In this section of the standard there are also requirements for transformers and motors under fault conditions, protection against overload, thermostats, the use of thermoplastics in the construction, etc.

Appendices

The contents of the appendices are as follows.

A	Tests for resistance to heat and fire
B	Motor tests under abnormal conditions
C	Transformers
D	Measuring instrument for earth leakage current test
E	Temperature rise of winding
F	Measurement of creepage distance and clearance
G	Earth leakage current for equipment intended to be connected directly to IT power systems
H	Ionizing radiation
J	Guidance on protection against ingress of water
K	Table of electrochemical potentials
L	Thermal controls
M	Examples of normal conditions for electrical business machines
ZA	Other international publications quoted in this standard
ZB	Special national conditions
ZC	National deviations
W	(National) A listing of the UK organizations which have supported the development of the standard
X	(National) A listing of the British Standard equivalents to the IEC publications and standards referred to in this standard

Interpretation of the standard

In a standard of this nature there are times when a user feels that a requirement may be interpreted in more than one way. In readiness for this the chairman of IEC TC74 set up a "Chairman's Advisory Panel" consisting of five experts who have participated in the development of the standard and of which the author of this article is a member. This panel is commonly referred to as the "Interpretation Panel" but strictly speaking it offers an opinion on the interpretation to be recommended to the inquirer; this opinion needs formal adoption at a plenary meeting before it becomes official. By providing the inquirer with a consensus of the five expert opinions a measure of confidence can be placed on their interpretation. This is an important point if production planning is involved.

Access to this service is through the national committee: BSI EEL/33/- in the case of the UK. In seeking assistance it is advisable to present the interpretation(s) being put on the point being raised. The BSI committee will usually be able to give an answer which settles the point. Only if the committee is unable to supply an authoritative answer will the question be passed on to the Chairman's Advisory Panel. When an interpretation question proceeds thus far the panel not only provides a response to the national committee but also considers whether the text needs to be modified in this area. There have been very few such enquiries up to the time of writing (1992).

Future developments

The text of BS 7002 (EN 60950) is based on the first edition of IEC 950, which was issued in 1986. Since then the IEC text has been modified by two amendment issues. These have corrected minor points which slipped through the process of combining the former two standards for office machines and computers and have also picked up some interpretation issues which arose. Users of BS 7002 are not disadvantaged by this since the implementation of the amended version is scheduled by a timetable which provides generous overlap, and is not retrospective. The modifications have the effect of making the requirements a little easier to meet and consequently anyone using the current BS 7002 should have little difficulty in changing over when it suits them.

Of more significance is the issue of the second edition of IEC 950, which appeared as IEC 950:1991 towards the end of 1991. In this edition there is a new section dealing with the safety requirements for connection of information technology equipment to the telecommunications networks. This new section has been prepared by a joint working group from both sides of the industry with a view to providing a standard which provides mutual protection of the telecommunications system on the one hand and the IT equipment on the other. In due course the text of this second edition will appear as a European Norm and a British Standard, and its adoption in place of BS 7002 will be phased with an overlapping timescale. Those using, or proposing to use, BS 7002 need not necessarily delay their plans by waiting for this version of the standard. There will be only minor changes to the computer and office machine sections; consequently if telecommunications connection is not involved the consequences are insignificant. However, where new products for telecommunications working are concerned it is advised that a copy of the new second edition of IEC 950 be obtained and applied to those products.

Summary

Legal and ethical requirements in EC countries require that those using IT equipment and electrical business equipment shall suffer no injury when using the equipment in accordance with the manufacturer's instructions. To achieve this degree of hardware safety it has been necessary to bring together many national standards and harmonize them into one document. There has been excellent cooperation among safety experts worldwide on this under the banner of IEC TC 74. A series of publications has been produced from the early 1970s onwards, each progressively improving the integration of the specific needs of various nations. BS 7002 reflects this by copying the 1986 harmonized text of IEC 950. The latest standard is IEC 950 which was published in 1991. This adds requirements for the safe connection of IT equipment to telecommunications networks. The BSI version of this is currently (1992) awaited; it is likely to be the same text in a BSI cover.

The ongoing advances in hardware miniaturization will inevitably call for a revision to the current standard. However, that standard will not be superseded quickly. It is IEC practice to schedule a period of overlap in the tenure of its standards so that manufacturers have time to migrate to the replacement standard if necessary.

Acknowledgments

The author wishes to thank the British Standards Institution for permission to quote extracts from their standard BS 7002, copies of which may be obtained from BSI Sales Department, Linford Wood, Milton Keynes, MK14 6LE, UK. He is also grateful for the assistance on the section on the history of the British Standard provided by the chairman of BSI EEL/33/-, Mr D.W. Farquhar.

Clearly there is a need for standards which address the safety and security aspects of IT systems. The contributions to this section have demonstrated this need and have shown that both standards and other guidance do exist which address the need. As with other aspects of IT, change and development is continuous. Both the contribution by Johnston and Wood and that by Fiddes have drawn attention to the changes to standards which are required to accommodate this.

Safety and security are clearly matters of considerable concern to those providing services, as has already been touched upon earlier. It is to the question of standards for professional IT services that we now turn.

References

Standards and standards body documents

BS 4644:1970 Safety of data processing equipment (replaced by BS 5850 and BS 6204)

BS 5750:1987 Quality systems – model for quality assurance in design/development, production, installation and servicing (British implementation of ISO 9001)

BS 5850:1981 Safety of electrically energized office machines (from IEC 380)

BS 6204:1982 Safety of information technology equipment including electrical business equipment (from IEC 435:1983, 2nd edn; replaced by BS 7002:1989)

BS 7002:1989 Safety of information technology equipment including electrical business equipment

[CAN 1989] Canadian standard CAN/CSA-C22.2 No 950-M89 Safety of information technology equipment including electrical business equipment (Canadian implementation of IEC 950)

EN 29001:1987 European norm corresponding to ISO 9001

EN 60950:1988 European norm corresponding to IEC 950

IEC 380:1985 Safety of electrically energized office machines, 2nd edn

IEC 435:1983 Safety of data processing equipment, 2nd edn

IEC 643:1979 Application of digital computers to nuclear reactor instrumentation and control

IEC 880:1986 Software for computers in the safety systems of nuclear power stations

IEC 950:1986 Safety of information technology equipment including electrical business equipment (replaced by 2nd edn)

IEC 950:1991 Safety of information technology equipment including electrical business equipment, 2nd edn

[IEC 1991] 65A(Secretariat)122, Software for computers in the application of industrial safety-related systems

[IEC 1992] 65A(Secretariat)123, Draft – Functional safety of electrical/electronic programmable electronic safety related systems: generic aspects

ISO 9001:1987 Quality systems – model for quality assurance in design/development, production, installation and servicing

Other references

[ACARD 1986] Advisory Council for Applied Research and Development (ACARD), Software: a vital key to UK competitiveness, Her Majesty's Stationery Office, London

[Baber 1991] BABER, R.L., Epilogue: future developments, in McDERMID, J.A. (ed), Software Engineer's Reference Book, Butterworth-Heinemann, Oxford

[Bennett 1984] BENNETT, P.A., The safety of industrially based controllers incorporating software, PhD thesis, The Open University, Milton Keynes

[CEC 1991] Information technology security evaluation criteria (ITSEC), provisional harmonized criteria, CD-71-91-502-EN-C, Commission of the European Community, Brussels

[EEMUA 1989] Safety related instrument systems for the process industries (including programmable electronic systems), Publication 160, The Engineering Equipment and Materials Users Association, UK

[Forester and Morrison 1990] FORESTER, T. and MORRISON, P., Computer unreliability and social vulnerability, Futures, June 1990

[Gilb 1977] GILB, T., Software metrics, Winthrop, Cambridge, Massachusetts

[Guardian 1990] News article, BR signalmen worked blind, The Guardian, 23 July 1990

[HSE 1987] Health and Safety Executive, Programmable electronic systems in safety related applications, Her Majesty's Stationery Office, London

[HSE 1988] Health and Safety Executive, The tolerability of risk in nuclear power stations, Her Majesty's Stationery Office, London

[IEE 1989] A study of the computer-based systems practices of UK, European and US industry, Institution of Electrical Engineers, London

[IEE 1991] Formal methods in safety critical systems, Public Affairs Report No 9, Institution of Electrical Engineers, London

[IGasE 1989] The use of programmable electronic systems in safety related applications in the gas industry, Institution of Gas Engineers, UK

[IUR 1986] Software design for computer based safety systems, Report No 9, Office for Research and Experiments of the International Union of Railways, Utrecht, Holland

[Jolly and Johnson 1987] JOLLY, M.E. and JOHNSON, S.W., Guidelines for the use of programmable electronic systems for reactor protection, Central Electricity Generating Board, London

[Jones 1986] JONES, C.B., Systematic software development using VDM, Prentice-Hall International, London

[Littlewood 1991] LITTLEWOOD, B., Software reliability modelling, in McDERMID, J.A. (ed), Software Engineer's Reference Book, Butterworth-Heinemann, Oxford

[MOD 1991a] Interim Defence Standard 00-55/Issue 1, The procurement of safety critical software in defence equipment, Ministry of Defence, UK

[MOD 1991b] Interim Defence Standard 00-56/Issue 1, Hazard analysis and safety classification of the computer and programmable electronic system elements of defence equipment, Ministry of Defence, UK

[Myers 1976] MYERS, G.J., Software reliability, principles and practices, John Wiley and Sons, Chichester

[NATO 1981] AQAP-13, NATO software quality control system requirements, NATO International Staff Defence Support Division

[New Scientist 1991] Airbus safety claim "cannot be proved", news article, *New Scientist*, 7 September 1991

[POST 1991] Safety critical systems, Parliamentary Briefing Note 20, Parliamentary Office of Science and Technology, London

[RTCA 1985] Software considerations in airborne systems and equipment certification, RTCA/DO-178A, Radio Technical Commission for Aeronautics, USA

[Stokes 1991] STOKES, D.A., Requirements analysis, in McDERMID, J.A. (ed), Software Engineer's Reference Book, Butterworth-Heinemann, Oxford

[Underwriters Laboratories 1989] UL 1950: Safety of information technology equipment including electrical business equipment, Underwriters Laboratories, USA

9

Standards for professional services

In a sense, standards for professional services are outside the mainstream of this book, not because they are not important, but because very often they are covered in ways other than the standards produced by the official standards bodies – for example by legislation. There are of course relevant standards, in particular quality standards such as ISO 9001 referred to in Section 6, but the major aspects are outside the conventional standards arena.

Nevertheless, standards for professional services are important for users, because however good the technical standards are from the user's point of view, their value will be diminished if the standards of professional conduct by those who provide services to the users are not of the highest. Therefore it was resolved that a section on these issues should be included here. It will consist mainly of two examples, one from the professional institution side and one from the trade association side. These are reproduced almost verbatim apart from minor presentational changes to reduce differences from the overall style of the book.

Professional associations in all areas have long been concerned with the standing of their profession and ensuring that their members behave in a professional and ethical manner, by establishing codes of conduct and codes of good practice. Those in the field of information technology are no exception. The following is the code of conduct established by the Association for Computing Machinery (ACM) in the USA, as enshrined in its Bylaw 17. (In 1992 a draft revision [ACM 1992] was published for comment by the ACM membership but the final version had not been published at the time this book goes to press.)

The ACM Code of Professional Conduct

Preamble

Recognition of professional status by the public depends not only on skill and dedication but also adherence to a recognized code of Professional Conduct. The following Code sets forth the general principles (Canons), professional ideals (Ethical Considerations), and mandatory rules (Disciplinary Rules) applicable to each ACM member.

The verbs "shall" (imperative) and "should" (encouragement) are used purposefully in this Code. The Canons and Ethical Considerations are not, however, binding rules. Each Disciplinary Rule is binding on each individual Member of the ACM. Failure to observe the Disciplinary Rules subjects the Member to admonition, suspension or expulsion from the Association as provided by the Procedures for the Enforcement of the ACM Code of Professional Conduct, which are specified in the ACM Policy and Procedures Guidelines. The Disciplinary Rules of the Code apply, however, only to the classes of membership specified in Article 3, Section 5, of the Constitution of the ACM[1].

Canon 1

An ACM member shall act at all times with integrity.

Ethical considerations

EC1.1. An ACM member shall properly qualify the member's expressed opinion outside the member's area of competence. A member is encouraged to express an opinion on subjects within the member's area of competence.

EC1.2. An ACM member shall preface any partisan statements about information processing by indicating clearly on whose behalf they are made.

EC1.3. An ACM member shall act faithfully on behalf of the member's employers or clients.

Disciplinary rules

DR1.1.1. An ACM member shall not intentionally misrepresent the member's qualifications or credentials to present or prospective employers or clients.

DR1.1.2. An ACM member shall not make deliberately false or deceptive statements as to the present or expected state of affairs in any aspect of the capability, delivery or use of information processing systems.

DR1.2.1. An ACM member shall not intentionally conceal or misrepresent on whose behalf any partisan statements are made.

DR1.3.1. An ACM member acting or employed as a consultant shall, prior to accepting information from a prospective client, inform the client of all factors of which the member is aware which may affect proper performance of the task.

---

1   That is, members with voting rights – Eds.

DR1.3.2. An ACM member shall disclose any interest of which the member is aware which does or may conflict with the member's duty to a present or prospective employer or client.

DR1.3.3. An ACM member shall not use any confidential information from any employer or client, past or present, without prior permission.

Canon 2

An ACM member should strive to increase the member's competence and the competence and prestige of the profession.

Ethical considerations

EC2.1. An ACM member is encouraged to extend public knowledge, understanding, and appreciation of information processing, and to oppose any false or deceptive statements relating to information processing of which the member is aware.

EC2.2. An ACM member shall not use the member's professional credentials to misrepresent the member's competence.

EC2.3. An ACM member shall undertake only those professional assignments and commitments for which the member is qualified.

EC2.4. An ACM member shall strive to design and develop systems that adequately perform the intended functions and that satisfy the member's employer's or client's operational needs.

EC2.5. An ACM member should maintain and increase the member's competence through a program of continuing education encompassing the techniques, technical standards, and practices in the member's fields of professional activity.

EC2.6. An ACM member should provide opportunity and encouragement for professional development and advancement of both professionals and those aspiring to become professionals.

Disciplinary rules

DR2.2.1. An ACM member shall not use his professional credentials to misrepresent the member's competence.

DR2.3.1. An ACM member shall not undertake professional assignments without adequate preparation in the circumstances.

DR2.3.2. An ACM member shall not undertake professional assignments for which the member knows or should know the member is not competent or cannot become adequately competent without acquiring the assistance of a professional who is competent to perform the assignment.

DR2.4.1. An ACM member shall not represent that a product or the member's work will perform its function adequately and will meet the receiver's operational needs when the member knows or should know that the product is deficient.

Canon 3

An ACM member shall accept responsibility for the member's work.

Ethical considerations

EC3.1. An ACM member shall accept only those assignments for which there is reasonable expectancy of meeting requirements or specifications, and shall perform his assignments in a professional manner.

Disciplinary rules

DR3.1.1. An ACM member shall not neglect any professional assignment which has been accepted.

DR3.1.2. An ACM member shall keep the member's employer or client properly informed on the progress of his assignments.

DR3.1.2. An ACM member shall not attempt to exonerate himself from, or to limit his liability to clients for the member's personal malpractice.

DR3.1.4. An ACM member shall indicate to the member's employer or client the consequences to be expected if the member's professional judgement is overruled.

Canon 4

An ACM member shall act with professional responsibility.

Ethical considerations

EC4.1. An ACM member shall not use the member's membership in ACM improperly for professional advantage or to misrepresent the authority of the member's statements.

EC4.2. An ACM member shall conduct professional activities on a high plane.

EC4.3. An ACM member is encouraged to uphold and improve the professional standards of the Association through participation in their formulation, establishment, and enforcement.

Disciplinary rules

DR4.1.1. An ACM member shall not speak on behalf of the Association or any of its subgroups without proper authority.

DR4.1.2. An ACM member shall not knowingly misrepresent the policies and views of the Association or any of its subgroups.

DR4.1.3. An ACM member shall preface partisan statements about information processing by indicating clearly on whose behalf they are made.

DR4.2.1. An ACM member shall not maliciously injure the professional reputation of any other person.

DR4.2.2. An ACM member shall not use the services of or membership in the Association to gain unfair advantage.

DR4.2.3. An ACM member shall take care that credit for work is given to whom credit is properly due.

Canon 5

An ACM member should use the member's special knowledge and skills for the advancement of human welfare.

Ethical considerations

EC5.1. An ACM member should consider the health, privacy, and general welfare of the public in the performance of the member's work.

EC5.2. An ACM member, whenever dealing with data concerning individuals, shall always consider the principle of the individual's privacy and seek the following:

> to minimize the data collected,
> to limit authorized access to the data,
> to provide proper security for the data,
> to determine the required retention period of the data, and
> to ensure proper disposal of the data.

Disciplinary rules

DR5.2.1. An ACM member shall express the member's professional opinion to the member's employers or clients regarding any adverse consequences to the public which might result from work proposed to the member.

The repetition in this Bylaw, for example about not misrepresenting one's competence, no doubt demonstrates the importance the ACM places on the principles of ethical conduct, and its anxiety to ensure that there is no danger that a relevant consideration will be overlooked simply because of the context in which it occurs. Professional IT bodies elsewhere have similar codes, the British Computer Society (BCS) in the UK for example [BCS 1992].

The effectiveness of such codes, as far as users of services are concerned, is limited by the fact that IT is a young profession, and its professional associations have a long way to go before they attain the status, let alone the statutory authority, of equivalent bodies in longer-established professions such as the law, medicine, accountancy, and so on. Membership of a professional association is not a requirement of employment in IT, and the proportion who are members is low, certainly in the USA and the UK, though it is significantly higher in some countries such as Finland.

In the mid 1980s the BCS took two major steps which could eventually change this situation. One was that it obtained recognition as a chartered engineering institution, meaning that members could aim for the additional qualification in the UK of Chartered Engineer (C.Eng.) alongside members of the established mechanical, civil and electrical engineering institutions – with the further possibility of European recognition. The other was the establishment of the Professional Development Scheme, a BCS-monitored scheme of professional training, leading to MBCS and C.Eng. as professional qualifications, which has begun attracting considerable interest both in UK and abroad. Both these point the way towards an eventual recognition of membership as being first a desirable, and later a necessary, requirement to undertake certain kinds of professional work.

However, the professional institutions deal with the individual members of the profession, whereas users commonly have to do business not with individuals but with companies. The Computing Services Association (CSA) in the UK has a Code of Conduct, adherence to which, as the CSA emphasizes, "is a condition of an organization continuing to be a member or associate of the Association". This provides our other example.

The CSA Code of Conduct

As a Member or Associate of the CSA we will endeavour always to act in a proper manner in our relationship with our Clients, our Employees, other Employers and with the Public by making the following commitments.

Clients

To express the terms of our agreements clearly and precisely, and then to fulfil these agreements in good faith by rendering services of at least the quality offered.

To help eliminate confusion arising from computing terminology and accept the responsibility for educating the layman in this regard.

To provide proper security for Clients' confidential information, records, documents and programs.

To ensure that if a Client is offered the services of any person, that person is at the time the offer is made employed by or otherwise properly available to the member under a contract for services.

Employees

To provide good and safe working conditions, scope for job satisfaction and equal opportunities for employment and promotion.

To work continuously to improve Employees' skills and technical competence.

To impress upon Employees and periodically remind them of the confidential nature of Clients' material and information.

To encourage professional behaviour and a high standard of service to Clients.

To ensure that Employees are acquainted with this code.

Other employers

To recognize that disparagement of other members of the industry is unbusinesslike and damaging to the reputation of the entire industry.

To ensure that no employee or prospective employee is encouraged to act in breach of any provisions of any existing or previous contract of employment with another employer, by way of an offer of employment or otherwise.

Public

To promote the effective use of data processing as an instrument for social and economic good, and to counter the confusions and misconceptions that sometimes accompany the use of computers.

To pledge our Organization to be a good corporate citizen, fulfilling its responsibilities to the communities which it serves, as well as the broader community of our society.

The CSA supplements its Code of Conduct by Codes of Practice for different areas of work, and interestingly supplements these with "briefing notes" for clients, to be sure that the implications are fully understood. The example which follows is the Code of Practice for consultancy, which is accompanied by briefing notes (not reproduced here) on "How to choose a consultancy" and "How to work with consultants".

CSA Code of Practice: Consultancy

Members of the CSA Consultancy Interest Group undertake to conduct business in accordance with the following Code of Practice, in addition to the overall Code of Conduct of the CSA.

Membership of the Consultancy Interest Group is open to all members of the CSA who so undertake, and who are competent to provide consultancy services: that is, impartial, independent, professional advice and assistance in any or all the aspects of the planning, implementation, management, control, security and performance improvements of computing and associated information technology.

Impartiality

1. When providing services as consultants, Members will at all times put the interest of their client first, and advise and act solely in his best interest.

Independence

Members may quite properly offer forms of service or supply in addition to consultancy services (such as bureau, turnkey, systems and programming or software products). If they do so, however, Members undertake the following.

2. Consultancy services will be separately identified and organized from other areas of the Member's services or products, and consultants will be free to act independently of these.

3. Consultancy services will be separately identified and organized from other areas of the Member's external business interests, contracts or arrangements, and consultants will be free to act independently of these.

4. Whenever a potential conflict of interest arises or may arise, this will be promptly disclosed to clients or prospective clients in writing.

Professionalism

In supplying their services as consultants, Members undertake the following.

5. They will accept only those assignments which they are qualified and competent to carry out.

6. They will provide written proposals for all assignments, including the objectives, terms of reference, fee rates or cost, and terms of business under which they are offering their services.

7. For any given assignment, they will make available staff competent to undertake the work, and exercise proper supervision and management.

8. They will accept responsibility for the work they undertake, including subcontracted work.

9. They will respect confidential client information to which they may have access, and require members of their staff to do so.

The moral for users seems clear: where standards for professional services, as well as technical standards, are important for you, ascertain that the people you deal with know about and abide by – and preferably have bound themselves to abide by – codes of professional conduct of the kind shown here. If nothing else, it is an additional assurance that, if you have specified conformity to technical standards as a requirement for your application, that requirement will be respected by the service supplier.

With that brief look at standards for professional services, we complete our review of user needs. The final section now returns to Peter Swann's query in Section 1 – how to ensure that "the users' votes are counted", i.e. how to see that users' needs are satisfied.

References

[ACM 1992] ACM proposed code of ethics and professional conduct, *Communications of the ACM*, Vol 35, No 5, pp 94-99

[BCS 1992] BCS Code of Conduct, *The Computer Bulletin*, Vol, No 4, pp 6-7.

10 The way forward

Much of this book has been concerned with the deficiencies of standards and of the standards-making process from the user point of view. In this concluding section the time has come to present some of the ideas which have been put forward to correct these deficiencies, though some have been alluded to earlier in passing. We begin with the INSITS conference in Braunschweig in 1989, an occasion often alluded to in the preceding pages, and from the proceedings of which [Berg and Schumny 1990], or papers directly resulting therefrom, some of the material in this book has been derived.

The conference was primarily concerned with the IT standardization process as a whole, but user needs figured prominently within it, so we begin by listing recommendations relating to user needs that emerged from a number of workshops which took place during the conference week.

Workshop W1 was entitled *Buyers, sellers and standards – what should both sides do differently?* and the whole report is worth reading. Of the five main recommendations, three refer to both vendors and users and one to vendors only, but the third is worth quoting in full:

> That large users, especially government users, such as the CEC, could sponsor and lead vendors towards providing standards across national boundaries, particularly those kinds of standards that make multinational operations more efficient. Scope for cooperation between the largest users internationally (especially private corporations) should be exploited. This is a call for a more coherent view of standards required, from large users.

All workshop reports were presented and discussed in open plenary session and the chairman of Workshop W1, Paul Reynolds, added some further points that arose at that time. Among them were:

> Unlike other large markets, the size of the IT "market" represented by user internal EDP expenditure (i.e. on staff) is equivalent in size to the strict "supply side", i.e. the vendors and software companies.... However, most discussion on IT markets defines the "market" as the strict supply side only. In IT it is necessary to give more emphasis to user behaviour and needs than is customary in evaluating these issues....

Given that IT is a special case,... governments (should) make legislative adjustments (e.g. in anti-trust law), and engage in actual *encouragement*, to ensure large users and national governments coordinate their requirements on standardization. .... the actions that governments take to promote their indigenous IT industry can be misguided, and ... a false conflict exists between this IT-government role, and the roles of anti-trust authority, standards authority, and procurer of IT equipment. By putting their full weight behind international cooperation on standards, governments would be automatically supporting their industry promotion and anti-trust objectives.

Workshop W3 was entitled *The role of the user in the standardization process* and the report is obviously of interest throughout. The main recommendation reads:

End users should form an international information technology standards user organization with the following mission:

Inform the user about current and planned standards activities through programmes sponsored by government agencies, vendor consortia, universities and standardization organizations,

Orient the standards development process by identifying and prioritizing the information technology standards required by the end user community,

Promote the adoption of information technology standards by outlining the concrete benefits of using standards.

Workshop W5 was entitled *Changing people's attitudes*, though the preferred term at the end was changing people's *perceptions* of IT standardization rather than their attitudes towards it. Of the seven "points for consideration" listed, the following seem particularly relevant to user perceptions (these were followed by discussion of how these aims might be met, and the report from Workshop W7, *Resources for standardization*, is also relevant):

In general (though with some exceptions), it is important to encourage a more positive attitude in the academic world to IT standardization, both for inclusion in courses and as a subject for research.

There is a need to persuade the press, particularly the trade press, to give more prominence to IT standardization. It is important, also, that IT standardization is put into context and that its significance is explained more fully.

Acceptance of standards would be promoted if both suppliers and users had more guidance on how best to exploit IT standards.

> Positive steps are needed to promote understanding within the IT community of the importance of standardization, and of the standards themselves; it is important that standards are seen as products to be sold. In particular, it is necessary to explain why the standardization programme is important, and to promote coherent understanding of it, especially within governments and in corporate management.
>
> There is a need to promote greater awareness of the interdependence of IT standards, and of the importance of conformity testing of standards, i.e. support should be committed to complete projects, covering all the standards involved, and including conformity testing.... Again, it is particularly corporate management and governments that need to be convinced of the importance of this aspect of IT standards work.

It has to be said that, in the time that has elapsed between the conference in 1989 and this book going to press in 1992, not a great deal has happened to make progress in any of the directions suggested by these workshops, certainly not on a worldwide basis, though some initiatives have been taken.

So what is the way forward? In a follow-up to his paper on the problems of software standardization presented in Section 6 of this book [Meek 1990d], **Brian Meek**, in a further paper [Meek 1990e], offered his views on the way forward as far as software standards are concerned, and this, with minor presentational changes, forms our first contribution. This too was based on a presentation by the author at the October 1989 SoftProd 89 seminar at Tampere, this time the closing summary; that summary, and hence the paper, also drew on material presented at a conference on *Standards for the 1990s* at Dublin, Republic of Ireland, in 1988 [ComputerScope 1988]. References to [Meek 1990d] can of course be taken as references to the contribution in Section 6.

The future of software standardization

Introduction

This paper follows up an earlier paper entitled *Problems of software standardisation* [Meek 1990d]. Ideally, a paper on "problems" should be followed by one on "solutions". The difficulty here is that some of the most deep-seated problems described in [Meek 1990d] appear to be either inherent in the nature of software or inherent in the nature of standardization. This paper, therefore, more modestly if only marginally so, discusses not "solutions" but "the future" – particularly hopes and fears for the future. It specifically avoids predictions or expectations for the future, since these can often be dominated by short-term factors which are very likely to render the discussion out of date before it appears in print. The paper attempts to address longer term factors.

Flexibility: the "flip side"

The paper on the problems of software standardization [Meek 1990d] argued that the problems are primarily rooted in the fact that it is indeed "soft" and not "hard", capable of unending variation, adaptation and extension, and inherently resistant to the concept of standardization.

While not seeking to qualify that judgement, it can be remarked that flexibility, while presenting a problem, can also be exploited. If software is so flexible and easy to adapt to the needs of users that it can be argued that it should not be constrained by standards, then by the same token, if after all the benefits gained from the constraints of standardization are recognized, it should be possible equally readily to adapt software to the need to conform to a standard.

Nevertheless, it is sometimes argued that the cost of conversion of software from an old standard to a new – or from no standard at all, to a standard – would be excessive. If the software has not been "engineered" but "crafted" (in a neutral sense of the term) then redesign to a new standard (or a first standard) might well entail a virtual total rewrite. An "engineered" product, however, should surely have made allowance for later revision and have either provided, or used in its development, tools to support revision.

Hence, the adaptability of software, hailed as one of its greatest virtues by some at least of those who argue against its being constrained by standardization, can be turned as a weapon against the opponents of standards. Either it is adaptable to standards, or it is not as adaptable as had been claimed. The opponents of standardization cannot have it both ways.

This is not to say that conversion costs are trivial: far from it. They are mentioned as something to take into account when considering revisions of standards [Rickert 1988, Meek 1988c] and apply to investment in applications using software as well as to the basic standardized software which those applications use. The references just cited are confined to revisions of language standards, but the issues addressed are certainly of direct relevance to software standards generally and, to some extent, of relevance to the establishment of new standards.

The earlier paper [Meek 1990d] argued that being an engineering discipline was something that software engineering still aspired to, rather than as yet been actually achieved. It cited the need for software engineering, if it is to be considered seriously as an engineering discipline, to use standardized tools and components; among other things.

Hence, a potential solution – or more realistically, partial solution – to the problems of software standardization could be the standardization of software engineering tools – especially CASE (computer aided software engineering) tools. At an extreme, use of such tools to produce standard-conforming products for a piece of software could be made a requirement, but even without that, it provides a standard means of assessing the costs involved in modifying products to meet a standard. Well-designed software tools aimed at minimizing costs of meeting user needs would permanently greatly limit such costs – because some users might well need, for their application, to conform to a standard!

Hence, vendors claiming that their software is well-engineered and readily adaptable would at least have a case to answer if they argued that the cost of conformity to a standard was too high. It would be that, or they would lose credibility for the claim. However, if they could indeed demonstrate that their products were well-engineered (using standardized tools) and still could not adapt to the requirements of a software standard at acceptable cost, then perhaps the proposed software standard itself could be called into question.

Seen in this light, CASE standards could act as monitors of the appropriateness of arguments both for the requirements of a proposed software and against them: they would arbitrate.

However, the success of any arbitration is to some extent dependent on the competence of the arbitrator: in this context, the quality of the CASE standards. This paper will not pursue the obvious regression any further, but merely note that the quality of CASE standards could have implications beyond the most obvious applications in the field of software products.

The future

The original title of this paper included the words "hopes and fears" – mainly because an unqualified title might have prompted an expectation that definitive predictions would be offered, or definitive solutions. Were predictions to play a major part then "hopes, fears and expectations" would have been a fairer subtitle. Indeed, "dangers and opportunities" is just as good – or even better, since the dangers at least, if not the opportunities, are likely to prove less ephemeral than the hopes, the fears and the expectations.

The dangers

The dangers standing in the path of software standardization (true, worldwide software standardization) seem to be threefold, and will be dealt with briefly in turn. Two are "political" (in very general terms), the other technical.

USA vs. Europe

One "political" danger is of a widening split between US national standards in IT and ISO international standards. There are a number of relevant factors. One, clearly, is the factor of economic and industrial competition, something which is exercising the minds of more forward-looking companies in the US following the European Community decision to move to a Single European Market in 1992. The establishment of European Norms (EN) has tended to concentrate their attention, since it appears as a potential challenge to the traditional US leading role in setting worldwide standards in the IT industry.

However, most important of all is the significant cultural difference between attitudes to standards in the US and in Europe. There are two main strands to this. One is that, for historical reasons of having had (until recently) a large enough internal market to be viable, with worldwide markets almost taken for granted as a corollary, the US industry has tended to think mostly in terms of national standards rather than international ones and has looked to ANSI rather than ISO. Europeans, in the IT field at least if not always elsewhere, have tended to look to international standards.

Much more important, since much more deep-rooted, is that in the US the attitude is that a standard should in general provide a basis, but be permissive, whereas in Europe the attitude is much more that a standard should be regulatory and place strict requirements on suppliers. Of course, the "regulatory" attitude is not totally absent from the US any more than the "permissive" attitude is totally absent from Europe, but the difference in cultural emphasis is often sufficient to be noticeable.

Suppliers vs. users

The second danger, also "political" in a way, is that the already apparent supplier/user divide in the standards-making arena will become wider, rather than being bridged. Users have notoriously found it hard to get their act together, and, except for very large corporations or for governments, do not individually exert a great deal of economic pressure compared with suppliers. Large corporations have in general sadly and singularly failed to exercise the power that they could command, being seemingly dominated by short-term factors and the wish to protect past (often non-standard) investment rather than in making sure that current and future investment benefit from standards. Governments, as major users themselves, are clearly best placed both to coordinate and to lead representation of user interests. However, often their attitude is all too ambivalent, through being concerned also to protect (or appear to protect) the interests (or perceived interests, or purported interests) of indigenous suppliers.

Governments have supported standards in the past, but mostly in the form of requiring conformity to relevant standards in public procurements; it has not extended significantly, and certainly not extended in any systematic way, to ensuring user-orientation of the standards themselves. I have long argued that regularizing of "existing practice" is a very inadequate basis for standardization [Meek 1988b] and more recently pressed the case for standards to be "product-oriented" rather than "product-based" [Meek 1990a]. *[See the contribution in Section 1 based on these two papers – Eds.]*

A product-oriented standard does not just codify existing technical practices, but is designed from the point of view of properties which a conforming product is required to possess. This places a more appropriate level of emphasis on conformity requirements and, of course, the need to be able to test for conformity.

The early programming language standards are typical codifying standards, defining just the language and syntax and semantics (and even that not very precisely) but leaving completely unmentioned many factors which determine whether or not conforming products, especially implementations, are usable. In the case of Fortran, the deficiencies were so glaring that it led to the development of another standard, BS 6832:1987, to help both users and implementors to specify the missing requirements.

A product-based standard in contrast, takes an existing, usually proprietary, product and models its specification on that product – including, often, design decisions taken for reasons quite divorced from the purpose of the standard, and even design infelicities (to use no stronger word).

The inadequacies of this approach are explored in more depth in the paper cited [Meek 1990a]. Examples of product-based standardization from the 1980s include SQL and the many activities based upon Unix and related products. The fact that Unix is (still) a trademark of the AT&T corporation illustrates further disadvantages of the product-based approach: the very essence of the standardization process is or ought to be complete openness, but inevitably there are doubts about this if the product on which the standard is based is subject to patents, or the documents defining the specification of the project are subject to copyright or non-disclosure restrictions. Nothing short of complete and unconditional release into the public domain is really satisfactory.

Earlier in this section, the importance of testing of conformity was stressed, and it can be readily acknowledged that support by governments of conformity testing of products for public procurements has had a very positive effect in promoting the acceptance of standards. Yet paradoxically, since it has not been accompanied by any systematic support for the inclusion of user-oriented requirements in standards, its effect on the quality of the standards themselves, before conformity testing becomes an issue, may actually have been damaging.

The reasons are not far to seek. Suppliers tend to resist the concept of independent testing and conformity validation, for reasons on which it is not necessary to elaborate. Hence, if suppliers have reason to believe that conformity testing is likely to be an important issue in public procurements following adoption of a standard, it can be expected that a commensurate amount of supplier effort in the standardization effort will be devoted to delaying adoption, and to weaken the conformity requirements.

Options and system dependence

Those who do seek to weaken the provisions of standards, for whatever reason, tend to do so on the basis of inclusion of options, leaving things system-dependent, or better still, not mentioned at all, to make it easier to achieve conformance for their products and preferably make it automatic because conformance clauses are so weak. Untold damage has been done to the benefits which standards could confer, solely as a consequence of this. The problems have been discussed in the cited earlier paper [Meek 1990d]; my fear is that the lessons of the past will not be learned and future standards will continue to be flawed in this respect.

The opportunities

Though these dangers are very real, there are also opportunities there to be taken, if there is the will to do so. Again, I shall pick out three, of which two are political.

European harmonization

Earlier, the danger of a division developing between the US and Europe was discussed, but this also has a "flip-side", and a much more positive one. It is clear that the European harmonization programme, in preparation for the Single European Market in 1992 and even more thereafter, is of interest far beyond the membership of the Community or the bounds of Europe, especially in highly international industries like IT. The political and economic drive towards harmonization is something which can be harnessed for the benefit of all. One is a drive towards standardization in areas that are currently an almost untouched jungle – European Commission IT standards guidelines issued in 1988 cited word processing packages and access to databases as examples [Computing 1988].

Another is the emphasis being given to "functional profiles". A functional profile consists of a usable combination of standards to meet a particular function, including choices of options to avoid incompatibilities which could arise if the options are selected arbitrarily. This can be regarded as rectifying deficiencies of past standardization, something which the Chairman of the main international IT standards committee, ISO/IEC JTC1, went some way towards acknowledging in his keynote address at the 1989 INSITS conference at Braunschweig [Rankine 1990]:

> Until recently, an activity that the international standards organizations did not address is how to decide which options are to be used from within the hierarchy of standards so equipment can be interconnected on a non-equivocal basis....
>
> The development of these "standards profiles" as they are now known has been taken up instead by relatively recently created organizations, namely, the Standards Promotion and Application Group (SPAG) in Europe, the Corporation for Open Systems in North America (COS), and the Group for the Promotion of Open Systems in Japan (POSI). These groups and others are agreeing on the test suites and procedures that are to be used in determining conformance to the OSI standards.
>
> There are some who argue that it would have been better to do all of this under the ISO/IEC umbrella so as to ensure international consistency through a proven consensus mechanism thus avoiding duplication of effort and the need for harmonizing results – a problem that is inevitably having to be solved via JTC1 anyway so as to ensure truly international solutions. Be that as it may, harmonized input from SPAG, COS and POSI, etc. must be

achieved and JTC1 has readied the mechanism for receiving this
and ensuring truly international solutions.

Nevertheless, such moves towards a more product-oriented approach, even if
remedial after the event, are welcome. The opportunity is there to build on this
further, and improve new standards, and revised standards, by making them
more tightly specified, and including fewer options (preferably none at all) and
stricter conformity requirements for products.

It is to be hoped that the functional profiles are specified well enough that those
virtues will become too obvious to ignore even by those with an instinctive
distaste for standards.

Internationalization

The international nature of IT has been mentioned several times, and it became
prominent as an issue in the later part of the 1980s, particularly over the
question of character sets and handling. Much of the previous discussion has
been in terms of the US and Europe, but important though that relationship is,
it leaves out most of the world. On character sets and related issues, however,
it has been Japan, China and other countries in Asia that have been prominent
– not surprising considering the unsuitability for their languages of approaches
based upon western alphabet style character-coding.

The twin opportunities here are to extend international understanding and
mutual effort to overcome problems, and to help those concerned with software to separate out levels of abstraction – to distinguish between functionality
and implementation of that functionality, and between functional services,
implementation and the means by which the services are invoked, presented
to and exploited by the user.

Far too many of the problems of software are caused by inability of people to
separate out levels of abstraction – e.g. in character sets to distinguish between
"A" and the ASCII code for it, let alone whether "A" is the capital roman letter
or the capital greek alpha (see discussion in [Meek 1990d]). The pressure
towards internationalization will, among other things, encourage more software suppliers to separate in their products the functionality from the
presentation, both to reduce costs through duplication and to expand acceptability to new markets. Even for English-speaking users, this could bring
benefit, because the same approach could allow different styles of interface as
well as different base languages, so that someone preferring (say) a
mouse/icon interface to a menu/command interface would not have to be
forced to use an uncongenial interface, nor use a package less suitable func-
tionally with a better interface, not to have to pay for multiple interfaces, only
one of which will be used.

This opens up a wide area which is fraught with difficulties. In internationalization alone, the differences in structure, semantics and style of different
natural languages render simple transcription from one to another an inadequate solution: for example, the commands of an imperative English-based

programming language like Cobol might be literally translatable into another language, but the form of expression be totally unnatural.

The opportunity is there, but if true internationalization is to be achieved, then a good deal of research is going to be necessary – a point which will be returned to in the next section. The hope is that the momentum behind internationalization will be suffice to ensure that the research is done.

Professionalism

If the future offers those two political opportunities, it also offers a professional opportunity. The two elements contributing to this are the new approaches to standards in terms of technical structure and approach, of which product orientation (functional profiles) and internationalization, and in terms of procedures, as exemplified by initiatives outside the conventional standards institutions (or conceived as alternatives to them) that have been a feature of the 1980s.

Standardization is traditionally seen as a voluntary activity. There is no obligation for individuals or organizations to participate in standards-making, and obligation to adhere to standards arises only when there is law to back the standards up, e.g. legislation on adherence to safety standards, or contractual law if conformity to standards is a requirement of a contract to supply goods or services or whatever.

There can be no quarrel with that as a general principle. The trouble is that for standards-making this seems to have led to a chain of association like this:

$$voluntary \rightarrow spare\text{-}time \rightarrow unpaid \rightarrow unimportant$$

where *unimportant* is in the professional sense: though there are exceptions, involvement in standards work is not normally regarded as advancing one's career or, in the academic world, enhancing one's status. Associated with this is the view that the only "professionals" in the standards world are the administrators in the standards organizations, responsible for procedures and format but not for technical content. The chain of association also carries the connotation "amateur": the professional administrators get training in standards rules and procedures, but the people who design and build the standards are expected to be able to do it without training for the task.

In a popular article [Meek 1988a] I have likened the writing of an IT standard to producing other IT products using a similar approach:

> Consider what would happen if you were MD of a software house and you were approached by some people who wanted a stock control package. Suppose that you assemble a group of volunteers all with full-time jobs, who know about stock control but have never written a program. You give them a Cobol reference manual (or tell them where to find one), they form a committee, meet every few weeks or months and otherwise work by corre-

spondence, when their other (paid) work, and the indulgence of their employers, allows. When at last they finish, you get a Cobol programmer to check their (untested) code and correct any syntax errors. Then you publish it.

I would guess that in such circumstances you would find that it takes years to produce; that the people who wanted it are unhappy with the end product; that many potential users ignore it; and you do not sell many copies. It is not surprising that, if you develop other things of similar complexity in a similar way you get similar results – and note that this does not involve any malign influences from vested interests. It is a tribute to the expertise and dedication of those concerned that some standards at least are still reasonably good.

The new initiatives give an opportunity to introduce a new approach to IT standards-making as a legitimate professional activity of similar status to designing and building any other IT product. The large, complex and interrelated standards needed by the IT industry demand no less.

They demand something else as well. The complexity of standards in this area, and the relatively new and fast-developing nature of the technology, mean that new approaches to standardization are needed, to an extent which demands not just revised procedures, not just a rethinking of approaches, but research. The variety of new developments in the 1980s, recognized by Rankine [Rankine 1990], illustrated both the inadequacy of what has happened in the past using established practices, but also that there is no very coherent view of how things should be changed. Even within the formal standards framework, various initiatives have occurred which can be broadly classified as "research". The research-related nature of the reference model for Open Systems Interconnection (OSI) [ISO 7498:1984] has long been recognized, but the activities of Technical Study Group 1 (TSG-1) of ISO/IEC JTC1, charged in the late 1980s with considering and reporting (with recommendations) on issues related to interfaces for applications portability, is a more recent example – and possibly even larger, given the virtually unbounded scope of "applications".

The OSI reference model is already recognized as a major achievement in the history of IT standardization, and TSG-1 has produced, on a shorter timescale at the time of writing, a substantial amount of useful work. Yet it has to be questioned whether an international standards committee or study group, acting under the constraints inherent in its status, can be regarded as an effective research mechanism, or even as a cost-effective research mechanism when measured against the costs. The initiatives referred to represent an opportunity to develop the idea of standards-related research projects, with appropriate research organizations awarded grants to carry them out. Research into technical issues would be of most interest to IT professionals, but there would be scope for research also into the mechanisms of standards-making, and into socio-economic aspects such as what determines levels of standards acceptance.

As for "appropriate research organizations", these could include existing academic institutions, and government or industrial research laboratories and institutes. But the opportunity also exists to establish an IT Standards Research Institute, something I proposed several years ago [Meek c1985] but did not then attract much interest. The climate at the start of the 1990s appears to be less hostile to such a concept.

Such an institute could be a new foundation, but would be easier to set up under the wing of an existing institution.

Choice of a host institution would have to be made with great care, whether it was a national or an international foundation. It would have to be seen to be free from undue influence from government or from IT supplier industry pressures; it would have to be intellectually "respectable" from the academic point of view, yet sufficiently practical not to be dismissed as "too academic" by the business world; it would have to be seen as technically competent by the world of manufacturing industry, including the IT industry, yet not be regarded by the commercial world as a collection of IT scientists and engineers insensitive to the needs of non- specialists. To achieve this calls for careful planning, but it is not impossible. Its very establishment would help to break down the absurd and unnecessary barriers in the IT world caused by the attitudes just alluded to and whose deleterious influence spreads way beyond standards.

Conclusions

These, then, are the dangers and opportunities, the hopes and the fears. Past experience does not offer many grounds for hope that the dangers will be avoided, still less that the opportunities will be taken, unless attitudes change [Meek 1990b, Meek 1990c] *[and see later – Eds]*. Yet the opportunities are there for everyone, even though some are better placed than others to ensure that they are taken, if they see them in time and have the courage to act. If those of us who share the hopes expressed here take whatever chances that arise, however limited, to realize those hopes, then perhaps some dangers will be avoided, and not all opportunities will be lost.

Some echoes of some of this will be encountered later; for example, the impact of European harmonization can be seen in the EWOS report on the *Framework for open systems* which appears near the end.

The role of governments

Contributions in earlier sections have indicated some progress on governmental action to promote standards, and not wholly from the point of view of protecting, and promoting the interests of, indigenous IT industries. Individual governments may be torn between such interests and the interests of users, but intergovernmental organizations naturally tend more to be concerned with the importance of standards for protecting investment on both user and indigenous supplier sides, and also with promoting interworking. As indicated in the preceding paper, the Commission of the European Communities (CEC) has been very active in attempting to promote the harmonization standards (of all kinds, not just IT) and, while one motive is undoubtedly to make the EC industries more competitive in world markets, since many of these industries are major *users* of IT products rather than producers, a side effect has been to render the IT standards part of the policy noticeably user-oriented in many of its aspects, as the examples quoted by Meek show.

On a worldwide stage, in 1991 the Organization for Economic Cooperation and Development produced a report on *Information technology standards – the economic dimension*, [OECD 1991] which considers in some depth the role of governments – both what they have been, and what they might be. This report, though not mentioning the Braunschweig INSITS conference, echoes many of the proposals which had been put forward there and have been cited previously in these pages. This is perhaps a further indication of an emerging general awareness, at the turn of the decade, among those thinking about IT standards policy, of what needed to be done. For example, in the *Policy proposals* section of the report, under the heading "Promoting interest in standardization", we find:

> Even greater efforts might be justified to promote users' participation, which might ensure the development of standards which will reflect, more adequately, from the outset, the diversity of needs (which include "user-friendliness" of systems as well as the special requirements of various professions and activities), and will thus facilitate the diffusion of new technologies.

Many INSITS participants might regard the use of "might" in this proposal to err on the side of bureaucratic caution, but they would certainly endorse the sentiment. Under the same heading we also find:

> Standardization questions should be included in educational and training programmes.... In universities, such programmes will make it possible to encourage research on the various dimensions of standardization.

This is further strengthened later under "Linking research and standardization", when discussing "fostering closer linkages between research and standardization activities":

> More efforts could be made at national and international levels, to strengthen these links in connection with major R&D activities...

Again, this echoes one of the recommendations from the INSITS Workshop W7. In the UK, DISC, the IT standards wing of BSI mentioned previously, in 1991 started conducting a survey of potential activities in this area, with the aim of drawing up a standards-related IT R&D programme. The survey stimulated much interest and many possible projects were identified. At the time of writing no programme has yet been published, let alone any funds made available to carry one out, but it does indicate active interest in pursuing such possibilities. Similarly, it is known that there have been some project proposals under the CEC's ESPRIT research programme which are standards-related to some extent. The economic climate in the early 1990s might severely limit what could be undertaken, but the climate of opinion for "fostering closer linkages between research and standardization activities" seemed more favourable than it had ever been.

Validation

If there is one area above all where government action is especially important, it is that concerned with testing and validation, a theme which has recurred from time to time throughout this book. Before considering what governments might do, it is worth spending some time discussing exactly why this is an important issue for users – in some ways, we have almost taken it for granted.

At first sight, it may seem that testing and validation services is a matter on which users had little to say. It is a job for professionals; it is a job, moreover, for professionals properly equipped for the task. The users simply sit back and reap the benefits.

That view is correct so far as it goes, but it begs a few questions. Firstly, users have need for *independent* and *disinterested* testing services. While it is perfectly possible for the industry itself – say through producer consortia – to set up testing and validation services, and self-regulation by the industry is better than no regulation at all, there would always be the residual doubt of whether findings are truly and totally independent, when it is clearly in the interests of those concerned generally to come up with favourable reports. While self-regulation often works adequately in most circumstances most of the time, there are enough instances of, say, self-regulating professions "closing ranks" to mean that one could never be sure. Involvement of users as monitors can help, but again there are instances in other walks of life of these being "token users", and so-called "watchdog" consumer groups in other industrial sectors sometimes seem to be "more growl than bite". Even independent inspectors cannot cover everything all the time. It is a matter, as with justice, of something not just being done but being seen to be done.

Users, or user consortia, could set up their own testing services, but users, even large corporate users, have many other calls on their resources. Much resource of time and money goes into IT procurements – often to decide how best to cope with *lack* of standardization – but even if much of that could be channelled into testing for standards conformity, it still entails duplication of effort. Much better to have independent testing services to serve the needs of all users, and governments are uniquely placed to provide these either directly or by placement of contracts or licences, having both the resources and (as users) the motivation.

In a way this may be regarded as pushing at an open door. In longer-established fields, such services have long been established, and in IT there is already a respectable track record for independent services such as those by BSI Quality Assurance and the National Computing Centre in the UK, by NIST in the USA, and numerous others in other countries. The difficulties that have been encountered seem mostly to have been caused, yet again, by the headlong pace of IT development. The standards have often lagged far behind the products and the testing services behind the standards.

It is sometimes suggested that in such circumstances "certification" is enough, that is that the producer makes an undertaking, with a guarantee of redress if found wanting, that the product conforms to a standard. Standards conformity is often seen as a selling point, and products often come out claiming conformity to given standards. The trouble with this is that the onus of proof of failure to conform still lies with the user – and the proof may be obtained the hard way.

Producers are naturally cautious about making such claims, if there are penalties attached. IT standards are notoriously complex in many areas, and it is a truism that testing can never *prove* conformity, merely try to demonstrate *lack of* conformity, failure so to do hence giving a greater sense of confidence in the product.

Whether to cover themselves, or simply to retain greater freedom of action than the standard will allow, producers sometimes announce products that "closely conform" to some standard or another. Some purists claim that "closely conforms to" is akin to "almost pregnant" – that it is all or nothing, in other words. Most users would not go that far; but what is essential is to have documented exactly where the divergences from the standard occur, what they are, and if possible how to work round it. Users can then decide for themselves how much, if at all, the divergences matter to them. But taking "closely conforms to" as "near enough", sight unseen, is a decidedly risky business.

The "purist" view tends to be used in the standards themselves, of course; conformity requirements are stated and no allowance is made for not meeting all of them and requiring documentation in such cases. (Testing services can sometimes fill the gap, if the product was submitted to testing.) Even when there are explicit levels and options, let alone things left "system dependent", there are not always adequate requirements for documentation.

This introduces the other main user need in this area – they need conformity rules that are testable, and so that validation tests the properties users want testing. Some deficiencies in this area have been pointed out earlier, for example in Section 3 concerning flexible diskettes – see the citation there from [Schroeder 1990] and others. As Tuinenberg has shown [Tuinenberg 1990], the testing agencies themselves have similar requirements for conformity rules in standards.

It is up to users to be vigilant when the standards are being formulated, and to keep up the pressure for the independent testing services. Much has been done from the latter part of the 1980s onwards in both areas, witness the number of standards projects relating to testing of existing standards (in an ideal world the original standards themselves might have had tough enough requirements built in from the start), and witness the establishment of GOSIPs (Government OSI Profiles – see for example [NIST 1992]) and collective efforts in Europe and elsewhere to establish testing centres. Perhaps the important thing for users is that this momentum be maintained. If governments do not do it, it is hard to see who will.

Though the role of governments is important, even vital, other things are needed. Workshop W7 at the 1989 Braunschweig INSITS conference was entitled *Changing peoples' attitudes*, as noted when its recommendations were discussed earlier, and **Brian Meek**, in a paper published in *Computer Standards and Interfaces* [Meek 1990c] to argue his personal view that, it was indeed "attitudes" and not just "perceptions" that needed changing. The next contribution is a version of that paper, abridged, updated and somewhat modified for the purposes of this book. Some echoes will be found of points made earlier in the book, e.g. in the contribution by Bevan in Section 7.

Changing attitudes

Workshop W7 at INSITS, mentioned earlier, concluded that it was perceptions, more than attitudes, that needed changing. This paper, however, argues that there are in fact wrong attitudes to standardization which are frequently encountered in the IT community, and that means of changing such attitudes deserve serious attention. A number of wrong attitudes are identified, and means are discussed of countering them directly, evading their harmful effects, or if necessary diverting them to advance rather than impede standardization.

The state of the IT standards world

In the world of IT, there seems to be widespread dissatisfaction with the world of IT standards. Some have gone so far as to describe it as being in a state of crisis, while many, though not going so far as that, have expressed varying degrees of concern about aspects of it. Concerns expressed have included the work programme expanding at an apparently uncontrollable rate, and the seeming inability (in the minds of many) of the traditional standards machinery to deliver the standards that are needed, of the quality that is needed, by the time that they are needed.

Concern that resources are not matching the need was a recurrent theme at informal gatherings of ISO committee participants through the second half of the 1980s, if not before. In the UK, the concerns resulted in what eventually became known as "Project DISC", the acronym DISC standing for *delivering information solutions to customers*. It arose from a workshop arranged by the IST/- committee in late 1987, and a subsequent study commissioned jointly by BSI and the UK Department of Trade and Industry (DTI).

The report stated unequivocally in its introduction that "the normal processes of IT standardization were not meeting the needs of those whom the standards should benefit". It made various recommendations for changes, as a result of which Project DISC, to provide a new framework for IT standardization in the UK, was begun.

After a gestation period, DISC (the "project" was dropped) was established as an autonomous wing of BSI and formally took charge of the IT work in BSI in 1990. It will probably not be until the mid to late 1990s that a verdict can be reached on whether the DISC experiment has succeeded or failed; what is of interest here is the evidence it provides of dissatisfaction with the status quo.

If one asks why there should be this dissatisfaction, there are many partial answers, which have been advanced many times: lack of resources; the perceived inability of conventional standards-making mechanisms to cope with the requirements of IT standardization, in particular its complexity; the use of standards committees as battlefields to promote commercial or national interests (or perceived interests).

This paper takes as established that the dissatisfaction exists and that it is sufficiently great and sufficiently widespread that it must be taken seriously. Rather than concentrating on its causes, the paper considers ways in which it may be removed, or at least reduced.

The interest groups

Two main interest groups contribute to the standards-making process, though the total number is perhaps three or four, as we shall see. The two groups that are directly affected at the technical level are, first, the suppliers and vendors, and, second, the purchasers and users. Those are obvious. However, the number becomes three if the standards bodies are included. Though with no direct interest in the content of the standards (except possibly, at a different level, as users), they do have a vested interest in maintaining their existence and influence, and are likely to have a tendency to guard the rules and procedures which they have built up in the past – mostly the non-IT past. The number rises to four if the general public interest is included. The general public may not be direct IT users, except virtually unconsciously when using cash dispensers, or cars, washing machines, video recorders etc. with embedded microprocessor controls. However, the cost to them of the provision of goods and services of all kinds increasingly now depends on the IT industry.

These groups are themselves not integrated, but disparate. Users tend to see suppliers as a united group "carving up" standards work to preserve vendor freedom against user interest. However, even if this rather cynical view is justified, at least in certain cases, the suppliers nevertheless are unlikely to be united in many other respects. Suppliers include not just manufacturers of conventional mainframe computers, minicomputers, and microcomputers, plus peripherals, accessories and consumables, but software houses and component producers – and dealers, or are they "users"?

As for "the users", whether or not one includes dealers, that vague term can be used to cover domestic PC owners, professional engineers or programmers (maybe even employed by an IT supplier), small businesses (again, possibly in IT but using other IT products), large corporations, public bodies, or national governments [see also Section 1 – Eds]. There are tensions and procedural disputes between standards bodies, so they themselves do not always form a united vested interest. As for the general public, if they are not in a state of total or near-total unawareness (blissful or otherwise) about IT standards, they are helpless and bewildered, and there is no possibility for their interests to be represented unless it be by governments or government agencies, by consumer groups, or by professional bodies.

The argument here is that the one common element between all of these groups is, simply: people. All of the groups, ultimately, consist of people, and people's attitudes affect things. If things are wrong with IT standardization, it is worth asking whether it is because people's attitudes to it are wrong; and if things are to be put right, then it is worth looking at what can be done by changing people's attitudes.

Wrong attitudes

A considerable number of wrong attitudes to IT standardization can be identified, and they are often interlinked. This part of the paper lists some examples.

Yes in theory, not in practice

One common attitude is that standards are all right in theory, but in practice are too much trouble to establish and implement. This is a common human failing, of muddling on with something known to be unsatisfactory because of the "threshold effect" of the pain and upheaval of making the change to something better – or it is socially or culturally unacceptable to go against established conventions. Examples can be found in all walks of life – domestic, social, political, administrative, industrial and commercial.

Yes, but not in my area

The second example of a wrong attitude is that standards are all right in other areas, but not in the particular area of interest of the person concerned. This is another common human failing, ranging from a simple assertion of individuality, through a genuine belief that one's case is special, to "special pleading" and ultimately to the arrogant belief that rules are only for other people to follow. It can be observed in everyday life in attitudes to no-smoking areas, or to motoring rules on speed limits or drink driving. Arguments about being a "special case" can almost always be made, but often through concentrating on differences while ignoring similarities or taking them for granted.

Yes, but not yet

The third example is accepting the need for standards eventually, but not yet:

it is "too early to standardize". Though sometimes rooted in a natural tendency to procrastinate and put off decisions, this is one argument that can have some factual basis. This particularly true in a fast-moving area like IT and may be inevitable in an area like software, which by its very nature is capable of unending variation and development. However, it has to be weighed against other factors.

Yes, but we cannot afford it

The fourth example is to profess the wish to standardize, but claiming that the costs of so doing cannot yet be afforded. Again, this may have a factual basis, but again needs to be weighed against other factors.

We must have "state of the art"

The fifth example is the protestation that it is vital to have the most "state of the art" products, which will inevitably be non-standard. Whereas the first four arguments were of the four of "yes but" excuses, this one is a direct anti-standardization argument. In fact, it is a variation of "we are special" with particular overtones.

"Standards inhibit progress"

The sixth and last wrong attitude is that standardization is a bad idea because it inhibits progress (a theme already mentioned by Nigel Bevan in Section 7). This is a variation, though a good deal more extreme, of the "too early" argument. It is often based upon incorrect perceptions both of standardization and of "progress" and the prerequisite for it.

Comments

Most of these attitudes are wrong attitudes, based on false assumptions or faulty reasoning, some totally, some at least in part. If there is some justification some of the time for some of them, it is usually a consequence of taking a narrow and not a wide view, a short-term and not a long-term view.

Some are not quite as simple as that: the idea that standards inhibit progress, for example, which is quite widespread, seems to be based not just on wrong attitudes but on bad experiences of poor quality standards which actually have had that effect. This indicates the need for professional forward planning and quality assurance for IT standards as well as for all other aspects of IT. However, changes within the standards-making process itself to improve quality and remove causes of (or excuses for) wrong attitudes are beyond the intended scope of this paper, which is concerned with direct ways of changing attitudes.

As already indicated, it is *people* who determine the attitudes of companies (both supplier companies and user companies), and the attitudes of governments. It is suggested above that most of the wrong and negative attitudes to standardization arise from people taking too narrow and shortsighted a view.

The justification for this suggestion is that, in many spheres, there is much evidence of ills caused, for example, by managers not looking beyond next quarter's sales, by politicians not looking beyond the next election or the next opinion poll or the next party reshuffle. The world seems to be full of people in positions of power who have narrow and short-term vision. This paper discusses how, nevertheless, attitudes to IT standardization can be changed for the better. The next three subsections suggest some possibilities.

Changing attitudes: frontal attack

The most obvious approach is to try to persuade people to take a wider and longer-term view. Experience suggests that this is not always successful and at best takes a great deal of effort, but the rest of this section suggests possible counter-arguments to those listed above, a "frontal attack" approach. Later subsections will discuss other approaches.

Yes in theory, not in practice

Countering that argument, that standardization is too much trouble, is not easy, but can be attempted by adapting the proverb "a stitch in time saves nine" and contrasting success stories of those who made a transition, and benefited as a result, with horror stories of those who made things worse and worse for themselves through delaying "taking the plunge". Analogies can be used from all areas, whatever is ready to hand and will strike a chord with whomever one is trying to convince. One technique is to try to discover if they had a "success story" themselves in making a transition which can be convincingly likened to adopting standards.

Yes, but not in my area

In its extreme form, the attitude that "standards are things for others, but we are not going to be bound by them", is probably irremediable by frontal attack. In less entrenched cases attempts can be made to counter it by stressing similarities rather than the differences that make the "special case", and pointing out that the benefits of standardizing on the basis of similarities outweigh the benefits of retaining the differences. The best is often the enemy of the good, and often the benefits of having the best are less than the compatibility benefits of having something less than ideal, but good enough. If ready-made clothes are good enough, then the cost savings may outweigh the (marginal) benefits of having something "bespoke" (i.e. "customized").

Yes, but not yet

The most direct way of countering the "too early to standardize" argument is to point out the disadvantages of leaving it too late. The economic aspect can often be the best to stress: the longer you leave it, the more investment will be made in incompatibilities and hence the greater will be the time and the cost both of deciding the standard and then converting to it. Against the danger of "locking" too early into something which is unduly restrictive can be set the relative simplicity of transition between an old standard and a new standard compared with the costs of transition between large numbers of unstandardized incompatible products to a standard that has arrived too late.

The growth of the overall market if standards are established early is an additional argument that can be used. A possible example is sound recording on disk. It can certainly be agreed that it has been the size of the 33-1/3 rpm LP disk market that generated the revenue to make the compact disk developments possible – and that the LP market itself developed on the basis of the earlier 78 rpm market with standardized record sizes and rotation speed.

Yes, but we cannot afford it

The most effective way to counter arguments of "we cannot afford it" is to ask those concerned to make a realistic estimate of the costs of lack of standardization. Too many of these costs tend to be overlooked, particularly those arising from the time that people have to spend worrying about the absence of standards, worrying therefore about which of the unstandardized alternatives to choose and coping with the incompatibilities between unstandardized things.

We must have "state of the art"

The argument about must having the "state of the art" is hard to counter, simply because the very nature of the argument indicates a general attitude of mind. The true counter-argument is really that many who claim that they have to have "state of the art" would be hard pressed to justify it – though of course, some have a genuine case. Often, the only hope is to persuade them to count the costs as well as the benefit of having "state of the art" rather than something standardized, but too often the true reasons are emotional and not rational.

"Standards inhibit progress"

Since the nature of software means that change and innovation are likely to prove never-ending, probably the most effective counter-argument is that lack of standards means continuing reinvention of wheels. The well-known contrast between the cost of developing software and its subsequent maintenance can be quoted. Part of the cost of maintaining an application programme is that its working can depend upon facilities which cannot be guaranteed because of lack of standards – so changes in an operating system, or even in a system-dependent feature of a standard language compiler, can entail consequent changes in the code.

Setting standards in a highly flexible and hence elastic and unstructured environment can be likened to cutting paths through a jungle or wilderness. The existence of paths enables you to go in the direction you want without having to go through the trouble of deciding the line and preparing the route of the path you wish to take. It may not be exactly what you have chosen, but it will get you close to where you intended much faster and much more safely than would have been the case had the mapped-out standard path not been there. It is also not a constraint because the flexibility of software will still be there – you can always move away from the path, or ignore it, if you so wish.

Evasion

Another approach is to accept that one is unlikely to be able to change the attitudes of such people, and hence one should try something else. One possibility is to try to evade such negative influences somehow, or to negate them by recruiting the support of those who do have a wider vision.

By careful project management, and training courses in standards development – too much standards work is done in an essentially amateur way – it may be possible to ensure that a standards committee is led and the work mainly done by people with broader and longer-term vision. This, however, would mean a significant shift away from traditional styles of standards-making. Also, it would be difficult to defend any major departure from the principle of open participation. It could be hoped that the voluntary nature of the activity would mean that people dominated by short-term interests would get frustrated by the long-term ethos, and drop out. One good argument for consciously promoting wider and longer-term vision is that currently it is all too often the people that do have such vision who get discouraged and drop out. Yet even a very strong shift in that direction would be unlikely to stop someone really determined to protect a perceived short-term interest.

Leverage

If frontal attack is likely to be of limited effectiveness, and evasion is difficult to carry out, the possibility remains of trying instead to find some means of leverage, to make use of people's concentration on short-term interests for longer-term purposes, to change negative attitudes to standardization into positive ones by providing short-term incentives and justifications.

The role of conformity and validation

The most-used method to date of directing people's short-term interests towards standards has been the use of conformity testing and validation of products, and of requirements for test reports and validation certificates in procurements. This has been most influential in public (i.e. government controlled or influenced) procurements, rather than in private procurements since (because of attitudes already described) the general tendency among users is not to put very much emphasis on standards.

Nevertheless, public procurements are large enough in most economies to "concentrate the minds" of relevant suppliers: the examples of Federal Information Processing Standards (FIPS) in the USA and the more recent initiatives of the Commission of the European Communities (CEC) on functional profiles and on testing services for conformity to standards are sufficient to make the point.

Unquestionably, insistence on testing and validation of conformity to standards is an important factor in making suppliers take standards seriously. The existence of independent and reputable testing services is an important factor in making users believe that they should take standards seriously. This is why initiatives, by the CEC in particular, to set up a network of accredited test centres is a major step forward. Yet in a way this somewhat pre-empts the issue. For the testing services to get enough work and hence survive, or even be launched at all, it is a prerequisite that there is sufficient of the right attitudes around, among users, to support them. The present services do excellent work, but the area covered so far (at the beginning of the 1990s) is very limited, after all.

The downside of conformity testing and validation requirements making suppliers take standards seriously is that the reaction may well be not one of changing suppliers' attitudes. There are certainly grounds for suspicion that, when some suppliers realise that they have to take standards seriously, the consequence is for them to put more effort not into supporting standards but into delaying tactics, inclusion of options, promotion of alternative standards, weakening conformity requirements, and so on. Further discussion may be found in [Meek 1990d].

It is emphatically not claimed that this is the case for all suppliers all the time: many have a good record in supporting standards. The point is simply being made that it is not an inevitable consequence of making people take standards more seriously that their underlying attitudes to them will be changed for the better.

With that proviso, albeit a major one, conformity testing and validation must be seen as an important potential influence in changing people's attitudes.

Other motivations

There are other potential motivations which it might be possible to utilize in order to change people's attitudes. Most of the power in standards-making lies with the suppliers and the direct users, especially the large-scale users. Suppliers on the whole are motivated by things like their share of the market, while users tend to be motivated by budgetary considerations. Such factors would seem to offer the best hope of finding the necessary leverage. However, if the quality of standards-making is to be improved, and since most standards-makers are provided by suppliers and users many of which are dominated by short-term interests, it might still be possible to attract better quality and longer-visioned participation by improving the professional status of standards-making within the IT industry. The individual people employed by suppliers and users to standards committees are not motivated only by the objectives of their organizations, but by status in their profession.

Governments are only entities with the power to create financial incentives for supplier and user organizations to take positive attitudes to standardization where they do not otherwise exist. However, the standards bodies, and still more the professional institutions, have the power to raise the professional status of standards-making. Because of the nature of such bodies, all have the capability to take a wider and a longer-term view, on balance, than the supplier and user organizations. The remaining difficulty is that nevertheless they too are full of people who take a narrow and short-term view of things.

A further possibility is to target the people in those organizations, rather than in the supplier, or even the user, organizations. If they are people with narrow and short-term vision, then one cannot expect all of them to be converted (though all publicity, like INSITS, helps), but the nature of the organizations they work for is more likely to be favourable to change and any tentative steps they may take internally have less likelihood of being dismissed out of hand.

Targeting and lobbying the key people in such organizations rather than in supplier and user companies is more likely to bring dividends for the same amount of effort. Individuals can be encouraged to take political or administrative or managerial risks in promoting new attitudes to standards.

As implied earlier, however, one can also search out, select, nominate, and provide back-up for, people on standards committees who have wider and longer-term vision; this is a role particularly appropriate for professional bodies.

Among such people, the following concepts can be promoted:

the cost of the IT standards programme in each country and worldwide is obvious, and is easily calculated; it is essential to make clear (especially to governments) the costs of lack of standardization;

it is vital to find incentives (in terms of financial support and of professional status) for people to participate in standardization (especially people with wide and long term vision;

it is essential to find incentives for people to use standards, to the extent where their collective purchasing power becomes vital to suppliers.

Concluding remarks

This paper is a revised and much extended version of some notes distributed at the Braunschweig INSITS conference to stimulate discussion. Those notes were not included in the INSITS Proceedings [Berg and Schumny 1990], which does, however, contain a report of the workshop [Meek 1990b], which should be read in conjunction with this paper [and see the discussion at the opening of the section – Eds]. The author would like to thank a referee for constructive criticisms which led to the inclusion of the subsection The role of conformity and validation, and to numerous other improvements.

So that paper again stresses the vital role of governments, and, as was said earlier, some initiatives have been occurring since the late 1980s. To conclude, therefore, we return to that theme, and present extracts from two "framework" documents published in the early 1990s, both of which relate to user requirements. The first is the *Framework for open systems* which was the final report from project team PT04 of EWOS, the European Workshop on Open Systems [EWOS 1991]. The project team was set up in late 1989 with terms of reference "to explore ways and means of improving the processes and procedures associated with the management of the development of functional standards" to quote from the management summary. To quote further from the management summary:

> ... the project team gathered information on the IT market and the position and importance of standards of all kinds to that market. An early conclusion was that standardization areas and priorities should be market-led but not market-dominated. This information provided the project team with evidence of the high expectations of users.

The members of the project team were Roy Dibble of the CCTA in the UK as chairman, G. Cadina (Hoechst) and S. Heine (IBM) from Germany, J. Piette of the CEC in Belgium, and C. Pilate (Bull) and F. Sztajnkrycer (Lore) from France.

The extracts presented below are Chapters 5 (Rationale), 7 (Findings), and 8 (Conclusions and Recommendations) from the project team's report, with the exception of two subsections which are specific to EWOS. Other EWOS-specific references have been retained to preserve continuity, and anyway some related to work of EWOS of relevance to this book. Some minor editing has been done to avoid confusing cross-references to parts of the report not reproduced here, and to ensure that presentation is not too dissimilar to the rest of the book.

The EWOS framework for open systems

Rationale

This section describes the changing environment which has led to a requirement for open systems standards in Europe. It examines the particular changes that are occurring in the IT sector and the resulting pressures on the standards development organizations. The section repeats statements made in other documents and its purpose is merely to set the scene for the report.

The project team set out to determine the reasons for these changes through the knowledge of its own members or in discussions with the leading experts in the field. The results of this work provided essential background information for the project team which helped it to assess the scale and significance of the challenge represented by the need to manage the development of open systems standards. The members of the project team were convinced that if open systems are to become a reality, this challenge must be overcome.

A changing environment

To obtain a complete picture of those issues that affect standards development it was necessary to examine a number of different factors.

Community level

At the community level, governments want to create open markets where tariff barriers and cartels have been removed. One important prerequisite for open procurement is the stipulation of common standards for products and services. This enables free exchange of goods between countries. The European Commission has paid particular attention to IT standards since the technology itself will be an important enabling mechanism in creating an open market.

Supplier level

The suppliers' main objective is to manufacture and sell products at a price the market can bear. They also attract customers, new and old, by producing new models in ranges of goods which have better facilities, features or performance when compared with their competitors. In the information technology market, the range of goods and services, fuelled by constant technological change, is so vast that many separate industries have been created (software, hardware, networking). Suppliers recognize the importance of standards and play a critical role in their creation and adoption. However, suppliers are constantly striving to find a competitive advantage and they will continue to introduce new techniques and technology that are not covered by standards. If a supplier is able to persuade a large number of customers to purchase these new goods a de facto standard is often created. In the past, if market pressure was sufficiently high or if the supplier recognized a need or advantage, an attempt was made to get the work adopted as a de jure standard.

Successful suppliers respond to market requirements. As the next paragraph indicates, more businesses are demanding open systems standards and suppliers have turned their attention to meeting this need.

Business user level

At a business level, information volumes continue to rise which increases the complexity of the tasks of managing and handling information. Success is often achieved through an organization's ability to manage information with automated systems. Business users are increasingly dependent on information technology (IT) systems which are located at the heart of their organizations. Many businesses cannot recover from a major failure in their IT systems and it is vital that appropriate IT strategies are matched against the organization's business objectives.

Many modern businesses rely on their ability to exchange information with their customers, suppliers and competitors. The days when companies could establish "islands of computing" are now in the past.

Business users have recognized the benefits that can be realized through the adoption of an open procurement policy which leads to the implementation of open systems and open infrastructure (computing, telecommunication and broadcasting systems). This policy offers potential benefits of flexibility, lower costs, increased choice and the prevention of either "lock-in" or "lock-out". Since business users or purchasers ultimately control the choice, selection and introduction of IT, the consequent development of standards should be demand or market-led.

End user level

End user expectations from the use of new and advanced technology continue to rise as they see systems offer new concepts which not only provide new forms of entertainment but practical means of handling information and communicating with others. They also see a mechanism for reducing the drudgery associated with the more mundane tasks. Information systems in all their various forms will become an important requirement in everyday life but they must be properly integrated into that life with proper attention being paid to social and economic issues. However, end users need and demand systems that are more easy to use. The availability and use of standards are required to address this problem.

Effect of new technology

IT technology is becoming increasingly complex and continues to advance at a seemingly amazing rate offering new levels of computing power, telecommunications bandwidth and storage capacity. Although there has been a promise of convergence between computer and telecommunications technologies, artificial separation continues to exist. These barriers need to be broken down or at least crossed if the full potential of multimedia information management techniques are to be realized. This includes computing, telecommunications (voice, data and image) and broadcasting (radio and television). There is a large requirement for the development of standards in each of these areas. Given the very large task and the potential overlaps, it is important that the standards development programmes should be managed and coordinated to prevent any nugatory effort being expended. The introduction of new technology is largely as a result of "supplier-push" with a requirement for appropriate standards appearing later in project life cycles.

Supply and demand

In the scenario described above, business users in particular are becoming more vociferous in expressing their requirements for new technology, applications, techniques and standards. The IT manufacturers and suppliers are keen to foster increasing interest in and therefore demand for new products and services. Both business users and IT suppliers are keen to create positions where they gain a significant competitive edge over their rivals. To achieve this position, both parties want to take advantage of new technology as soon as possible.

Many of the classic examples of competitive edge have been achieved through the use of technology to lock customers into one source of supply. However, the business user, having achieved a short-term advantage over his competitors, seeks an enduring process and long-term stability. In many situations there is a requirement to exchange information in electronic form between customers, suppliers and competitors. These requirements from communities of interest have led to increasing emphasis being placed on the creation of open standards.

The creation of monopoly situations also means lack of competition which leads to increased prices and inferior products and services. They also place a severe constraint on business flexibility.

Open procurement often leads to a multivendor situation where the requirements for intercommunication and interworking can only be satisfied by the use of appropriate IT standards. All of these needs have led the market to the conclusion that open systems standards must be produced. Open systems standards cover all aspects of information handling; including communications, system interfaces, information exchange, application portability, management, security and user interface.

Open systems standards

The requirement for the IT standards development community to give a high priority to all forms of open systems standards will introduce a fundamental change in this area. It will result in a complex and onerous management task which will be exacerbated by the many pressures that the standards-makers will face:

> IT standards are becoming more complex;

> the breadth of coverage of standards and therefore the number of standards is increasing;

> testing of products against standards to check conformance and interoperability is becoming more difficult;

> updating and maintenance of standards will become an onerous task as numbers and complexity increase;

> more and better standards will be demanded by both suppliers and users in a shorter and shorter timescale.

Users have consistently argued that their needs and requirements have not been properly recognized by the standards-making community. Suppliers have also claimed that the burden of supplying the resources for standards development falls upon their organizations. Both groups argue that standards take too long to produce and that the significant time lag behind technology causes severe problems.

These views have created a situation where users and suppliers have formed pressure groups either to create standards or to influence the development of standards. A quite different standards-making environment is evolving from the rather static scene that was in place only a few years ago. Within this dynamic and largely uncoordinated periphery surrounding the formal de jure standards-making process, there is a raft of activity covering de facto, proprietary and emergent standards. All of the standards-making bodies are covering a mixture of base and functional standards or profiles of standards. In this situation there is a constant threat of duplication of effort, selection of incorrect priorities or programmes of work.

The foregoing paragraphs illustrate the fact that the open systems standards-making processes are:

difficult;

different;

demanding.

They also indicate a requirement for improved process and procedural management and an increased level of coordination of the work at international and sectoral levels. If these actions do not occur, members of the project team believe that further fragmentation of the standards work will occur.

As a result of the project team's investigations, it emerged that not only is the IT standards development task becoming difficult, different and demanding, a move from OSI to open systems (embracing OSI) will result in more standards and therefore the involvement of more people, which will significantly increase the management task. The project team was conscious of the fact that questions will inevitably arise on the scale of the problem. However, without undertaking a more detailed study it has proved to be impossible to provide accurate figures covering the number of standards, increased complexity or number of development staff.

[The last subsection of this chapter, on the effect on EWOS, is omitted here – Eds.]

Findings

Introduction to the findings

The preceding section provided an overview of the review and consultation processes conducted by the project team. The project team reached a conclusion that no organization had either produced a final result or had planned a programme of work which satisfied the terms of reference and objectives established for project team PT04. However, a number of organizations had developed partial solutions that went some way towards addressing the problems and objectives outlined in those terms of reference. The project team would draw on the experience and results of that work, where appropriate.

At the outset of its activity, the project team looked at a number of potential options for work which might provide a more formal approach to the identification of new standards requirements, their priorities and the processes and procedures associated with the management of the development of standards. These options, each of which was examined as a separate entity, included:

review of existing EWOS technical strategy;

review of potential work plans;

construction of a more forward-looking technical strategy;

compilation of a generic technical model or framework;

studies of user requirements.

The project team was aware of the limitations of its resources and expertise in its small team of six people working on a part-time basis. It rapidly reached the conclusion that it was unlikely to be able to develop a technical strategy, in isolation, in the complex area of functional standards and profiles. Any minor deviation of accuracy or any recommendation that could not be realized would be rapidly identified by the EWOS or other standards experts in a particular field. Although one possibility that could have been adopted would have been to coopt experts from each area of endeavour or specialism and construct a technical strategy in a piecemeal fashion, this concept was rejected since it would have been too expensive in both time and money.

From its coarse analysis of the potential options, the project team examined ways and means of making some progress towards meeting a number of the key issues. An early conclusion was to avoid specific technical details wherever possible and thus prevent unnecessary or nugatory discussion and debate. Selected approaches would therefore be based on generic solutions. The main output from the project team would consist of tools and aids to assist the management and planning for the development of standards.

The following three examples illustrate some of the early analysis that was undertaken by the team prior to reaching a decision to proceed on the combination of the three aids indicated later in this section.

Framework

A concept that has been adopted in other fora is to construct a technical model or framework that could be either specific or generic. This approach might offer longer-term benefits but the project team concluded that on balance it would not be the most cost-beneficial approach at this stage. It is recommended that EWOS consider the extension of the principles set out under the subsection on the conceptual model (see below) to develop a generic, technical framework in the future.

Advantages

    Single representation of the information system

    Improves understanding at all levels

    Assists future planning

    Provides indication of coherence

    Indicates completeness of standards of all types

    Management control and planning aid

Disadvantages

    High level of difficulty

    Requires lengthy analysis and high manpower resources

    Unsure of format; narrative, graphical, tabular

    Multiple perspectives of problem

    Unlikely to obtain universal agreement

    Potential for multiple levels of abstraction

User requirements list

Another popular approach to the planning problem is to rely completely on market influence and let that dictate the course of standards development. The market position could be illustrated by a user requirements list which would be a stand-alone document. This approach, although representing market requirements, takes no account of the degree of difficulty or resources needed to meet those requirements.

Advantages

    Relatively easy to compile

    Provides a "real world" perspective

    Can readily be expanded to cover any area

    Comprehensible by all parties

Disadvantages

    Users unable to articulate requirements

Multiple perspectives of needs – who is the user?

Need glossary of terms

Multiple potential lists without some structure

Requires analysis to determine technical specifications

Priorities need to be identified

Does not consider development problems

Technical strategy

A third potential activity for the project team was to develop a technical strategy for EWOS with help from experts in the major areas of standardization. Whilst it was accepted that a single work item which resulted in a technical strategy for EWOS would be the ideal solution, it was felt that this was beyond the capability of the project team, in resource and timescale terms. A technical strategy produced in isolation from user requirements could lead to the use of incorrect priorities.

Advantages

Provides a rapid, pragmatic solution for EWOS

Indicates areas of high technical priority

Based on a detailed knowledge of standards

Takes into account the practicability of developing standards

Scope limited only to the knowledge of the strategists

Disadvantages

Open to dispute from experts

Constrained by views of developers, does not necessarily identify gaps

Provides no link to user or market needs

Difficult task – constrained by timescale and resources

Having rejected a number of potential solutions based on a stand-alone approach, the project team examined the idea of a combination of aids. It also constrained its review, not only to realistic options that could be tackled within its timescale and budget, but to those areas where the work would enable useful aids to be defined. The report contains recommendations for future work to be undertaken if the full benefits of the approach are to be realized.

With these caveats, the project team focused its attention on more enduring aids which were oriented towards the development of structures that could be enhanced or developed, not necessarily the production of a total solution.

The project team concluded that four key areas of work were likely to yield maximum benefits:

(a) conceptual model (a high level view which provides a reference source for common understanding of issues and terminology);

(b) technical structure (a hierarchical structure within which user requirements can be specified);

(c) process method (an incremental approach to the construction of a framework);

(d) management organization (an indication of where and how the tools and aids indicated in (a), (b) and (c) might be deployed).

The following paragraphs describe each of these key areas of work in more detail.

Conceptual model

Description

Based on the definition of an open system it is possible to construct a conceptual model at the highest level of abstraction. It has the following components and interfaces:

components: application, application platform

interfaces: application interface (Applications Program Interface API)

interface to the external world (Platform External Interface PEI)

Figure 10.1 shows one possible graphical representation of a high level model.

Two forms of communication can be derived from Figure 10.1:

application to application platform (services) (through the API); and

application to application (through the PEI).

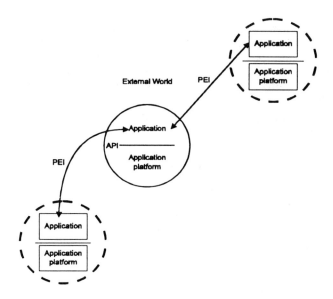

Figure 10.1 *Graphical representation of a high level model*

A first level of refinement of the model, shown in Figure 10.2, is to distinguish between the standard and non-standard portions of the interface. This introduces the concept of direct mapping from standard interface to standard interface and indirect mapping from standard interface to non-standard interface or vice versa. The latter requires some form of conversion or adaptation.

A second level of refinement is to allow a multiplicity of applications on the same platform thus introducing local application to application communication through the same application interface (API) and remote application to application communication through the interface to the external world (PEI).

The last level of refinement is necessary to introduce the human user to the model. The user is described in terms of the following characteristics:

skill;

culture;

knowledge;

experience;

cognition;

senso-motoric;

handicap.

Although at a logical level a user communicates with an open system through an application, in reality the physical interface from the external world is through the application platform. It is that part of the PEI which the user sees and through which a person is able to invoke any function of an open system necessary to support the user's task represented by the application component.

Using the principles described in the preceding paragraphs, Figure 10.1 can be expanded to form the representation in Figure 10.2.

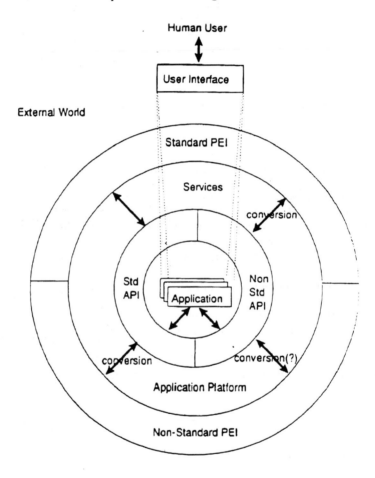

API: Application Program Interface
PEI: Platform External Interface

Figure 10.2 *The conceptual model*

Purpose

The purpose of the conceptual model is twofold:

It should enable the general concepts of an open system to be described in common terminology to establish common understanding.

It should establish the ground rules and the starting point when developing more detailed technical models. It should be emphasised that more than one technical model could be constructed.

Using the basis of the conceptual model, details need to be worked out in the following areas:

subcomponents of application (although necessary, not yet considered);

services provided by the application platform;

types and structure of interfaces;

type of relations between the components, e.g. client/server, master/slave, peer/peer, synchronous/ asynchronous, etc. (not relevant to this activity).

Interface classification

The key elements for standardization are the interfaces, which were identified earlier as the API and PEI.

The PEI is shown in the conceptual model to be the interface between the services provided by the application platform and the external world. The particular services supported via the PEI comprise:

user interface;

information interchange; and

communications.

The user interface enables the physical interaction between the human being and the application platform.

Information interchange facilitates data transfer to external storage media where the format is required to be standardized for interoperability.

Communications services are provided in support of the information interchange between an internal application and an external application where protocol, syntax and format have to be standardized for interoperability.

The API is shown as the interface between the application software and the application platform. It is possible to classify the services supported via the API as:

user interface;

information interchange;

communications; and

system internal resources and services.

An API is required to provide access to external world services. While there is a one-to-one correspondence in classification, there may not be a direct correspondence in implementation. For example, access to a remote file via Network File Service (NFS) uses services associated with the application platform's internal resources. However, implementation makes use of the communications service provided by the PEI.

An additional API is required to provide access to services associated with the application platform internal resources, the fourth item in the list of APIs above. This interface has two parts:

representing services for which language independent specifications may be written;

containing the language specifications.

Definitions of services at this interface take the form of language specifications, language independent service specifications, and language bindings. Language independence facilitates the management and development of standards.

General

These descriptions are in accordance with the key results from ISO/IEC activities and proposals for conceptual models that have been made in international fora, notably ISO/IEC JTC1/TSG1. Further work on the conceptual model is required in those areas listed above. However, the concept could be taken further to explore the possibility of producing a technical model or framework which was rejected as a component of the project team's work due to the project's timescale and the high level of effort required. The project team looked in some detail at the IEEE Posix work on the MUSiC model. It considered that whilst MUSiC offered a useful and simple means of mapping the conceptual model onto supporting technical services, it would be more beneficial as a management aid or check. More work on this subject is required.

Technical structure

The terms of reference indicated that the project team should ensure that full cognisance should be paid to the need to identify market requirements. It was not possible or indeed practicable to conduct a market survey to establish user requirements for open systems within the project team's work. However, members of the project team examined the results of surveys carried out by a number of bodies and concluded that it was necessary to develop a classification or taxonomy for this activity. An agreed classification system would ensure that all organizations work from a common base of information. If the concepts shown below are accepted, EWOS should encourage other organizations to adopt the same definitions. By adopting a classification system of this kind, it should prove to be possible to classify user requirements rapidly and effectively. Equally people using the aid should be able to determine the presence or absence of standards by using the full flexibility of the structure. The technical structure is not however a total solution for determining gaps, priorities and dependencies in standards development by itself. It should be employed in conjunction with the other aids.

In summary therefore a classification system (taxonomy) should:

adopt a market oriented classification;

provide a means to represent user requirements within a technical framework;

have a hierarchical structure (see also a later *Comment*);

provide a direct path to a declaration of the presence or absence of base standards;

indicate the current work of standards-making bodies.

The classification system consists of three levels:

domains;

subdomains;

technical items.

Domains

The proposed list of domains is the following:

A.   Operating system services.

B.   Administration and management.

C.   Application development environment.

D.   Data management services.

E.   Information interchange.

F.   Network and communications services.

G.   User interface.

H.   Distributed applications.

I.   External environment.

Using this list of domains, the current activities of some of the formal standards-making bodies in these areas has been constructed; see Table 10.1.

Table 10.1 *Standards activity*

DOMAINS	IEEE	NIST	FWOS	ISO
A. Operating Systems	*	*		*
B. Administration and Management	*	*	*	
C. Application Development Environment		*		
D. Data Management Services	*	*		*
E. Information Exchange	*	*	*	*
F. Network and Communications Services	*	*	*	*
G. User Interface	*	*		*
H. Distributed Applications	*	*	*	*
I. External Environment		*		

Subdomains

The domain list can be further enhanced to form a subdomain list. This
paragraph indicates the type of subdomain that would be included under each
domain. A further expansion is shown in Appendix E [*not included here – Eds*].
In each case the submission is a worked example and should not be viewed as
a definitive or exhaustive list. If the approach is deemed to be acceptable and
useful, more work needs to be done.

A.   Operating system services

These are the essential services provided by the applications platform, representing the basic functions such as:

kernel operations, e.g. process and task management, generalized input-output, memory management;

shell and utilities, e.g. job control, editor;

scheduling;

checkpoint/restart.

As the fundamental base services are part of this category, and over time they may be extended to incorporate services which today are seen in other domains, e.g. data management, it is important to manage and harmonize the standardization work in this domain. Users seek comprehensive and reliable services from the operating system, e.g. support for online transaction processing and real-time, better diagnostics and recovery mechanisms, dynamic reconfiguration at a system level.

B.   Administration and management

These services depend substantially upon facilities provided by the operating system services. Administration and management provides the tools which use, for instance, the information collected by the operating system to assist with administration and management of both application platforms and networks. The functions cover:

backup, restore and archiving;

system configuration management;

file system management;

naming/routing;

network management;

user account management;

security management.

Users require that all administrative tasks should be performed effectively and efficiently. Furthermore the user interface to the administration tools should be consistent throughout the system whatever the source of the hardware and software components that comprise the system.

C.   Application development environment

The services required in this area are important to support the complex needs of system and software development, which is a major area of expenditure for large organizations. The domain is also of significant interest to software vendors as it provides the enabling technology, in conjunction with acknowledged development methods, for all applications. It provides tools, e.g. CASE tools, for editing, debugging, configuration management, version management, languages including 4GL, and object-oriented development tools. It is not generally regarded as a high priority area but the Portable Common Tool Environment (PCTE) work of ECMA is likely to be an important development.

D.   Data management services

This domain provides services which give application programs the ability to create, alter, or delete tables, records and fields and to insert, select and update data in structured components such as indexed files or relational or object-oriented databases. The functions include:

file management, e.g. ISAM;

data dictionary;

distributed database;

database access and manipulation, e.g. SQL.

There has been little attention paid by standards development bodies to this domain as a whole although some components such as SQL and Data Dictionary have received attention at international level, supported by emerging groups of vendors such as SQL-Access to advance the delivery of standards.

E.   Information interchange

This area provides support for the exchange of information between applications or components of applications and more particularly addresses the data formats that need to be standardized to ensure that information can be interchanged effectively. A number of activities are in progress with standards development organizations enabling transfer and interchange of compound documents, graphical data, tables, trade data, etc supported by standards such as:

ODA/ODIF;

SGML;

EDI/EDIF;

CGM.

With a potential increase in the number of different and incompatible products, a priority for this domain is to ensure the harmonization of evolving profiles.

F.   Network and communications services

These services are needed to transport data between the external world and the applications platform, between platforms, and between applications on different platforms. Equally the services manage the data communications infrastructure. User requirements indicate a need for improved conformance and interoperability testing based on International Standardized Profiles (ISPs). Users also require a standard API to the communications services which support:

file transfer;

messaging;

directory;

terminal access.

The existence of protocols such as TCP/IP, considered to be the de facto standard by many Unix users, require assistance to be provided to facilitate migration to OSI protocols.

G.   User interface

From a user perspective, the user interface is considered to be the most important domain that requires improved progress on standardization especially with regard to establishing a consistent "look and feel" interface. The scope of the domain is broad, covering keyboard layout; selection tools, e.g. mouse, tablet, trackball; window management; toolkits for the applications developer. Popular products such as MOTIF from OSF and Open Look from UI are emerging as de facto standards at the terminal, supported by the X-window protocol and Xlib evolving as a de facto standard from the X Consortium. The basic services required include:

window services;

toolkit;

command language;

dialogue;

graphical user interface.

H.   Distributed applications

The increasing trend towards use of distributed systems encouraged the classification of this area as a separate domain. The user requirement is for a distributed computing environment within which the whole network is transparent to the user. It relies significantly on other domains such as the operating system services, applications development environment, and information interchange requiring discrete facilities such as:

remote procedure call (RPC);

name server;

transparent file access.

I.   External environment

This domain embraces physical components such as:

peripheral controllers;

magnetic media;

optical media;

ports;

cables.

More work is required to address a number of environmental issues including cabling strategy, ergonomics, safety, electronic emission.

Technical items

There is a third level within the technical structure which identifies the fundamental technical items which comprise the subdomain and at which level base standards can be identified. An example of the structure at this level is provided in Appendix F [not included here – Eds] which looks at the subdomain of message handling and languages, providing a direct link between a technical item and base standards.

Comment

Although the preceding paragraphs provide an indication of a possible structure, the project team was conscious of the fact that there will be a debate on the classifications used. This is inevitable since some subdomains can appear under multiple domains. It is also apparent that technical items have potential connections with several subdomains. These linkages can be built into the classification system. The primary objective is to provide a straightforward structure into which user requirements can be categorized.

There are also some issues that are applicable to most if not all of the domains, e.g. security, management, internationalization, which must be taken into account in the structure.

Process method

Introduction

The project team concluded at an early stage that it would be impossible, given the timescale and resources assigned to the activity, to produce a detailed Framework for Open Systems which either covered all of the existing EWOS work on standards or the full spectrum of open systems. This conclusion was reached after reviewing the progress of other groups who had started work in this area and assessing the technical complexity of the task.

However, the project team considered that there was a potentially viable approach to the problem which might enable the project team to meet some of the requirements of its terms of reference. Although it was clear that there would not be an opportunity to construct a fully developed framework, it was possible to move towards a final objective by adopting an incremental approach to the problem.

Objectives

The process method will be used when EWOS considers that work in an area of standardization should be undertaken. EWOS will need to examine the set of standards that currently exist in the technical area and carry out some analysis to determine whether or not those standards adequately cover all of the identified requirements. In addition, it will be necessary to assess the demand for standardization in a particular technical area and its relative priority. Finally, EWOS needs to identify what other work is being progressed in this work area by other standards bodies.

To meet these objectives it is necessary to adopt a systematic approach to the construction of a framework, called the *process method* in this paper. The components of the method are described in the subsection *Process method steps* below.

A technical area is selected (domain, subdomain or technical item). Its internal components and their interfaces are defined. In addition it is important to ensure that a technical area is not analysed in isolation since it exists in an environment and needs to cooperate with other technical areas. Cross-boundary issues such as applications program interface (API), management, security, data formats and testing need to be considered as well as interfaces between technical areas. The external environment might exhibit different attributes according to the nature and use of the information system.

From the analysis of the internal components and interfaces in a technical area and its relationship with other technical areas in an external environment, missing areas of standardization can be identified. It is also possible to confirm that a consistent and usable set of standards exists covering all identified user requirements.

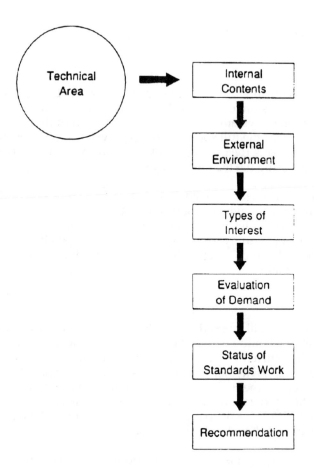

Figure 10.3 *The process method*

Following the analysis in the process method, a final recommendation to EWOS can be made.

Process method steps

The process method consists of a series of steps, each of which requires a task to be performed. The steps are illustrated graphically in Figure 10.3 and the tasks at each step described in the following paragraphs.

Technical area

A *technical area* is defined as a domain, subdomain or technical item identified in the classification system: the *technical structure*. It is an area that is meaningful to an end user, product or service provider or to the developer of standards.

Internal contents

The purpose of this task is to identify and define the component parts and their interfaces in the technical area. If the area is large, i.e. a domain or subdomain, further levels of decomposition might be required.

External environment

This task is most important since it determines the relationship between the technical area under scrutiny and all other technical areas. The analysis can be undertaken using the technical structure as a guide or by examining real or potential system designs.

Types of interest

Following the analysis of the technical area and its relationship with other areas, it is necessary to review other types of interest that might be present. Typical considerations might be:

user interface;

programming interface;

data structure and format;

security;

management.

A list of those cross-area items that need to be considered for each component must be constructed.

Market demand

A statement of user demand and priority for each area is required based on the final output of the work in the technical structure. In addition an indication of the current availability of products complying to relevant standards is needed.

Status of standards work

The current status of standards development for each component and interface within a technical area is required. Both de jure and de facto standards development activities must be taken into account and statements on the progress at international level (ISO, CCITT), at regional level (CEN-CENELEC, ETSI, EWOS, AOW, NIST) and in other areas (IEEE, X/Open, OSF, UI, APIA, NMF etc) must be made. Typical responses might include:

under consideration;

part of work programme;

work in progress;

work completed.

Recommendation

As a result of the analysis of the information determined at each step of the process method, it is possible to come to a conclusion which results in a recommendation to EWOS. A number of possible alternatives might result:

contribute to the work of other standards-making bodies;

liaise with other groups;

launch a project team;

create a new expert group;

start work on a new work item.

Rigour of the method

Although it was not possible for the project team to produce a framework which addressed all of the technical items currently covered by the EWOS work programmes, some particular examples were used to explore and demonstrate the rigour of the method. For this purpose, Message Handling System (MHS) covering MHS 84, MHS 88 and Directory, Human-computer Interface, and Open Document Architecture have been chosen. To ensure that all aspects of the method were tested, the analyses provide an illustration of the use of the process method for technical items, subdomains and domains. *[The results of those analyses are described in an appendix to the report – Eds.]*

Way forward

The examples shown *[in the appendix – Eds]* indicate the concept of the incremental approach to the construction of a framework at different levels. It is clear from the results that a valid analysis can only be undertaken with the help of an expert in the appropriate area of standardization.

A useful picture can be established and it is recommended that this work is extended to cover other areas.

Summary

Each of the three aids – conceptual model, technical structure and process method – will require maintenance in the future. The technical structure and the process method in particular are dynamic systems that will require constant update.

It must be emphasised that the project team has only been able to devote a limited amount of time and resource to each of the aids. In the case of the conceptual model, the initial work could be extended but the main objective in the future will be to establish agreement to the concept by organizations in other parts of the world who are undertaking similar work. Therefore the project team's efforts have been restricted to work at a high level where there is a strong likelihood that the conclusions will not be the subject of debate. Many of the ideas have been based on existing work in JTC1. Although early attempts were made to produce technical models and it was thought that such models could be useful, the resulting output would undoubtedly be subject to challenge and debate.

[The last subsection of this chapter, on organization, is specific to EWOS and is omitted here – Eds.]

Conclusions and recommendations

Conclusions

1. From the analysis of the current and future market conditions it was concluded that the effect on IT standards development would be significant. It was further concluded that standards development would become different, more difficult and demanding.

2. With the advent of a requirement for open systems, IT standards are required across the whole panoply of IT systems. EWOS will need to address the full scope of open systems as indicated by its title. This requirement will be a natural progression from its work on OSI functional standards. It will require a change to the EWOS terms of reference.

3. Business users and purchasers control the choice, selection and introduction of IT systems and should be consulted to determine the key areas for standardization and their priorities.

4   The convergence issue of major technologies (computing, telecommunications, broadcasting) needs to be constantly reviewed and the development of standards drawn together if the advantages of multimedia systems are to be realized in the future.

5. If EWOS engages in all of the prospective work, the number of standards to be developed and the number of people involved will increase significantly. In conjunction with these increases the problems of priorities, control and management become more onerous.

6. EWOS must also play an active role in coordinating both the de jure and de facto standards activities. This will necessitate an increased liaison role in an attempt to persuade all of the current and future bodies involved in standards development at all levels to work in concert. It is important to prevent any duplication of effort when so much needs to be achieved.

7. EWOS should ensure that IT users are made aware of its achievements and aspirations. This will require a marketing exercise, and without that effort, users will turn to those organizations who produce de facto standards and who are far more vociferous.

8. To address the increasing management and control of the development of standards processes, better aids and tools are required and the work of the project team is justified.

9. The project team were unable to find any evidence of a relevant development that would satisfy the EWOS requirement for a framework.

Recommendations for specific future work

1. The work on the three tools or aids (conceptual model, technical structure, process method) should continue until each tool is complete. A maintenance schedule or policy should be developed for each tool. This will require the continuation of a project team with maintenance to be undertaken by an independent group.

2. To ensure that the areas of standardization and priorities are identified, it is recommended that market surveys are undertaken. The most cost-effective approach is to use existing work which is available from other sources. However, the project team recommends that more than one source of information is used. A more costly but impartial way forward would be for EWOS to conduct independent surveys.

3. It is also recommended that the present EWOS organization is modified to take full advantage of the use of the management tools. The project team advocates the addition of a separate Group, called EMG in the Report, to maintain the tools and provide management support and control in support of EWOS activities.

4. The project team also recommends that other business-oriented functions such as an annual business plan and marketing should be considered by EWOS to ensure that the availability of functional standards is made known to a wider community of interest.

5. EWOS should consider continuing the work on Frameworks not only to finalize the early concepts derived by PT04 but also to develop a generic technical model or framework.

6. Early effort on the process method has indicated that gaps exist between areas of standardization and concerns exist as to whether an item of work falls within OSI. There is a particular and specific concern over the development of Application Program Interfaces (APIs) as an example. This and other items prove the worth of the analysis and the conclusions should be examined by the appropriate expert group.

7. On the specific issue of PT04 [the project team which produced this report – Eds], it is recommended that the present work is terminated.

Global recommendations

1. All the recommendations concerning tools, aids, processes and procedures should be discussed with other international standards developers, but particularly the other regional workshops, in an effort to create a common, agreed set of working methods. This liaison is most important since it potentially produces common ground from which the harmonization of programmes can be achieved.

2. The project team recommends that EWOS continues to monitor any new worldwide activities on Frameworks and that the Workshop attempts to use its influence to align the work.

Prioritization

The clear priority for the way ahead, if EWOS accepts these recommendations, is to continue the work established by the project team. If the concept of the three tools is agreed, the details of the technical structure and the process method must be finalized as a matter of urgency. Of the two tasks, the former is the less onerous and should reach a relatively stable position. For the process method, the early task is to substantiate the rigour of the model by using more examples.

Having reached a conclusion on the practicality of the approach, this should be followed by adopting the incremental approach to framework development across all of the areas currently addressed by EWOS. The latter activity will take some time and effort and will only reach a successful conclusion if the technical experts play a full part in the process.

These are the priority tasks but clearly other recommendations can be carried forward in parallel with this work if they are deemed to be appropriate.

The current activity of the Framework for Open Systems project team PT04 should be terminated. New terms of reference should be constructed for the continuation of the work covered by the specific recommendations listed in this section *[of the report – Eds]*. A new project team, with some common membership to ensure continuity, should be formed to undertake the new work programme.

As our final contribution, we present here some extracts from the BSI/DISC Draft for Development *A framework for user requirements for information technology* [BS DD210:1992]. One of DISC's innovations has been the establishment of a Business Strategy Forum (BSF) to set the agenda, i.e. priorities, for IT standards work in the UK, and the framework for user requirements was drafted by one of its working groups. Most BSF members are representatives of major supplier or large corporate user companies.

As the name indicates, the whole of the document is of relevance to the theme of this book, but the extracts here are sufficient for immediate needs. Readers are strongly recommended to obtain and review the entire publication.

"Drafts for Development" are BSI publications which are of a provisional nature because their subject matter is still under technical development requiring wider exposure. Hence this framework document is not, and must not be regarded as, a British Standard. Instead it should be applied on a provisional basis, so that information and experience of its practical application may be obtained. A review of the Draft for Development will be carried out not less than two years after its publication, i.e. not before 1994.

The parts reproduced here ("clauses" in BSI terminology, as will be seen from the text) are Clauses 1 (Scope), 3 (Overview), and 4 (The framework for user requirements, i.e. the specification itself). Annex B (Using the frameworks) is also included here because it relates the framework for user requirements to other frameworks. The text is reproduced here almost verbatim apart from the omission of clause numbers, which would here be confusing, and some consequential changes to cross-references; the incorporation of some definitions from Clause 2 into the text; some minor presentational changes to bring it more into line with the rest of the book; and editorial explanatory remarks (in square brackets and italicized).

The BSI/DISC framework for user requirements

Scope

This Draft for Development is a document that describes a framework for user requirements for Information Technology and presents some general guidance on the application of such a framework. It does so by proposing a way in which an enterprise (i.e. the user) can identify its needs for the services that IT might in future provide, and can describe those needs in business terms. However, it is not a tutorial document and does not provide detailed guidance relating to the processes appropriate to specific needs.

This framework for user requirements encompasses any IT required to support those activities of an enterprise that manipulate or depend on information in some way.

Overview

Objectives of the framework for user requirements

Information technology is becoming an increasingly important factor in supporting enterprises to achieve their business objectives. This is so much so that enterprises, in forming their corporate strategies, need to establish an information strategy to assist the development of both an infrastructure and a set of facilities for managing information. The capability of the technology, together with the availability or lack of appropriate standards can, and does, influence or inhibit the development of information and hence corporate strategies.

The high level business need is for standards to help enterprises and people to work together in using information. This framework comprises constructs and processes that will support that need, allowing strategic considerations and business needs to be expressed at an appropriate level of detail and the standards-making process to be influenced accordingly. These requirements need to be expressed in common terms, and preferably to call up a common set of building blocks. In this framework for user requirements, the common building blocks are provided by the concept of *generic IT services* (see below) which are invoked to satisfy requirements where possible.

This framework for user requirements therefore has the following specific objectives:

(a) It should enable an enterprise to express its particular requirements for information systems.

(b) It should enable enterprises to express their requirements collectively, and to do that in a way that makes it possible for others to ascertain the needs and priorities for standards.

This framework should also assist enterprises to achieve competitive advantage through flexible exploitation of common components.

The need for a related framework for standards and technology

There is a need for standardization in the area of information systems and in how particular and general statements of requirements are interpreted. An additional framework, "a framework for standards and technology", would help to meet this need.

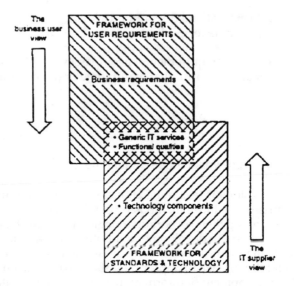

Figure 10.4 *The two frameworks*

This Draft for Development does not describe a framework for standards and technology in any detail but recognizes the need for its existence. Work is going on elsewhere (for example work in a European Workshop on Open Systems expert group, in CCTA's Framework for Open System Standards project and in the IEEE Posix Open Systems Environment project 1003.0) on the equivalent of a framework for standards and technology, and close liaison will be maintained with such activities. *[See the EWOS contribution earlier in this Section, and the contribution by Cannon in Section 6 – Eds.]* For a description of the relationship between the two frameworks and the simultaneous processes that operate upon them, see Annex B *[the subsection "Using the frameworks" below – Eds]*.

The two frameworks are related through the concepts of generic IT services and their functional qualities as shown in Figure 10.4 *[Figure 1 in BS DD210:1992 – Eds]*.

The generic IT services are clearly defined in a form that is meaningful to business and are also structured sufficiently unambiguously to link directly to a framework for standards and technology that will allow the IT suppliers to select standards and specifications for use in products with a view to meeting these business needs.

Generic IT services are thus pivotal in linking the two frameworks and, for an explanation of this pivotal role, see Annex C *[not included here – Eds]*. With the guidance of these two frameworks, businesses can express needs in their own terms and are shielded from the complexities of the component technologies; on the other hand, the suppliers of those technologies can decompose the business needs more easily into product specifications.

Identifying user requirements

This framework for user requirements promotes the development of consolidated statements of requirements that:

(a) are based on the business needs of enterprises;

(b) are expressed in terms of technological capability meaningful to such enterprises (i.e. not at the detailed level of more technical standards);

(c) show the relative importance and value placed on particular attributes of generic IT services;

(d) are classified so that the need for corresponding standards can be identified.

Formally basing user requirements on the aggregated needs of several enterprises would require the following.

(1) A process of enterprise analysis for each enterprise which is carried out typically in terms of strategic business factors, business functions and business data (as described below).

(2) A determination of business systems needed by the enterprises.

(3) An analysis and aggregation of those needs in terms of requirements expressed in a common format, for supporting generic IT services also expressed in a common format.

(4) An assessment of priorities and organizational/distribution requirements typically derived from an analysis of business plans for each business function.

(5) An assessment of priorities that relates to the corresponding generic IT services.

These business-oriented concepts are illustrated in Figure 10.5 [*Figure 2 in BS DD210:1992 – Eds*]. They help to ensure that user requirements are based on the elicited needs of enterprises, without implying any particular approach to decomposition.

In practice, different organizations have different structures and therefore may select an approach which is more or less rigorous when analysing their requirements. This Draft for Development does not prescribe any approach for an enterprise, neither does it expect an enterprise to allocate the effort needed for such an analysis if it is not already available. However, enterprises should be able to identify and relate to the concepts of business functions, business data and business systems that would result from such an enterprise analysis.

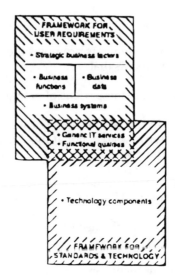

Figure 10.5 *The concepts of the framework for user requirements*

Benefits of using the framework

The concepts contained in this Draft for Development may help enterprises to appreciate the overall role that can be played by IT in their business. These concepts may also be helpful in the various business processes of developing a mission statement, a business strategy, an IT strategy, a strategic infrastructure and a realignment to the business strategy. However, the essential requirement for this Draft for Development is that it be adequate to support users in determining and representing their requirements, and to do so in a way that will influence the standards-making process.

The framework for user requirements

The concepts of the framework

General

A number of concepts are involved in making up a framework for user requirements. This set of concepts comprises strategic business factors, business functions (with their related business data and business systems), generic IT services, and functional qualities. The definition of these terms are the following:

> *strategic business factor*: a characteristic of an organization that determines how it operates by encapsulating a principle or ethical value that can be used to guide courses of action;

> *business function*: a discrete group of related activities that supports one aspect of the mission of the enterprise;

business data: the set of enterprise-relevant data which is a common resource for business functions;

business system: a system which performs one or more of the tasks of one or more business functions by transforming a set of inputs, using a set of rules and procedures, to produce a set of outputs;

generic IT service: a designated grouping of IT-based components, providing a commonly needed group of capabilities which are comprehensible from both user and supplier viewpoints;

functional quality: an attribute of a generic IT service that determines inter alia the level of service required and the type of information on which that service operates.

Together they should enable an enterprise to identify the processes and mechanisms related to the IT that it needs. These concepts are detailed below.

Implementation of the concepts

One starting point for the development of a strategy for IT would be for a particular enterprise to interpret its mission statement in terms of business objectives, key business processes and existing resources. At an appropriate stage, this interpretation process would develop into an analysis of specific requirements for business functions, business systems and supporting IT services. The enterprise could then identify the strategy and the appropriate IT components necessary to support it.

The concept of strategic business factors

Since strategic business factors are those characteristics of an enterprise that determine how it operates, the process of enterprise interpretation and analysis should be guided by the strategic business factors of the enterprise which in combination represent the ethos of the organization. For example, a desire for local autonomy and accountability would emphasize the need for standards for distributed processing, while a centralist approach might emphasize tightly controlled development of highly reliable corporate databases. Enterprise interpretation and analysis should result in a set of identified business functions and systems that form a major input to the development of a strategy for IT.

The choice of particular capabilities required in generic IT services should be guided by lower level interpretations of the enterprise's strategic business factors and by more process- and user-oriented considerations such as the need for timeliness of information and the ability to evolve. Further, more detailed examples are given in Annex D.1 *[of the full document – Eds]*. IT can be a key enabler of a new culture in supporting enterprise objectives.

Strategic business factors are essentially qualitative, so they are not used directly in this framework for user requirements. However, an enterprise may find it helpful in assessing the required functional qualities for each generic IT service to review that service against its own strategic business factors.

The concepts of business functions, data and systems

The concept of business functions

A business function is a discrete group of related activities that supports one aspect of the mission of the enterprise. In total, the business functions provide complete support to the mission. Each business function therefore describes a convenient grouping of functionality that is seen as necessary because of the essential nature of the business, for example sales/marketing, product development or information management. Other examples are given in Annex D.2 *[of the full document – Eds]*.

Business functions may or may not be equivalent to a departmental role. They are essentially independent of the organizational structures that undertake them. Because of this, they provide clear pointers to the types of information systems that are needed for the enterprise to further its mission, to support its values and to achieve its objectives.

A review of business functions provides an opportunity to analyse core processes of the organization and exploit IT to re-engineer these processes (and conversely to avoid automating old, suboptimal processes).

Several decomposition levels of business functions may be identified and, at the lower levels, common, cross-functional activities are likely to appear. Examples might be production, quality assurance and payment. If these are to be managed cross-functionally, they place additional user requirements on the business systems and generic IT services which support them.

The concept of business data

Business data is that information which is needed for the activities of business functions, for example information about products, services, customers, suppliers, employees, locations, equipment and skills.

Needs for information and for processing that information are in some sense dual, and requirements can be identified from either viewpoint. Establishing the requirements for business data is crucial to the understanding of requirements for business systems and generic IT services. Requirements to share business data across business functions, organizational units, locations and even different enterprises can be particularly revealing. Further examples of some common types of business data are given in Annex D.2 *[of the full document – Eds]*.

Business data can be of different kinds and of different qualities. It can encompass pure data (raw facts), structural data (data about the form or meaning of data), information (summarized/processed data as in a monthly sales report), knowledge (human interpretation of multiple channels of information) and wisdom (knowledge combined with experience and vested in people or expert systems). It can also be represented in many different forms and stored on, or carried by, many different kinds of medium.

Business data is a resource of the enterprise and like any resource requires management, operations (including maintenance), standards, ownership and monitoring. These requirements can also generate needs for business systems or functional qualities of business systems (see below).

The concept of business systems

A business system performs one or more of the tasks of one or more business functions by transforming a set of inputs, using a set of rules and procedures, to produce a set of outputs. The need for business systems may be identified directly from the needs and policies of the enterprise, e.g. requirements for global communications or for a common infrastructure. Typically business managers are directly responsible for business systems. Examples of business systems, such as administration, production and sales are given in Annex D.2 *[of the full document – Eds]*. Business systems themselves make use of generic IT services (see below).

A business system can also provide a way of expressing commonality of activities between business functions, which may be helpful in progressing to the generic IT services.

How business data and business systems are deployed to support particular business functions will vary according to a specific enterprise's needs and perceptions of an appropriate span of control. However, it should be noted that there are advantages in separating business systems from the underlying business data, so as prevent the data from being tied to a specific system and to allow it to be reusable. Such an architecture poses particular requirements for standards.

The need for generic IT services can also be identified from a strategic analysis of corporate requirements. One approach would be to identify the need for individual applications, personnel and computing resources to be linked to the corporate infrastructure in order to add value to the operations of the enterprise. This leads to identification of necessary capabilities and standards for data interchange and interoperation. The form of interaction, and therefore the interface, will vary according to the type of information source and destination (i.e. personnel, machines), and the appropriate form for the information to be exchanged (i.e. media, etc.).

The strategic value of the exchange increases as its information content increases and as compass of the groups involved increases from individual, to team, to strategic business unit, to intra-enterprise, to inter-enterprise.

Such considerations may lead to selection of a set of enterprise-wide standards and identification of a number of shared IT-based services which, in combination, provide a strategic infrastructure, rather than a specific business function.

The concept of generic IT services

A generic IT service is a generalized grouping of information-handling capabilities that can be packaged and tailored to provide an operational service or some other service commonly required by business systems. The details of a generic IT service will include a list of its basic capabilities and the functional qualities provided by the service.

A generic IT service is conceptual; it is an abstraction which gives a label to the common characteristics of a set of information-handling services, where these characteristics are comprehensible from the point of view of both user and supplier of the technology and, in that sense, look both ways. Different enterprises, users and suppliers may express these characteristics differently even though the underlying business and technological requirements may be the same or similar. However, it is fundamental to this framework for user requirements that the label, i.e. the name given to a particular generic IT service, is common to all.

The information-handling capability of a generic IT service relates to some essential characteristics of manipulating information, communicating information or controlling business processes that depend on information. The expression *manipulating and communicating information* should be interpreted in a broad sense; it includes the recording, storing, recovering, transporting, transforming/processing, analysing, structuring, managing, ageing, reconciliation and presenting of information. The capability relates to the organization and management of information as a resource, as well as the provision of functionality based on the manipulation and communication of information. The expression *controlling business processes* includes monitoring and activation, as well as control itself.

Each identified generic IT service is one for which standards requirements can be recognized by users. These services are independent of any particular business system, although they might be specialized to provide a domain-specific IT service. They will be implemented (i.e. engineered as a specific IT system or systems) within an enterprise by procurement from its suppliers or directly by its implementors.

An initial list of generic IT services is given in Table 10.2 *[Table 1 in BS DD210:1992 – Eds]*. This list will be enhanced and refined using responses to this Draft for Development and to a questionnaire (see under *Users of the frameworks* below).

The list is given here in full because of the pivotal role of generic IT services, on the one hand between the enterprise (i.e. the user) and the standards-maker, and, on the other hand between the two frameworks (see also Annex C *[of the full document – Eds]*). Two of the categories (IT service management and applications development environment) are "cross-category" which means they can apply to and be used by the other generic IT services.

Table 10.2 *Generic IT services*

Title	Description
Message distribution	Providing mechanisms for sending and receiving messages of limited structure
Batched data transfer	Providing mechanisms for the structured, bulk transfer of data, e.g. files, within or between organizations
Data exchange	Providing mechanisms for sending and receiving structured and unstructured information prior to presentation
Integrated data query and update	Providing the basic processing functions of read, write, create, update, delete, compare, move and copy, etc. for data items
Source data capture	Providing appropriate mechanisms for gathering the required data prior to its input for processing
Data storage and retrieval	Providing mechanisms for holding large quantities of structured and unstructured data
Data and service safeguarding	Providing mechanisms for controlling access to data and preventing its corruption or loss
Executive information extraction	Providing business managers with flexible access to and presentation of information required for reviewing the business
Mathematical calculation	Providing the basic functions required for intensive numerical processing
Business information management	Managing the integration of information elements within an organization's information systems(s) (e.g. repository, strategy planning) and managing the interrelationship between other information services
Information presentation	Providing information in, for example, a publishable form via a variety of media (paper, sound, video, graphics, image)
IT service management	Managing, integrating and accounting for the services, systems and resources used by all other generic IT services
Applications development environment	Providing the mechanisms to allow the controlled development, distribution, maintenance and replacement of applications which realize the functionality of generic IT services

The concept of functional qualities

A functional quality is a characteristic of a generic IT service that identifies some key issue of particular relevance for standards. These functional qualities need to be identified for each business system to which a generic IT service is relevant. These qualities might be specific to a business system or business function, or they might be enterprise-wide.

As with generic IT services, functional qualities may be seen from both business and technological perspectives. Because of the need to combine requirements, functional qualities should be measurable, wherever possible. Because of the different perspectives, this Draft for Development contains two kinds of functional qualities, one business-oriented and the other technological. In reviewing an enterprise's needs, it may be easier to identify requirements the choice of business-oriented functional qualities by using strategic business factors as a guide. However, it may be easier to express values for these needs by using a technology-oriented list that proposes, where appropriate, discrete choices for functional qualities, i.e. by operating in the same way as a multiple-choice questionnaire.

Examples of business-oriented functional qualities are business criticality and usability. Examples of technology-oriented functional qualities are scalability, timeliness, non-denial of service, throughput, and level of security. Annex D.3 *[of the full document – Eds]* gives further examples and sets out possible metrics or discrete choices for each functional quality listed.

Functional qualities allow the aggregation, or clustering, of requirements. In addition, situations can be identified where sets of functional qualities are required for a particular class of user service, for example one that it would be useful to differentiate from an otherwise similar service.

Using the frameworks

Necessary processes

DISC's mission is to help enterprises to improve their operational effectiveness by accelerating standardization in information systems, by promoting standards and by making them easy to exploit. In support of this mission, DISC is developing a way by which enterprises in general, and DISC members in particular, can influence the content of, and the priorities within, the UK standards programme related to IT. At an appropriate time, it is intended to bring the work forward to ISO. The framework for user requirements described in this Draft for Development will allow business managers to express their requirements in business terms. The development of a complementary framework for standards and technology will allow technical managers to express these as requirements for appropriate technologically-based services. Standards-makers will then be able to adjust the pace of this process and content of standards accordingly.

Two associated processes are needed, when using the frameworks, in order to meet the objectives. They are as follows.

(a) *Identifying user requirements*

Identifying user requirements is the process which elicits the requirements of individual, or groups of, enterprises and aggregates these into generic user requirements. It should be possible for this process to make use of concepts from the framework for user requirements, both in the description of the process and in the expression of the resulting requirements.

(b) *Defining standards requirements*

Defining standards requirements is the process which interprets generic user requirements into requirements for standards, and categorizes them in terms of available standards and sets of standards or profiles. It should be possible for this process to use concepts derived from the framework for standards and technology and development of this process will depend on the availability of an adequate framework for standards and technology.

These two processes are illustrated in Figure 10.6 [*Figure B.1 in BS DD210:1992 – Eds*].

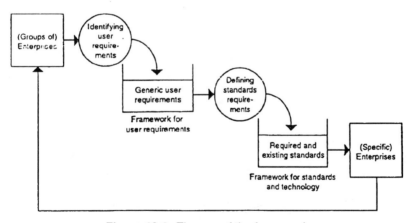

Figure 10.6 *The use of the frameworks*

Two further processes are needed to realize the objective of allowing enterprises to exploit common components. They are as follows.

(c) *Identifying appropriate standards*

Identifying appropriate standards is the process which allows an enterprise to identify what standards and profiles are appropriate to meet specific business needs for information systems and, conversely, what information systems are made feasible by available standards and technology. It should be possible for this process to make use of concepts from the framework for standards and technology and it is therefore not described further in this Draft for Development.

(d) *Identifying appropriate services*

Identifying appropriate services is the process which enables an enterprise to identify what IT services and systems are appropriate to meet its business needs.

These various processes should overlap in time and should be undertaken by different groups of people as described in (a) to (d). The two frameworks are constructed from a rather small and stable set of generic categories, but the number of elements within any one category is not fixed and will vary over time. In particular, the initial lists of generic IT services and their functional qualities, described above, will evolve as each process exercises the framework(s) on which it depends, possibly showing the need for new entities. The evolution (progressed by different groups at different times) will require that the overall task of managing the entities represented in the frameworks and of adjusting the processes that use them is coordinated. This coordination will be carried out initially by DISC for the UK.

The relationship between the frameworks

Figure 10.7 *[Figure B.2 in BS DD210:1992 – Eds]* represents the relationships between these two frameworks. While both have value and purpose in their own right, they should be regarded as interlocking elements to the general DISC objectives of identifying user requirements, interpreting them as requirements for setting standards, representing available standards, and providing ways in which enterprises can use and benefit from those standards, in turn generating new enterprise requirements.

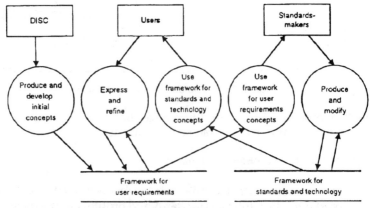

Figure 10.7 *The relationships between the two frameworks*

Figure 10.7 also shows the way in which an initial set of concepts seeds the framework for user requirements. Development of the framework exists in the continuing cycle of applying it and in the dialogue between users and stand-ards-makers.

Users of the frameworks

The framework for user requirements, and the framework for standards and technology, together with the four processes described above, are needed to support two communities. These are as follows.

(a) *DISC, its various working groups and members*

DISC is the organization that has to interpret the needs in terms of a prioritized work programme, and make developed standards accessible for use by UK enterprises.

In particular, the DISC Framework Working Group is providing an initial set of generic constructs and using these to create a questionnaire that will be used for consultation with relevant enterprises. Consolidation of the returns will be used to develop general statements of user requirements. Later (in combination with the Priorities Working Group), the Framework Working Group will be analysing, aggregating and prioritizing these con-structs into a list of standards requirements and a work programme. DISC and others will populate that list of require-ments with standards profiles and base standards.

(b) *Enterprises and industry groupings*

IT users, consisting of individual enterprises and industry group-ings, need to express collective requirements and to derive benefit from the use of standards.

In particular, IT users will find that the framework assists in producing statements on requirements and functional qualities for generic IT services, probably grouped into consolidated re-quirements through industry groupings. Enterprises will later exploit the populated standards list to identify usable standards, new requirements and improved generic constructs for this framework for user requirements.

Aggregating requirements

Figure 10.8 *[Figure B.3 in BS DD210:1992 – Eds]* illustrates the process of aggregating enterprise needs.

In practice groups of enterprises, organized into trade associations or other organizations having a common interest, will generally provide the collective input that directly affects the content of the relevant set of generic IT services

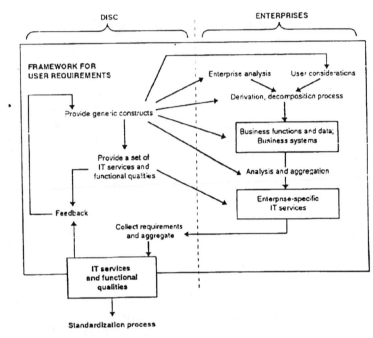

Figure 10.8 *Aggregating enterprise needs into requirements for generic IT services as input to the standardization process*

(as outlined in Figure 10.8). Examples could include electronic funds transfer, point of sale or electronic data interchange.

It is beneficial to most individual enterprises to participate because of the common disciplines and feedback accruing from the use of this framework for user requirements.

Benefits of using the framework

For a specific enterprise, the benefits of using the framework for user requirements are as follows.

(a) To clarify business objectives and the relationship between these and the use of IT as part of an enterprise's business, quality and management processes.

(b) To create a disciplined approach that will help enterprises to establish their information management requirements.

(c) To conduct a business analysis of customers' needs, especially in areas of interworking and cooperation.

(d) To provide a common format for determining what standards are needed in the many different information handling systems within an enterprise, so reducing costs and easing transition to new requirements and the use of new standards.

(e) To obtain competitive advantage as standards development responds to corporate strategies.

(f) To allow later development of a process by which individual enterprises can identify those standards that are available and appropriate to their needs.

Currently, mapping the global user requirements to technical standards requires a high level of expertise which may not be available in every organization.

For the standards-setting process, the expected benefits of applying the concepts and processes of this framework for user requirements are as follows.

(1) To allow a consultation process to be established which uses the framework to derive overall statements of requirements.

(2) To allow a standards-setting programme to become more aligned to the needs of the market and to develop appropriate standards more quickly.

(3) To support a feedback mechanism that alerts standards-makers to requirements.

The three concepts of business requirements, standards and technology evident in items (1), (2) and (3) are mutually linked. Business innovation may arise from technological innovation and then demand standards to make the use of that technology more effective. Business demand for unavailable technology can initiate suppliers' searches for technological innovations. The availability and prospect of appropriate technology and identifiable standards influence enterprises to aspire to new systems capability. For these reasons it is necessary to identify and represent the capabilities both of standards (existing and developing) and of technology so that they can be mutually used and exploited.

The concepts contained in this Draft for Development should also help enterprises to appreciate the overall role that can be played by IT in their business and should assist in developing a mission statement, a business strategy, an IT strategy, an IT design infrastructure and a realignment to the business strategy. However, it is essential that this Draft for Development is adequate to support users in determining and representing their requirements.

Use of checklists and examples

The various lists and examples (see Annex D [of the full document – Eds]) should be helpful to the iterative, parallel processes that lead to expressions of enterprise needs in terms of generic IT services and their qualities. Iteration arises because of the evolutionary nature of business strategies and the use of IT in supporting those strategies. It also arises because of the impact that enterprise controls have on the process (e.g. budgetary controls) and the implicit delays. Other factors are as follows:

(a)   the need for short-term solutions;

(b)   the need to match requirements arising at different organizational levels and in different business functions;

(c)   the influence of the structural nature of the organization (e.g. hierarchical or otherwise);

(d)   the installed base of systems and equipment;

(e)   the need to reconcile user needs against what suppliers state is possible;

(f)   the need for collaboration with partners in business alliances.

Reconciling the existing and the desired strategic infrastructure of an enterprise with the demands of specific business functions within it also leads to iteration. This Draft for Development does not prescribe any specific approach to determining IT Infrastructure requirements.

These, then, are two frameworks in the context of which it is intended that IT standards work will be done through the 1990s. Both address user requirements, that from DISC doing so specifically, and both in relation to corporate user requirements. In fact the EWOS framework pays somewhat more attention to requirements of individual users than does that from DISC, perhaps reflecting the provenance of the documents. It will not be until the late 1990s, after the frameworks have been in use for a period of years (and no doubt modified), that it will become clear whether this apparent difference of emphasis means anything much – or, for that matter, whether the exercise has been successful generally. Of course, corporate users ought to recognize that concerns of individual users, i.e. their workforce, of the kind addressed earlier particularly in Section 7, are also important to their businesses. However, corporate entities have other things on their corporate minds additional to the welfare and working conditions of their staff, so this cannot be deemed automatic.

Nevertheless it is clear from much in the preceding pages that the only real hope, for all users, of exerting influence over the IT standardization process is by collective pressure from governments and large user companies. And, as pointed out earlier, in the end all these corporate entities are composed of individual people. As IT becomes more pervasive, perhaps the best hope is that most of these, even in the top echelons, will become individual users themselves, and experience the problems themselves. That could be the best guarantee of progress; though user concern about the standards of catering does not invariably transfer out of the board dining room to affect the works canteen.

It will not be until the 21st century that it can be judged whether the 1990s is the decade of user achievement. What *is* clear at the beginning of the decade is that it is one of user opportunity. Coincidentally, as these closing words are being written, SPAG in Brussels is launching EPHOS (European Procurement Handbook for Open Systems) and its associated PSI (Process to Secure Interoperability), referred to by Dr Nottebohm in Section 4. The stated aims are very much in line with many of the user arguments presented in this book.

The opportunities are there. It is up to users – all users – to take them.

References

Standards and standards body documents

BS 6832:1987 Method of specifying requirements for Fortran processors

BS DD210:1992 Draft for Development: A framework for user requirements for information technology

ISO 7498:1984 Open Systems Interconnection – basic reference model

Other references

[Berg and Schumny 1990] *see general bibliography*

[ComputerScope 1988] Conference report, *ComputerScope* (Dublin), July/August 1988

[Computing 1988] Press report in *Computing*, 2 June 1988

[EWOS 1991] Final report on the framework for open systems, Document PT4 P032, European Workshop on Open Systems

[Meek c1985] MEEK, B.L., paper privately circulated in the early to mid 1980s

[Meek 1988a] MEEK, B.L., Where the blame lies for bad methods [original title Reforming the standards scene], *Computer Weekly*, 11 February 1988

[Meek 1988b] MEEK, B.L., Is standardisation just regularisation?, *Computer Standards and Interfaces*, Vol 7, No 3, pp 257-259, see also Section 1

[Meek 1988c] MEEK, B.L., Language standards committees and revisions, *Sigplan Notices of the ACM*, Vol 23, No 12, pp 134-142

[Meek 1990a] MEEK, B.L., Product-based v. product-oriented standards, in [Berg and Schumny 1990], pp 95-97, see also Section 1

[Meek 1990b] MEEK, B.L., Changing people's attitudes (workshop report), in [Berg and Schumny 1990], pp 457-460

[Meek 1990c] MEEK, B.L., Changing people's attitudes: personal views, *Computer Standards and Interfaces*, Vol 10, No 1, pp 29-36

[Meek 1990d] MEEK, B.L., Problems of software standardisation, *Computer Standards and Interfaces*, Vol 10, No 1, pp 39-43, see also Section 6

[Meek 1990e] MEEK, B.L., The future of software standardisation, *Computer Standards and Interfaces*, Vol 10, No 2, pp 125-131

[NIST 1992] MEEK, B.L., The GOSIP testing program, National Institute for Standards and Technology, USA, *Computer Standards and Interfaces*, Vol 14 No 1 pp 46-48

[OECD 1991] *see general bibliography*

[Rankine 1990] RANKINE, L.J., Information technology standards: can the challenges be met?, in [Berg and Schumny 1990], pp 41-48

[Rickert 1988] RICKERT, N.W., The role of the language standards committee, *Sigplan Notices of the ACM*, Vol 23, No 4, pp 51-55

[Tuinenberg 1990] TUINENBERG, H.A., Conformance testing of IT implementations, in [Berg and Schumny 1990], pp 73-83

Index

Principal entries and full references in bold.
Entries relating to figures and tables in italic.